PORTRAITS OF A GENERATION

PORTRAITS OF A GENERATION

EARLY PENTECOSTAL LEADERS

EDITED BY

James R. Goff Jr. and Grant Wacker

With an Afterword by David Edwin Harrell Jr.

THE UNIVERSITY OF ARKANSAS PRESS
Fayetteville
2002

06 05 04 03 02   5 4 3 2 1

Designer: John Coghlan

⊚ The paper used in this publication meets the minimum requirements
of the American National Standard for Permanence of Paper for Printed
Library Materials Z39.48-1984.

Library of Congress Cataloging-in-Publication Data

Portraits of a generation : early Pentecostal leaders / edited by James R. Goff,
Jr. and Grant Wacker ; with an afterword by David Edwin Harrell, Jr.
    p. cm.
  Includes bibliographical references and index.
    ISBN 1-55728-731-7 (pbk. : alk. paper)
    1. Pentecostal churches—Biography. 2. Pentecostal churches—History.
I. Goff, James R., 1957– II. Wacker, Grant, 1945–
    BX8762.Z8 A33 2002
    289.9'4'0922—dc21

                                                            2002012302

For
Merian Zeller
and
Carolyn Forehand Castania
Gifted Women, Quiet Leaders

CONTENTS

ACKNOWLEDGMENTS

Our friendship began in the fall of 1979 on the campus of Duke University where, as student and teacher, we shared both a background and an interest in Pentecostals. This book grew out of ideas held separately and then merged over time in the best tradition of both the academy and personal fellowship. All of the authors included in this volume have helped shape our understanding of early Pentecostalism, and they share much of the credit for our work over the years. A special word of thanks goes to Ed Harrell, Jim's doctoral mentor at the University of Arkansas in the early 1980s and no less a friend and inspiration to Grant. He has taught us both, and his wisdom has informed this collection of essays.

Throughout this project, our colleagues in the history department at Appalachian State University and in the divinity school at Duke University have supported us. The undertaking also received support from a summer 1999 grant from Appalachian's University Research Council. From the beginning, Larry Malley and others at the University of Arkansas Press have encouraged this endeavor and have helped turn it into a book. Monica Phillips served as copyeditor and, for her diligence and cooperation, we owe a debt of thanks. Carol Shoun, administrative assistant at Duke Divinity School, and Laura Wacker Stern, a ministerial student at Candler School of Theology, proofread the manuscript. Elesha Coffman, a doctoral student in the Graduate Program in Religion at Duke, produced the index.

Finally, we wish to thank our families for their enduring support. In gratefulness for that support, we honor two special persons, Grant's mother, Merian Zeller, and Jim's maternal aunt, Carolyn Forehand Castania. They represent the Christian tradition of gifted women, quiet leaders, at its best. The foundation they provided in our lives and the examples they set, both inside and outside of church, have made us stronger.

James R. Goff Jr. and Grant Wacker
June 2002

INTRODUCTION

By James R. Goff Jr. and Grant Wacker

In 1980 the noted American religious historian Peter W. Williams judged Pentecostalism "*the* popular religious movement" of the twentieth century.[1] If Williams's claim seemed persuasive in 1980, it seemed even more persuasive twenty years later, especially if one focused on movements within the Christian tradition. At the beginning of the new millennium, the reported membership of the main Pentecostal denominations totaled more than ten million in the United States alone. If we add the souls in the older Protestant denominations who embraced Pentecostal or Pentecostal-like beliefs and practices (often called charismatics), and the Roman Catholics who embraced similar beliefs and practices (also often called charismatics), the figure would easily reach twenty, perhaps thirty, million. In the year 2000 U.S. converts, coupled with Pentecostal and charismatic Christians outside the United States (especially in the Third World), yielded a figure exceeding a half billion, making them the largest collection of Christians on the planet outside the Roman Catholic Church. All of those numbers may have swelled in the telling, perhaps wildly so, yet other studies consistently suggest that by the year 2000 Pentecostals and charismatics claimed a massive slice of the Christian pie, both in the United States and abroad.[2]

Social standing followed numbers. In 1978 the *Christian Century* ranked healing evangelist Oral Roberts as one of the ten most influential religious leaders in the United States. Two decades later *Christian History* magazine judged Azusa pioneer William J. Seymour one of the ten most influential Christians of the twentieth century.[3] Run-down urban missions and back-woods huts increasingly competed with opulent suburban churches. Rough-tongued country preachers found themselves progressively eclipsed in the public eye by flamboyant television evangelists. The press's interest in the tradition, aroused by the scandals of the 1980s, surged when John Ashcroft, son and grandson of Pentecostal preachers and a lay exhorter himself, won confirmation as U.S. attorney general in 2001. The meteoric rise of this Yale-educated lawyer, governor, and senator made clear that the Pentecostal-charismatic movement had become a permanent and largely accepted fixture of American life. Often journalists' columns focused on the real or alleged antics of Pentecostal celebrities. Yet behind those very public and sometimes sorry tales lay the private stories of millions of ordinary believers whose commitment to the work of the church typically dwarfed the involvement of mainline Christians.

Who were the men and women who helped form the Pentecostal movement in the early decades of the twentieth century? Almost all traced their roots to a succession of white-hot revivals that blazed across the radical evangelical subculture in the United States just before and after 1900. Some looked to fire-baptized meetings in the upland South in the 1890s, some focused on stirrings in eastern Kansas in the early 1900s, and some found their origins in interracial gatherings in southern California in 1906. Converts soon organized themselves into scores of fellowships, as they preferred to be called. The largest of the mostly white bodies included the Assemblies of God, the Church of God (Cleveland, Tennessee), the Pentecostal Holiness Church, the International Church of the Foursquare Gospel, and a cluster of sects that coalesced after World War II into the United Pentecostal Church. The largest of the mostly black bodies included the Church of God in Christ, the Pentecostal Assemblies of the World, and the United Holy Church. The largest Latino body was the Apostolic Assembly of the Faith in Christ Jesus.

What did early Pentecostals believe and practice? In the beginning they often dubbed their halls Full Gospel Tabernacles, which meant that they preached the "full" gospel that the mainline denominations seemingly had elided. This full gospel included four enduring convictions: (1) salvation through faith in Jesus Christ, (2) baptism of the Holy Spirit with the necessary evidence of speaking in tongues, (3) divine healing of the physical body through the power of Christ's atonement, and (4) the assurance of the Lord's soon return. In the 1910s a significant minority of Pentecostals—perhaps 20 percent—grew convinced that God had fully manifested Himself in the person of Jesus Christ. Known as "Oneness" believers, these stalwarts formed themselves into the Pentecostal Assemblies of the World, the Apostolic Assembly, and the United Pentecostal Church, among other bodies.

JAMES R. GOFF JR. AND GRANT WACKER

The full gospel metaphor rightly suggests that early Pentecostals represented the confluence of (at least) four distinct theological traditions. We might picture those traditions as separate though frequently overlapping streams that had been crisscrossing the American religious landscape for many decades. The first stream, both theologically and historically, emphasized heartfelt salvation through faith in Jesus Christ. This notion dated back to the Great Awakening in the mid-eighteenth century (if not earlier), when it was commonly called the new birth. Like their evangelical forebears, Holy Ghost saints made salvation the nonnegotiable marker that divided Christians from non-Christians.

The second stream, Holy Ghost baptism, was more complex. Several closely related though historically discrete tributaries constituted it. The earliest tributary started in England in the eighteenth century with John Wesley's notion of entire sanctification. Though the new birth signaled the true beginning of the Christian life, Wesley preached, corrupt desires persisted. This "inbred sin" needed to be eradicated in a lifelong process of moral cleansing. But in mid-nineteenth-century America many Wesleyans, led by the evangelist Phoebe Palmer, came to view entire sanctification less as a process and more as a definable state that one entered by faith at a moment in time. Many called it the second blessing.

Oberlin perfectionism formed a second tributary. Flowing from the teachings of Oberlin College president Charles G. Finney and other Reformed (or broadly Calvinist) writers just before and after the Civil War, this notion also emphasized a life-transforming experience after conversion. However, Oberlin perfectionists understood this postconversion experience not as the eradication of inbred sin but rather as the ability to consecrate one's life wholly to Christ's service.

A third tributary surged across the Atlantic from the annual higher life conferences at Keswick, England. Higher life teachers urged that the second experience in the order of salvation was properly understood as a *series* of experiences that equipped believers for extraordinary feats of witness and service. They called it an enduement of power. "Baptism with the Spirit," the American higher life preacher Reuben A. Torrey testily remarked, "is not primarily intended to make believers happy nor holy, but to make them useful."[4]

Lines blurred. By the end of the century Christians in all three of these tributary traditions had come to label the postconversion experience (or experiences) the baptism with the Holy Ghost. But where holiness Wesleyans spoke of purity, Oberlin perfectionists and Keswick higher life advocates more often spoke of power. Grassroots believers typically talked about purity and power in a single breath.[5]

Divine healing and anticipation of the Lord's soon return represented the third and fourth streams of the full gospel. Divine healing was as old as Christianity itself, but European and American radical evangelicals departed from historic Christian doctrine (which had enjoined elders to anoint and pray for the sick). They insisted, instead, that if one's faith was strong enough, Christ's atonement on the cross provided automatic healing for the body just as it provided automatic healing for the soul. In the same years, anticipation of the Lord's soon return expressed itself in the language of dispensational premillennialism. The latter called for an imminent secret rapture of the saints, immediately followed by seven years of terrible tribulation, the Second Coming of the Lord, the millennium, and final judgment.

A restorationist yearning to recover the supernatural power and miracles of the New Testament church complemented the full gospel, more as a premise or pervading outlook than as an explicit affirmation. Many radical evangelicals expected that the "former rain," the signs and wonders described in Acts, would soon be fulfilled by the "latter rain," a final outpouring of the Holy Spirit's glory at the close of history. The exact origins of this influence are hard to pin down, but nineteenth-century Protestantism brimmed with restorationist impulses that strongly affected other indigenous groups, including the Churches of Christ and the Latter-day Saints. Religious outlooks and practices initiated in West Africa, and mediated through black evangelical Christianity in the United States, may have played a formative role as well.

As the century drew to a close a small number of radical evangelicals longed for more than the full gospel. Though prescriptions varied, all sensed the possibility of a spiritual experience more intense, more palpable than anything they had known. So it was that, just after the turn of the century, one tiny band, huddled in a Topeka, Kansas, Bible school, grew particularly interested in the miracles described in Acts. Led by an itinerant Methodist healer named Charles Fox Parham, the seekers read that on the Day of Pentecost Jesus' followers experienced Holy Ghost baptism and "began to speak with other tongues, as the Spirit gave them utterance." This simple story, which had fascinated Christians for nearly nineteen hundred years, raised a question as disturbing as it was provocative. If speaking in tongues accompanied Holy Ghost baptism on the Day of Pentecost, why not now? Indeed, if then, why not always and everywhere?

For the Kansas zealots the answer presented itself with the force of an epiphany: speaking in tongues *always* accompanied Holy Ghost baptism, first as an audible sign of the Holy Ghost's presence, second as a tool for evangelism. This claim, unique in the entire history of Christianity, defined a rare, fairly difficult physical activity as a nonnegotiable hallmark of a fully developed Christian life. Not incidentally, it also marked believers who did not speak in tongues as second-class Christians. By definition they had not received the coveted baptism experience.

From these inauspicious beginnings the Pentecostal message spread slowly but steadily, mainly among old-stock whites, hard-working plain folk.[6] Initially it made news in the Kansas press; then it shriveled and nearly died. In 1903 Parham salvaged the revival by returning to a divine-healing ministry. Two years later he took the Apostolic Faith—his label—to Houston. In Houston an African American evangelist named William J. Seymour embraced the message and carried it to Los Angeles, where his preaching sparked the now famous Azusa Street revival in the spring of 1906. In the meantime, Parham's disciples bore the Apostolic Faith to Chicago and then to urban centers of the Northeast. By the early 1910s the revival had reached most parts of the United States, Canada, and northern Mexico, claiming 50,000—possibly 100,000—converts.[7] Though the stirring would remain preponderantly old-stock white, after 1906 it acquired a conspicuously multiethnic face.[8] And though a disproportionate number would hail from the South, a slight majority lived north of the Mason-Dixon line, with especially strong showings in the Chicago and New York City areas. By 1958 Henry P. Van Dusen, the president of Manhattan's prestigious Union Theological Seminary, would dub Pentecostals, along with disparate holiness and millenarian groups, an emerging "third force in Christendom."[9]

At first blush, this book would have puzzled early Pentecostals. After all, when it came to leaders, what was there to write about? In their minds they had none, or at least none worth mentioning. The Holy Ghost ran everything. Of course certain men and women *seemed* to manage things. But appearances were deceiving. In reality the figures that stood behind the pulpits, or edited the periodicals, or planned the meetings were only yielded instruments—vessels, they liked to call themselves—awaiting the Lord's bidding. In believers' eyes autocrats and bureaucrats filled the ranks of other traditions but not theirs. The revival had come into existence without human direction and, thankfully, it had operated that way ever since.

First-generation Pentecostals' conviction that their movement had tumbled from the skies as a "sacred meteor," untouched by human hands, was to some extent an accident of circumstance. For different reasons, three of the persons most likely to hold the honor of founding figure—Charles Fox Parham, William J. Seymour, and Aimee Semple McPherson—slipped from contemporaries' recognition. By 1907 Parham's reputation had fallen victim to unsubstantiated but damaging rumors of sexual misconduct. His insistence on conditional immortality (annihilation of the wicked) did not help matters, nor did his fiercely combative attitude toward rivals. By 1910 Seymour had disappeared into obscurity because of factionalism at the Azusa Mission, his own apparent lack of leadership aspirations and, undoubtedly, whites' unwillingness to credit him with a founding role. If those factors were not enough, his later denial of the doctrinal cornerstone of Pentecostalism—tongues as the necessary initial evidence of Holy Ghost baptism—made it unthinkable that he would stand as the movement's creator. McPherson came closest to being regarded as the movement's organizational architect, for her real-life achievements proved astonishing by any reasonable measure of such things. But her gender, divorces, ecumenical dalliances, flamboyant style and, in the eyes of many, controversial personal behavior rendered her a dubious pioneer.[10]

Nonetheless, the main reason saints remained convinced that they possessed no leaders to speak of stemmed from their view of themselves in the grand scheme of history. When they looked back at their own beginnings they were pleased to discover that they had no founders—no Martin Luther, no John Wesley, and certainly no Joseph Smith. The reason was clear. Just like the Bible itself, the Pentecostal revival had come directly from the divine hand, in essential points already fully formed. One Azusa pioneer made the point with memorable simplicity: "The source is from the skies."[11] Even Holy Ghost historians, who of all people should have known better, fell into step. In 1915, in one of the earliest attempts to survey the movement's history, the China missionary M. L. Ryan put the point as plainly as the language permitted: "This great world-wide movement did not originate with man. It has no great earthly leader. It is not a religious organization. It will not be organized."[12] A half dozen years later another chronicler, likely the Church of God's general overseer, A. J. Tomlinson, waved aside any suggestion that human directors had played a significant part: "The Holy Ghost Himself has been the leader."[13] As late as 1961 the Pentecostal historian Carl Brumback published *Suddenly . . . From Heaven: A History of The Assemblies of God*. Perhaps more than he realized, Brumback's main title exemplified one of the revival's deepest assumptions.

If in Pentecostal eyes the movement lacked mortal founders, it also lacked mortal managers. The Lord Himself had guided it from beginning to end. In a reminiscence significantly titled "The Holy Spirit Bishop of the Church," Azusa leader William J. Seymour averred that every assembly's first action was to make sure that the "Holy Ghost [was] installed as the chairman." Whenever a group of worshipers lost their spiritual effectiveness, he charged, it was because humans tried to direct their own affairs.[14] Such views were not restricted to individuals either. Organized sects said the same. For example, the congregated divines of the first General Council of the Assemblies of God trumpeted that they remained free—gloriously free, it seemed—of earthly directors. "[T]his great movement of God has no man nor set of men at the head of it but God to guide and mold it into clean cut Scriptural paths by the Holy Spirit."[15]

It should be noted that Pentecostals were not simply saying that they lacked a single dominant leader. Rather they were saying that they possessed no leaders at all. A complete "absence of human machinery" was how Rochester Bible Institute teacher Elizabeth V. Baker described the revival's structure.[16] Kansas City's A. S. Copley, among the most thoughtful of first-generation writers, similarly asserted, without a trace of irony, that the "Apostolic Faith movement is not an organization or controlled by man in any way, but is under the direct control and supervision of the Holy Ghost."[17] This premise explains why some periodicals refused to list a human editor. As the premier issue of the *Latter Rain Evangel* made plain in October 1908, no person's name would appear on the masthead because the magazine would contain nothing of human origin.[18]

Yet we dare not take Pentecostals solely at their word. The ideal of a leaderless movement, however genuinely held, did not square with social reality. Considered whole, the evidence leaves little doubt that strong, determined, clear-eyed leaders orchestrated the revival from first to last. And they did it just as Christian orchestrators had always done: by inspiring the cooperative, squeezing the uncooperative, and cajoling the undecided. Moreover—and this is the key point—Holy Ghost officials knew how to transform coercive power into moral authority. If the essence of leadership was the ability to persuade people to do what needed to be done, the essence of effective leadership was the ability to persuade them to do it of their own accord. And in this respect the revival's torchbearers proved skillful beyond their grandest dreams.

Two qualifications about the terrain ahead are needed. First of all, our subject is leaders, not clergy. Though most leaders were clergy, and many clergy were leaders, the overlap was never exact, especially for women. Even if it had been, the subjective authority associated with leaders almost always authenticated the objective authority associated with clergy, not the reverse. The second qualification is that three of the most important figures, Charles Fox Parham, William J. Seymour, and Aimee Semple McPherson, do not appear in this volume. After decades of unmerited neglect, they have recently received extensive treatment in other media.

The essays that we commissioned for this book focus on important but comparatively unstudied individuals, or on individuals who have not received examination in the context of Pentecostal cultural history. It should be stressed that our choices are symptomatic, not exhaustive. They represent the availability of materials and the interests of researchers. They also represent both sexes and the variety of theological ideas, denominational families, social locations, geographical origins, and races and ethnic identities that formed the movement's constituency. In some cases the primary sources are plentiful. In others they are so sparse that the authors were forced to take a "life and times" approach to reconstruct lives, as best as possible, from the data that could be located. In all cases the authors tried to present the basic factual details of their subjects' lives and also to place their stories in a larger interpretive framework. The aim, in short, was to ask not only "what?" but also "so what?"

The twenty essays gathered in this volume make clear that the Pentecostal sky was studded with stars, luminaries of the flesh-and-blood variety, and their trajectories both illumined and ordered the world around them. Together they defined the movement's identity. Their stories beckon.

JAMES R. GOFF JR. AND GRANT WACKER

Forerunners

John Alexander Dowie, circa 1900. Courtesy of the Flower Pentecostal Heritage Center, Springfield, Missouri.

John Alexander Dowie: Harbinger of Pentecostal Power

Grant Wacker, Chris R. Armstrong, and Jay S. F. Blossom

On a fall Sunday afternoon in 1905, John Alexander Dowie stepped onto the platform of Shiloh Tabernacle in Zion City, Illinois, a community forty miles north of Chicago on the Lake Michigan shore. The thousands in attendance considered Dowie—garbed that day in the vestments of an Old Testament high priest—Elijah the Restorer and the First Apostle of the Christian Catholic Apostolic Church. He owned the 6,500 acres of farms and homes around the tabernacle, as well as the stores and the village bank. The people awaited Dowie's pronouncements in awed silence. But on that fateful Sunday afternoon, at a moment of triumph, the prophet of Zion suffered a crippling stroke, extinguishing his followers' hopes and his own ability to create a utopia on the prairie.[1]

Though the prophet died, broken, in 1907, his influence continued. Many first-generation Pentecostal leaders had spent time in Zion or had experienced significant contact with Dowie. Others had read about his work in Dowie's widely circulated newspaper, *Leaves of Healing*. More significantly, early Pentecostals embraced Dowie's conviction that Christian faith required claiming the supernatural gifts that God had amply given. Though Dowie did not originate or systematize these ideas, he did disseminate them widely. Early Pentecostal leaders rarely mentioned Dowie's influence on their own movement because of rumors about financial and marital irregularity that enveloped his final years. Nevertheless, his influence proved substantial.

Speaking His Joy Abroad

Born in Edinburgh, Scotland, in 1847, Dowie immigrated to Australia as a lad, returned to Scotland for theological training at the University of Edinburgh, then made his way back to Australia in 1872. Dowie's formal ministry started with a call to the Congregational Church at Alma in 1872, and then a church in a Sydney suburb before year's end. Two years later he migrated to nearby Newton, where he counted among his parishioners professors and students of Camden College, the theological seminary of the Congregationalists in Australia. He soon married his cousin Jane Dowie. The years in Newton also marked the beginning of the central feature of Dowie's ministry: faith healing. In 1876 a plague swept over eastern Australia and within weeks the young minister officiated at forty funerals. According to Dowie's account, one day, at the home of a woman who was dying of the plague, he prayed for her and she instantly recovered. "And this," remembered Dowie, "is the story of how I came to preach the Gospel of Healing through Faith in Jesus."[2] Two years after this pivotal event Dowie withdrew from the Congregational Union because that denomination seemed "terribly overladen with worldliness and apathy."[3]

Like Dwight L. Moody, Dowie was drawn into revivalism, initially in Sydney, then Melbourne. In the first several years he suffered extreme deprivation, recurring marital difficulty, the death of a daughter, and a humiliating defeat in a bid for Parliament. But in 1883 Dowie established the Free Christian Church in Melbourne, soon organized a Divine-Healing Association, and launched a vitriolic pulpit attack on local liquor interests. He so provoked those interests that they purportedly dynamited his tabernacle and arranged to have him thrown in jail for thirty days for breaking the ordinance against street meetings.[4] The publicity was priceless. His following in Melbourne swelled into the thousands.

Things were good in Australia, but throughout his life Dowie showed a propensity for moving on. In the summer of 1886 he experienced a vision telling him to carry "leaves of healing from the Tree of Life to every nation."[5] In 1888 Dowie and his family left Australia for San Francisco. In the United States Dowie's fame as a healer spread quickly. Large numbers reportedly made the pilgrimage to his headquarters in the Palace Hotel in San Francisco.[6] He spent the next two years itinerating up and down the Pacific coast, holding divine-healing meetings and organizing branches of the (now) International Divine Healing Association, with himself as president. Everywhere Dowie went he took care to establish this organizational structure for the proper funneling of funds after he left. In 1890 Dowie started a healing campaign in the Midwest, sometimes cooperating with denominational clergy. That summer he set up a tent at Western Springs, near Chicago, and established his residence in Evanston. Little is known about his activities in these years, except that he traveled extensively in Canada and the eastern United States, carefully establishing institutional branches of the International Divine Healing Association.[7]

Dowie's sensitivity to public relations proved worthy of a P. T. Barnum. When the Chicago World's Fair opened in 1893, he set up his operation across the street from Buffalo Bill's camp. Dowie's tabernacle became known as "The Little Wooden Hut," and even his detractors acknowledged that he preached night and day, seven days a week, and thousands came to hear him. In April 1894 Dowie moved his operation to downtown Chicago and converted his private residence into "Divine Healing Home No. 1," a hostel where sick people could take board and room at a reasonable rate, study the Bible, and pray with others for healing. From this small headquarters, Dowie launched himself into the leadership of the divine-healing movement in the United States.

Municipal authorities viewed these events warily. The confinement of people with contagious diseases and broken bones aroused public ire. In the fall of 1894 the *Chicago Tribune* announced that the State Board of Health was preparing to investigate Dowie for practicing medicine without a license. In early 1895 the Board of Health passed a hospital ordinance that required that any dwelling used for the reception and care of the sick must be licensed and attended by a licensed surgeon. Dowie refused to comply on the grounds that his hostels were "not hospitals. . . . No 'medicine' is used. No 'treatment' is given. . . . Divine healing has no association with doctors and drugs, or surgeons and their knives."[8] Legal confrontations followed. Dowie was arrested May 1, 1895, and convicted of practicing medicine without a license. He appealed and a superior court dismissed the case. Immediately he was rearrested for violating the new hospital ordinance. The outcome again was conviction in lower court and dismissal in superior court. The city repeatedly arrested him on various technicalities of the ordinance but all were dismissed and the ordinance itself eventually was declared unconstitutional.[9] Dowie claimed that in 1895 he was arrested nearly one hundred times, spent portions of 126 days in court or jail, and spent $20,000 in his own defense. The chief significance of these events is that through them Dowie garnered national publicity beyond his wildest dreams. That some of the newspaper attacks seemed libelous hardly mattered.[10] Like some other countercultural movements, Dowie's band not only thrived on opposition but also interpreted it as confirmation of its own moral rectitude.[11]

In Chicago, Dowie's energy seemed limitless. He renovated an auditorium seating eight thousand that he called Central Zion Tabernacle. During this period he also bought or built several ancillary structures, such as the Zion Printing Plant, Zion College (a ministerial training school), Zion Day School, Zion Orphanage, Zion School for Deaconesses, charity outlets such as the Zion Home for Working Girls and the Zion Home for Hope for Erring Women, and a dozen or so branch tabernacles throughout the city. One opponent attributed his growing outreach to an "epidemic of credulity."[12] In 1895 Dowie withdrew from his own creation, the International Divine Healing Association, and the following year called a general conference of believers to announce the organization of the Christian Catholic Church, a new body that would "carry out in the letter and in the Spirit the organization of the New Testament."[13] Up to this point he had encouraged his disciples to remain in their parent denominations, but he could no longer endure divided loyalties.

Perhaps the last significant event of Dowie's life prior to the founding of Zion City was the three-month "Holy War" he launched in 1899 against the "Hosts of Hell in Chicago." Crusading, as he put it, against the apostate clergy, the lying press, the medical butchers, the dispensers of distilled damnation, and most anyone who had crossed him, Dowie so antagonized blocs of people that he was stoned in Oak Park, Illinois, and nearly lynched in Hammond, Indiana. One widely advertised sermon, titled "Doctors, Drugs, and Devils," reportedly elicited a reception committee of two thousand medical students who set off stink bombs and shouted him off his own platform with threats of physical violence. Again, these tactics by the opposition guaranteed Dowie's apotheosis among his own people—and not incidentally gave him an opportunity to harvest a handsome profit on the sale of the story of "*Zion's Holy War against the Hosts of Hell in Chicago* . . . price $.50, postpaid."[14]

The Beautiful City of God

Dowie's plans for a theocracy had started to take tangible form as far back as 1895 when he tried to buy a large tract at Blue Island, several miles southwest of Chicago. The plan failed, possibly because word of the deal leaked and prices rose. Undaunted, he regrouped and prepared his masterstroke. In 1898 Dowie launched the "Seventies," battalions of evangelistic workers, whom he sent on evangelistic missions into Chicago. Beginning as six separate units, they eventually expanded into a legion of ten thousand who reportedly visited every house in Chicago eight times with Zion literature. They also established thriving branches of Dowie's own newly formed sect, the Christian Catholic Church, in the Midwest, the northeastern United States, and even Europe.[15]

The following year Dowie quietly secured options on thousands of acres on Lake Michigan, halfway between Chicago and Milwaukee. In the summer of 1900, ten thousand of Dowie's followers journeyed from Chicago to Zion City for the dedication of the tabernacle site and to catch their first glimpse of the land.[16] Meanwhile, Dowie had begun negotiations to buy an entire lace factory from an English businessman, and reconstruction of the disassembled plant began later that year.

In 1901 the *Zion Banner* reported that 6,500 acres had been topographically surveyed with 500 acres subdivided for business and residence use. The Zion Land and Investment Association, a corporation owned entirely by Dowie himself, secured a water supply, laid out streets and sidewalks, and established a general store, a livery stable, several depots and warehouses, coal and lumber yards, a small brick factory, and shops for a blacksmith, barber, harness maker, and cobbler. A tent city to accommodate twenty thousand and outdoor seats for fifty thousand were brought in for the dedication of the tabernacle.

By March 31, 1902, the date of the completion of Shiloh Tabernacle and the formal incorporation of the city, two thousand people had moved to Zion after securing long-term revocable leases from Dowie's corporation. All of them enjoyed the economic benefits of living in a communitarian system—guaranteed employment and profit sharing from Zion businesses. All were also bound by the structures of a theocracy in which Dowie stood as sole interpreter of God's rule. Democracy had no place in Zion City. "There will be No Municipal Elections in Zion City," Dowie pronounced. "If you cannot stand the rule of God, then you had better go to Waukegan, where I guess the Devil rules."[17]

Though Dowie had disavowed his qualification for the apostolic office in 1896—partly because he lacked the gift of tongues, and partly because he felt he lacked a "depth of true humility . . . true abasement and self-effacement"—by 1899 he had changed his mind. At that point he decided that if he was not an apostle, he at least represented the prophet that Deut. 18:18 and Mal. 3:1–3 described. On June 2, 1901, Dowie revealed that he was also the third and final manifestation of the Prophet Elijah. Acceptance of Dowie as Elijah the Restorer now constituted a requirement for continued fellowship with the Christian Catholic Church and for residence in Zion City. Dowie required all members of the Zion Restoration Host (the former "Seventies") to sign pledges accepting the proclamation.[18]

On September 18, 1904, Dowie took another and more controversial step. With eight thousand followers watching, he ascended the pulpit of Shiloh Tabernacle and announced, "I declare in the name of the Lord Jesus Christ, in the power of the Holy Spirit, in accordance with the Will of God our Heavenly Father, that I am, in these Times of Restoration of all things, the First Apostle of the Lord Jesus Christ, in the Christian Catholic Apostolic Church in Zion." Henceforth he signed his name simply "John Alexander, First Apostle," perhaps intending to link himself with biblical heroes like Moses, who lacked surnames. In any event, he would proclaim: "Clothed by God with Apostolic and Prophetic authority, I now have the right to speak as the instructor of nations."[19]

Though Dowie's increasing megalomania invited the ridicule of unbelieving observers, his utopian community at Zion attracted many thoughtful Christians. For many, the promise of economic security proved appealing. Significantly, Zion City's motto was "Where God rules, man prospers." Dowie promised his followers a generous share in the profits produced by the bank and the lace factory, both of which he owned outright. He allowed them to sell their real-estate leases at fair market value, albeit only to other believers. And he discouraged people from obtaining outside mortgages, or even outside insurance, because everyone in Zion would be his brother's keeper.[20]

Dowie fashioned all of this within a larger restorationist theology. Along with the first-century church's practice of healing, he wished to restore for the benefit of his followers "the Primitive Practice . . . of trading for the Advantage of the Kingdom of God." To do so was not simply a happy side-benefit of true belief, but an essential part of the cosmic battle of good versus evil. Unless Christians created wealth in God's way and used it for his purposes, the church would continue to stand threatened by the huge fortunes of anti-Christian capitalists. Dowie taught that Christians could combat the evil conglomerates of tobacco, liquor, and pharmaceuticals only by a group ethos that ensured both a commonality of the spirit and a proportionate return of the community profit to all. Rather than communism, this was profit shared by the faithful in a "community which preserves personal rights both in property and in person."[21]

Beyond the initial stock offering, Dowie sought to ensure the smooth running and ample returns of his grand machine through the mechanism of the tithe. Hardly an issue of Dowie's weekly *Leaves of Healing* passed without some minor jeremiad about tithing, sometimes recalling the stories of Achan in the Old Testament and Ananias and Sapphira in the New Testament. "All I have to say is this," ended one typical harangue, "I will find you out some day, and if ever I do, that will be the last of you, so far as your connection with Zion is concerned, you . . . hypocritical pretenders." Virtually every issue of his newspaper included letters telling of healing and financial rewards that had come to those who diligently tithed, gave, and invested in Zion. The letters were headed by inspiring boldface pronouncements: "TITHING MAKES A VAST DIFFERENCE IN MONEY MATTERS; INCOME TREBLED IN TWO YEARS; BUSINESS INCREASES EVERY SEASON WHEN TITHES ARE PAID." Dowie possessed many talents, but subtlety was not one of them.[22]

Nonetheless, by 1903, financial difficulties had started to surface in Zion City. Church-owned industries began to shut down. Within the next two years the bank stopped paying interest and disallowed withdrawals. Then, on November 28, 1904, the prophet ordered every person in Zion City to make a deposit. The final blow came when it was revealed that Dowie had secretly tried to borrow seven million dollars, using the homes and businesses of Zion City as collateral.

Despite suffering a stroke in the fall of 1905, Dowie continued his efforts, which he had started the year before, to purchase a large tract of land in Mexico for a new planned community. While he was in Mexico in the spring of 1906 he instructed Wilbur Glenn Voliva, his overseer for Australia, to return to Zion City to take charge, with full power of attorney. Seeing that Zion City teetered on the verge of legal bankruptcy and that Dowie was telegramming almost daily demands for money, Voliva and the other resident overseers decided to sell Zion. On April 1, 1906, 3,500 church members gathered in Shiloh Tabernacle to affirm the sale by a 95 percent majority, and Voliva dispatched a telegram to Dowie informing him that he had been removed from office and from all involvement in the Christian Catholic Apostolic Church in Zion. Auditors found that, at the time of the vote, Dowie's personal account at Zion City Bank was overdrawn $475,000. The deficit of Zion Institutions and Industries was $2,529,765. Of the millions invested by the faithful, all seemed to have evaporated. While financial troubles mounted, Dowie also suffered estrangement from his family in the midst of rumors of infidelity. He returned quietly to Zion City, his health declining, and died surrounded by few friends on March 9, 1907.[23]

Marching to Zion

After the prophet's death, his critics and disillusioned followers alike tended to see him as an eccentric, a swindler, or both. But, during the 1890s and early 1900s, the Dowie faithful viewed him as a credible leader. They both invested in his enterprises and contributed to his mission work. By the thousands they moved to Zion City to be a part of his holy enterprise. Their acceptance of his claims rested on several factors.

First in Dowie's own consciousness ranked divine healing. Until the last few years of his life, when he became entangled in the momentum of his own apotheosis, the simple desire to heal people, the opportunity to alleviate physical suffering, seemed the preponderant passion of his life. Like other radical evangelical teachers of the late nineteenth century, Dowie differentiated his own gift of healing from that of the Christian Scientists by emphasizing the reality of sickness and the powerlessness of autosuggestion. But Dowie also differed from other radical evangelicals like A. B. Simpson and A. J. Gordon in his insistence that disease was essentially the same as sin; it manifested Satan's interference in human affairs. Thus, he directly and explicitly tied the act of healing to the efficacy of Jesus' atonement for sin.[24]

Though detractors believed that Dowie's moral character deteriorated in later years, in the practice of healing, at least, he always maintained scrupulous integrity. There is no evidence that he ever accepted payment for praying for an individual's restoration. He always insisted that repentance for sin must precede such a prayer, and he frequently refused to pray for people if he doubted that they had undergone conversion. "I had been working with these godless Christian Scientists, and church members, and fine-feathered birds with polluted hearts," he once lamented after turning away a group of supplicants, "and I was tired."[25] Till the end of his life Dowie steadfastly maintained that he himself held no ability to heal and that he served only as the instrument of divine power.

Numerous examples show how physical healing created loyal followers out of would-be skeptics. For example, Charles J. Barnard, head of the Zion City Bank, had previously been a member of an Oak Park, Illinois, Presbyterian church and chief clerk of the National Commercial Bank of Chicago. Barnard's daughter suffered from curvature of the spine. Her parents had taken her to the most eminent osteopaths in Chicago, but her condition deteriorated. As a last resort, Barnard took her to Dowie, who laid hands on her and prayed. "Instantly," Barnard testified, "her pain departed from her and to this day it has not returned. Her back became straight, and she is today a healthy, happy, and entirely well young woman. . . . [I]s it any wonder to you that we follow Dr. Dowie with undying love, and obey his wishes even before they are uttered, if we can guess them?" A great many of Zion City's residents testified that they had become followers after similar episodes, and even those who left Zion City and the Christian Catholic Church rarely renounced their belief in Dowie's ability to heal.[26]

The second factor that drew Dowie's followers was prosperity. To whatever extent he mulcted the people of their earnings and savings, many undoubtedly did experience a temporary prosperity as they gave up tobacco, liquor, gambling, worldly amusements, and expensive medicines. Further, Dowie exhorted his flock to achievement. Christian exhortations to poverty as a virtue, he said, were an "infernal lie," and hundreds of letters regularly printed in Zion publications testified that readers believed themselves better off financially than they had been in "the world."[27]

A third factor that drew followers to Zion City was perhaps even more important than the promise of prosperity—Zion City's status as a haven from worldliness. To those believers trying to move on to perfection but beset on every side with the temptations of a filthy world, Dowie offered the sanctifying equivalent of a monastery, but without the onerous requirements of poverty and celibacy. Within Zion City, Dowieites could be free from many of the temptations that the outside world offered. More important, they could protect their children from those same temptations through Zion's kindergarten-to-college educational system. Dowie and his followers instinctively defined morality in terms of external holiness.

Morality as a quality of being, or as a theoretical framework for resolving life's dilemmas, remained an abstraction alien to his mentality. Though Dowie's conception of morality presupposed conversion, and certainly entailed positive elements such as helping out a neighbor, it was primarily a set of specific proscriptions—what might be called "visible puritanism." The proscriptions in Zion City were essentially the same as in a thousand radical evangelical churches (no smoking, drinking, cardplaying, gambling, theaters, dances, profanity, cosmetics), but to these Dowie added the eating of pork products and shellfish, the use of medicines or physicians, and participation in "secret societies." Hardly a page of Zion literature failed to excoriate such evils.[28]

A fourth factor contributing to Zion City's growth was Dowie's political ideology, which leaned toward progressivism. Although it is hard to separate Dowie's own beliefs from those of his followers, there is no evidence that Zion City's defectors left because of disagreements over political outlook. Zion's publications revealed a complex and, at many points, surprisingly liberal outlook. For example, Dowie stridently opposed the Spanish-American War of 1898 and American imperialism in general. In 1901 he berated the government for financing "murder by wholesale in Cuba and in the Philippines." In 1905 he complained, "This Republic has pounced upon innocent peoples and annexed them, without consulting their feelings in the matter. . . . The Filipinos never asked to be annexed; they had done nothing to justify their annexation." In context, Dowie's opposition to racial bigotry proved especially striking. In an 1898 sermon he lamented that "with all America's greatness there is a black blot across the flag. Oh, friends," he continued, "why fight for the black man and his liberty in the Philippines and Cuba, and down there in North and South Carolina allow him to be shot at the polls." One observer reported that Dowie defended miscegenation and called for a marital merging of all races in Zion City. He promised that when the Apostolic College was appointed at least one of its members would be black, because "Primitive Conditions Exclude Race Prejudices." (By "primitive," Dowie meant the primal, or original, blueprint laid out in the New Testament church.) Dowie opposed labor unions, but mostly because they induced workers to accept their status as pawns in the capitalistic-trade union system. He was never reluctant to rail against the corporate interests, which he decried with unveiled hostility. "If the law against trusts were to be enforced, as it ought to be," he argued, "John D. Rockefeller would be looking at the world through prison bars today."[29]

Although Dowie was technically a premillennialist—he believed that Jesus Christ would return at any moment and establish a millennial rule on earth—his political progressivism trumped the negative view of history that many radical evangelical premillennialists accepted. While many saw the sin-sick world deteriorating to the point that God would have to intervene and take true Christians to heaven, Dowie averred that "never was there more of God [in the nation] than today. . . . [O]ur people are being led into the right way, and prepared to be brought into a City of Habitation where God wants them to be."[30] The prophet taught that the establishment of offspring Zion communities around the globe would invite the Lord's Second Coming and launch a new dispensation of history. Dowie's followers likely believed, as he did, that they would be active participants in the great drama of the end times. Indeed, their own town, Zion City, would stand at the center of world events. Since Zion City constituted a new Jerusalem, in which the rules and laws were consonant with the practices of primitive Christianity, at the most fundamental level the world was improving, not growing more corrupt.

Dowie's inclination to view Last Things in a redemptive rather than punitive framework may explain why he taught the heterodox doctrine of universal reconciliation. Dowie denied the eternality of hell and placed it in a dispensational schema. Since sin, he believed, was essentially sensual, repentance for sin must be coerced through sensual punishment. Thus the fires of hell existed only to burn a sinner's rebellion into submission. When that goal was accomplished for all people, hell itself would pass away.

Another factor that contributed to Dowie's appeal to his followers lay in his manifest public relations skills. The Zion prophet capitalized on his devotees' perceptions of him as a selfless and humble leader in order to bring the Zionites into what one supporter gladly acknowledged was "marching order, ready for whatever command may come from the lips of their leader; full of confidence in him as God's servant, chosen for this great work, and determined to obey, no matter what the cost."[31] To buttress his authority, Dowie not only published testimonials from his most loyal followers, but also adduced independent witnesses to his own visionary powers. On Sunday, July 21, 1901, for example, he imported one Mr. Irving Ward, L.L.B., of New York City, "to whom has been given a wonderful vision of Elisha, proclaiming the appearance and Declaration of Elijah the Restorer. . . . He will tell of his vision and of the message which was delivered to him at that time."[32] More subtly, Dowie and his acolytes habitually blurred the distinction between official Zion policies on one hand and an ultimate value reference on the other. For example, when Zion lawyers won a suit against the federal government (which had tried to prevent the importation of skilled Zion lace workers), he portrayed the event as the result of God's direct intervention for Zion against the forces of evil: "From the very first day when the World, the Flesh, and the Devil learned that Zion proposed to establish Lace Industries at Zion City, these powers of evil have been fighting tooth and nail to prevent it . . . [but] God has once more manifested His presence and power in Zion by giving her glorious victory over all the power of her enemies."[33]

Numerous other public relations tactics emerged as well. For example, Dowie made use of provocative attacks on other denominations, Catholics, Masons, medical doctors, public figures, and the Chicago press. Whether he actually believed all the things he said is hard to determine.[34] What can be assumed with reasonable certainty, however, is that Dowie's torrent of invective galvanized his community by creating the appearance of conspiratorial opposition and by sharpening his followers' insider-outsider consciousness. In addition, Dowie used a variety of minor though cumulatively effective image-building devices to attract attention to himself and his movement. He stamped each prayer request at the exact time that the prayer was offered, thus implying that healing might occur at the time the prayer was made. He recorded prayers for specific ailments on phonograph records, allowing followers to write in and request, for example, an arthritis phonograph prayer.[35] He arranged with the railroad for discount fares to Zion City for special events,[36] and on most Sundays he chartered a special excursion train from Chicago to Zion City for a fare of fifty cents.[37] Beyond these publicity gimmicks, face-to-face recruitment became the hallmark of Dowie's Christian Catholic Church. Though the imperative for giving witness was inculcated into every convert,[38] the Zion Restoration Host proved especially effective in this respect. Apparently organized along the lines of the Salvation Army, the Restoration Host may have had thousands of members worldwide. Many issues of *Leaves of Healing* included a tabulation of the Restoration Hosts' successes for the most recent week. These descriptions revealed that members were expected to make their living independently of the church—preferably in some vocation that entailed wide personal contact, like door-to-door sales. Yet it also is clear that the Restoration work was not an avocation, but the main reason for existence.[39]

Dowie himself remained convinced of his unique providential mission, and that conviction formed a sixth reason for his remarkable success in attracting followers. This assumption explains how a man could say that every line of his newspaper *Leaves of Healing* was directly inspired by God and that the paper constituted (after the New Testament books of Acts and Revelation) the seventh gospel: "We have never written a line," he said as early as 1897, "without the sweet consciousness of the overshadowing of the Power of the Highest. . . . These Leaves of Healing are God's own work, as much as any of the six Gospels preceding."[40] It would be a mistake to view the Zion situation as an instance of a cunning genius manipulating hapless pawns. A more realistic interpretation would see both Dowie and his followers as self-conscious participants in a particular kind of "cognitive closure," to use the phrase of anthropologists Luther P. Gerlach and Virginia H. Hine. According to Gerlach and Hine, cognitive closure describes the sense of finality that true believers feel when they embrace "a conceptual framework that fully satisfies [their] need for explanation and meaning." After this point, while secondary beliefs may develop and even change, bedrock beliefs remain unquestioned.[41] This pattern may explain why Dowie's followers could accept sobering admonitions with apparent equanimity. "When you are competent to instruct your instructor; then you are fitted to teach me Theology. It does seem to me to be a piece of audacious impudence for a layman of exceedingly limited education to pose at once as the instructor and detractor of the First Apostle. I wish to say that I will suffer no such criticism."[42] Once most of Dowie's followers turned their backs on the skeptics and put their trust in him as their leader, those followers seemed willing to go wherever he led.

Fairer Worlds on High

Though most (perhaps all) Pentecostals eventually repudiated Dowie's extreme views about himself, many adopted and adapted ideas and methods that he had helped pioneer. For example they too taught that physical healing was available to all believers through the atoning death of Jesus. Some followed him in urging that financial prosperity was to be joyfully accepted and perhaps even sought. Like many radical evangelicals, first-generation Pentecostals also tried to create havens from worldliness within their own homes and churches, and though Dowie had not been the first to teach holy living, early Pentecostals could recognize in Zion City an attempt at consecrated living on a grand scale. A few of the Pentecostal faithful even agreed with Dowie's refusal to eat pork or shellfish.

Early Pentecostals also shared some of Dowie's ideology—initially they joined him in opposing war and race prejudice, although within a few years most succumbed to the influence of American society at large. And while most Pentecostals refrained from direct political involvement, they resembled Dowie in their opposition to unions and their suspicions of big business. Like him, they espoused a premillennial eschatology and believed that Jesus Christ might return at any moment, though none endorsed the location-specific details of Dowie's futurist vision. At the same time, several influential Pentecostal leaders, including founding architect Charles F. Parham, paralleled Dowie in adopting unorthodox views of the state of the lost after death.[43]

Along with some of Dowie's theological agenda, early Pentecostals shared his gift for public relations. Like him, they spent much time promoting themselves using inexpensive newspapers and magazines, tracts, and flyers. They did not fear to attack members of other denominations, and they warned that their opponents would suffer the pains of hellfire. Like Dowie, early Pentecostals viewed all opposition, trivial or large, as satanic, but also like Dowie, they felt no need to spend all their time damning their enemies, for they had a positive message to proclaim. While they did not enjoy the organization of the Zion Restoration Host, Pentecostal missionaries were as vigilant and tireless as Dowie's Christian soldiers. To Dowie's message of physical healing, moral uprightness, and impending judgment, they added speaking in other tongues, which they understood to be the initial evidence of the believer's baptism in the Holy Spirit. They taught that the primary purpose of Holy Spirit baptism was to give the recipient power to fulfill the command of God—chiefly to spread the Pentecostal message around the world.

The connections between Dowie and early Pentecostalism ranged beyond theological and ideological agreements. Apostolic Faith pioneer Charles F. Parham had visited Dowie's Chicago headquarters in 1900, shortly before his own faith work in Topeka, Kansas, became a center for

GRANT WACKER, CHRIS R. ARMSTRONG, AND JAY S. F. BLOSSOM

the tongues movement. Parham returned to Zion City in 1906, this time hoping to bring his new teaching to a community that was receptive to supernatural power and perhaps to draw the Christian Catholic Church under his own Apostolic Faith banner. In an interview with the *Daily Sun* of nearby Waukegan, Parham stated, "Before I came, I [found] that the characteristic spirit of the city was that of selfishness and bigotry. But now I think that this spirit is softening." He added, "There is no compensation for me. I am not making money, neither am I proselyting [*sic*], but I am for the spiritual salvation of Zion."[44] Just a few weeks later, the *Daily Sun* revealed that a "'gift of tongues' . . . is the latest phase of the Parham apostolic movement at Zion City." The newspaper account noted that at least twenty-four persons had spoken in tongues, including Hubert Grant, the former stenographer for Dowie himself. "[H]e stopped, a pallor swept across his face and he commenced to talk in a strange language. After he had spoken some time it was declared that he was speaking Chinese," to which "Elder Simmons," a former Baptist missionary present at the meeting, attested. The newspaper account concluded that Dowie's appointed successor, Wilbur Glenn Voliva, "has been much concerned by the inroads made upon his flock by Parham. It is only a few weeks ago that the leader of the cult came to Zion City from Topeka, Kan., claiming he had been told in a vision to go and save the people of Zion City from their sins."[45]

Subsequent issues of the Waukegan newspaper related further details of Parham's meetings and his split with Voliva. On October 22, the newspaper reported that twenty deacons and twelve deaconesses of the Christian Catholic Church had sided with Parham and were expelled from leadership in the Christian Catholic Church. By October 24, Parham had left town, but on November 5, the paper claimed that the "Parhamite colony in Zion City" was still growing, and on December 18, the paper reported that "[t]he Parhamites now claim between 500 and 800 followers."[46]

During the following year the Pentecostal group in Zion City became increasingly well established. A congregation organized in spite of opposition from Voliva, and Zion City became one of the centers for spreading the new message. Parham himself traveled to many branches of the Christian Catholic Church, and other Zion City residents also spread Apostolic Faith doctrines. Parham later reported that thousands of Dowieites worldwide eventually accepted the "full gospel."[47] The historian

Edith L. Blumhofer has chronicled the stories of several residents of Zion City who later became influential Pentecostals. Their number included Helen Innes, the daughter of convinced Dowieite John Innes, who moved his family to Zion City in 1901 as part of the first group of settlers. Helen Innes attended the city's schools and in 1921 married Joseph Wannenmacher, a Hungarian immigrant. Together the two founded a Hungarian mission in Milwaukee that later became the most important Assemblies of God congregation in that city.[48]

Still another daughter of Zion was Marie Burgess, who moved with her parents to Zion City in 1901. Burgess's sister had claimed healing at Dowie's hands, and the family became convinced of the truth of the prophet's message. Marie Burgess herself, already a young woman at the time of her family's move to Zion, took employment as a food demonstrator. When Charles F. Parham began his meetings in Zion City in 1906, Burgess was curious and began to attend. On October 18, 1906, her twenty-sixth birthday, Burgess received Holy Spirit baptism and spoke in tongues. She soon traveled to New York City at Parham's request to preach the Apostolic Faith message there, and she established a Pentecostal mission, Glad Tidings Hall, on Forty-second Street. Following Burgess's marriage to Robert Brown, a Methodist immigrant from Britain, the two served as joint pastors of the congregation in New York and participated in organizing the Assemblies of God denomination in 1914. Like Joseph Wannenmacher, Robert Brown served as a general presbyter of the denomination. When he died in 1948, Marie Burgess Brown invited her nephew to assume the copastorate of the congregation, but she continued her leadership until her death in 1971.[49]

Other members of Dowie's congregation also became leaders in the Pentecostal movement. John G. Lake, a Zion City resident, became a well-known evangelist and organized a Pentecostal denomination in South Africa. Another son of Zion, Gordon Lindsay, edited the *Voice of Healing* magazine and founded the Christ for the Nations Institute in Dallas. William Hamner Piper founded the Stone Church in Chicago, an independent congregation that quickly embraced the Pentecostal message, and edited the *Latter Rain Evangel*, which spread news about the Apostolic Faith around the country. Still another Dowie partisan, J. Roswell Flower, established a competing periodical, the *Christian Evangel*, which later became the *Pentecostal Evangel*, the weekly voice of the Assemblies of God, which he also helped organize in 1914. Along with two other former Dowieites (Cyrus Fockler and Daniel C. O. Opperman), Flower was part of the original eight-man executive presbytery of the fledgling denomination. He also attended the organizing meeting of the National Association of Evangelicals in 1942, where his commitment to ecumenical cooperation ensured that the Assemblies of God would support interdenominational organization among conservative Protestants.[50]

Parham's claim that thousands of Dowieites became Pentecostal believers is impossible to verify, but plausible. Perhaps even more important than such flesh-and-blood connections are Dowie's indirect influences on a movement that sprang up just as his own theocracy self-destructed. His emphasis on physical healing, his ideology, his gift for self-promotion, and his hotheaded condemnation of worldliness passed to his own followers, many of whom became active in Pentecostalism. Through them, Dowie's distinctive beliefs and practices contributed to the available fund of ideas from which early Pentecostals fashioned their own theology and worldview. More important, Dowie's utter self-confidence and his manifestly sincere belief that he was supernaturally chosen by God to usher in a new apostolic era foreshadowed the Pentecostals' conviction that they served as harbingers of the end times.[51]

E. L. Harvey, circa 1920. Courtesy of the author.

E. L. Harvey: The Price of Discipleship

William Kostlevy

"There is a religion of happiness, and I know that if I ever get religion I want to get their particular brand," wrote novelist Jack London after attending religious services conducted by the Metropolitan Church Association (MCA) in 1905 in Boston. As a socialist with considerable contempt for established religion, London was an unusually sympathetic observer of one of the most controversial religious bodies of the early twentieth century. Noting the joy on the faces of the "poorly clad" converts, London praised the MCA evangelists' "common-sense" remarks and "biting metaphors" and seemed especially delighted with the evangelists' depiction of Boston's churches as "steepled clubhouses." For the Burning Bush movement, as the MCA was popularly known because of its controversial periodical, the *Burning Bush,* such praise by outsiders was rare. Nevertheless, London understood the unusually powerful attraction of Holiness radicalism to thousands of young women and men during the first two decades of the twentieth century.[1]

Willingly surrendering personal property and family ties, young Holiness radicals cast their lots with dozens of Holiness-related communal societies that flourished in the early twentieth century. Only a few of these societies, such as Frank Sandford's community at Shiloh, Maine, and John Alexander Dowie's community at Zion, Illinois, have attracted the attention of scholars. And, even in these cases, scholars have tended to view them more as exotic cults than as expressions of mass social protest. Although hardly conventional, the Burning Bush community in Waukesha, Wisconsin, was one of the largest and most durable communes in American history.[2]

The principal founders of the Burning Bush movement were Edwin L. Harvey and his wife, Gertrude Ford Harvey, and wealthy Chicago bond salesman Marmaduke ("Duke") Mendenhall Farson. Although all three were members of the affluent Western Avenue Methodist Episcopal Church, they came from quite dissimilar homes. While Farson and Harvey were both sons of Methodist ministers, Gertrude Ford was reared in an affluent home. Converted in his youth, Harvey became a class leader, secretary for Chicago's sixty-six Methodist youth organizations, and the leader of a group of devout young people committed to evangelistic outreach. His interest in evangelism came naturally. His father, Daniel Harvey, a deliveryman in Chicago, supplemented his income each summer through the sale of household products to downstate farm families and, in the process, spent as much time dispensing evangelical Christianity as selling his wares. A member of the church's social elite, Gertrude Ford spent her youth in "the usual round of strawberry suppers and ice cream socials." In spite of her family's deep roots in Methodism (her mother had even attended the prestigious Johns Street Methodist Church in New York City), Ford remained unconverted and, like most of the members of the Western Avenue Church, indifferent to the spiritual needs of Chicago's poor.[3]

In 1884, shortly after his conversion while attending the Des Plaines (Illinois) Camp Meeting, Duke Farson joined Harvey's youth-centered evangelistic team. In 1887, Farson married Annie Butcher, a musician, and in 1890 Harvey and Gertrude Ford were married. Shortly after the Harveys' marriage, Edwin Harvey and Duke Farson purchased property on Chicago's near south side and built a little red church, which was deeded to the Rock River Conference of the Methodist Episcopal Church. Farson was listed as pastor of the church, and Edwin L. Harvey served as Sunday school superintendent. In the spring of 1894, even as the devastating depression of 1893 paralyzed Chicago, Harvey acquired property for a second church on the city's northwest side. Located over five miles from the nearest Methodist Church, the Metropolitan Methodist Mission opened in July 1894 in a four-story brick building constructed at a cost of about $50,000. Again Farson was the pastor and Harvey, Sunday school superintendent.

Initially the mission closely resembled the social settlement model pioneered by Jane Addams at Hull House and included such activities as cooking and sewing classes for mothers and young girls. The culmination of the mission's first year was a spectacular tent revival that left a permanent mark upon the mission. "Five hundred were at the altar in four weeks," Gertrude Harvey remembered in 1920.[4] Evangelistic efforts and visitation among the sick and needy replaced such mundane and temporal activities as the teaching of cooking and sewing. Especially noteworthy was the mission's Sunday school, which, in only a year's time, reached an average attendance of five hundred children. Drawing primarily the children of Norwegian, Swedish, and German immigrant families, Harvey, always an entrepreneur, hired a bus and after Sunday school at the Western Avenue Methodist Church took as many teachers as were willing to teach at the Metropolitan Mission. While many of the parents of the Sunday school students were attending non-English-speaking churches, Harvey, who had cards printed by the thousands promising prizes and entertainment, managed a Sunday school that used the methods of tabloid journalism and dime novels to present an evangelical message to children who were hardly welcome in Chicago's largely suburban Methodist churches. As Duke Farson's son Bernard remembered years later, the "children were a tough lot, and Ed [Harvey] sometimes said it needed two teachers for one pupil." Within two years, Sunday school attendance was averaging more than eight hundred. Adult church membership was more modest; meeting before the Sunday school in an anteroom, the worship service attendance averaged about 150.[5]

Notwithstanding the unconventional character of the Metropolitan Methodist Mission, by the summer of 1897 Harvey and Farson were rapidly establishing reputations as leaders of Methodism in the greater Chicago area. In recognition of his business acumen and service to Methodism, Harvey was chosen as secretary of the Des Plaines Camp Grounds, while Farson became one of the most important financial contributors to Methodist missions and a frequent speaker in Chicago-area Methodist churches.[6]

In spite of the success of their ministry and the deep piety of the two men, the Metropolitan Methodist Mission remained aloof from the most potent religious renewal movement of the late nineteenth century—the Methodist-dominated Holiness movement. Nevertheless, Harvey in particular longed for a deeper religious experience.[7]

Agitated over the lack of depth of his religious experience, Harvey invited popular and controversial Holiness evangelist Beverly Carradine to conduct meetings at the Metropolitan Methodist Mission in November 1897. An ordained minister in the Methodist Episcopal Church, South, Carradine was noted for his public attacks upon the dress, lifestyles, and social activities of wealthy urban Methodists.[8]

For Edwin L. Harvey, the struggle for entire sanctification was both intense and fraught with numerous apologies, restitutions, and repeated trips to the altar. Finally, on November 28, 1897, he received the second blessing. The cost was high. For him, entire sanctification entailed a literal surrender of worldly possessions. He committed everything, including his wealth, to the ministry.[9] The extent of his understanding was clearly expressed in a 1909 account of the experience.

> Brethren, it is not necessary to write the date down in your Bible, because the Lord says He will put the sanctification right in your heart and then you will not forget it. He will brand you the same as a farmer brands his cattle. A farmer takes the animal, throws it in, ties his feet together and burns his initials right into him. That animal will not forget it, and it will not wash off. Before I was sanctified I used to give the Lord five per cent of my income and then ten per cent and then fifty per cent, but before I could get sanctified I put everything on the altar.[10]

The most notable feature of Harvey's early ministry was his insistence that authentic Christian witness included physical demonstrations. Although shouting, crying, laughing, running, and other physical manifestations had characterized Methodism and the Holiness movement over the previous century, Harvey insisted that "Pentecostal jumping" itself was a sign that a person was entirely sanctified. As Jack London noted, Burning Bush worship united devotional exercises, vaudeville, and elements of African American minstrel shows. It seemed to London a right mix of comedy, religion, and exercise. In fact, London believed that Burning Bush worship was inherently subversive to the social order. Its very insistence that all, regardless of education, race, gender, or social standing, must surrender the appearance of outward control to the subjective experience of Holy Spirit baptism was radically egalitarian. Given such a reality, it was perhaps inevitable that the movement's most insistent and thoughtful champions of demonstrative worship were its most educated members.[11]

Separating from Methodism in the fall of 1900, the Metropolitan Holiness Church (soon renamed the Metropolitan Church Association) entered 1901 intent on fanning the flames of revival. In March, a scheduled ten-day evangelistic campaign turned Chicago upside down. Attracting front-page coverage in Chicago newspapers, the revival resulted in an estimated 2,200 conversions. Deeply impressed with Harvey's ministry, Cincinnati publisher Martin Wells Knapp suggested that the Chicago church was, in fact, the normative Pentecostal church described in Acts 2. In December, Harvey, now billed as the "Chicago Whitefield," was the star attraction in a ten-day evangelistic campaign in Boston. Drawing front-page coverage in Boston newspapers, Harvey, Quaker evangelist and Knapp associate Seth C. Rees, and the team of evangelists from the Chicago revival took Boston by storm. Speaking to an estimated crowd of seven thousand people, Harvey suggested that the modern theologically trained minister and those deceived by the latter's ministry were destined for hell.

Building on the movement's remarkable evangelistic success in May of 1902, the MCA launched a periodical, the *Burning Bush*. Noted for its muckraking format, which featured front-page cartoons attacking opponents and popular religious figures, the *Burning Bush* became the most notorious Holiness publication of the era. In turn, the MCA became so identified with the periodical that it became known as the Burning Bush movement.

Imitating the success of the developers of mass circulation periodicals, Harvey and Farson almost inadvertently discovered a nearly insatiable market for stories concerning ecclesiastical scandal, self-aggrandizement, and compromise. The ease with which the MCA adopted journalistic exposé, the chief weapon of Progressive reform, may surprise those who continue to understand evangelicalism and the Holiness movement primarily as expressions of a cultural retreat from modernity. However, as heirs, with the muckrakers, to a common Protestant cultural legacy, the MCA believed, as did Progressive Era journalists, that while exposé was an end in itself, it would naturally lead to repentance and conversion. As the *Burning Bush* editorialized in 1904, "if exposing sin is 'opposing everybody' then they [the MCA] are guilty and we are glad they are. Let the truth be told if every holiness(?) movement must die as a consequence."[12]

In spite of the *Burning Bush*'s initial promise to expose sin, the periodical only gradually adopted a full-fledged muckraking format. With its first named attack on a Holiness ministry, Cincinnati's God's Bible School, in September 1902, the *Burning Bush* began a steady drift toward a tabloid design that included such standard muckraking features as the printing of private correspondence, the naming of names, and the use of cartoons. In October 1902, the *Bush* commissioned its first cartoon critical of American Christianity, an attack that depicted worshipers departing a simple church structure for ornate steepled churches designated Methodist, Baptist, and Presbyterian.[13]

On January 29, 1903, the *Bush,* employing a professional cartoonist whom critics claimed was unsaved, began its most notorious feature—full front-page cartoons caricaturing prominent evangelical leaders, especially Holiness evangelists. Among the prominent figures lampooned in "the Church Situation" were the one-time ally Seth C. Rees and John D. Rockefeller, whose sin lay in his refusal to give up his wealth. For individuals immersed in Holiness movement personalities and ideas, the cartoons made written text redundant.[14]

The cartoons caused an immediate sensation. Similar to the disclosures of the crimes and human foibles of political and social elites in the muckraking journals, their genius rested in part on exploiting the celebrity status of the subjects under scrutiny, a status many Holiness evangelists had masterfully cultivated in an age when Protestant evangelists such as D. L. Moody and Sam Jones were major cultural figures.[15]

For their part, the leaders of the MCA never denied that the source of the inspiration for their cartoons was the secular press. However, they also insisted that Old Testament prophets such as Ezekiel and Jeremiah employed similar pictorial images. Further, they argued that the ideas behind their cartoons were not the inventions of clever minds but were given by God to Farson and Harvey. Their contribution was merely to engage individuals with appropriate skills to translate "God's" messages into *Burning Bush* cartoons.[16]

The MCA's transition from a radical, but still conventional, evangelical denomination to a utopian religious community began at the church's 1902 camp meeting held at scenic Buffalo Rock, near Ottawa, Illinois. The ten-day encampment featured the preaching of Harvey, Farson, popular Holiness evangelist and founder of the Pillar of Fire Church Alma White, and, most notably, *Burning Bush* editor W. E. Shepard. Typical of such camp meetings, excitement increased as the meeting moved toward its conclusion. During an early Saturday morning service, Gertrude Harvey publicly announced that she would sell her spacious Chicago home and give the proceeds to support the ministry of the MCA. Deeply moved, others followed suit. Among the properties deeded to the MCA were several homes and a farm. In all, over $100,000 worth of property was surrendered to the trustees of the MCA.

Returning to Chicago, the Harveys sold their home and even their business. The proceeds were poured into the expanding ministry of the MCA, which now included the periodical, an orphanage, a home for unwed mothers, a Bible school and missionary training home, and several churches in northern Illinois. The individuals left without homes moved into the recently established Bible school. Although still not completely committed to the notion that private property was sinful, an intentional community began taking shape in Chicago.[17]

Moving gradually beyond the position that possessions could be idols that might threaten one's sanctification experience, the Bible school did not fully implement the "apostolic" practice of "having all things in common" until 1904. By August 1904, the *Burning Bush* was insisting that, "while people who do not have the Holy Spirit may give, those who do give all." By November of that year, E. L. and Gertrude Harvey had gone on record as saying that God, in these last days, was calling out a people willing to lay "down their money and their reputations and their lives." Although forced to admit that the actual surrender of one's wealth might not be an immediate possibility, especially given the greatly overcrowded Bible school, the *Burning Bush* began to insist that those remaining in temporary management of God's possessions must give all above immediate living expenses to the ministry of the Lord.[18]

Although the task of moving from a rapidly growing evangelical denomination of five hundred adult members scattered over six states to a centralized utopian religious community appeared daunting, the MCA was remarkably well equipped for such a transition. The growing theoretical commitment to communal living was aided by a pressing need to relieve overcrowding at the Bible school and an equally desperate need to expand the overtaxed printing plant in Chicago. Further, unlike many budding communal groups, the MCA possessed considerable capital from the sale of Harvey's hotels and the strong sales of the *Burning Bush,* the MCA's popular songbooks, and the recently established line of Scripture calendars. These publishing ventures also provided employment for individuals and families willing to "forsake all" and move to a denominational center that, unlike Chicago, provided adequate space for the movement's present and future needs.[19]

Last, but certainly not least, the MCA possessed the considerable managerial experience and skills of F. M. Messenger, who, as the general manager of a textile mill in North Grosvenor, Connecticut, had supervised 1,800 workers. Although largely unknown today, Messenger was one of the most remarkable products of the late-nineteenth-century Holiness movement. Messenger became a member of a company-sponsored Methodist Episcopal Church in the early 1880s. Although remembering himself as a "rank backslider," addicted to tobacco and unedifying conversation, upon assuming management of the mill, Messenger immediately embarked upon a campaign to rid the company town of liquor, violence, and sexual immorality. By the turn of the century, he had turned North Grosvenor into a remarkable anomaly—an industrial town without liquor and pool halls. Losing confidence in Methodism, Messenger organized an independent Holiness congregation in North Grosvenor in 1899. Emerging as one of the most militant Holiness champions in New England, he made what proved to be an unfortunate decision to invite the MCA to conduct evangelistic meetings in North Grosvenor and, as a result, was terminated as plant superintendent in 1903.[20]

Messenger sold his property and began life in the increasingly crowded MCA community in Chicago. He immediately assumed a prominent role. Rapidly emerging as the de facto editor of the *Burning Bush* and principal daily director of operations for the MCA, he became the primary architect of the MCA's implementation of a full-scale utopian community.[21]

With proceeds from the sale of the MCA's Buffalo Rock, Illinois, camp in the fall of 1905, Messenger engineered the purchase of a large abandoned resort hotel, the Fountain Spring House, in Waukesha, Wisconsin.[22] Located nineteen miles west of Milwaukee, Waukesha was a city of seven thousand people, easily accessible on inter-urban trolley lines. Known as "the Saratoga of the West," Waukesha boasted mineral springs that made the city a favorite vacation site in the years following the Civil War. The Fountain Spring House, the city's most famous resort, had opened its doors in 1874. The four-story structure was 450 feet from north to south. Its 450 rooms could accommodate 850 guests; its dining hall could comfortably seat 500. The grounds included a golf course, stable, racetrack, bathhouse, artificial lake stocked with trout, and one of Waukesha's famous springs. After intense negotiations, the property, which had been valued at $400,000, was purchased for $80,000.[23]

During the winter of 1905–6, the MCA began to transfer its varied ministries to its new home. Among the first to arrive were the orphans, who occupied a section of the Fountain Spring House with ample space for playgrounds. In the weeks that followed, the dining room was transformed into a church, while rooms previously dedicated to instruction in dancing became classrooms for the Bible school. Finally, in March 1906, the editorial offices of the *Burning Bush* and the printing plant relocated to their new home in Wisconsin. The move signaled a fundamental shift in the ministry of the MCA. Going beyond conventional ecclesiastical understanding, the MCA was no longer content with urging Christians to organize independent congregations. Faithful Christians, following the apostolic precedents established in Acts 2, were urged to sell their possessions and join the rest of God's people at the Fountain Spring House. Although continuing the church's tradition of aggressive evangelism, including the operation of urban missions and the dispatching of evangelistic teams wherever requested, the MCA had ceased to be a conventional Protestant denomination.[24]

As might be expected, not all those involved in the ministry of the MCA were willing to accept the full implications of Burning Bush communalism. Especially noteworthy for the subsequent history of the MCA was the loss of nearly all the members of the MCA's Los Angeles mission to Pentecostalism during the Azusa Street revival in 1906. In December 1905, Harvey dispatched two of his most successful evangelists, A. G. and Lillian Garr, to Los Angeles. As leaders of the MCA's extended and successful ministry in Danville, Virginia, the Garrs had created enormous conflict and publicity with an all-out war on tobacco, the basic staple of the local economy, demonstrating mastery of the Burning Bush strategy of direct confrontation. In California, they chose to concentrate on a social problem that was particularly prevalent—divorce. Their concern was the Church of the Nazarene's practice of allowing the remarriage of the so-called innocent party in a divorce. Initially, the response seemed gratifying. Herbert Buffum, a young Nazarene minister who had vigorously opposed MCA preaching, became one of the first converts.[25]

In spite of the initial success, the mission failed to attract the notoriety the Garrs and the MCA so prized. In early June, A. G. Garr locked the doors of the mission and led his remaining followers to an independent mission in a renovated church on Azusa Street, where both he and Lillian Garr spoke in tongues on June 14, 1906. With the closing of the Los Angeles mission, the Burning Bush movement's Los Angeles campaign had come to an unexpected conclusion.[26]

Convinced that the tongues they had spoken were Indian and Chinese dialects, A. G. and Lillian Garr immediately laid plans for a trip to the Burning Bush Mission in India. Surprised to find themselves unable to converse with the natives, the Garrs simply redefined the meaning of "tongues" as a heavenly language signifying that one had received the "Baptism of the Holy Ghost." They then spread the Pentecostal message among students at Pandita Ramabai School and among other missionaries in India and China. The Burning Bush mission in India remained unaffected.[27]

The real significance of the Harveys and the Burning Bush movement's encounter with Pentecostalism may be the impact the MCA had on the Pentecostal movement. Especially pivotal was the defection of A. G. Garr and the remaining members to the Azusa Street Mission. All evidence suggests that Garr's contingent arrived at Azusa Street at a point when the early enthusiasm generated in the wake of the San Francisco earthquake had subsided, and that real expansion of the Azusa Street revival occurred after Garr's experience of speaking in tongues. Further, other elements of the revival, such as demonstrative worship, its interracial character, and its formulation of the fivefold gospel, bear the unmistakable imprint of the Burning Bush movement, especially as emphasized in the MCA's ill-fated California campaign. It is especially noteworthy that the MCA position on divorce and remarriage, the particular emphasis of the MCA Los Angeles revival, became a prominent feature of the Azusa Street revival. In part, this was probably coincidental. William J. Seymour, the African American leader of the revival, shared the MCA's roots in Holiness radicalism. Having attended God's Bible School and having stayed in Denver at Alma White's Pentecostal Union on his way to California, he was a part of the radical network. Seymour's opposition to divorce and remarriage and his emphasis on restitution for past wrongs, both special emphases of the Burning Bush movement but not of the God's Bible School tradition, suggest that the doctrinal roots of the Azusa Street revival are in the MCA's California campaign. In fact, the message propagated by Seymour was identical with MCA teaching, with the exception of his teaching concerning the gift of tongues as the evidence of Holy Ghost baptism and his greater emphasis on racial equality. (One also finds similarities in the first Pentecostal group to break with Seymour during the Azusa Street revival, Florence L. Crawford's Apostolic Faith Church of Portland, Oregon. The doctrinal emphases of Crawford's movement, in its formative period, are virtually identical to Burning Bush teachings in 1906.) Regardless of the appeal of its other doctrines, as the twentieth century would demonstrate, the MCA's most prominent doctrine, "forsaking all for Jesus," would find only luke-warm support in the burgeoning Pentecostal movement. Although both movements turned to the book of Acts, Pentecostalism would take its cue from Acts 2:4, the Burning Bush movement from Acts 2:44–45.[28]

The MCA's war on Pentecostalism was just beginning in the fall of 1907. During the following decade, the "tongues movement" would be excoriated mercilessly in the pages of the *Burning Bush*. Fittingly, as muckraking-era journalists, the editors of the periodical wasted little time in beginning a full-scale investigation of Pentecostalism and its principal adherents. In January 1907, the *Burning Bush* published the first of several devastating exposés on the new religious phenomenon. Drawing on extensive investigations in Los Angeles, Topeka, and Zion City, Illinois, where MCA leaders interviewed Charles Parham, the early leader of the Apostolic Faith movement, the MCA, noting with considerable glee a dispute between Seymour and Parham, charged the latter with doctrinal irregularities and ethical lapses. Among the heresies identified were Parham's belief in the annihilation of the wicked, his opposition to demonstrative worship, and his support for tithing. The ethical lapses appear to have been of a financial nature. Taking special pleasure in Parham's attacks on the Azusa Street revival and in his descriptions of the emotional excesses of former MCA member Glenn A. Cook, the *Burning Bush* noted that Parham's actions and words bore an uncanny resemblance to those of the "fanatical" prophet from Maine, Frank Sandford.[29]

Other exposés followed. Especially significant for the history of Pentecostalism was a September 1907 issue of the *Burning Bush* that reprinted a *Zion Herald* account of the arrest of Parham on a charge of sodomy. Reaching a different audience from the *Zion Herald* account, the *Burning Bush* story, which was published during the crucial period when the Holiness movement was coming to terms with Pentecostalism, was certainly a factor in the Holiness movement's rejection of the new religious experience. During the next several years, the *Burning Bush* vigorously exposed any signs of Holiness movement compromises with Pentecostalism, especially Holiness periodicals carrying reports of avowed Pentecostals or of Pentecostals speaking at Holiness camp meetings.[30]

In addition to attacks on Pentecostalism, the *Burning Bush* continued its emphasis on forsaking all. Harvey never tired of insisting that "capitalists were responsible in a measure for the privations, the sufferings and even the death of many poor." As he asserted, "we preach every rich man into hell, just where Jesus preached him." "Jesus said the rich man could hardly get into heaven," the *Burning Bush* editorialized in 1906, concluding that "we believe his only way is to sell out and go in poor."[31]

The communal theology of Harvey and the Burning Bush movement did not remain static. Initially employing the language and logic of consecration and surrender, Harvey wrote of sanctification in 1904: "you think [holiness] is the nicest thing in the world—and it is, but it costs everything you have and that is what you do not know." Gradually, however, the language and logic of consecration was supplemented by other reasons for Christians to sell all and join the faith community in Waukesha. As early as December 1904, Harvey was insisting that in the normative church, as described in Acts 2:44–45, Christians were to surrender all worldly possessions. Further, employing the humanitarian approach, Harvey insisted that "any man having wealth, who loved his neighbor as himself, would soon get rid of his property, endeavoring to relieve the needs around him." Other voices, in typical Holiness fashion, asserted that the MCA teaching on possessions faithfully represented the teachings of John Wesley. In defense of Wesley, Burning Bush songwriter F. M. Lehman turned to Jesus' demand that anyone wishing to be a disciple must "forsake all" (Luke 14:33).[32]

As the Lucan text assumed primacy in the defense of their distinctive doctrine, the MCA began to subordinate the logic of consecration to the teaching of Scripture while increasingly turning to the example of Jesus as the basis for the church's position. As Jesus had voluntarily given up his special status in heaven, becoming homeless in the process, his followers, the MCA insisted, would do the same. As MCA leader Charles Hollingsworth argued in 1909, "giving all is but a natural consequence of getting a glimpse of Jesus."[33]

Increasingly, Harvey and *Burning Bush* writers turned to the substantial body of New Testament teaching that denounced wealth, those who possessed it, and the illusion of security it provided. Among the favorite scriptural defenses of their position were the Sermon on the Mount (Matthew 5), the Parable of the Rich Fool (Luke 12:13–21), the Story of the Rich Young Ruler (Luke 18:18–30), and appropriate attacks upon wealth and the wealthy in 1 Timothy, James, and 1 John. In marked contrast to the more established denominations and significant elements in the National Holiness Association, the MCA insisted that no rich person could be saved and further radicalized their contention by defining riches as anything more than the necessities and conveniences of life. Although acknowledging that on rare occasions one might meet a rich person who was generous, the *Bush* insisted that "you will find they never have salvation." With biting sarcasm, an editorial, aptly entitled "Millionaires Praise the Lord," reminded readers that the only rich person Jesus depicted in eternity was unfortunately lodged in hell (Luke 16:19–31). "Rich Methodists are going to find, when it is too late, that there is a dire and fearful punishment that lasts throughout eternity," the editorial concluded. Although insisting that the ministry of the Burning Bush movement was not to the rich, the *Bush* did note that Jesus had a message for them: rich people could not "enter the kingdom of Heaven any more than a camel can go through the eye of a needle." The rich did have an option. They could, following such Scripture passages as Matt. 19:29, Luke 14:33, and Luke 19:8–9, give up their wealth and join "the Lord's poor" in Waukesha.[34]

Beginning in 1913, with an ill-fated attempt to establish a second community in Bullard, Texas, the MCA's once solid financial bases began to erode. By 1925, the combination of community indebtedness and Harvey's now chronic poor health forced the founder to resign as MCA president. On January 22, 1926, E. L. Harvey died. Although ostensibly a tribute to his ministry in Chicago, Waukesha, and elsewhere, the founder's funeral in the Fountain Spring House and burial in Waukesha's Prairie Home Cemetery provided community members with an opportunity to justify publicly their own affirmation of Holiness radicalism and their decision to cast their lot with the mission of God's "peculiar people" in Waukesha. Although most of those in attendance were MCA faithful, much of the attention of the congregation was directed toward two visitors. One was the stately F. M. Messenger, now board chairman of the Church of the Nazarene. Messenger had unceremoniously left the MCA in 1913 in a dispute over the production and sale of gospel art calendars and had established a publishing company that would make him a millionaire by the time of his death in 1931. The other was an African American from Chicago whom Harvey had visited years earlier in the Cook County jail. Although the man had been on trial for murder, Harvey had become convinced of his innocence and was instrumental in his acquittal. Years later, Harvey's nephew, Edwin F. Harvey, remembered the "broken-hearted Negro, stretched out full length beside the coffin, sobbing out his heart." As Harvey recalled, the man softly repeated, "no one ever loved me like that man." As my interviews with MCA survivors suggest, although sixty-five years later few would accept all aspects of the founder's theology or the communal teaching he espoused, the affection for Harvey expressed by the African American mourner reflects the predominant sentiment of those in the Burning Bush movement.[35]

In North America, the Metropolitan Church Association experienced a steady decline in membership after the 1920s. The 1936 U.S. census of religious bodies reported that in the previous decade the MCA had closed seven missions and lost more than 150 members. Other indications of the church's waning influence in North America included a rapid decline in attendance at the annual camp meeting. The crowds, which had exceeded three thousand people at the time of Harvey's death, had fallen to a mere six hundred worshipers by 1940. Abandoning demonstrative worship in the early 1940s, the MCA became increasingly difficult to distinguish from other Holiness groups.

In 1956, the MCA, significantly reduced in membership and no longer able to maintain its aging facility in Waukesha, sold the Fountain Spring House. Relocating to Dundee, Illinois, the group continued to market books, religious art, gift products, and, interestingly enough, a gospel art calendar published by the heirs of F. M. Messenger. In 1961, the MCA reported 443 members in fifteen North American churches. By 2000, the MCA operated a single church in Milwaukee.[36] The Holiness radicalism of E. L. Harvey had become a distant memory.[37]

Charles Price Jones, circa 1910. Courtesy of Bishop Victor P. Smith, chairman of the National Publishing Board, Church of Christ (Holiness) U.S.A., Decatur, Georgia.

Charles Price Jones: Image of Holiness

Dale T. Irvin

Jesus only is my motto, Jesus only is my song,
Jesus only is my heart tho't, Jesus only all day long.
None but Jesus, Savior, Captain, None but Jesus help me sing;
Fill me ever with Thy presence, Jesus, Jesus, Lord and King.[1]

So wrote Charles Price Jones in his signature hymn, "Jesus Only," which was first published in 1899 in his hymnbook by the same title. Jesus alone was to be his guide: "Only He to choose my changes." Jesus alone was worthy to be worshiped: "Jesus only let me see."[2] From his perspective, the early Pentecostal doctrine of tongues seemed to shift the focus of Christian attention away from Jesus by placing an inordinate emphasis upon the gifts of the Spirit. Jones opposed the radical rupture that the Azusa Street experience represented in Christian life, advocating instead a more progressive form of sanctification. The exuberance of the burgeoning Pentecostal movement seemed to him to be antithetical to the decorum he associated with social and moral improvement in the African American community. Thus it is more than a little ironic that Jones came to play a major role in advancing the early Pentecostal movement. In 1897 he organized an annual Holiness convocation in his church in Jackson, Mississippi, in order to further the work of Christian sanctification among the churches. From that convocation emerged two new denominations after 1907: the Church of Christ (Holiness) U.S.A., which he continued to lead until his death in 1949, and the Church of God in Christ, the largest predominantly black Pentecostal denomination in North America. Jones himself went on to become relatively obscure, his legacy outside the Church of Christ (Holiness) confined mostly to historians of the Holiness and Pentecostal movements. He deserves a wider hearing, however, for his contribution to the southern Holiness revival at the end of the nineteenth century and to the Pentecostal movement in the twentieth.

The Making of a Holiness Preacher

Charles Price Jones was born in northern Georgia on December 9, 1865.[3] As a child, he benefited from the attention of several gifted teachers and developed a notable love of books before setting off on the road in his late teens. Conversion came in 1884 on Cat Island in the Mississippi River in Arkansas, where he worked picking cotton. Jones was baptized and the following year joined the local Baptist church. Feeling called to Africa as a missionary, he sought out the counsel of E. C. Morris in Helena, Arkansas, who convinced him to enroll first in the Arkansas Baptist College, which he did in 1888. Jones never did make it to Africa as a missionary, but he devoted himself for the rest of his life to ministry among those who were sons and daughters of Africa in the United States.

While a student in college, he accepted his first pastorate and was ordained by the dean of the college, C. L. Fischer, a graduate of Morgan Park Divinity School in Chicago (now part of the University of Chicago). Jones's visibility among black Baptists in the South quickly grew, aided by his reputation as a preacher and his work as editor of the *Baptist Vanguard*, the Arkansas Baptist state paper. The year 1891 marked his graduation from Arkansas Baptist College and his marriage. That same year he met Joanna P. Moore, a white northern Baptist missionary who had worked extensively among African Americans in the South for several decades. Sister Moore, according to one source, prophesied in 1891 that "God is going to fill you with the Holy Ghost."[4] The promise struck home, for despite his demonstrated intellectual and pastoral gifts, he still "yearned for apostolic life and power."[5]

In 1894, while serving as pastor of the Tabernacle Baptist Church in Selma, Alabama, Jones entered this new stage of spiritual experience, which he variously referred to as the experience of holiness, of being sanctified, and of being filled or baptized with the Holy Ghost. He also called it a fuller realization of Christ dwelling within, or the fullness of the Spirit. Holiness for Jones brought the capacity not only for overcoming sin but also for healing from physical disease. He recognized in this experience an effective means of spiritual empowerment for his own life and ministry and for the churches of the South, which he perceived to be in need of revitalization. During this period of intense spiritual wrestling, Jones also received a revelation from the Holy Spirit that he should begin to write hymns, resulting eventually in an extensive body of hymnody.[6]

The following year he was called to serve the Mt. Helm Baptist Church in Jackson, Mississippi, where he continued to teach his message of sanctification. Another revelation from the Spirit led him to call a Holiness convocation at the church in 1896. Around the same time, Jones began to bring out a bimonthly publication entitled *Truth*, a paper that soon proved to be an effective vehicle for publishing the call to the convention.

The first meeting of the convocation was held at the Mt. Helm Baptist Church in June 1897. It continued to meet annually thereafter, becoming the organizing nucleus for the Church of God in Christ and the Church of Christ (Holiness) U.S.A. Participating in that first year's convention were, among others, Charles H. Mason, with whom Jones had already worked in revivals and church planting, and J. A. Jeter, who had been a deacon in St. Paul Baptist Church in Little Rock when Jones was the pastor in his college days, and would later, with Mason, visit the Azusa Street mission in Los Angeles.

The experience that Jones, Mason, Jeter, and others were teaching was not without its critics. Holiness doctrines were meeting with increased resistance within the churches as Baptists and Methodists in the South began to exclude from membership persons who claimed a distinct experience of sanctification or Christian perfection. Jones even reported several incidents of violence directed against him for his teaching.[7] Opposition arose on several points. For one thing, Jones himself acknowledged that he put much more emphasis upon the person and work of the Holy Spirit than did the denominational churches.[8] Moreover, like many others within the Holiness movement across the United States, Jones linked the experience of personal sanctification with the goal of realizing the unity of the church. Many churches in the South, including the black Baptist congregations, were concerned with strengthening their institutional identity during this period, and this in turn meant increased attention to denominational distinctives. The Holiness movement cut against the denominational grain, challenging a separate Baptist identity by calling for the unity of the churches.[9] In the context of southern African American Christian experience, argues David Daniels, the Holiness movement also represented a renewal of the vitality associated with the noninstitutionalized form of

Christianity found in slave religion, over a Baptist denominational identity that was largely a post–Civil War development among African Americans in the region.[10]

Jones recognized the legitimacy of other churches outside the Baptist association that practiced baptism by immersion and pursued spiritual sanctification. At the same time, he began to question on biblical grounds the use of the term *Baptist* in identifying one's church or faith. The Baptist churches stood upon the authority of Scripture, but he found no scriptural support for naming the church Baptist. The use of the term was less than four centuries old, he argued, whereas the true church of Christ went all the way back historically to the time of Jesus and the Apostles. In the New Testament, believers were told to do all in the name of Jesus. The term *Baptist*, on the other hand, referred specifically not to the work of Jesus and the Holy Spirit but to John, who came before Jesus.[11]

The controversy around these convictions erupted at Mt. Helm in 1898 when Jones led an attempt to change its name officially to the Church of Christ, dropping the denominational nomenclature. Several members of the church sued in court to block the change on the basis of Mt. Helm's charter. The case was first decided in Jones's and the majority's favor in a lower court. But then in 1901 the decision was reversed in the Mississippi state supreme court, which, despite a subsequent vote by the church to rescind the name change, ruled that the majority had violated the church's charter and ordered them to vacate the premises. The majority of the members left with Jones to found Christ Temple Church in Jackson.

The building they erected in 1903 continued to serve as the meeting place for the annual Holiness convocation. The convocation became in effect the gathering point for an association of churches spread across several states during the first decade of the twentieth century. Individual congregations referred to themselves as "Church of Christ" or "Church of God." Jones served as general overseer of the association, while C. H. Mason served as overseer of Tennessee and J. A. Jeter as overseer of Arkansas.

Jones and Mason parted ways after 1907. The denomination Jones went on to build on the foundations of his annual convocation came to be known as the Church of Christ (Holiness) U.S.A. The church was episcopal in its structures, and after 1927 Jones himself carried the title of senior bishop.[12] Nevertheless, he did not entirely abandon his earlier Baptist identity. In a short article from around 1907, written in response to an inquiry about the various other Holiness movements of his day, he noted the following: "As we now stand we might be called 'Higher Life Baptists,' our doctrine differing very little from that advocated by A. J. Gordon, F. B. Meyer, Evangelist Torrey, Chas. H. Spurgeon and others. Only like the Christians (sometimes known as Campbellites), we beleive [*sic*] that we ought to HONOR THE NAME of Christ as it is honored in the New Testament and not put human nicknames on Christ's bride, since there is only one name by which we may be saved."[13]

C. P. Jones and the Emergence of Pentecostalism

It is in his relationship to Mason that the importance of C. P. Jones for the history of early Pentecostalism is primarily to be found. There is some historical basis for arguing that William J. Seymour at least knew of Jones and his Holiness work, and perhaps that Seymour had even met Jones prior to the 1906 Azusa Street revival, but the evidence is slim. Jones and Mason, on the other hand, were colleagues in ministry from the days when Jones was in Arkansas. They had an active theological relationship for at least fifteen years prior to Mason's trip to Azusa Street, where he received the gift of tongues, an event that would prove to be decisive in separating the two. The various accounts of the events surrounding Mason's visit to Azusa Street in 1907 and Jones's theological response to the Pentecostal understanding of tongues and Holy Spirit baptism call for careful delineation.

The year 1906 found Jones in a spiritual state of general dissatisfaction. The previous year had witnessed the burning of his church, Christ Temple, at the hands of a white mob. According to Jones, the governor of Mississippi himself had played a role in inciting the event. Jones's prominence as an African American church leader was without doubt the major reason for the attack. The fire destroyed not only the church building but also Jones's printing plant, two thousand recently arrived copies of his new hymnal, and what he estimated to be thousands of dollars of office material.[14] A new, brick structure was erected the following year in 1906. But the struggle must have taken its toll on him, and by his own account he was in need of a renewal of the Holy Spirit.[15]

This experience of a renewal of the Holy Spirit occurred at a time when a wider discussion concerning the work of the Holy Spirit was emerging among the leaders of the convention. At the center of their conversation was the question of what properly constituted the baptism of the Holy Spirit. Most agreed that, "after repentance and forgiveness of sins of the past, the new convert should receive the Holy Ghost as keeping power from committing known sins henceforth, and that the fruits of the daily life are the evidence of either having thus received Him or having not so received Him."[16] According to one source, however, Jones began to doubt that they had as yet received the fullness of the Spirit. "Here he saw that a jug could be full of water and not be in the water."[17] It is significant that it was Jones who was remembered as having first raised the possibility and need of a further experience of the Spirit. When word came to both Jones and Mason of the events of Azusa Street, Mason decided to go, taking along with him two other members of the convocation, J. A. Jeter and D. J. Young.

Years later Jones recalled his distress over the reports of Mason's experience at Azusa Street. He was staying in Americus, Georgia, at the home of a supporter when he saw a copy of the Azusa Street paper, *Apostolic Faith*, with Mason's testimony in it. Mason seemed to be saying that he had not received the Holy Spirit prior to his experience on Azusa Street and speaking in tongues.[18] To Jones, this was tantamount to denying Christ. "Now Christ and the Holy Ghost are one, the Holy Ghost is the Spirit of Christ (1 Pet. 1:11), and when one who has asked and received the Holy Ghost (Luke 2:1–13) lets some sort of spirit cause him to deny the witness of the Spirit that he has received in order to get that other spirit, I ask you what has he done?"[19]

Regarding the practice of speaking in tongues, Jones did not reject the experience per se. By his own admission, he had at first welcomed the reports of the revival he read in the *Apostolic Faith*. Even after his break with Mason, he accepted the possibility of a legitimate gift of tongues while rejecting what he took to be the exuberance and "extravagances" associated with Azusa Street and the new Pentecostal movement.[20] He also rejected the doctrine of initial evidence, arguing that on the Day of Pentecost tongues were not given as an evidence of the Spirit but as a means of communication. Thus he wrote, "I believe God's gift of tongues shall some day be restored to the church, but it will not go with a false doctrine. Why should there not be people who now speak with tongues? But they would not call a nervous gibberish a tongue, nor would they call it an evidence or **the** evidence, or the only evidence; for the Bible does not."[21]

Upon the return of Mason, Jeter, and Young from Los Angeles in 1907,

Jones sought to head off the teaching and practice regarding tongues within the churches in their convocation. The issue erupted that August at their gathering in Jackson, however, leading to a split between those following Jones (who now included Jeter) and those siding with Mason. A new round of court cases ensued, with Mason's party eventually winning control of a large number of the churches associated with their work.[22] In 1909 Mason organized a new convocation under the name he had received some years before in a prophecy, "The Church of God in Christ." Jones reorganized the churches and pastors that had sided with him as the Church of Christ (Holiness).

Excursus on Jones and Seymour

One question remains concerning Jones's relationship to, and possible influence upon, William J. Seymour, the leader of the Azusa Street revival. Writing several years later, Jones claimed to be familiar already in 1906 with the writings of Charles Parham, whom he credited with being the originator of the doctrine of tongues as the initial evidence of Holy Spirit baptism.[23] He claimed as well to have met in Denver the first person to speak in tongues in 1901 under Parham's teaching, Agnes Ozman, without being convinced of the genuineness of her experience.[24] Regarding Seymour, Jones only said that during the 1906–7 period he had read his *Apostolic Faith* papers, deciding after an initial positive response not to distribute them any longer.[25] In an article responding to an inquiry concerning the relationship of his own work to that of other Holiness groups around the country in the first decade of the century, Jones listed "The Tongues cult started in Kansas a few years ago under a man named Parham" as one such movement with which he was familiar. He continued, "Afterward, in 1906 I believe, it broke out afresh in a colored mission in Los Angeles, California. It became immediately almost a world-wide sensation and many good and earnest people were deceived by it."[26] It is noteworthy that in this early report Jones made no mention of Seymour by name. Indeed, I know of no direct reference by Jones to having met Seymour, even though such a claim would certainly have fit his pattern of relating firsthand experiences with those involved in events about which he was writing.

Despite this silence, recent Pentecostal historiography has often directly linked Seymour to Jones. Most claims for a direct relationship are dependent on Douglas J. Nelson's 1981 dissertation, "For Such a Time as This."[27] The basis for Nelson's assertion of direct influence in turn lies in a footnote found in a 1914 A.B. thesis by C. W. Shumway that was completed at the University of Southern California. Shumway conducted interviews through the mail and in person with a number of Pentecostals, among them Seymour. According to Shumway, "In the winter of 1904–5 [Seymour] went by 'special revelation' to Jackson, Miss., to receive spiritual advice from a well-known colored clergyman there. There he was grounded more firmly in his millenarianism and he came away a more firm believer than ever in the value of 'special revelations.'"[28] From an interview conducted in 1979 with Elder C. C. Carhee in Los Angeles, Nelson stated that he was able to confirm that the clergyman was C. P. Jones.[29]

One would be hard pressed to imagine Seymour traveling to Jackson, Mississippi, in the winter of 1904–5 to meet with an African American clergy member other than Jones. By that time Jones was among the most widely read black Holiness teachers in the country, and the convocations at Mt. Helm were drawing people from considerable distances. Yet, when writing of Seymour several years later, Jones did not indicate that he had met the leader of the Azusa Street revival in person.

What kind of spiritual advice might Seymour have received from Jones? Jones strongly advocated the doctrine of special revelations, or what might more generally be known as the gift of prophecy among Pentecostal and charismatic believers today. This would seem to support the argument for Seymour having met with Jones. On the other hand, Jones did not appear to place much emphasis upon millenarianism, making it hard to reconcile Seymour's statement with Jones's teachings.[30] In many ways Jones's Christocentric doctrine was closer to that of William Durham, whom Seymour later opposed theologically within the Pentecostal movement. Jones even used the phrase "finished work" at times to describe the sufficiency of Christ for the fullness of salvation, a phrase that came to be associated closely with Durham's position. Of course one could argue for Jones's influence upon Seymour being experienced indirectly through his earlier relationship with Mason, belying Nelson's claim for a direct relationship. But still that report of a 1904–5 visit to Jackson, Mississippi, cannot be ignored.

A possible explanation lies in a small report found in the December 29, 1904, edition of *Truth*.[31] There one reads a published invitation to "the ministers" (presumably those who have identified themselves with the work and whose names were printed in the same edition) to come "to the class in January. It begins the 15th and goes on 10 days, maybe two weeks." It is possible that it was this ministers' seminar offered in January 1905 in Jackson that Seymour recalled a decade later as having attended. The notice makes no mention as to the identity of the leader of the class, but it is a safe assumption that Jones was involved. It is quite conceivable that during this class a discussion of millennial teaching occurred that could have impressed itself upon Seymour's thinking.[32] Most important, such a hypothesis offers the possibility that Jones's emphasis upon the gift of prophecy or special revelations was indeed significant for Seymour and his own eventual understanding of the ministry of the Holy Spirit in the church.

One final connection needs to be noted regarding Seymour and Jones. In 1917, Jones organized a new congregation in Los Angeles and began to shift the center of his own ministry to that city where he eventually permanently located. Seymour was still serving during these years at Azusa Street, which by then he had incorporated as a local church. Although their joint tenure in Los Angeles only lasted five years (Seymour died in 1922), it is possible that the paths of these two African American church leaders crossed on some occasion. If this were not so in life, however, it makes even more ironic the resting place in which their bodies were laid in death. Professor Cecil M. Robeck of Fuller Seminary has pointed out that both William J. Seymour and C. P. Jones were buried in the same cemetery in Los Angeles, less than one hundred feet apart.[33]

A Practical, Christ-Centered Spirituality

The two major court decisions that affected the early institutional development of the Church of Christ (Holiness) provide a symbolic framework for situating the theological perspective of C. P. Jones. The Church of Christ took its name neither from John the Baptist nor from the day of Pentecost, but from Jesus Christ himself. Jones often pointed to his "Jesus-only" theology as being what was at stake in the conflicts the church was going through. The Baptist churches seemed to him to be exalting the work of John the Baptist rather than Jesus. Likewise, according to Jones, the Pentecostal movement lifted up various experiences of the Holy Spirit, such as occurred on the Day of Pentecost, at the expense of emphasizing the life, ministry, and death of Jesus Christ. Jesus alone determined Christian identity; Jesus alone was to be the center of all theological reflection.

Jones did not deny the distinctive personhood of the Holy Spirit or the doctrine of the Trinity. On the contrary, he affirmed both in no uncertain terms. The Holy Spirit was the subject of the first booklet he published in 1896 and of numerous sermons over the years.[34] Jones followed C. L. Fisher in emphasizing the distinct agency of the Holy Spirit in Christian life and the work of the church.[35] At the same time, he did not conceive of the work of the Holy Spirit to stand apart from Jesus Christ. "The Savior in this wonderful dispensational administration of the Spirit thoroughly and personally identifies Himself with the Holy Spirit . . . Our Savior and the Spirit are one. The Holy Spirit is Christ at work in the world saving men in his divine, invisible, omnipresent and almighty aspect."[36]

The Holy Spirit who enlivens and empowers the church is the Spirit of Jesus Christ. Through the Holy Spirit, Jesus Christ continues the work of salvation he began in the flesh. The sacrificial work of propitiation Jesus finished on the cross, but the sanctifying work through the Holy Spirit he continues in the church. Jones employed the terminology of a "second blessing" to describe the distinct baptismal experience of sanctification that "adds such glory to sainthood."[37] Nevertheless, he emphasized that it was Jesus Christ, and not the Holy Spirit, who was to be the focus of spiritual reflection. By his own admission it was a theological stance closely related to that of the Christian Alliance, whose founder, A. B. Simpson, had articulated a doctrine of the "fourfold Gospel" emphasizing the work of Jesus Christ as savior, sanctifier, healer, and coming King.[38]

According to Jones, the baptismal experience of sanctification brought about a cleansing that enabled a believer to live free from sin by being fully in Christ. The Christian who had the mind of Christ had thus "*ceased* from sin."[39] The finished work of Christ's death removed both our sins and our sinful nature.[40] The mode of sinlessness, or perfection, one attained was entirely of Christ, never of one's self, he said. "It is God's business to make the mystery effective," and ours only to claim victory through faith in Christ. "Christ in us is the hope of glory," he concluded.[41]

Jesus was the divine teacher whose word brought freedom. On the cross he pronounced his work to be finished; in the church he continued to communicate that perfection to all who would receive it. The effect was quite practical. Christians could truly overcome sin through Jesus Christ.

Perfection was a matter of the Holy Spirit leading one deeper into the life of Christ, a life of righteousness and love, which were the fruits of divine activity in the world. In this way Jones connected Jesus' work of atonement with experiences such as divine physical healing. The order of salvation included finished and continuing dimensions, both of which required emphasis. Jones affirmed the distinct nature of the experience of the second blessing and the baptism of the Holy Spirit, and at the same time he recognized the need for a continuing work of the Holy Spirit that from time to time could become more pronounced in one's life. On these issues he was siding with those who taught a progressive, rather than instantaneous, doctrine of sanctification.

When it came to consideration of specific works and gifts of the Spirit in the Christian life, Jones taught that one ought to avoid forms of exuberance that could be considered excessive, for they led to placing an unspiritual emphasis upon the gifts rather than the Giver. He encouraged vitality in worship. Yet in a 1903 article he wrote the following: "Many of us have made the mistake of supposing that to be full of the Holy Ghost, one must be mentally unbalanced, obstreperous, defiant of authority and generally noisy and self-demonstrative. Not at all. There is no person as sound-minded, gentle, quiet, unostentatious and free from the selfvaunting spirit as the *truly* sanctified Christian. . . . Be not extravagant in testimony or sermon or prayer; do not think the most power is in the most noise. Be sober. Noise is good in its place, but the word says be sober."[42]

It is important to note here that Jones wrote this passage some three years before the Azusa Street revival began. Given this orientation to worship and personal spiritual demeanor, it is easy to see why he responded negatively as he did to the reports of Azusa Street. Almost immediately he rejected much of what he observed and heard reported concerning the early Pentecostal movement and speaking in tongues. He called the "Tongues cult" of Parham and Azusa Street "a spiritual fake supported by false interpretations and false applications of scriptures."[43] The gift of tongues in the book of Acts, he believed, referred to known human languages or empowered modes of speech, such as when one who had not previously demonstrated oratorical skills could proclaim the gospel with power. Jones did not reject the sincerity of those who embraced the new Pentecostal doctrine. He referred at one point to the leader of the Azusa Street revival as "Brother Seymour," even though he rejected his teaching regarding tongues.[44] In fact, Jones accepted the possibility of a gift of known tongues given to the church for carrying out its ministry and mission. His argument was against unknown tongues being the initial or biblical evidence.

One further issue concerned Jones regarding what he thought to be one of the excesses of the Pentecostal movement, namely the role of women in ministry. He was forthright in his rejection of women preaching or serving in pastoral leadership in the church. On several occasions he cited the exuberant worship services he had observed women leading as a reason for rejecting their ministry. He also referred to biblical texts in support of his position.[45] One might argue that Jones was not entirely consistent in this regard, for he did not object to the active work of Joanna P. Moore, with whom he was involved in ministry.[46] Jones's concerns about women's leadership seem to have been focused on issues of respectability and decorum, which in the end were also those he raised against forms of worship that encouraged dancing, shouting, or any other behaviors that he considered excessive.

On the positive side, Jones consistently argued for dignified worship and an informed faith. Throughout his ministry he taught that Christian holiness was a matter of empowerment, stressing the themes of spiritual cleansing, intellectual advancement, and moral betterment. Empowerment for living entailed resistance to the forces of oppression that confronted Americans of African descent in particular. Looking back upon his life in 1927, he recalled the terrors of Jim and Jane Crow racism that allowed whites to murder blacks without consequence, often forcing blacks during the 1880s into a "practical slavery without the master having any particular responsibility for his slave."[47] In this situation, religion offered hope for life in heaven and justice on Judgment Day. "The hope God gives the ignorant and the oppressed is a precious thing," he noted.[48] Such hope, however, did not come without moral effort and persuasion. Providing moral direction, especially for those of African descent in America, was the purpose of one of the major works Jones published in his lifetime, *An Appeal to the Sons of Africa*. Its pages were particularly addressed to "that distinct part of heterogeneous American citizenship, the despised, honored, feared, petted, loved, hated and *sometimes,* too-much noticed black people."[49]

The opening poem of the volume was occasioned by the report of two lynchings in the Midwest. In the lines of the poem itself, Jones called upon those "of ancient Ethiopic blood" to recognize that "We are the lowliest class, but then / God's nobles come from lowly men."[50] Africa once swayed the world, and the history of its ancient civilizations was one filled with grandeur. It was destined once again to be a place of higher culture and prominence. The degradation of the present condition of Africans in America could thus be no more than a "school ground,"[51] preparing them for what God intended to be a greater existence. "Africa's sons, we plainly see / That *in us* wise divinity / A holy purpose has. Let's find / The wisdom of the heavenly mind."[52] Because of severe oppression, African Americans were going to be held to a higher standard of judgment and subject to greater difficulties than other classes might be. Nevertheless, Jones did not despair of victory. Elsewhere in the volume he wrote the following: "This poem is intended to teach that we must not let hardship discourage us but oppose force with stronger force and arduous difficulties with indomitable perseverance; that is, labor to *win any how* and stop not till we win."[53]

The overall message of *An Appeal* was one of resistance through moral improvement and personal betterment. Jones exhorted those of African descent not to stoop to emulate the viciousness of their oppressors and not to follow the ways of the dominating class, but to take up lives of industry and virtue. Holiness coincided with a program of empowerment and victory through suffering and virtue: "But know, dear Afric's sable sons / Not pompous talk, not Gatling guns, / Not lodges, politics nor creeds, / Not gold, nor culture, *power* breeds / So much as *rugged honesty* / With God and man."[54] Along these lines, Jones was concerned that more secular civil rights organizations would prove ineffective if they failed to attend to spiritual dimensions. In the pages of *Truth* he wrote that the Negro Congress ought to be a place of fasting and prayer, for if the people acknowledged God, God would help their cause.[55] Political freedom and Christian holiness were for him inextricably bound.

In the end it was a message addressed to more than those of African descent. Jones was not a racial separatist in his ideology, but he joined an Ethiopic or Africanist perspective and an integrationist vision that sought to speak not only to African Americans but to all people. The poem "The Bond of the Races" articulated well his hope for improved relations between blacks and whites, particularly in the South. Recognizing the enduring legacy of their past relations as master and slave and the continuing divergences in social status, Jones asserted that there was nevertheless an underlying common humanity among blacks and whites and that they would one day dwell together in justice and peace.[56]

This vision of empowerment and inclusion was reflected in practical ways in Jones's ministry. He participated in collaborative efforts and preached at convocations such as that of the predominantly white Holiness Pentecostal Mission in Nashville in 1902.[57] On various occasions he included white speakers at his own programs and was interested in furthering the interracial aspects of the Holiness movement. He was realistic in his assessment of what was possible in America at the turn of the century; but his was no less a vision of integration and inclusion than the one that was later identified with William J. Seymour and the Azusa Street revival.

As noted, the name of Charles Price Jones has been greatly eclipsed from the historical record of Holiness and Pentecostal movements in the past century. Nevertheless, his legacy merits remembrance. His emphasis upon the centrality of Jesus Christ within the Christian higher life, his advocacy of an integrated and progressive mode of sanctification, and his vision of social equality are still viable ingredients of any movement for Christian renewal today.[58]

Frank Sandford: Tongues of Fire in Shiloh, Maine

Shirley and Rudy Nelson

On the weekend of June 9 and 10, 1900, a group of seven people, including a young Bible student named Charles Parham, made their way east from Topeka to Kansas City and joined some forty others in a chartered railroad car on its way from Tacoma, Washington, to Shiloh, also known as the Holy Ghost and Us Bible School, on a hilltop in Durham, Maine, thirty miles northeast of Portland. The Tacoma Group was only the latest wholesale addition to the burgeoning movement led by Frank Weston Sandford. In 1892, Sandford had left the Free Will Baptist ministry in Maine, going off on his own to test what God could do with a man who would "step out in absolute abandonment to His will, His word, and His providences."[1]

Parham did not stay long. The record indicates that on July 18 he was a member of a group of seven that left Maine with Sandford on a mission to Winnipeg, Manitoba. Within a month, Sandford returned to Maine, but Parham severed his ties to Shiloh and went back to Topeka to start his own school.[2] However, if in the annals of Shiloh, Parham rates only a passing footnote, the influence of the brief Shiloh experience on Parham—and indirectly on the Pentecostal movement in America—is quite another matter.[3]

On the evening of January 1, 1901, during a service in Parham's Bethel Bible School in Topeka, a young woman student received Holy Spirit baptism, evidenced by "speaking in tongues"—a historic moment generally identified as the beginning of the modern Pentecostal movement in America. Other students, and eventually Parham himself, experienced the same phenomenon. From this point on, Parham began to affirm the gift of

Frank Sandford, represented as David the Shepherd, 1903. Courtesy of the author.

tongues in his preaching ministry. Vinson Synan notes that this pivotal event took place just six months after Parham left Shiloh. The temporal closeness of the Shiloh sojourn would not, of course, by itself imply a causal connection. But Synan is clear about the significance of Shiloh: "While in Shiloh, Parham heard glossolalia for the first time when several students came down out of a 'prayer tower' speaking in tongues after several hours of intercessory prayer. Returning to Topeka, he felt that there was still something beyond the experience of sanctification, perhaps a charismatic baptism in the Holy Spirit, that would be needed 'to meet the challenge of the new century.'"[4]

Actually, glossolalia had broken into Shiloh's world at a New Year's Eve watchnight service one year earlier. When "the gift of tongues" descended, Sandford reportedly was astonished to look around and count 120 people present, exactly the number gathered at the first Pentecost in Acts. Unlike the later watchnight service at Parham's school in Topeka, however, this event was not a harbinger of things to come. Whatever happened at Shiloh on December 31, 1899, Sandford insisted (to the local newspaper) that "speaking in tongues" did not mean the "unknown tongue" referred to by the Apostle Paul, but currently known foreign languages.[5] There is no evidence that Parham disagreed, or that he intended to open a school where glossolalia was more acceptable, or that he said as much to Sandford. The problem for Sandford was more likely that Parham chose to leave, whatever the reason. According to Frank Murray, his biographer, Shiloh's leader, "well aware of the excesses and shameful practices then often associated with Pentecostalism, always felt that Mr. Parham, who for months had professed the strongest loyalty to Shiloh, fell into a snare by breaking away."[6] In other words, Parham slipped into error because he left Sandford's side.

There is more than a hint in Murray's allegation that Parham's real offense had a lot less to do with "excesses" related to speaking in tongues than with his real failure—defecting from Shiloh. As for the "shameful practices" that Sandford is said to have imputed to Pentecostalism, Shiloh was not immune from the same charges, often having to fend off the accusation, because of its boisterous and spontaneous worship services, that its adherents indulged in their own brand of "shameful practices." Here, too, we must look for a more convincing explanation of why Sandford turned his back on a movement with which he shared so much.

FRANK SANDFORD: TONGUES OF FIRE IN SHILOH, MAINE

There is no convenient litmus test to simplify the search. In his valuable essay on history writing among early Pentecostals, Grant Wacker observes that "the early periodicals make it clear that the boundary lines that defined who was in or out were extremely porous," although there was "substantial consensus about the theological inner core." He uses Shiloh as an illustration: "Through the 1890s and 1900s all of the characteristic beliefs and practices of pentecostalism, including resurrections from the dead, took place at Shiloh. All, that is, except speaking in tongues. Although primitive pentecostals disputed the theological meaning and linguistic nature of tongues, none doubted that it was a coveted part of Christian experience. Clearly the absence (or, at most, minimal role) of tongues at Shiloh precluded it from serious consideration as a fountain of pentecostal revival."[7]

As we have seen, there is clear evidence that glossolalia did make an appearance at Shiloh, but Wacker is correct in claiming that it played a minimal role. While not undercutting at all the significance of the fact that Sandford settled on a negative view of glossolalia, we shall try to show that the fundamental difference between Sandford's movement and the movement that became known as Pentecostalism goes much deeper than the tongues issue. What distinguished them finally had much more to do with Sandford's authoritarian leadership and his steadily intensifying personal obsessions—especially his narcissistic identification with certain biblical figures and his conviction that Shiloh was the key to history's apocalyptic consummation.

The Beginnings

First, we need to explore the common ground between the two movements. Like so many others in the early days of American Pentecostalism, Frank Sandford was profoundly influenced by the Holiness teachings, perfectionism, and the Higher Life movement. In 1887, as a twenty-seven-year-old pastor of a small Free Will Baptist church in Topsham, Maine (not to be confused with the southern strain of Free Will Baptists), Sandford read a book that changed his life. Hannah Whitall Smith, a well-bred Quaker woman from Philadelphia, had become popular—along with her husband Robert Pearsall Smith—in England and America as an advocate of the Higher Life, sometimes called the Victorious Life or the Deeper Life. Sandford, although a successful and highly regarded pastor, was constantly nagged by the conviction that there must be something more to the Christian life and ministry than he had yet experienced. Hannah Whitall Smith, in her book *The Christian's Secret of a Happy Life,* assured him that there was and that it was his for the asking.[8] The secret lay not in personal struggle but in a joyful "letting go," reckoning on God's power, responding obediently the moment one was sure of God's will. This was exactly the message for which Sandford had been waiting. Closing the book, he made a vow, "like a drunkard signs a pledge," as he put it, never to doubt God but to obey immediately and without hedging, as soon as His leading was clear.[9]

For the next few years, that vow brought him into the circle of many others in the Holiness movement on the same spiritual quest. D. L. Moody's "College of Colleges," held each summer on the grounds of his academy at Northfield, Massachusetts, was one stop on the way. A center of the Higher Life movement, Northfield was also a driving force in the revived interest in foreign missions. In the summer of 1887 some four hundred people gathered there, under the leadership of men like Robert Wilder of Princeton and John R. Mott of Cornell, for the second annual meeting of the Student Volunteer Movement, with its stirring challenge, "The evangelization of the world in this generation."[10] Later that summer, as a guest at Maine's Old Orchard Beach camp-meeting grounds, Sandford sat under the tutelage of A. B. Simpson, founder of the Christian and Missionary Alliance, whose emphasis on divine healing held out the possibility that Sandford, too, might claim the gift of healing in his own ministry.[11] Then in 1888, while at one of the popular Niagara Falls Prophecy Conferences, the intricate strands of biblical interpretation concerning the end times were woven into his network of interests.[12]

The kind of ministry that these influences would mold for Frank Sandford began inauspiciously. He resigned from his church, cut loose from the Free Baptist denomination, and with his new bride—the former Helen Kinney, a returned missionary whose wealthy parents were followers of A. B. Simpson—set out by faith to do evangelistic work in the state of Maine, with no salary and no home. Looking back on these months, Sandford called them with humor their "shabby period."[13] Even in these humble beginnings, however, his eyes were set on a wider ministry. Following Christ's apostolic commission in Acts ("Ye shall be witnesses unto me both in Jerusalem, and in all Judea, and in Samaria, and unto the uttermost part of the earth"), he thought of Maine as his Samaria, but his heart was already set on the uttermost parts of the earth.

This time was also a period of self-doubt. Sandford was troubled that he had not experienced a dramatic infilling of the Holy Spirit, as had so many others in the various Holiness communities. For several weeks in the winter of 1894, the Sandfords and a few of their friends spent morning after morning in an abandoned church, kneeling on the floor, consecrating and reconsecrating themselves, waiting for some empowering experience that did not come.

When it did come, in August 1894 at Old Orchard Beach, its mode was quiet, rational, and unemotional. Stephen Merritt, known in Holiness circles around the world for his teaching on the Holy Spirit, pointed out to his listeners that Jesus had promised the Holy Spirit to anyone who asked. One should not demand proof of fulfillment—a disparagement of God's faithfulness—but rest confidently in Jesus' promise. That is exactly what Sandford did. "AUGUST 2ND, SETTLED FOREVER," he wrote in his Bible. It was a pact with God, made "without the slightest feeling or emotion," to be led and controlled by the Holy Spirit.

From a historical perspective, when we look back on Sandford's further interpretation of the experience, a small warning flag goes up. "The Guest," he wrote, "told me that he was in all the experiences of life, making them all work together . . . He said I need have no responsibility whatever, but simply respond to His movings."[14] "No responsibility whatever." It is God the Holy Spirit who controls. In Sandford's circumstances at the time, that was a relatively benign conviction. Hannah Whitall Smith would surely not have questioned its validity. But a little further down the road Frank Sandford was destined to open a Bible school, build a community with several hundred residents, and establish a worldwide missionary emphasis with branch headquarters in England and Palestine. Faced with the prospect of making controversial decisions that profoundly affected the lives of all who joined him in his ministry, it would often become very convenient for him to disclaim any personal responsibility and place it all on "the Guest."

In this early stage, however, Sandford's ministry launched into several years of extraordinary success and rapid growth. Deciding that no existing Christian training school was completely faithful to the whole Bible, not even Simpson's in New York, A. J. Gordon's Missionary Training School in

Boston, or the Bible school in Chicago later named for D. L. Moody, he announced on October 2, 1894, his thirty-third birthday, that his Bible school would open the very next day. (From that time forward, his own birthday became a date of great significance.) Starting from the smallest of small beginnings—classes on that first day consisted of Sandford and one student sitting on the floor of his sister's attic in Brunswick—the Holy Ghost and Us Bible School soon had ten full-time students, all with free tuition and, like the Sandfords, trusting God for their living expenses. He demanded that every student be baptized—or rebaptized if they had already experienced baptism in their own churches. The stains of defunct denominationalism needed to be washed away. God was doing a new thing at Shiloh. In the winter of 1895 Sandford published the first issue of a monthly magazine: *Tongues of Fire from the World's Evangelization Crusade on Apostolic Principles*. It is significant that those early publications included extensive reports on "the gift of foreign tongues" exhibited by a young woman named Jennie Glassey, loosely affiliated with Sandford.[15]

By January 1896, with the prospect of more students and a growing number of interested followers, Sandford claimed to have received an order, couched in scriptural words and coming directly to him from God, to "arise and build." But where? In February, with a recent convert who had made available to the group his entire farm in the nearby town of Durham, Sandford stretched out in prayer on the frozen ground of a sandy hill overlooking the Androscoggin River and heard the answer, again in the words of Scripture: "In the mountain of the height of Israel" (Ezek. 17:23).

One afternoon in late March, the day before construction was to begin on the project, Sandford received an unexpected and important visitor. Holman Day, a popular young journalist with the local paper, the *Lewiston Evening Journal,* rode up on his horse and asked for an interview.[16] What transpired in the next few hours proved to be significant for Shiloh's future. It also gives us a good sense of Sandford's brash but charming personality and, in the bargain, a clue to the style of leadership he was developing, not problematic at this point perhaps (only a cloud the size of a man's hand), but an omen of stormy times to come.

The two men, the evangelist and the journalist, immediately took to each other. Day appreciated Sandford's "touching romanticism" and also his candid admission that he was "scared." "God has told me to build a five-story building up there," he said, pointing the reporter to the bald, sandy hilltop just outside the window, "and—well, here is my entire capital." He dug through his pockets and came up with three cents. However, claiming that when God gives an order he knows how to furnish the means, Sandford assured Day that they would break ground the next morning. When Day, not a religious man himself, asked how God gave these orders, Sandford replied that he heard words in the "inner consciousness," which, he maintained, is exactly what the Bible means when it says that "the Lord spake" to various people. Actually, Sandford added, God speaks to a great many people today. "The trouble with most folks is they won't listen."

Later the same afternoon, examining the drawing Sandford had made of the towering building he hoped to erect, Day expressed serious reservations about the suitability of the construction site. When he also remarked how incongruous it seemed that the evangelization of the world should somehow emanate from a small town in Maine, Sandford amiably classed him with all the world's doubters: "You believe neither God nor His prophet. Well, time will tell. In fact, I here and now constitute you our chronicler. Come to us from time to time, and see what God will do for those who put absolute reliance in His Word." Day readily agreed.[17]

True to his promise, for the next several years Day wrote occasional articles, chronicling the rapidly evolving conditions on the Durham hilltop. Although by this time other journalists were mocking the "Holy Ghosters" as a bunch of religious fanatics, Day's articles assumed a generally sympathetic tone.

For Shiloh's part of the bargain, Sandford, whose sense of the dramatic rivaled that of Aimee Semple McPherson, provided Day with some great raw material. On July 4, 1897, more than a thousand people (by Day's count) gathered on the grounds to celebrate the completion of Shiloh Proper, the building whose plans Day had skeptically perused on his first visit. The visitors slept in tents and at nearby farmhouses and ate free food provided by the school. Parties arriving by train were met at the Lisbon Falls Depot by a gold-and-white four-seated "gospel carriage" pulled by two white horses (Grace and Glory) in white harness, a gift from a converted horse dealer. At one o'clock, exactly a year "to the minute" from the cornerstone dedication, Sandford climbed to the top of the five-story turret, stood under the shining gold dome, and flung out a "Victory" banner while the crowd below burst into a hymn of triumph. Two years later, when the Shiloh Extension was dedicated, the building itself, an architectural marvel, played the starring role. As they watched this one rise and spread to its full stature, plain-living Maine farmers must have thought they were dreaming. One of Shiloh's later chroniclers called the massive structure "a hybrid of a Maine resort hotel and a vision of the New Jerusalem."[18]

Small wonder that the name Shiloh, initially intended only for the building, came to stand for the entire movement. The name stuck for other reasons, too. Clearly it was much easier to handle than "The Holy Ghost and Us" and "The World's Evangelization Crusade." The most important reason, however, lay in the meaning of the word itself. An Old Testament term that literally means "rest" and "peace," *Shiloh* had through the centuries accrued additional connotations. For Sandford, the most significant of these derived from the word's first appearance in Scripture: "The sceptre shall not depart from Judah, nor a lawgiver from between his feet, until Shiloh come: and unto him shall the gathering of the people be" (Gen. 49:10). As Sandford interpreted that passage, Judah symbolized Christ. Therefore Shiloh must be the forerunner of Christ's Second Coming. In those days of the movement's exciting growth, along with a growing—if still inchoate—conviction of its key role in the consummation of history, the name Shiloh suited Frank Sandford just fine.

A History of Crises

It has often been pointed out that the Japanese word for crisis is made up of two characters: danger and opportunity. Hardly a stranger to crisis, Shiloh had always managed not only to survive hard times but to prosper. The crises that began to emerge in 1899 raised the stakes to a new level. On the positive side, Shiloh's ministry took on cosmic dimensions that transcended even the task of worldwide evangelization, with Sandford's own status as leader expanding commensurately. On the down side, the insidious dangers inherent in overreaching began to erode the foundations. While these crises, entangled in related circumstances, defy a neat sorting out for separate examination, we can identify three critical clusters of events. Within each cluster we shall discuss the events chronologically, but, since the clusters themselves overlap in time, we will have to turn the clock back once or twice to see a particular situation developing.

The first two clusters connect directly with Sandford's quest for personal apostleship. He began to discuss the quest publicly, as early as 1893, when he chose the name for his small band of followers, "The World's

Evangelization Crusade on Apostolic Principles." But it was not until 1899 that he believed all the pieces had come together. True, he never doubted the indwelling presence of "the Guest" since he had received Him in 1894, and he could look back gratefully on a number of impressive personal victories. He had not only cast out demons and acted as the human agent in divine healings; in 1899 he had successfully institutionalized Shiloh's healing ministry with the erection of "Bethesda," a hospital with a difference, where all medicines were banned and licensed doctors allowed only for diagnosis and consultation. What Sandford still lacked, he thought, was "the seal of apostleship," some transforming experience that would place him on the same level as the apostles in the early church, empowered to perform what Acts repeatedly called "signs and wonders." "The Olive Mills affair" provided that opportunity, and it identifies our first cluster.

In the summer of 1899, the same year that Bethesda opened, Olive, one of his favorite students, became seriously ill with what she identified as a recurrence of cerebrospinal meningitis. When Sandford was told in the middle of the night that she had died, he went to her room with two other ministers and, to his dismay, concluded that their diagnosis was correct. In desperation he placed his hands on her head and ordered her back to life. She quickly regained consciousness and within two hours was up and dressed, convinced that she had indeed died and been summoned back from the very threshold of heaven's gate. Sandford had raised her from the dead.[19]

The ambiguities involved in this kind of power soon caused problems. One tangible and far-reaching result was the imposition, in September 1900, of an official top-to-bottom chain of authority, descending from God the Father to God the Son to the God-chosen "prophet" (Sandford). Then in order came the ordained ministers, husbands, wives, and finally children. Sandford rhapsodized on the beauty of this remarkable divine plan: "I saw that as the woman took her place, obedient at every point and turn to her husband, and as the woman and man took their places obedient to the men of God, and as the men of God took their places, obedient to my Lord, that my Lord took the whole company of us and stepped in behind His Father, obedient at any point."[20] Conversely, what was perceived as disobedience even at the lowest level constituted actual disobedience to God at the top and often exacted a fearful penalty. A "Fair, Clear and Terrible" purge in November of that year called the entire community to account for alleged spiritual failings in a grueling examination of external behavior and inner spirituality.

Two years later, during a smallpox epidemic in what came to be known as the "Black Winter," Sandford ordered the "Nineveh Fast," modeled on the days of repentance in the city of Nineveh following Jonah's preaching. At Shiloh this meant a seventy-two-hour period, during the first thirty-six hours of which every living being at Shiloh, including animals, infants, and the sick, were to go without food and water. For those who were ill, the man of God held the power of life and death. In any given case, if healing did not occur after the prayer of faith, one always had an escape hatch: The answer to prayer is sometimes negative; it is God's will that finally rules. That was elementary Christian theology. But what if the leader should decide, for any number of possible reasons, to withhold the prayer of faith?

That was what happened to Leander Bartlett, a lad of fourteen who had made the mistake of confessing to a friend that he planned to run away. The time was particularly unfortunate for such a show of independence, for Sandford perceived that through the smallpox epidemic God was punishing the entire Shiloh community for spiritual declension. Disobedience of the rules laid down by the man of God demonstrated Leander's unworthiness to receive the healing prayer and, we might add, the miracle of resurrection. For he did die—not of smallpox but of undiagnosed diphtheria—and became the major focal point of a landmark trial in Maine's legal annals, with multiple charges brought by the Androscoggin Humane Society and the Cumberland County Conference of Churches. In Leander's case, the indictment charged Sandford with manslaughter. In the court's judgment, the decision hinged not on whether Leander received proper medical care (he obviously had not) but on whether the medical care Sandford did believe in—the prayer of faith—was offered on behalf of the patient. Although the jury returned a verdict of guilty, later appeals trials and hung juries that could not decide the slippery issue of "culpable indifference" dragged the case out for years until, in 1906, Sandford was finally judged not guilty.[21] Years later, in his most serious encounter with the legal system, he would not be so fortunate.

For the beginning of the second cluster of events, we must go back to 1893, years before the Olive Mills raising, when Sandford's early commitment to discovering "apostolic principles" clearly places him within the movement that Edith Blumhofer calls "Restorationism," a term for the complex of views that "molded the subculture in which Pentecostalism flourished." Blumhofer defines it as "the attempt to recapture the presumed vitality, message, and form of the Apostolic Church."[22] That this was Sandford's goal is evident not just from the group's first name but from his desire to perform the same signs and wonders as the first-century apostles. Blumhofer's term *Restorationism* gives us an apt label.

Sandford's task now was to discover Shiloh's exact role in the Restoration process. To that end, in January 1898 he heard another message from the voice of God, this one in a new mode; no longer was the content confined to words of Scripture. During a prayer meeting late in the evening, the inner voice he identified as God's said the words "Boston next" and "February fifth." Within days he was on his way to Boston, and by February 13 he had set up branch headquarters there. To be sure, we can hardly consider this an anomalous move—a rural religious sect storming the citadels of Satan. But in April the voice gave a far more radical order: "Jerusalem next." With the Spanish-American War on—to say nothing of the time and money required for a transatlantic voyage during a time of great financial need—Sandford claimed to wonder if he might have heard the voice of Satan rather than the voice of God. But a cryptically whispered message earlier in the month, about which he had said nothing to anyone, tipped the balance. At that time God had said, "Remove the covering," a condensation of Isa. 25:7: "Remove the covering cast over the face of the earth." Sandford claimed to be mystified by this instruction, but the Jerusalem order seemed to be a part of it. So off he went, with one trusted colleague, to the Holy Land.

Once Sandford reached Jerusalem, the pieces soon fit together in a stunning revelation. For some time he had been reading the published works of C. A. L. Totten, a professor of military science at Yale, who had developed a theory—not taken seriously by most historical and biblical scholars—that the true Israel was not the Jews of the present time, apostate descendants of the tribe of Judah, but the ten northern tribes carried into exile by the Assyrians in 721 B.C. Through comparisons of Old Testament prophecies and subsequent historical events, Totten concluded that the true Israel survived as the modern nations of England and America, the heirs with whom God would now keep His everlasting covenant.[23] At the height of nineteenth-century Manifest Destiny, this theory resolved a contradiction for Sandford—how to be patriotically true to secular America and spiritually true to biblical revelation. Anglo-American Israel would defeat the ungodly kingdoms of this world and help bring the Jews back to the Holy Land, where eventually all twelve tribes would be united under one head, as the prophet Hosea had foretold. Now at last he understood the divine mandate to "Remove the covering." The covering was the carnal earthly perceptions that made it impossible for humanity to comprehend spiritual truth, and it was in Jerusalem that the removal process would begin. But it would not be accomplished "Til Shiloh come," the words that had been carved and gilded across the white pulpit in Shiloh chapel. Shiloh was the crucial link to everything. The Shiloh of the Old Testament actually referred to the Shiloh of the sandy hilltop in Durham, Maine—and it would restore the kingdom to Israel, an objective (one could argue) even more important in the divine plan than restoring the primitive apostolic church.

Even as raising Olive Mills from the dead, with its seal of apostleship, would embolden Sandford in the following year to impose increasingly arbitrary and authoritarian regulations, so this new sense of Shiloh's cosmic significance, as the restorer of the Old Testament kingdom, would also result in even more radical declarations and decisions. These measures gradually brought Sandford to the margins of sectarian Christianity, increasingly distant not only from mainstream Protestantism but also from Pentecostalism. Having equated Shiloh, Maine, with the Old Testament Shiloh, Sandford now began to find himself in the biblical prophecies— each discovery, of course, validated by direct personal revelation from God.

It is not surprising that the first of these identifications was with the prophet Elijah, whose name (for biblical literalists in this turn-of-the-century era) hovered in the air between the Old and New Testaments. Malachi ended with these words: "Behold, I will send you Elijah the prophet before the coming of the great and dreadful day of the Lord; and he shall turn the heart of the fathers to the children, and the heart of the children to their fathers, lest I come and smite the earth with a curse." Alexander Dowie, whose work Sandford closely followed for a time, had recently announced that he was the second Elijah. At 4 A.M. on the morning of November 23, 1901, pacing the Jerusalem Turret at the top of Shiloh Proper, Sandford heard a message that "went down to the depths of my soul": "Elijah is here," and then, in a few moments, "Testify." And testify he did—before the students in the morning chapel. When a reporter later asked Sandford what he thought of Dowie's claim, he replied, "All I know is that God said to me, 'Elijah is here' and I presume He knew what He was talking about." One immediate result of this revelation was the right to level prophetic denunciations not permissible for an ordinary Christian. "I warn every lying editor," he told reporters, "that I will bring swift and awful witness against them for all the lies they have written about this man of God for the last eight years. Now I promise every such man that before long he will meet the God of judgment." Sandford acknowledged that he himself was not immune from the serious implications of his role as the returned Elijah. He would die a martyr's death. It was commonly thought that in history's final drama, as revealed in Revelation, one of the "two witnesses" put to death by the anti-Christ on the streets of Jerusalem would be Elijah.[24]

The biblical identifications did not cease with Elijah. Several additional fragmentary messages, tantalizingly mysterious, accumulated in the following months: "Prepare a throne," "Occupy till I come," and "Renew the Kingdom." Then, in Jerusalem on October 2, 1902, the morning of his fortieth birthday, Sandford heard the whispered word "Beloved," an unmistakable clue as to which direction the wind was blowing. "Beloved" was the meaning for the word *David* in Hebrew—and the heroic David, far more than Elijah, was the Old Testament character Sandford most admired, "the man after God's own heart." Opening himself to further divine illumination, he was soon rewarded with two more messages. The first, "I give to Jerusalem one that bringeth good tidings," was a fragment from Isaiah. The second, "I have found David," from Psalm 89, proved to be the Rosetta stone that showed Sandford how all his private revelations fit into God's master plan. Both of these passages had always been interpreted as heralds of the coming Messiah. Now, however, it was clear that he, Frank Weston Sandford of Shiloh, Maine, had been divinely called, along with his loyal followers, to prepare a throne for the renewal of David's kingdom and occupy that throne until the return of David's greater Son, as if Jesus Christ had said, in so many words, "Save my seat till I come back." To mark the occasion, fourteen Shilohites sat for a photograph on the roof of the Jerusalem headquarters. Sandford declared that "the Kingdom of our Father David, Rent and Shattered for Nearly Thirty Centuries, is today renewed" and immediately jettisoned Shiloh's ponderous official names in favor of simply "The Kingdom," the name by which it is still known today.[25]

Although in theory, of course, God was the ruler of this kingdom, Sandford more and more began to resemble a dictator. This was never more evident than in March 1904, when a ten-foot scroll, called "The Pledge of Loyalty," was unfurled in chapel for all present to sign. Most of the articles were standard evangelical fare, but among the final items was a touchstone that clearly set a course for the Kingdom's future:

> I believe not only in the Father—the only Potentate—and in Jesus Christ—the King whose millenial [sic] reign is to prepare the globe for the great God—but also in the prophet-prince-priest who is to prepare the Kingdom for the Christ; I believe in the man who as prophet is called in the Bible "Elijah," and as prince is called "David," and as a priest is called "Tsemach" or "The Branch." I believe that Frank W. Sandford of Shiloh, Maine, U.S.A. tells the truth when he makes proclamation that God said to him, "Elijah is here. Testify," and again "I have found David," words spoken as applying to himself personally. I believe in and accept him as such.[26]

For the third cluster of critical events in this phase of Shiloh's history, it would be difficult to avoid the label *Coronet,* a famous racing yacht much admired among the seagoing rich. Sandford purchased it in 1905 for $10,000, raising the money by the usual method, prayer, this time forty days and nights of it. If there were questions among the faithful about the incongruity of such an icon of conspicuous consumption in juxtaposition to the almost perpetual poverty on the Durham hilltop, they tended to vanish at the sight of the *Coronet* sailing smoothly into the harbor at South Freeport, Maine. In some respects, that moment could be seen as the high watermark of Shiloh's life—a symbol of the world's wealth commandeered for Christ to transport missionaries around the world.

The *Coronet* did sail around the world all right, but the strategy of evangelization employed on its journey will not be remembered as a great achievement in the history of missiology. Starting from its berth at Jaffa in the Mediterranean, the plan was to anchor off the coast of the various heathen nations where Satan held dominion and, like the children of Israel marching around the walls of Jericho, claim the country for Christ. If that seems like much too neat and easy a way to fulfill the missionary mandate—no interaction with the sweat and grime, the disease and hostility, of the all too real ordinary people in the non-Christian world—it has a curious logic if one accepts Sandford's apocalyptic assumptions. The task of evangelizing the world in the time-honored way, in what he was convinced were the rapidly approaching end times, was in fact humanly impossible. Anchoring offshore and praying for the population shifted the responsibility to God, who alone could accomplish the task. No one asked why such intercessory appeals could not be raised to the heavens from the prayer towers back at Shiloh. When this "chain of prayer" voyage was completed in July 1909, Sandford retrieved a copy of the missionary pledge he had signed two decades earlier at Northfield ("I am willing and desirous, God permitting, to be a foreign missionary") and wrote underneath it, "I am that. So much so that what was home is now foreign and what was foreign is now home."[27]

One might almost say that in these years Sandford spent so much of his time on the yacht that the Kingdom's real nerve center was neither Durham nor Jerusalem but his cabin in the *Coronet* on the high seas. Moreover, in 1911 certain developments having to do with real or threatened defections of important members gave him ample reason to think of the boat as a sanctuary. Knowing that the maritime authorities were waiting for him to land, he heard the voice of God give the order "Continue," even though the boat at the time was seriously overloaded, sixty-two persons in a space designed for thirty. After months of cruising around the Atlantic, in a badly damaged craft, often woefully short of drinking water and food, in September Sandford and his *Coronet* party played out what would become Shiloh's endgame up and down the stormy waters of the North Atlantic coastline. When two of the crew instigated a mutinous demand to head for home, Sandford finally capitulated, though he considered the request inspired by Satan. Contrary winds of gale force, however, kept pushing the boat farther out to sea. Consequently, by the time the *Coronet* limped into harbor at Portland, four men had died of scurvy and many others were seriously ill. Within days, two more of the crew died. Sandford was arrested, charged with causing six deaths, and taken to the city jail. At the trial in December, the jury returned a guilty verdict within an hour and Sandford was sentenced to a term of not more than ten years in the federal penitentiary in Atlanta, Georgia. Shackled to two common criminals, he rode the train south in defiant optimism. "Every roll of the car wheel is a ring of triumph," he said. "When men are willing to suffer 'the loss of all things' for the absent King, then the Almighty has a clear field and conquest is certain."[28]

That is not quite the way things worked out. When Sandford was released from prison seven years later and returned to the Shiloh hilltop, it was soon clear that there was no possibility of just picking up where he had left off. While the vision of the restored Kingdom was still very much alive, the massive Durham installation had become a dead weight. So when the divine command came in 1920, in its usual terse language, to "Retire," Sandford was in no mood to question it. His followers left the community to rejoin the larger world in a diaspora they referred to as "The Scattering." The Kingdom survived as a tightly knit association of churches in several parts of the country. Sandford lived out the rest of his life in secretive semiseclusion on a farm in western New York State. He died on March 4, 1948, not violently on the streets of Jerusalem, as he had expected, but in his armchair, surrounded by a handful of devoted followers.

Conclusion

Let us return to the question we raised at the outset. Why did Frank Weston Sandford not become a Pentecostal? He shared many influences and convictions with other Holiness leaders, some of whom became leaders in the Pentecostal movement. And, except for the de-emphasis and virtual disappearance of speaking in tongues, the religion practiced at Shiloh had much in common with Pentecostal worship. What were the distinctive factors that turned Sandford and the movement he founded in a different direction?

In his social history of Pentecostalism, *The Vision of the Disinherited*, Robert Mapes Anderson stresses that the first adherents of the movement in America were drawn almost exclusively from the economically, racially, and ethnically marginalized.[29] Harvey Cox, in *Fire from Heaven*, makes the same point in theological and intellectual terms: "But while contingent after contingent of young seminary graduates tried to impart the latest ideas from Europe to their suspicious congregations, the Pentecostal revolution, a genuinely American spiritual revolution if ever there was one, was bubbling up from underneath."[30] Although occasionally the movement has spawned autocratic leaders who have developed their own personal empires, the opposite tendency has generally prevailed. Dennis Smith, writing about Pentecostalism in Guatemala, has dubbed the more common trend the "Amoeba School of Church Growth."[31] If there is dissatisfaction with a minister's accumulation of power in a particular congregation, within a few months there will probably be three new churches. This suggests that close to the heart of Pentecostalism lives an independent spirit we might without exaggeration call antinomian.

If the picture we have developed of Frank Sandford puts one single trait above all others into sharp focus, it is his authoritarian style of leadership. Although early unshackling himself from the conventional expectations of the Free Will Baptist denomination, he molded a community far more restrictive than any denomination, forming a group of followers from whom, as God's appointed prophet, he demanded absolute obedience. An exemplar himself of New England antinomianism in the tradition of Anne Hutchinson and Roger Williams, he viewed matters differently from a position of power. Not surprisingly, he perceived the merest trace of an antinomian tendency in others as the ultimate satanic threat. It was Sandford who heard those succinct messages from the voice of God—"Jerusalem next," "Remove the covering," "Elijah is here," "I have found David." Others at Shiloh received messages, too, and that was all right if they fit the master plan being revealed to the man of God. But if anyone's leadings contradicted what had been revealed to Sandford, as he had to explain to one of his gifted female associates in England, she would have to recognize his special role as God's agent and ultimately just accept his authority.

With this dominant character trait in mind, we can see glossolalia once again rising to the surface as a hallmark, the absence of which distinguishes Shiloh from Pentecostalism—but not for the obvious theological or hermeneutical reasons. Frank Sandford's theological creed, so focused finally on his and Shiloh's role in the fulfillment of prophecy, could have easily made room for speaking in tongues. And the scriptural evidence was ambiguous enough to permit considerable latitude. What Sandford could not abide was the personal spiritual freedom implicit in glossolalia. The practice of tongue speaking has persisted, says Cox, "because it represents the core of all pentecostal conviction: that the Spirit of God needs no mediators but is available to anyone in an intense, immediate, indeed interior way."[32] Sandford realized, perhaps subliminally, that, if speaking in tongues were to become an accepted part of worship at Shiloh, it would be only a matter of time before his total control would be undermined and the Kingdom's special role in history's climactic events jeopardized.

Today the churches of Shiloh's Kingdom are virtually indistinguishable in faith and practice from many other evangelical churches. As a matter of fact, although Frank Sandford's vision of the movement's apocalyptic significance lives on in those we might call the movement's "strict constructionists," for others it has steadily receded into the hazy past. Whether among third and fourth generations of families with a long Shiloh history or new members attracted to the group for what it represents now, the historical events of long ago and the claims of the founder excite little or no interest.

For some of the movement's leaders, however, these matters demand more than a perfunctory allegiance. The strict constructionists still follow Sandford's insistence on closed communion, require special "restoration baptism" of new members, and maintain the distinction Sandford insisted on between the Kingdom and the Church. In the last few years, however, under pressure from those we might term the "loose constructionists," the Kingdom Board of Ministers has sought to bridge this gulf and lay these issues to rest. While affirming Sandford's ministry, they have allowed that, with regard to such special claims as his identification with Elijah or David, "a certain amount of ambiguity seems unavoidable and each person needs the freedom to come to his own conclusion."[33] As for the affiliated churches and chapels, the Kingdom Executive Committee has offered them three options: (1) remain in the Kingdom; (2) choose spiritual independence but retain some affiliation with the Kingdom organization; (3) become completely independent.[34]

So, while we are probably not justified in pinning the label antinomianism on these recent developments, they surely exemplify a more democratic spirit than the authoritarian regime that prevailed when Frank Sandford was alive. But the changes cannot be ascribed to glossolalia, since neither strict nor loose constructionist heirs of Sandford's movement practice speaking in tongues. One suspects, however, that many members of both groups would probably be surprised to discover how much of their heritage they share with today's Pentecostals.[35]

Alma and Kent White with their sons, Arthur *(top)* and Ray, shortly before their separation, circa 1909. Courtesy of Pillar of Fire Archives, Zarephath, New Jersey.

Alma White: The Politics of Dissent

Susie C. Stanley

On October 9, 1928, Alma White created a media event by disrupting Aimee Semple McPherson's sermon at the Royal Albert Hall in London when she stood and shouted, "Could not Mrs. McPherson explain her kidnapping incident on the Pacific coast?"[1] In an interview following the confrontation, White called McPherson a sorceress and a deceiver and criticized her theology, informing reporters that "her doctrines are unorthodox and unscriptural."[2] White particularly opposed McPherson's acceptance of glossolalia, or speaking in tongues.

Alma White founded the Pentecostal Union in 1901, yet she unequivocally opposed glossolalia, the hallmark of the Pentecostal movement that emerged later that decade. White, along with other Wesleyan/Holiness adherents, had used the *Pentecostal* label long before it became synonymous with the Azusa Street revival. While they initially sought to maintain use of the term without its association to glossolalia, within fifteen years they gave up and abandoned *Pentecostal,* both in the names of their groups and as a self-description. White adopted the title Pillar of Fire to designate her organization.

Why did White choose to reject Pentecostalism rather than accept it? This chapter explores several reasons for her unmitigated opposition. First, White's perspective cannot be divorced from her estrangement from her husband, Kent, which his acceptance of glossolalia exacerbated. Second, she challenged the movement on theological and moral grounds. Last, she did not want her group's reputation to be tarnished by association with Pentecostalism.

Scholars have portrayed White as a "vitriolic critic of Pentecostalism" and "the most critical anti-pentecostal writer of the century."[3] While it would be difficult to support the second designation statistically, White definitely deserves a place high on the list of those who vociferously denounced the new movement. In fact, White maintained that God had raised up her church "to expose the devil as he appears in the disguise of the Holy Ghost in this tongues sorcery."[4]

Melvin Dieter and Donald Dayton are among those who have documented the close relationship between the Holiness movement and Pentecostalism.[5] Dieter contended the two are fraternal twins sharing "basic theological and experiential commitments."[6] Wesleyan/Holiness believers emphasized Pentecost for several reasons. Many related it to the experience of holiness or sanctification, the second work of grace that followed conversion. White argued that Jesus' followers who had gathered in the Upper Room in Jerusalem experienced holiness when they received Holy Spirit baptism at Pentecost, but Holiness understanding of Holy Spirit baptism did not include glossolalia. White, along with other Holiness adherents, also pointed to Pentecost to justify the ministry of women.[7]

The Pentecostal movement did not deny the importance of Pentecost as understood by Wesleyan/Holiness believers. However, followers added one element. For Pentecostals, glossolalia evidenced Holy Spirit baptism. Some Holiness believers embraced Pentecostalism, viewing the movement as a natural progression of God's work among Christians. Others, such as White, denounced the movement in no uncertain terms. Before outlining White's basis for waging war against Pentecostalism, it is necessary to gain a sense of who she was and the extent of her ministry.

"A Cromwell in Skirts"

Mollie Alma Bridwell was born in Lewis County, Kentucky, in 1862. She was the seventh child of William and Mary Ann [Harrison] Bridwell, who had ten other children, six daughters and four sons. She experienced conversion on November 8, 1878, while attending a revival conducted by William Godbey, a Methodist Episcopal evangelist, at a nearby schoolhouse.

Within a week after becoming a Christian, Alma felt called to become a minister. However, since her denomination, the Methodist Episcopal Church, South, did not ordain women, she reluctantly set aside her original calling and substituted teaching in its place. Alma taught school in Kentucky before moving to Montana in 1882. While teaching at Bannack, she met Kent White in 1883. Kent and Alma conducted a courtship by correspondence, resulting in their marriage in Denver, Colorado, on December 21, 1887. At this time, Kent was completing ministerial training at the University of Denver. The Colorado annual conference of the Methodist Episcopal Church ordained Kent a deacon in 1889 and assigned him to serve congregations in Lamar and Las Animas, Colorado. Two years later, Kent was ordained an elder and transferred to Morrison, Colorado.

During this time, White began seeking the experience of sanctification. It was after reading Martin Wells Knapp's *Out of Egypt into Canaan* that White consecrated her life on the altar of Christ and claimed sanctification by faith on March 18, 1893. White's experience paralleled Phoebe Palmer's explanation of how sanctification could be achieved: "There are but two steps to the blessing: ENTIRE CONSECRATION is the first; FAITH is the second."[8]

White believed, with Palmer, that it was necessary to testify publicly in order to retain sanctification. The progression from testifying to preaching was a short one. She began to fulfill the calling to ministry that had been impressed upon her years earlier as a teenager. White preached her first sermon during the fall of 1893 at Erie, Colorado, where Kent had been transferred. She assisted in a revival at Pleasant View, Colorado, later that same fall. Soon she began receiving requests to speak at other locations. In the spring of 1894, she conducted "independent" services without the assistance of Kent or other male ministers at a rented hall in Lafayette, Colorado, followed by several revivals in rural schoolhouses in the state. The experience of sanctification and the accompanying empowerment of the Holy Spirit enabled White to preach the gospel fearlessly.

It is difficult to determine precisely the extent of Kent's cooperation with Alma in her early evangelistic work. The fact that he initiated several revivals and Alma joined him later indicates that he was recognized as an evangelist in his own right. The Whites began full-time evangelistic work after Kent left the pastorate in 1895. Alma often led eighteen to twenty services a week during 1896. Between 1896 and 1899, she conducted more than three thousand services.

Alma and Kent opened their first mission in Denver soon after moving there in 1896. The Whites relied on Holy Spirit guidance and believed that God would provide the means to keep their missions open. Within two years, Alma was supervising five missions, two in Denver and one each in Leadville, Colorado City, and Cheyenne. In 1899, she also founded a missionary home and training school in Denver to train gospel workers and missionaries to staff her missions.

White formally organized her mission work on December 29, 1901, calling her group the Pentecostal Union. One reason she founded the Pentecostal Union was her revulsion against Methodism. White denounced her former denomination: "[I] drank from the Methodist brook, but when the waters became stagnant and the odor of death ensued [I] had to remove the rubbish so the water of life might break forth in another place or perish."[9] Consequently, White and four other members were ordained elders in the Pentecostal Union on March 16, 1902.

Kent White initially opposed the formation of the Pentecostal Union and was not a charter member of the group. Nevertheless, he relinquished his Methodist clergy credentials five days before the Pentecostal Union was incorporated on March 19, 1902.[10] Only one reference has been found to explain Kent's action: "He says he left the church because of its corruption and failure to live up to its tenets."[11]

The Pentecostal Union and the Metropolitan Church Association, also known as the Burning Bush after the name of its magazine, cooperated extensively between 1902 and 1905, holding joint revivals in the United States and London. The two groups were similar in significant ways. Both split from the Methodist Episcopal Church and proclaimed a conservative message that they equated with primitive Methodism. The two groups stressed the doctrine of holiness. The Pentecostal Union also adopted the lively worship style of the Burning Bush.

Conflict over a piece of property near Bound Brook, New Jersey, ended the cooperative work of the Pentecostal Union and the Burning Bush in the fall of 1905. Caroline Garretson, owner of the land, donated the property to both groups in two separate transactions. A bitter fight ensued with Alma White and leaders of the Burning Bush justifying their respective claims to the land. Ultimately, White maintained ownership of the contested property, where she established Zarephath, which became the new headquarters of the Pentecostal Union.

Outreach and evangelism were crucial components of White's ministry. Along with revivals, she edited several journals, which her members sold door to door, and she authored more than thirty-five books. She was among the first to recognize the potential of utilizing the airwaves for evangelistic purposes. Her denomination received a license in 1927 to operate a Denver

AM station and purchased a second station that began broadcasting from Zarephath in 1931.

White's group achieved an organizational milestone in 1918 when it formalized its structure by adopting a church discipline written by White's son, Ray. During the camp meeting that summer at Zarephath, White was consecrated bishop, thus becoming the first woman to serve as bishop in the United States. Her mentor, William Godbey, attended her consecration.[12] White presided over the Pillar of Fire until her death at the age of eighty-four in 1946. At that time, there were more than fifty branches and approximately five thousand members. Family members maintained leadership of the Pillar of Fire until 1984.

White was a fighter. A reporter labeled her "a Cromwell in skirts."[13] The designation aptly describes a woman who not only attacked sin but also battled those who opposed her right to preach and those who sought to take over her organization, including her husband. "A Cromwell in skirts" also evokes her deportment with respect to other battles she waged. Her aggressive sectarianism motivated her to take on all perceived opponents vehemently. White's anti-Catholicism and antisexism have been documented elsewhere. The remainder of this chapter will focus on her anti-Pentecostalism.

White's association with William J. Seymour began during the spring of 1906, prior to the outbreak of the Azusa Street revival. Seymour, an African American Holiness minister, visited the Pentecostal Union Bible School in Denver on his way to Los Angeles as a candidate for the pastorship of a Holiness church. In spite of his unkempt appearance and his race, White invited Seymour to eat with her and other residents of the Denver mission and asked him to pray at the end of the meal.

White had worked with African Americans, including Rebecca Grant in a revival in July 1895 at Longmont, Colorado,[14] and with Susan Fogg in revivals in New England during December 1902 and in Colorado in the spring of 1903.[15] Derogatory references to African Americans were infrequent in White's books. The scarcity of racist comments in her voluminous writing does not excuse White's prejudice but suggests that racism did not figure prominently in her message.

Four years after meeting Seymour, White recorded that during his prayer she felt "serpents and other slimy creatures were creeping all around me . . . In my evangelistic and missionary tours I had met all kinds of religious fakirs and tramps, but I felt that he excelled them all."[16] Surely, this was not White's initial perception of Seymour or she never would have extended hospitality to him. Her later disregard for Pentecostalism rather than racial prejudice probably shaped her perception of Seymour.

From White's mission in Denver, Seymour continued on to Los Angeles and became the major catalyst in the Azusa Street revival. White traveled to Los Angeles in March 1907 to observe the revival. Mincing no words, she claimed that Pentecostalism "has proved to be the greatest religious farce that has ever camouflaged under the name of Christianity."[17] White recorded her observations in the tract *What I Saw in a Tongues' Meeting*. In her words, it was "a so-called Pentecostal service" whose origin was "from the under-world."[18] White freely sprinkled inflammatory adjectives such as "gibberish" and "counterfeit" throughout the tract. She passed judgment on Pentecostal believers, claiming "none are truly converted" and that most "have nervous trouble or defective mentality at some time." She also maintained that there were "disreputable characters" in their midst and that some "teach and practice free-lovism." No documentation supported her assertions.

Fighting a Disloyal Partner

White's battle against Pentecostalism acquired a personal dimension when her husband embraced its doctrine. This tension stemmed from long-standing conflicts between Kent and Alma. Kent found fault with Alma's early preaching, which led to heated arguments. Specifically, he objected to her hermeneutics and accused her of detecting the doctrine of holiness in biblical texts that contained no bearing on the topic. The disagreements over Alma's use of holiness metaphors continued with different sermon texts. Alma described Kent's hostility during the first year of her preaching: "As time went on and the battle became fiercer he would often endorse my messages in public, but in private would take a stand against me and contend to the bitter end . . . Often he would keep me awake more than half the night discussing my interpretation of the Scripture, declaring that the commentaries would not sustain me."[19]

Kent had threatened to leave the family several times during the early years of Alma's ministry. On one occasion, coworkers convinced him to stay. Two other threats resulted when Alma opened the Denver mission and when she began discussing the possibility of establishing her own church. Despite the ultimatums, Kent remained with his family.

From Alma's initial assumption of leadership, Kent questioned her claim to be spiritual head of the Pentecostal Union. Alma, however, believed that God had chosen her to lead the group and that her husband was the person best qualified to supplement her labors. According to Alma, Kent wished to assume preeminence in the Pentecostal Union based solely on his status as her husband: "But he not only insisted that he was the head of the home government (which was not disputed), but that he should be the head of the movement which God had used me to launch out, whether he merited the place or not. He persisted in confusing the home government with that of the church . . . His attitude was that on account of his sex he should be the head, that it was the wife's duty to submit to a place of subordination."[20] In short, Alma resisted Kent's assertion of authority over her organization. One can imagine the resentment Kent must have harbored because of his wife's refusal to grant him the position of leadership he coveted.

Kent began attending Pentecostal meetings while in Denver during the fall of 1908. When he returned to Zarephath, where the family was then living, Alma welcomed him, but her hunch that he was preparing to leave her permanently proved to be accurate. He formally severed his ties with the Pentecostal Union on August 11, 1909, as a result of an argument over an editorial Alma had written denouncing the Pentecostal movement. She rejected the Pentecostal identification with the latter rain prophesied in Scripture. On the contrary, Kent believed the latter rain referred to the Pentecostal movement. At this point, Kent defended Pentecostalism on biblical grounds although he had not yet spoken in tongues. Despite the history of strife, Alma begged Kent to stay: "At times I would weep until my tears ceased to flow, but my entreaties were unheeded."[21] Nevertheless, Kent departed two days later, rejecting her uncompromising opposition to speaking in tongues. While the relationship between the two had been strained throughout their twenty-one years of marriage, the doctrinal dispute over glossolalia provoked Kent ultimately to carry out his threat to leave. Alma was devastated: "This was a day never to be forgotten—a Gethsemane to my soul. I felt as if I were walking through the valley and shadow of death."[22]

Writing Kent the day after he left, Alma expressed her love and pleaded with him to come back.[23] On August 20, she wrote: "Apart from religious controversy I am your wife, and my love for you is stronger and deeper than the day you led me to the altar, and promised to cleave to me forever."[24] Kent wrote back on September 1: "But, Alma you cast your husband's testimony aside as unworthy, and God took me away from you . . . It is not that I do not want to come home, but He will not let me until there is a change . . . Now there are people in the Church who will accept the truth as soon as you get out of the way." Kent also enclosed Pentecostal tracts with the letter and instructed his wife to read them: "Now Alma, if you love me you will write and tell me what pieces you have read as required, and who else reads them."[25] Despite Kent's assertion, no one left the Pentecostal Union to follow him.[26] Some support for Pentecostalism among Alma's followers surfaced, however. In an undated letter to Kent, church member H. D. Ingersoll wrote the following: "In regard to the Tongues Movement, I have always believed there was grounds founded upon the scripture for such an experience and thought probably some among them were honest and sincere and their testimonies worthy of consideration."[27]

When Kent left Zarephath, he went to his mother's home in Beverly, West Virginia. Alma traveled there on September 21. Kent offered Alma a home in West Virginia where she could live while he looked for a job, but Alma rejected the proposal and returned to Zarephath.[28]

Alma persuaded Kent to go with her and several of her followers to conduct a revival in London later in 1909. When Alma returned to the States the following January, Kent remained in England and joined the Apostolic Faith Church under the leadership of William O. Hutchinson in Bournemouth, where he received the gift of tongues on July 7, 1910.[29]

Alma went to great lengths in her efforts to convince Kent to end their separation. Yet she was adamant that it could take place only if Kent renounced Pentecostalism. Kent was equally insistent that Alma accept his view; neither was willing to compromise. Alma visited Bournemouth twice in December 1910 and again in February 1911. He returned home with her in 1911 with the stipulation that she was to speak only with his permission. Two months later, he put his hands over her mouth to silence her when she rejected the claim made by Pentecostals that the latter rain mentioned in the Bible referred to them. Kent again left, returning sporadically to visit Alma and their sons over the next one and one-half years. He served an Apostolic Faith congregation in Chicago for a year before returning to England in 1914.

Braving submarine attacks during World War I, Alma traveled to

Bournemouth in 1915 and was given lodging at one of Hutchinson's houses. Kent was not there at the time, but she visited a meeting at Emmanuel Hall, where the leader spoke against her. She claimed his comments were so hostile that his people asked him to apologize. At one point, she asked to speak and permission was granted. When she said she wanted Kent to return to the United States with her, she was commanded to sit down. At another service, when she attempted to make a public statement, Hutchinson ordered her to leave the hall. Instead, she "stepped in between the seats, [and] continued to expose the demon worship of this so-called apostolic movement."[30] As she spoke, Hutchinson ushered people out, but twenty-two stayed to hear her. When Alma returned to her room, it was locked and her luggage was outside. After this visit, Kent wrote her: "God help me I am not going to leave the fountain of living water for any flesh or human relationships."[31]

After a visit in 1916, Kent wrote Alma: "Why hitch up two horses again that are contrary and will not pull together? Better they work single and far apart."[32] Despite her attempts, Kent refused her peacemaking efforts, maintaining his resolve to return only if she renounced her faith and accepted his theology. Alma, in spite of her love for Kent, refused to make this concession, even though she had made seven trips abroad seeking reconciliation.

Alma suspected that the Apostolic Faith leaders intended to take over the Pillar of Fire, as her group was now known, and use its properties as a base to expand their operations in the United States and England. Her fears intensified when Kent and leaders from his church arrived in the United States in October 1920. In December 1920, Kent came to Zarephath in search of letters and documents.[33] Alma deduced from statements Kent had made that he intended to gain control of some Pillar of Fire holdings through legal claims he would pursue in civil court. Kent planned to base his case on his belief that his role in the early years of the church entitled him to a share of its current property holdings. In anticipation of this threat to her church and in order to establish her sole right to Pillar of Fire properties, Alma filed a legal complaint in the New Jersey courts that charged Kent with desertion. Alma insisted: "I wanted no divorce; but when it was made known to me his intention was to break up our organization I felt that the time for action had come."[34] The presiding judge dismissed Alma's case in October 1921. Nonetheless, Alma welcomed the outcome for the publicity it gave to her cause. Taking Kent to divorce court was a humiliating experience for her, but she thwarted the scheme to take possession of her church.[35] Although unpleasant, the case and the publicity surrounding it served Alma's purposes by providing the opportunity to substantiate her claim that the Pillar of Fire was hers and hers alone: "It was shown that our society was in no way indebted to him [Kent] or under any obligation to help him financially in the course he had taken."[36] The court testimony demonstrated that the success of the Pillar of Fire had depended solely on Alma's efforts. As a result of the court case, the Pillar of Fire Church remained firmly in Alma's control.

Most of the information regarding Kent and Alma's estrangement comes from Alma's perspective. A few isolated letters, however, provide Kent's viewpoint. Kent wrote Alma's brother, Charles Bridwell, in 1918: "You better try and get Alma to come make her home with me. You folks can run that work. I miss her more than words can tell."[37] In a letter to their son Arthur in 1938, Kent bemoaned Alma's treatment: "I was assailed as deluded and possessed of an evil spirit. No greater disgrace and shame could come to a man from a wife than this." His feelings were transparent: "I now cry out in my tears! O why should it be that I had to lose Alma, my Girlie! O my! O my! This letter makes my heart ache." Arthur had invited Kent to come to Denver, but he refused: "Why should I return to an institution where there is no fellowship, no love, no respect, no faith in me?"[38]

In July 1940, Kent traveled to Denver, where Alma and her grown sons then lived.[39] Suffering from a serious throat ailment, Kent recorded a reunion that was less than conciliatory: "After dinner I got into an altercation with Alma on old conflictions in past and I did not mend it. She is harassed with an awful spirit of denunciation against the tongues as corrupt and devilish and she rages against the people who have them as deluded and of the devil. I was sorry I said a word." The following day, Kent wrote in his diary: "There is an evil spirit in Alma raging against the tongues . . . She has imbibed this bitter defiant spirit and it raged against me this P.M."[40] According to several sources, Alma and Kent reconciled shortly before his death on July 30.[41] Even so, it appears that Kent died without renouncing his belief in glossolalia.

Battling Pentecostalism

Alma had written *Demons and Tongues* in 1910 after one of her unsuccessful attempts to convince Kent to return from England. This diatribe repeated the claims she made in the 1907 tract mentioned earlier. She was not afraid of exhausting intemperate language: "The slimepits of Tongueism, where all kinds of heresies are fostered, cannot be too vividly pictured."[42] She shared her opinion on the origin of tongues and briefly addressed theological and moral issues.

White was blunt in her assessment of the origin of Pentecostalism: "The tongues movement with its so-called pentecostal baptism, and also other spirit movements, are of the flesh and of the Devil."[43] She utilized the following phrases to emphasize her point: "a Satanic trap," "hallucination of Satanic powers," "a Satanic delusion," and "the Devil's propaganda."[44] White traced Pentecostalism to spiritism or witchcraft rather than viewing it as an outgrowth of Holiness doctrine.[45] She claimed that Pentecostalism was "a counterfeit religion."[46]

White's theological critique argued that at Pentecost those who had been baptized with the Holy Spirit spoke in real languages since everyone could understand the message of the gospel in their native tongue. No unknown tongues or languages were heard among Jesus' followers at Jerusalem on the day of Pentecost. Rather than seeing the Pentecostal movement as a new outpouring of the Holy Spirit's work, she judged that it was a direct fulfillment of 1 Tim. 4:1: "Now the Spirit speaketh expressly, that in the latter times some shall depart from the faith, giving heed to seducing spirits and doctrines of devils."[47] Significantly, she persisted in using the term *gibberish* in reference to glossolalia.[48]

Challenging Pentecostalism on moral grounds, White referred to the Azusa Street mission as a "hot-bed of free-loveism."[49] She opined that "the familiarity between the sexes in the public meetings has been shocking, to say the least."[50] She quoted Nettie Harwood, one of her members who visited Azusa Street and observed that "kissing between the sexes is a common occurrence in the Tongues meetings."[51] This was, in fact, the "holy kiss" practiced in the New Testament church (Rom. 16:16). White also accused members of being bigamists.[52] While White did not name names or provide specific examples to support her case, there were instances of moral lapses among prominent Pentecostals.

White's judgments against Pentecostal believers echoed her comments on their spiritual and emotional conditions mentioned in her tract. In her view, none had "truly repented of his sins" and many suffered from nervous prostration.[53] There is one possible allusion to Kent: "I know of some who have become so hardened under the influence of the demoniacal power that they are entirely unlike what they once were. They turn away in cold indifference from those who are suffering on their account and manifest no sympathy toward those whose hearts they are breaking or have broken."[54]

The foregoing information from *Demons and Tongues* summarizes White's negative attitude toward Pentecostalism and its adherents. Her opposition led her to take drastic measures to disassociate her religious organization from the movement. White feared that her group would be discredited if it were confused with Pentecostalism. Pentecostals were derisively called "holy rollers" because of their lively worship. Because Pillar of Fire members jumped and skipped during worship, they, too, were sometimes called "holy rollers." In the early years of the Pentecostal Union, Denver newspapers had nicknamed members of the group "Jumpers" because of their boisterous worship, which included holy jumping.[55] White described a revival in Denver in 1904: "Another Pentecost had come, and the saints shouted and leaped for joy while souls that had been bowed down in grief were being liberated."[56]

Because of the similarity in worship practices, it was logical to assume that White and her followers had been caught up in the Pentecostal fervor. In a 1937 interview, White attempted to downplay any resemblance between the two worship styles: "We won't stand for anyone calling us 'jumpers' or 'holy rollers.' That doesn't belong to us—it belongs to those quacks in Los Angeles."[57] White was so intent on differentiating her group from the Pentecostal movement that she relinquished the nickname "Jumpers" that she had been proud to claim for her group during its formative years. She expressed her anxiety about being confused with Pentecostals: "My greatest concern was for the reputation of our society on which there had never been a stain or a real cause for reproach. We had been misrepresented by our enemies, but there was nothing to substantiate their statements. Now I feared our movement would be confused with this latter-day sorcery, and that more harm would result than could be lived down in the next quarter of a century."[58] White was embarrassed by being associated with Pentecostals, much like Pentecostals today are embarrassed by the excesses of some charismatics. Despite White's disclaimer, the worship styles of the two groups were similar. White, in fact, admitted: "Of course sometimes our people get happy and skip around a bit. There is some demonstration."[59]

SUSIE C. STANLEY

White's decision to abandon the name Pentecostal Union offers a second example of her effort to avoid any confusion between her group and Pentecostalism. Her organization officially became the Pillar of Fire in 1919. White offered two reasons for the name change. First, *Pillar of Fire* had replaced *Pentecostal Union Herald* as the title of the church's periodical in 1904, so it was a name already associated with White and her followers. Second, and uppermost in her mind, was "the fact that the 'Tongues' movement with all of its heretical aspects revealing its Satanic origin functioned in many places under the name of 'Pentecostals.'"[60]

Concern that her group's reputation would be tarnished by association with Pentecostalism was one factor that fueled White's opposition to the movement. Personally, the ongoing conflict with Kent significantly contributed to her rancor.

Alma White attacked all rivals with fervor. Her campaign against Pentecostalism was no exception. She maintained that she wrote *Demons and Tongues* to recover "some from the snare of the devil and be a warning to others."[61] However, she seemed oblivious to the fact that her hostile tone and vocabulary, much less her name-calling, would prevent her from achieving her goal. Unfortunately, Pentecostals sometimes knew how to respond in kind. For example, Herbert Buffum "categorized White's polemics as 'turkey-buzzard vomit' splattered upon 'God's elect and *select* people.'"[62]

While it is easy to list the reasons White rejected Pentecostalism, it is difficult to rank her motivations. Despite the decades of marital discord, theological convictions were crucial. Also, as an independent "Cromwell in skirts," she fiercely defended the Pillar of Fire from real and perceived antagonists. White's attitudes undercut the emphasis on love that she herself made the hallmark of holiness. Her fierce attacks on Pentecostalism, the "fraternal twin" of the Holiness movement, reflect the hostility that separated the two groups for decades. Evidence that the historic enmity had begun to break down became evident in 1998 when the Society for Pentecostal Studies and the Wesleyan Theological Society met jointly for the first time. In a spirit of civility, the two societies worshiped together and explored both their shared heritage and their distinctives in workshops and plenary sessions. The descendants of Aimee Semple McPherson and Alma White are learning to embrace each other as siblings rather than as enemies.[63]

Visionaries

Minnie Florence Abrams, circa 1893. Courtesy of the United Methodist Church Archives, Madison, New Jersey.

Minnie F. Abrams: Another Context, Another Founder

Gary B. McGee

Rushing to the quarters of Minnie F. Abrams at 3:30 A.M. on July 29, 1905, the matron of a girls' dormitory at the Mukti Mission told her that one of the girls had suddenly awakened "with the fire coming down upon her." The girl had prayed before going to sleep that she might receive Holy Spirit baptism. The matron related how she "saw the fire, and ran across the room for a pail of water, and was about to pour it on her when I discovered that she was not on fire." When Abrams arrived, "all the girls . . . were on their knees, weeping, praying and confessing their sins. The newly Spirit-baptized girl sat in the midst of them, telling what God had done for her and exhorting them to repentance." One of the more celebrated events of the great revival in India (1905–6), this "case of the burning bush" prompted confessions and repentance.[1]

Carried in mission magazines, the story put Abrams in the limelight of Protestant missionaries in India. Yet, like other Holiness and Pentecostal women missionaries whose activities have often been overlooked, underestimated, or simply forgotten, only a few scholars would recognize her name today. In the small number of instances where they have gained attention, the scope of their legacies has sometimes been narrowed to inspiring believers to missionary service or fundraising to support charitable ministries that they pioneered. In the case of Abrams, historians have mentioned her name only briefly in connection with the revival in India and her contribution to the Pentecostal Methodist movement in Chile. The only institution that bears her name is the Minnie Abrams Memorial Chapel, next to her gravesite, in the city of Uska. Even the obituaries published in major mission periodicals avoided reference to her significant leadership in the Pentecostal movement.

Nevertheless, her endeavors, perspectives on mission, and theology open a new vista of Pentecostalism outside Euro-America, one that challenges traditional assumptions about origins and uniformity in belief. The revival in India serves as a reminder that the first decade of the Pentecostal movement still contains potentially fruitful areas of study that await exploration. The story and legacy of Abrams, which rival the often lionized accomplishments of others in the Pentecostal "Hall of Fame," are the subjects of this essay.[2]

Preparation for a "Useful Life"

Minnie Florence Abrams was born on a farm on August 2, 1859, near Lawrenceville, Wisconsin, the third of four children in the family of Franklin and Julia Ann Abrams. According to the Minnesota Census for 1870, the couple had journeyed from New York to Wisconsin, where their first three children were born. By 1863, they had relocated to Medo Township in Blue Earth County, Minnesota, and resumed farming.[3] Franklin also traveled as a lay preacher in the region (at some point licensed by the Methodist Church), and Julia Ann "devoted her life to the cause of missions, the WCTU [Women's Christian Temperance Union], and religious work." As one familiar with the family said, "With such surroundings, it was but natural that the daughter early in life should have dedicated her life to the Master's work."[4]

Growing up in the village of Mapleton, her horizons gradually extended far beyond the fence lines. In her youth, Abrams attended a congregation of the Church of the United Brethren in Christ, whose Minnesota Conference had been organized in 1857 and consisted predominantly of rural congregations.[5] She later remembered making a decision to follow Christ at eight and a half years of age.[6] The call to mission dated back to her Sunday school days when she thumbed through the pages of the denominational *Missionary Visitor.*

At age nineteen, Abrams matriculated at the nearby Mankato Normal School (now Mankato State University), where she studied from 1878 to 1882 to prepare for a career in teaching. With a strong concentration in mathematics and science, she graduated with a "higher degree" that qualified her to teach on the high school level. She also joined a Methodist

Episcopal church, an easy transition given the likeness in theology and organization of the two denominations. After teaching in a public school at Owatonna, she then moved to Minneapolis in 1884 to another teaching position and for several months continued her teacher-education studies at the University of Minnesota. Setting the course of her future vocation, she also became a member of the Minneapolis Branch of the Woman's Foreign Missionary Society of the Methodist Episcopal Church.

Having been called "to go to India to preach the Gospel," she obeyed when "the Lord told me to go to the Chicago Training School [for City, Home, and Foreign Missions]" to pursue specialized training.[7] Lucy Rider Meyer, a leader in the Methodist deaconess movement, opened the school in 1885 to offer women instruction in theology (Bible, church history, doctrine) and practical skills (methods of teaching the Bible, nursing, elementary medicine, etc.) for home and foreign service. While deaconess leaders envisaged the movement for nurses, teachers, and pastoral helpers, most opposed the notion of training women to become evangelists. Nonetheless, from the school's founding Meyer trained deaconess evangelists by inserting "a little innocent modified homiletics" into the curriculum.[8]

Lacking the necessary funds to enroll, Abrams wrote to the school and asked if she could work for her room and board in return for classroom instruction. But owing to the brevity of the program, school officials considered this impractical and denied her request. Fortunately, someone contacted a donor in Oak Park, Illinois, who then provided the money for her to enter the first class. At the opening in December 1885, the lectures on foreign missions given by William E. Blackstone, a well-known Methodist layman, promoter of missions, and author of the widely read *Jesus Is Coming* (1878), probably reaffirmed her calling. Isabelle Horton, Meyer's biographer, noted that "Mrs. Meyer was used to say, that when Mr. Blackstone's lecture was on India every student came forthwith and offered herself for the work in India." Similar responses occurred when he appealed for missionaries to other countries such as Korea and Japan.[9] Like other young women at the time, Abrams chose the "useful" life of a missionary.

Although not organically connected with any mission society, the school prospered with the encouragement of the Chicago City Missionary Society, the Woman's Home Missionary Society of the Methodist Episcopal Church, and, important for Abrams, the Woman's Foreign Missionary

Society (WFMS). "The school has never had a dollar of endowment," wrote Meyer three years subsequent to its launching, "nor has it ever paid a dollar of salary."[10] She and her teachers urged students to give sacrificially to missions, and Abrams gave half of her meager income to "help India."[11] Furthermore, those who intended to serve overseas were challenged to live on partial support to expedite the sending of more women. But after living abroad, she contested the wisdom of this appeal through articles written for church papers and letters to Meyer, having observed the human costs firsthand.[12]

Institutional Work and Itinerant Evangelism

Following graduation, the Minneapolis Branch commissioned Abrams as one of its first two "deaconess missionaries." Paying for the steamship ticket and clothing expenses herself, she set sail on October 12, 1887. Disembarking at Bombay (now Mumbai), she immediately began serving at a girls' school started by Sarah M. DeLine, who had inaugurated Methodist educational work there in 1884. Though Abrams had originally been sent to do evangelism, she conceded that "God saw that I was not ready for it, so [he] kept me in training."[13] She helped expand the enterprise to include an orphanage and boarding school. Within six years the operation had added two more day schools, a house-to-house visitation program, as well as open-air evangelistic meetings.[14] During this time, she had the unenviable task of trying to learn the Marathi language while assisting at all three schools. For her and many other women, ministry in a foreign land focused on educational training—a vital component in the nineteenth-century "Woman's Work for Woman" missiology.[15] Along with being housemother, teacher, physician, seamstress, and financial manager, she was expected to give spiritual guidance to the girls. In due course, the regimen took its toll and Abrams left in ill health for the United States in 1892; she returned to Bombay sixteen months later. (Later furloughs included a fourteen-month visit to the United States in 1900–1901 and an approximate two-year furlough in 1908–10.)

Regardless of the successes of her institutional endeavors, Abrams longed for more active involvement in evangelism. Yet the stereotypical role of a woman missionary limited her opportunities. Driving her zeal were sights of the masses living in heartbreaking conditions. Under the cover of darkness, she ventured into opium dens and saw the emaciated bodies of people enslaved by their addictions. "Oh, how my heart cried out," she recounted, "and how I longed to be able to bring the message of life to these people in all their darkness."[16] Despite the presence of many missionaries among the millions in Bombay, she knew "they couldn't reach the thousandth part of the people with the sound of the Gospel."[17] Like other missionaries at the time, she found little if anything of worth in the non-Christian religions.

Finally, Methodist Bishop James M. Thoburn appointed her as a conference evangelist for the Poona area of the Bombay Conference in 1895. No one had been more influential in promoting the deaconess movement than Thoburn, having recognized early in his career the value of deaconess evangelists on the India field.[18] The new appointment transferred Abrams from institutional responsibilities to full-time preaching and evangelism. She remained in this capacity for four or five years. Florence Sterling, a friend and colleague, accompanied her for the first year but then married. Abrams continued in village evangelism, going "hither and thither, accompanied only by native helpers."[19] While the contributing factors remain unclear, she dramatically changed the course of her ministry by severing her connections with the Methodist Church and the WFMS in 1899 to become an independent faith missionary and work at the Mukti ("Salvation") Mission in Kedgaon, near Poona, approximately 120 kilometers southeast of Bombay. The renowned Indian Christian Pandita Ramabai had established it in the preceding year.

Both Abrams and Ramabai agreed that the decision had been of divine origin. According to Rachel Nalder, the American representative of the Mukti Mission, "[Ramabai] wanted a woman who would come and be her Bible teacher, one who understood the scriptures thoroughly, and He called out Minnie F. Abrams. . . . She came to Ramabai and said, 'Ramabai, God distinctly said to me, 'Go to Mukti,' and I do not know what it means, but I had to come.' Ramabai said, 'Praise God, we have prayed for you for seven years.'"[20] (By saying that she had prayed seven years for an assistant, Ramabai referred back to her earlier institutional ministry in Bombay, the Sharna Sadan [abode of wisdom], a school for the training of young Hindu widows, later relocated to Poona.)

Whatever physical rigors Abrams may have experienced in her itinerancy or possible conflicts that may have arisen with her Methodist superiors faded into the background as she chose "to follow the Cloudy Pillar" into "faith mission work."[21] Previous concerns about limited financial support aside, she flourished in this environment. "God had a way of subduing me and He did it," she later recounted, "*and when I was subdued I found myself a faith missionary,* working under an East Indian woman, Pandita Ramabai, who was also living by faith."[22] She functioned as pastor, Bible teacher, and administrative assistant over what soon became a world-famous charity that eventually cared for thousands of child widows and famine victims. Most important, Mukti gave her the chance to train women evangelists.

True of other faith ventures that survived, the Mukti Mission built a network of supporters. Funds came as a result of promotional efforts in Europe and Australia, in addition to the help of the American Ramabai Association, set up in 1896 after a visit by Ramabai to the United States.[23] Even though the faith principle rested on prayer and belief in God's miraculous provision, the faithful back home usually required some direction as to where their monies were most needed. Hence, Ramabai published the *Mukti Prayer-Bell* and traveled abroad to describe the activities at the mission and raise money. Periodicals also serialized her life story to help the cause. Even so, faith ministries like Mukti struggled without the financial guarantees that stood behind the denominational missions.

Revival Power and Evangelism

Before the end of the nineteenth century, a significant number of missionaries in India had embraced Wesleyan Holiness and Higher Life teachings on the baptism and gifts of the Spirit. According to Wesleyan Holiness writers, the postconversion baptism in the Holy Spirit brought deliverance from the sinful nature and power for Christian living; Higher Life advocates considered it full consecration for empowerment in evangelism. Abrams did not testify to her own sanctification until 1896, one year following her appointment as a conference evangelist. Unfortunately, she left no details as to the circumstances of her Spirit baptism. Later, after the revival began at Mukti in June 1905 that brought a new spiritual awakening to her own life, she admitted that her previous experience had been without "the fire" of the Holy Ghost (Matt. 3:11).[24]

Whether or not Holiness teachings in the WFMS influenced her to seek the second blessing, the seed had been planted long before her arrival in India. Along with other factors, the itinerant ministries of prominent

American leaders furthered its growth. These included William Taylor, later Methodist missionary bishop for Africa; Amanda Berry Smith, a Holiness evangelist of African descent who came in 1879 and traveled widely preaching on Holy Spirit baptism; as well as John S. Inskip, president of the National Association for the Promotion of Holiness, who toured a year later. Upon reaching Bombay, Inskip and his associate William McDonald learned that "most, if not all, of the preachers of the South India Conference, were earnest in their advocacy of holiness, and were anxious that we should make it the theme of our preaching while in India."[25]

The seemingly impossible challenge of world evangelization troubled radical evangelicals like Ramabai and Abrams whose millennial clocks ticked only to the midnight hour of Christ's imminent return. How could the "Great Commission" of Jesus (Matt. 28:19–20) be completed in the few remaining days, months, or years of human history? They found the answer in the end-times outpouring of the Holy Spirit, predicted in Joel (2:28–29). Wesleyan Holiness and Higher Life believers had long prayed for its fulfillment and urged their people to seek Spirit baptism. Only the fires of a Pentecostal revival could move the Protestant mission enterprise ahead of its conventional practices, which had garnered only 3.6 million converts by the end of the century.[26] Looking beyond the commonplace to the scenes of apostolic power portrayed in the Acts, they anticipated that the Holy Spirit would inspire the personnel and provide the spiritual equipment necessary to finish the task. When Ramabai visited England in 1898, she received an invitation to attend the annual Keswick Convention. Given five minutes to speak before the nearly four thousand people present, she asked them to pray for an "outpouring of the Holy Spirit on all Indian Christians." In response to her appeal, they prayed that God would raise up 100,000 male and 100,000 female Indians to preach the gospel in the power of the Holy Spirit to their own people.[27]

Learning of the R. A. Torrey and Charles Alexander crusades in Australia in 1903 and the revival that followed, Ramabai sent her daughter, Manoramabai, and Abrams to investigate the factors that had brought it about. But it was news of the Spirit's outpouring in Wales (1904–5) with its enthusiastic phenomena and sizable number of conversions that sparked revival in March 1905 among tribal peoples in the Khassia Hills of northeast India, at Mukti three months later, and at other mission stations across the subcontinent. After the "fire fell," Abrams and forty-eight "praying bands," each comprised of approximately fifteen young women, went out twice weekly to the surrounding countryside to preach in the villages. Mukti would do its part in preparing a corps of the requested 100,000 female evangelists.

Public confessions of sins and prayer storms (hours of public worship spent in loud and fervent prayer) were the most notable features of the awakening. Baptist, Presbyterian, Methodist, Anglican, Lutheran, Christian and Missionary Alliance, as well as other missionaries described unusual occurrences. These included visions, dreams, angelic visitations, a "burning" sensation, laughter, exorcisms, prophesying, and even miraculous provisions of food, paranormal happenings more acceptable in the worldview of India than of the West. Though such incidents perturbed Abrams at the outset, she set aside her own ethnocentrism to allow them so long as believers were seeking a deeper relationship with Christ.[28] She also knew that comparable things had taken place in the ministry of John Wesley.

But critics condemned her teaching on fire baptism since it seemed to require a burning sensation as proof of reception. A writer in *Dnyanodaya*, the Anglo-Marathi newspaper published by the Ahmednagar Mission of the American Board of Commissioners for Foreign Missions, chastised it as "sensuous and superstitious. . . . pure heathenism in Christian dress." However, an editorial in the *Indian Witness*, the official Methodist periodical for India, defended it by comparing the fire to Wesley's heart being "strangely warmed" at Aldersgate.[29] Abrams herself likened it to the testimony of Madame Guyon, whose "troublesome faults" were "consumed like chaff in a great fire."[30] All the same, this did not make her view parallel to the fire-baptized theology of Benjamin Hardin Irwin, whose concept of postconversion experiences highlighted fire baptism for empowerment as another work of grace following the second one of sanctification. This notion had gained currency in radical Holiness circles in America and helped lay the theological foundation of the Pentecostal movement.[31] Shy of this approach, Abrams maintained that the fire represented the fullness of the second work of grace.[32]

In the spring of 1906, she penned the first edition of *The Baptism of the Holy Ghost and Fire* to encourage believers to seek purity of life and power to evangelize. It combined Wesleyan Holiness and Higher Life themes of purification and empowerment. After an initial printing of 10,000 copies, two Christian newspapers, *Bombay Guardian* and *Christian Patriot*

(Madras, now Chennai), serialized it for their readers. The *Indian Witness* (Calcutta) also published it, evidence that Abrams had remained on good terms with the Methodist Church.

With other radical evangelicals, Abrams believed that miraculous interventions of supernatural power—the "signs following" (Mark 16:17–18)—were indispensable for completing the Great Commission. Indeed, she contended that they had reappeared in some circles.[33] Anticipation of the restoration of apostolic power continued to run high at mission stations across the country. When Abrams took ten young women with her to the American Presbyterian mission at Ratnagiri, the missionary A. L. Wiley announced that "the Spirit worked marvellously." In addition to believers falling down, swaying, shouting, and crying in the services, "many have seen visions of various kinds—Christ on the Cross, angels with drawn swords, fire, etc. Many have experienced inward burning, marking the cleansing by the Spirit of burning (Isaiah iv: 4) and his empowering for service."[34]

Nevertheless, some felt that the revival had fallen short of the outpouring of the Spirit as recorded in Acts. Indian Christians had queried Abrams: "If this is the work of the Holy Spirit, why do you not speak with new tongues, heal the sick, cast out devils and work miracles?"[35] Ever a seeker, her expectancy of such phenomena contributed to the beginning of the Pentecostal movement in India in July 1906, a development that arose independently of key events in the United States: most notably, the first Pentecostal revival of the twentieth century at Topeka, Kansas, in January 1901, where Charles F. Parham framed the "classical Pentecostal" doctrine that God would bestow unstudied human languages on Spirit-baptized Christians for gospel proclamation in the mission lands; and the internationally influential Azusa Street revival in Los Angeles, California (1906–9), led in part by the African American William J. Seymour.

Restoration of the Gift of Tongues

While Pentecostal-like phenomena had been present since the beginning of the Indian revival in 1905, the more controversial speaking in tongues came later. Still, it was a point of discussion. For instance, the *Christian Patriot* reprinted an article in April 1905 by Robert A. Hume, an American Congregational missionary at Ahmednagar, in which he warned of a "widespread misapprehension" about the work of the Holy Spirit. He specifically referred to the notion that preaching should be "attended by some remarkable signs corresponding to the tongues of fire upon the heads of the disciples, and accompanied with some unusual power of utterance like the gift of tongues." Though originally written for an American audience, an editorial note commented, "much of it applies also to India."[36]

Others had a more positive outlook. Reflecting on the revival at the Asansol District Conference in the fall of 1905, Methodist Bishop John E. Robinson reported: "So powerful was the manifestation of the presence of the Holy Spirit . . . that it would not have surprised me had I seen tongues of fire descend upon the disciples present, or had I heard them 'speak in other tongues as the Spirit gave them utterance.'"[37] In October, the *Christian Patriot* printed a story by the British writer Jessie Penn-Lewis in which she raised the topic of tongues by telling of a recent trip to Wales. There she heard of a visiting Dutch pastor who had miraculously preached sermons in English on two occasions. Because of this "remarkable manifestation of the Spirit," she declared: "Truly we are having the marks of Pentecost among us, and if the Church of God will be willing and obedient in this time of His power we shall see greater things than these in the days to come. Let us cast aside all unbelief and hesitation, in obedience to the Holy Ghost, and abandon ourselves to God, that He may manifest through us to an unbelieving world the *truth* of His written Word in its record of His supernatural power."[38] While she later castigated the "tongue movement," this early endorsement, along with Hume's and Robinson's comments, probably intensified the debate. To be sure, the gift of tongues had been a point of interest in radical mission circles since the 1880s, but their value had centered only on preaching in unstudied languages, as Penn-Lewis's account showed.[39]

Reports of tongues started two or three months after Anglican missionaries (Church Missionary Society [CMS]) at Aurangabad in the Deccan region of south India invited a praying band from Mukti to visit their station in April 1906. Abrams led the group of two boys, eight girls, and another woman missionary. Fifty preachers and mission workers from eleven churches in a forty-mile radius attended, with many schoolchildren. The revival that ensued stretched from the planned ten days to forty-eight. However, not all of the Anglicans were pleased. "The preachers thought we had come to break up their church order, and to take their prayer-book," Abrams wrote. "They objected to the loud simultaneous prayer and other demonstrations of the Spirit, and to public confession of sin, but more than all to the fact that women dared to set themselves up as teachers." Despite the criticisms, "God won the victory in answer to intense prayer," and "the meetings grew in fervor as the days went by."[40]

This revival proved to be a catalyst for the speaking in tongues that took place later among students who had attended the meetings. The testimony of a "pupil teacher" who returned home from Aurangabad in June to the Zenana Bible and Medical Mission orphanage at Manmad prompted a revival where one or two girls likely spoke in tongues.[41] However, the best-known episode took place in early July when other girls returned to the CMS boarding school in Bombay. Their enthusiasm stirred others to prayer and confession of sins. Several girls spoke in tongues, including a nine-year-old named Sarah. Canon R. S. Heywood (later Bishop of Mombasa, Kenya), thinking it might be analogous to what took place on the Day of Pentecost, found someone who could interpret Sarah's words and who then announced that she was "pleading with God for [the conversion of] Libya."[42] Months later, "Miss Lambourne" of the boarding school, reflected: "It is with reverence and awe that we retrace in our hearts the paths by which God led us last June, July and August. The Holy Ghost as the Lord and Giver of Life was so manifestly revealed to us all. Four girls, to whom was given a special power of prayer, still continue to pray daily, pouring out their young hearts in intercession for the coming of Christ's Kingdom."[43]

Such incidents pressed Maud Wiest to editorialize in the September 1906 issue of the *India Alliance,* a publication of Christian and Missionary Alliance: "Those who are following through the papers the reports of the revival movement in India cannot but be struck with the likeness of many things . . . to apostolic times and events, and the records frequently read like a continuation of the Acts of the Apostles." Spiritual gifts, "scarcely heard of in the church for many centuries," had now been given to "simple, unlearned members of the body of Christ. . . . Healings, the gift of tongues, visions and dreams, discernment of spirits, the power to prophecy and to pray the prayer of faith, all have a place in the present revival."[44]

Though Wiest mentioned tongues without reference to preaching in new languages or to having a normative function for Holy Spirit baptism, this mixture of supernatural ingredients caught the attention of leaders at the Apostolic Faith Mission on Azusa Street, where a Pentecostal revival had been in progress since April. In the November 1906 issue of the *Apostolic Faith* (Los Angeles), the publication of the mission, an excerpt of her editorial appeared with a preface stating that "news comes from India that . . . tongues [are] being received there by natives who are simply taught of God."[45] Another such discovery took place months later when Lillian Garr, accompanied by her husband, Alfred, arrived in Calcutta at the turn of 1907; she notified Azusa that Pentecostal revival had preceded them, having "already broken out among the natives, and some were speaking in tongues."[46] Indeed, they heard reports, "coming in from all over the world," about how people were speaking in tongues "even before they [had] heard of the Los Angeles meeting." Such news came from Russia, Canada, the United States, Burma, and India.[47]

From July to the end of 1906, Pentecostalism spread among Indian believers. The extent, locations, and the Indian leaders involved cannot be determined since mission publications, as well as Pentecostal periodicals, did not usually publish the number or names of Indians who spoke in tongues. Reflecting on the change in the revival scene in early December 1906, an editorial in the *Indian Witness* commented that "no phase of the present revival movement in Asia has received such severe criticism as the unusual and marked physical manifestations which have so often followed its outbreak in different localities." While noting that they may be "strange and incredible" to some, they should not be discounted because "one should recall similar experience[s] of Bible characters, visions and trances and unknown tongues and that the promise through Joel includes 'all flesh.'"[48]

The occurrences of tongues at Manmad and Bombay were followed by accounts of the same at the Mukti Mission in late December 1906. Having read about the Los Angeles revival in the pages of the *Apostolic Faith,* Ramabai and Abrams acknowledged that "the deeper fulness of the outpouring of the Holy Ghost accompanied by the gift of tongues . . . had not yet been received" there. Consequently, they encouraged the faithful to "tarry" anew (Luke 24:49). Before Christmas, seekers, claiming divine empowerment, spoke for the first time in languages they had never studied, among them English, Kannada, and Sanskrit. Unintelligible or "unknown" tongues could also be heard. A number of girls acquired the gift of interpretation and others that of healing.[49] Abrams herself testified to singing "a little chorus, in Hebrew, of praise and invocation to the Triune God, which was attended with great power." On the next day, she sang another chorus in another language.[50] Ramabai did not speak in tongues, but commended the experience (Manoramabai had spoken in tongues).

In the second edition of her *Baptism of the Holy Ghost and Fire* (December 1906), which first mentions the restoration of tongues, Abrams made no reference to their utility for preaching or requirement for Holy Spirit baptism. Instead, if spoken publicly, their value depended on someone present who either knew the language or had the gift of interpretation.[51] When uttered in private, tongues, now understood as unintelligible expressions of deep piety by the speaker, denoted prayer in the Spirit to God; in turn, this brought power to preach the gospel.

When comparing tongues with prophecy, Abrams said the latter was the "gift most needed, and most to be sought after," following Paul's evaluation in 1 Cor. 14:1.[52] The value of prophecy (spoken in one's own language) focused on preaching. According to Ramabai, some exercised the gift "so that they could give God's messages in very clear language, taught by the Holy Spirit. The believers and unbelievers were moved alike by these messages, and a deep spiritual work began in our midst."[53]

In light of this, neither Abrams nor Ramabai registered tongues as indispensable to every instance of Holy Spirit baptism as did their American counterparts (for example, Parham, Seymour, and Alfred G. Garr). Instead, those who were Spirit baptized obtained spiritual power and the gifts of the Spirit. This explains why Abrams's second edition notably lacked any reference to Parham's "Bible evidence" doctrine, later popularly called the "initial evidence." She remained consistent with her Wesleyan heritage by teaching that "perfect love" as defined in 1 Corinthians 13 represented the "highest form of Pentecostal power anywhere expressed in God's word or in the life of the Christian." Hence, "such love, preaching the word, that word being confirmed by signs, the Lord working with them, Mark 16:20, will stir the non-Christian world."[54]

Both views on tongues found expression at Mukti. In a letter to the editor of *Confidence* (UK), Abrams wrote that some believed it to be the only sign of the experience, "while others of us feel that . . . all may and should receive this sign, yet we dare not say that no one is Spirit-baptized who has not received this sign." In assessing what effects the two opinions had in the lives of the faithful there, she concluded: "We see the same gifts and graces and power for service in those who hold these different beliefs, and, so far as I know, we are as yet working in love and unity for the spread of this mighty work of the Holy Ghost."[55]

Leaving in 1908 for a promotional tour of the United States with Manoramabai, Abrams visited important centers of Pentecostal activity, including Carrie Judd Montgomery's Home of Peace in Oakland, California; Elmer K. Fisher's Upper Room Mission in Los Angeles; and Elizabeth V. Baker's Elim Tabernacle in Rochester, New York. At the Stone Church in Chicago, she received a warm welcome from the pastor, William Hamner Piper, who denounced the "Bible evidence" doctrine as "false teaching."[56] During one of her sermons, she added fuel to the debate in America by declaring, "God's rule [is] to give speaking in tongues at the time or sometime after one's baptism, but I think I see from the Word of God that He has exceptions."[57] (Did Abrams consider Ramabai an exception?) By this time, however, the voices of Abrams, Piper, and others were being drowned out by a growing host of Pentecostals who rejected such a possibility.

"Classical Pentecostalism" Arrives from America

The visit of the Garrs to Calcutta in January 1907 conveniently coincided with a missionary conference. As the meetings drew to a close, many felt the anticipated cloudburst of "latter rain" had missed them once again. Max Wood Moorhead, a Presbyterian missionary with the YMCA in Ceylon (now Sri Lanka), sighed, "We were all about as hungry and dry as when we started."[58] Meeting with the missionaries offered Garr the opportunity he wanted to tell of the recent events in Los Angeles. At the invitation of Pastor C. H. Hook, he then began to hold services at the historic Carey Baptist Chapel in the city. There he taught the Pentecostal doctrine of tongues as conceived by Parham, stating unequivocally that without tongues one had not experienced Holy Spirit baptism and could not be considered Pentecostal. To some of the missionaries who had witnessed the revival since 1905 and applauded its influence on Indian Christians, Garr's narrow definition was outrageous. In this way, he alienated missionaries sympathetic to Pentecostal phenomena who had not spoken in tongues themselves.

Although holding steadfastly to the evidential part of Parham's thesis on tongues, for a pragmatic reason (he could not speak Bengali, after all) and theological reasons, Garr modified it within a few weeks. While retaining tongues as crucial to Holy Spirit baptism, he said nothing about their capacity for preaching. Though still the "tongues of men and of angels" (1 Cor. 13:1), their exercise served primarily for personal prayer and public worship. He now marveled at the "blessedness of His presence when those foreign words [flow] from the Spirit of God through one's soul, and then are delivered back to God in praise to Him or in edification to others [through the gift of interpretation] or in prophecy."[59]

The debate over tongues ignited the first major theological dispute within the Pentecostal movement, several years before better-known quarrels surfaced in the United States, controversies that later forged the identities of Pentecostal denominations. What missionary Robert E. Massey trumpeted as the "Great Issue" over the evidential function of tongues appears to have started first in India, and then in North America and Europe. "Tongues is *the essentially* important issue in the present Revival," he warned as late as 1909, "and Satan will use all his forces to get us to compromise at this point. Shall we be true to our convictions? We will by the grace of God."[60] Indeed, Moorhead's periodical, *Cloud of Witnesses to Pentecost in India* (1907–ca. 1910), which printed Massey's statement, helped keep the devil from the door by advancing the American view of tongues to counter deviant teachings. Abrams could not have missed the point.

It is significant that when she told the story of how Pentecostalism came about in India, Abrams described the outpouring of the Spirit as coming in several "waves," beginning with the events of 1905. Then "God sent another wave upon us with the gifts of the Spirit, . . . a mighty wave of speaking in other tongues, and a mighty wave of interpretation; He used the Spirit of prophecy in witnessing to the heathen."[61] Pointedly missing are references to the Garrs, the Calcutta revival, and the controversy over tongues speech.[62] She undoubtedly lamented the division and acrimony that arose over the new insistence on tongues.

Ironically for Abrams, Ramabai, and many others, Moorhead credited the Calcutta revival as the beginning of the "first general outpouring of the Spirit" in India. Through his published articles and those of Garr, Calcutta became the birthplace.[63] Over the years, as historians assumed that Indian Pentecostalism emerged as a direct result of Azusa Street and proclaimed the latter as the "Jerusalem" of the worldwide movement, its actual beginning became invisible.[64]

Legacy in Mission and Theology

With a premonition that she had only two more years to live, Abrams went back to India in late 1910 intent on engaging in frontline evangelism. Like other Holiness and Pentecostal women ministers, she believed that the "promise of the Father" (Acts 1:4) gave her equal opportunity with men in preaching the gospel. Earlier in the year when visiting St. Paul, Minnesota, she had attended a regional convention of the Laymen's Missionary Movement, only to be disheartened at hearing that "the evangelization of the world was a man's job."[65] Having faced these sentiments before, she dismissed the remark, knowing that the Great Commission could not be accomplished without women. Later, when preaching at the Stone Church in Chicago, she referred to the hundreds of young women evangelists at Mukti, happily adding, "You know I only asked [the Lord] for 50."[66]

She returned with seven new "baptized in the Spirit" recruits: Edith Baugh, Blanche Cunningham, Lillian Doll, Minnie L. Houck, "Miss Bristol," "Miss Dempster," and "Miss MacDonald." Ramabai called them the "Phillipus Class" because, "like the daughters of Philip, they are to be evangelists" (Acts 21:9). To facilitate their endeavor, Abrams organized the party as the Bezaleel Evangelistic Mission (Exod. 31:2–3), perhaps the only women's mission society founded by Pentecostals.[67] As they journeyed north to the city of Uska near the border of Nepal, she left behind the controversy over tongues to pursue her first love—the evangelization of unreached peoples. With north India especially resistant to Christianity, intense opposition faced them. Difficulties in travel, the heat, and various trying circumstances increased their hardships. During a vacation in the mountains with her friend Alice E. Luce, both women became ill with malaria. As a result, Abrams died at age fifty-three on December 2, 1912.[68]

In analyzing the role of women in mission, the historian Dana Robert suggests that "women provided Pentecostalism with its first missiology, its first missionary training programs, and its first senior missionaries in the field."[69] In this light, Abrams deserves the accolade as the most prominent of the veteran women missionaries, virtually all of whom were in India, who moved "from the woman's missionary movement through holiness to Pentecostalism" in the first decade of the century.[70] Although Robert's thesis underrates Parham's contributions, it unveils a largely neglected aspect of Pentecostal mission history that promises fresh and possibly groundbreaking insights.

GARY B. MCGEE

The first edition of her *Baptism in the Holy Ghost and Fire* (ca. May 1906) affected the Indian scene, and when she sent a copy to Willis and Mary Hoover, Methodist missionary friends in Chile, it added to the tinder that sparked the large Pentecostal movement in that country in 1909. (Significantly, Willis Hoover, like Abrams, did not insist that speaking in tongues had to accompany every occurrence of Spirit baptism.)[71] Just as important, its revision in December 1906 provided Pentecostals with their first expanded theology of mission. As her missiology matured, she taught that Holy Spirit baptism is the "revelation of the triune God in us and through us to a dying world." That exposition formed a Pentecostal inter-pretation of *missio Dei* (the activity of God himself in mission continued through the Holy Spirit in the church).[72]

The association of Abrams with schools and charitable institutions, along with her intense zeal for evangelism and expectancy of "signs and wonders" (Acts 5:12–15), modeled a Pentecostal adaptation of "Woman's Work for Woman." Through balancing institutional ministry with gospel proclamation, she avoided a false dichotomy between them. Her story illus-trates the notable and creative achievements of women who shaped the progress of Holiness and Pentecostal missions. Her successful efforts at preparing and leading both Indian and American women in evangelism reveal a woman of strong faith and fortitude. Behind her resolve stood an uncompromising belief that the outpouring of the Holy Spirit had over-flowed the embankments of ecclesiastical caste systems that had tradition-ally denied them the prospect of preaching.

In addition to her missiology, Abrams made a vital contribution to the theological formation of Pentecostalism, though it represented a minority position, illustrative of the diversity of thought in the movement. When tongues followed the Aurangabad conference, it marked a new and virtu-ally predictable turning point in a long-standing quest for spiritual power among many evangelical missionaries and Indians. After news arrived in the fall of 1906 telling of the Azusa Street revival and more people began to speak in tongues, their concept of its meaning and purpose differed in crucial respects from that taught at Azusa.

Following her death, the *Bombay Guardian* praised Abrams as "a woman of unusual ability and force of character, and when she realized a course of action to be right, she followed it without questioning; she was also a woman of faith, and it was this rather than her strength of character and will which enabled her to accomplish the work she did among India's women."[73] Notwithstanding the sincerity of this tribute, it obscured the radical nature of her ministry and the stature of her leadership as a founder of the Pentecostal movement.[74]

Frank Bartleman: Pentecostal "Lone Ranger" and Social Critic

Augustus Cerillo Jr.

Frank Bartleman, pioneer Pentecostal evangelist, journalist, and social critic, arguably ranked as one of the most significant early American Pentecostal leaders. As a tireless evangelist, he preached the new Pentecostal message on the streets of the nation's cities and in countless Holiness churches, conventions, and camp meetings in the United States and around the world. A gifted and prolific writer, he regularly published his thoughts and observations about the new movement in the Holiness and Pentecostal press. Probably he is best remembered for his comprehensive, colorfully detailed and engaging accounts of the rise, impact, and significance of the Azusa Street revival in Los Angeles in 1906. Bartleman thus greatly contributed to the diffusion and growth of the fledgling pre–World War I Pentecostal movement and, most important, shaped all subsequent accounts of the origins of Pentecostalism. As a social critic, Bartleman also provided the nascent Pentecostal movement with detailed suggestions about what he considered the radical social, economic, and political implications of the revival.[1]

The Formative Years: Early Life and Ministry to 1904

On December 14, 1871, on a farm near Carversville in Bucks County, Pennsylvania, Frank Bartleman was born to Frank Sr., a German immigrant, pottery maker, and farmer by trade, and Margaret (Hellyer), an American of English and Welsh descent and former schoolteacher. According to Bartleman's reconstruction of his early life story, neither of his parents was a church member, but, as he recalled, his adored mother, desiring her children "to go right," said nightly prayers with him and his

Frank Bartleman, 1906. Courtesy of the Flower Pentecostal Heritage Center, Springfield, Missouri.

four brothers and sent Frank to Sunday school.[2] Plagued by poor health—
"I grew up practically an invalid," Bartleman wrote in his 1908 memoir—
the young Frank found work on the family farm physically difficult, so
much so that at times he "lost all interest in natural life."[3] If childhood on
the family farm was later remembered as a time of constant toil by this
"different" member of the physically hardy Bartleman family, school
loomed as a bright spot, where the evidently intellectually gifted Frank
earned grades that "hugged the 100 mark closely." Not until he turned
nineteen did Frank have the physical and emotional strength to break free
of his father's domineering control and low opinion of his prospects in life
and his own boyhood fear of early death. "Ambition for the first time began
to be born," he recalled. "I realized that I was now a man grown, an independent being. My life began to unfold."[4]

Despite this uncharacteristic optimism about his prospects, Bartleman's
early adult life was anything but spectacular. He held a number of low-
paying odd jobs and in November 1892, at nearly twenty-one years old, he
moved to nearby Philadelphia, then the nation's third largest city with a
population of about one million. During the day he worked at a wholesale
shoe store. In the evening he studied grammar and arithmetic at Temple
College (later Temple University), founded by Russell H. Conwell, the
nationally well-known social reformer, lecturer, prosperity preacher, and
pastor of the Grace Baptist Church, then the largest big-city social service-
oriented church in the nation. Bartleman attended services at Grace Baptist,
and, he later remembered, at this time in his life he experienced a great
hunger for God. On October 15, 1893, sitting alone and miserable in his
boardinghouse room, guided only by God, as the spiritual loner told his
conversion story, he was "gloriously saved." "The matter was finally settled,
the darkness gave way, floods of light illuminated my whole being, the
burden rolled off."[5] Following his conversion he was baptized by Conwell
and encouraged by the pastor to prepare for ministry.

Convinced that God wanted him in the ministry, the fiercely motivated
twenty-two-year-old convert was licensed to preach by Grace Baptist, took
evening Bible and theology courses at Temple, ministered among the city's
poor, distributed gospel tracts throughout Philadelphia, and in a burst of
faith threw away his medicine and trusted in God for physical healing. Not
surprisingly, on July 1, 1895, some twenty-two months after his conversion, Bartleman quit his job at the shoe store, a move his father pronounced

"insane." For the next couple of years Bartleman worked at odd jobs and willingly lived at a survival level and, as he indicated in his 1924 autobiography, saw his health deteriorate. He finished his second, and last, term at Temple and continued to minister where he could, including a short stint with the Salvation Army, whose ministry among the urban poor he appreciated.

In July 1897 the unemployed preacher headed for Chicago to fulfill a long-standing wish to study at Moody Bible Institute. On the trip to the Windy City, he walked more than three hundred miles and depended on the kindness of strangers for food and an occasional place to sleep. But after only a few weeks at the school, he opted to engage in evangelism with the Institute's Gospel Wagon. Over the next two years he made two preaching trips through the staunchly segregated southern United States, the first one with the Gospel Wagon primarily among black folk whose hospitality and friendship he accepted despite the racial mores of the region. During a second ministry tour, a solo venture confined to white southerners, he claimed a crisis of faith. On March 4, 1899, ill and tired in body, only one dollar in his pocket, alone and friendless in Mobile, Alabama, the twenty-seven-year-old Bartleman, unable to pray, thought he had been abandoned by God. In a rented room, for a moment—tempted by the devil, he would later state—he considered killing himself with the gun he carried for protection against dogs. Fortunately for the tired preacher, before he could pull the trigger, "sleep at last mercifully dropped the curtain on the near tragedy. God had 'given his beloved sleep.'" After this near suicide experience, if Bartleman's own reconstruction of his state of mind can be believed, the malaria-infected, tired, and penniless wandering evangelist, in the company of a Brother Garrow and family, made the arduous thousand-mile trip to Pennsylvania, ultimately settling in Pittsburgh on July 25, 1899.[6]

Over the next two and one-half years, Bartleman continued in his wandering ways even as his personal life changed significantly. He ministered for a time at the Hope Mission in Pittsburgh, where he met Anna Ladd, a coworker he married on May 2, 1900. When refused ordination by the Baptists because he lacked a seminary education, Bartleman, at the urging of a friend, and without any apparent theological motivation, joined the Wesleyan Methodists, who secured for him a pastorate in Lovells, Pennsylvania. After a year, the Lovells congregation refused to renew

Bartleman's tenure as pastor. Unable to gain a new appointment at the annual Wesleyan Conference, Bartleman and his undernourished and sickly family, now increased by the birth on April 30, 1901, of their first child, Esther, moved to Youngstown, Ohio. Soon after, the family moved to Pittsburgh and then, in April 1902, to Denver, Colorado, where Frank hoped the higher altitude would restore his failing health and where he had secured a ministerial job at Alma White's Pentecostal Union Home. Unfortunately, the family's hopes for a healthy life and successful ministry in the Rocky Mountain State did not materialize. Their three-month stay at the home, under the autocratic rule of Alma White, as well as their remaining time in Colorado, proved to be a physical, emotional, and spiritual disaster. The Bartlemans lived like vagabonds, moving from city to city, often with little money in their pockets or food on their table. Frank secured odd jobs here and there and preached when he could in Wesleyan or Free Methodist churches or camp meetings and in downtown Holiness missions, saloons, houses of prostitution, jails, and hospitals. On March 27, 1903, slightly less than a year after arriving in Colorado, Frank, Anna, and little Esther happily left Denver by train for Sacramento, California, where Frank was to minister in one of T. P. Ferguson's Peniel missions.[7]

Initially the Golden State proved inhospitable to the Bartleman family. After a few months Frank resigned from the Peniel mission, whose staff he found incompetent, and intermittently preached in missions in several northern California cities, taking on odd jobs to support his family, now increased by the birth of their second child, a girl they named Ruth. In December 1904 Bartleman again moved his family, this time south to Los Angeles, a rapidly growing city of more than 100,000. "The Spirit had led us to Los Angeles for the 'Latter Rain' outpouring," he later wrote. He had just turned thirty-three.[8]

The Making of a Pentecostal Leader, 1904–1935

Life in the City of the Angels proved no easier for the Bartlemans, who continued to experience poverty, hunger, and sickness. On January 7, 1905, at four in the morning, their firstborn, Esther, always physically fragile, died. "I was staggered, stunned," by her death, the heartbroken father confessed in 1908. Despite his personal sorrow, Bartleman interpreted his little girl's death in larger cosmic terms, as God's wakeup call to prepare him to participate in the end-time revival that he believed was imminent. "My own awakening, or reawakening to this plan," he confided, "was brought about through the loss of my little girl." The day after Esther's death, God informed Bartleman that He had taken Esther, as Bartleman put it, "to get my heart to Him in a new, deeper way."[9] After burying little Esther, the grief-stricken father pledged his "life anew for God's service."[10]

Throughout 1905 and 1906 Bartleman's life routines followed earlier patterns, only more intensely so. He gave up all secular work to live entirely by faith, which meant the Bartleman family constantly lived on the edge of extreme poverty. What outsiders undoubtedly considered spousal and parental neglect or even child abuse was, in Bartleman's view, a spiritual adventure of trusting in God and his people to supply the family's material needs. He threw himself into a frenetic pace of ministry, preaching on the streets of Los Angeles and Pasadena and in any mission that would give him a pulpit, prophesying of a coming Pentecost. When not engaged in public ministry or attending services at local churches, he prayed, sometimes all night at home or in an accommodating Holiness mission. "It seemed as though I carried a nation on my heart," he was to write of these months of intense intercessory prayer before the Pentecostal outpouring. "In fact I did," he boasted in his 1908 autobiography. In the midst of his "soul travail," as Bartleman referred to his prayer vigil, he became earthy enough to father with Anna a third child, a boy.[11]

During these months preceding the Azusa Street revival, Bartleman also wrote and published at his own expense gospel tracts, and he sent a steady stream of articles to several Holiness magazines reporting on the spiritual activities taking place in the Los Angeles area. So confident was he that an unusual revival was imminent, he boldly wrote in the November 16, 1905, issue of the *Way of Faith*, "'Pentecost' is knocking at our doors. The revival for our country is no longer a question . . . Los Angeles, Southern California, and the whole continent shall surely find itself ere long in the throes of a mighty revival, by the Spirit and power of God." In March 1906, one month before the Azusa Street revival, he published *The Last Call*, a tract in which he predicted a soon-to-occur end-time global revival.[12]

Although on March 26 and again on March 28 Bartleman attended William J. Seymour's cottage prayer meetings on Bonnie Brae Street, he was not present on April 9, when some of the participants received Holy Spirit baptism and spoke in tongues, thus igniting the historic Azusa Street revival. Nevertheless, in his influential autobiographical constructions of the origins of Pentecostalism in Los Angeles, Bartleman interpreted his fifteen-month prayer crusade as a key catalyst behind the outbreak of the revival. "Many and marvelous were the experiences in prayer and preparation before God finally secured the little simple, humble company who received the Spirit in April, 1906," he remembered. "I threw myself full length in a last agony of prayer, my strength all gone, to reach this, and it came. *My work was done. That particular burden left me then.* It remained largely now for others to carry it on. I was so exhausted I could hardly live. I had prophesied of the final outpouring also, just before it came."[13] Bartleman the journalist additionally promoted the Los Angeles revival as the foundational event in the more general history of the beginnings of Pentecostalism in early twentieth-century America. In the October 1906 issue of the *Apostolic Light,* a Holiness publication, he referred to Los Angeles as the American Jerusalem. Three months later in the *Way of Faith,* a magazine published by Holiness leader J. M. Pike in Columbia, South Carolina, Bartleman further characterized the Pentecostal movement as "the rising of a new order of things out of the chaos and failure of the past."[14]

Although Bartleman followed Seymour and his multiracial congregation from Bonnie Brae Street to their new location at 312 Azusa Street in downtown Los Angeles, he apparently did not become a regular at Seymour's church, often visiting other missions where Pentecostal revivals were occurring. On August 12, 1906, Bartleman, the fanatical antiorganizational man, disillusioned with the Azusa Street Mission because it had placed a sign on its building identifying itself as an "Apostolic Faith Mission," opened his own nameless Pentecostal mission in a recently vacated church building at the corner of Eighth and Maple Streets. Bartleman's landlord gave him the money for the first month's rent. Surprisingly, although now a Pentecostal pastor, Bartleman still had not spoken in tongues, and apparently he had not thought it necessary to do so.

On August 16, in his own mission, Bartleman received the Pentecostal baptism and spoke in tongues, the experience lasting for about fifteen minutes. Years later he claimed, "The whole utterance was a complete surprise to me." He also stated that he "never sought it as a definite experience" but only "wanted to be yielded fully to God." "But beyond that," he wrote, "I had no real definite expectation or desire. I wanted more of Him, that was all." Whatever the reasons for Bartleman's lack of urgency about seeking the new Pentecostal Spirit baptism, he certainly viewed the experience as a turning point in his life and ministerial career. "From that time the Spirit began to flow through me in a new way," he wrote. "Messages would come, with anointings, in a way I had never known before, with a spontaneous inspiration and illumination that was truly wonderful." He even claimed that, as a result of his baptism, languages came easy to him and he learned to sing in the Spirit.[15]

Spiritually invigorated and motivated by his Spirit baptism, Bartleman soon embarked on a career as a traveling Pentecostal evangelist, entirely dependent on freewill offerings for travel and living expenses and donated quarters to sleep each night. In a two-year period he made two coast-to-coast trips, one lasting from March 1907 to December 1907 and the other from March 1908 to February 1909. With the exception of a few camp meetings, Bartleman's itinerary followed the nation's towns and cities, the nodes of the nation's railroad system. On both occasions he took his family with him, each time, when geographically convenient, leaving them for extended stays with either his parents in Michener, Pennsylvania, or his in-laws in Peekskill, New York.

Bartleman's two preaching tours, at whatever cost in personal and familial well-being, and obviously stamped by his own style of ministry and personality, nevertheless revealed much about how post–Azusa Street Pentecostalism nationalized. As Bartleman crisscrossed urban America, he was on occasion able to preach at newly established urban Pentecostal missions and churches. The great majority of his meetings, however, took place in existing Holiness missions and camps and in Christian and Missionary Alliance churches, which, at least during his first trip, were still open for Pentecostal penetration. From Bartleman's accounts it is not always clear whether those inviting him to preach understood that he was to bring the new Pentecostal message. He often came unannounced and, given the participatory nature of Holiness services and even of camp meetings and conventions, voluntarily spoke. Unless confronted, Bartleman preached the new Pentecostal message. To some extent, then, the popular hayseed image of Pentecostalism approximated reality by the 1920s and 1930s. In its formative pre–World War I years the new religious movement was very much an urban phenomenon. The nation's towns and cities served as the nodal points for the diffusion of Pentecostal religion and the creation of personal and institutional networks that were beginning to provide the rudimentary Pentecostal movement a measure of cohesion and structure.[16]

Following his second evangelistic tour, Bartleman picked up on his routine of visiting the Los Angeles–area missions and unexpectedly even got to preach in Hawaii during May and June 1909. The family, now enlarged by the birth on October 14, 1909, of another daughter, Lois, continued to suffer from a lack of money for food and rent, but Bartleman still refused to ask anyone directly for money and persisted in trusting the Lord to prompt individuals to give him offerings. Despite his desperate financial situation and the consternation of friends, Bartleman, alone, audaciously left Los Angeles on Thursday, March 17, 1910, to undertake, entirely by faith, a global missionary trip. What possibly could have driven Bartleman to leave behind his family and friends and embark on a global tour as a "lone ranger" evangelist without the financial means both to support his wife and children in his absence and to pay for his trip? On his way east he explained to a congregation in Chicago's Stone Church that he loved "the will of God better than wife and babies." Moreover, the Lord had shown him that—if he were not to go—his ministry at home would come to an end. In a later book describing his missionary journey, Bartleman admitted that at the time of his trip he simply was worn out and needed a restful change in his life, evidently including time away from his wife and children.[17]

Throughout his trip, Bartleman combined sightseeing and preaching in Pentecostal churches. He returned to the United States in February 1911, ten pounds heavier and miraculously with all of his and his family's expenses having been met. Less than two years after his return, in October 1912, Bartleman, again by faith, embarked on another trip to Europe, only this time with his wife and children along. For almost two years the family lived in Europe, forced to return to the United States only by the outbreak of World War I. After his first trip abroad, Bartleman published a detailed account of his travels and ministry.[18]

On returning to the United States on October 10, 1914, Bartleman again made his home in Los Angeles, where he remained for the rest of his life, mainly ministering in downtown missions. No doubt his hard-hitting attacks against U.S. participation in World War I, apparent acceptance during the war years of the divisive new Oneness, or Pentecostal Unitarian doctrine of the Godhead, and his nonglamorous urban mission work during the 1920s and 1930s contributed to his growing marginalization from the evolving Trinitarian Pentecostal mainstream. Yet, still considering himself a Pentecostal elder statesman, Bartleman continued to publish tracts and magazine articles lamenting what he believed to be the spiritual declension of the two-decades-old Pentecostal movement and commenting on national social and moral trends. He died in Los Angeles on August 23, 1936.[19]

The Pentecostal "New Order" According to Frank Bartleman

The new Pentecostalism, in its fluid primitive stage, meant different things to different participants. For Bartleman it meant the arrival of God's new order in both sacred and secular history. Absolutely convinced that he was living in the last days—the literal end of history—before the return of Jesus Christ, he believed that the Lord consciously had bypassed society's elites and instead had given the socially and economically marginal Pentecostals—a "new order of priests"—the task "of bringing the last gospel witness before the end."[20]

Bartleman also saw in the heady first days of the Azusa Street revival signs of the arrival of a new Pentecostal society. In his colorfully detailed and engaging descriptions of services at the Los Angeles mission, he approvingly noted how they were characterized by a radical racial and social egalitarianism. "The 'color line' was washed away in the blood" was how he pithily described the interracial nature of the meetings. He admitted that "Brother Seymour was recognized as the nominal leader in charge" but lauded the participatory nature of the services and Pentecostals' dependence on the direct leading of the Lord. Bartleman elaborated: "The Lord was liable to burst through any one. It might be a child, a woman, or a man. It might be from the back seat, or from the front." And, he added, "it made no difference." The meetings—the singing, testimonies, praying, preaching, even the starting time—as described by Bartleman paradoxically were "spontaneous" yet "ordered of the Spirit." The programless services, he wrote, "were Holy Ghost meetings, led of the Lord"; they were "controlled by the Spirit, from the throne."[21]

If Bartleman's construct of the Pentecostal meetings is to be taken literally, he implied that when Pentecostal worshipers entered the mission they entered into a spiritual state where they cast off their personal, social, and

AUGUSTUS CERILLO JR.

114

material identity and collectively sought a direct experience of God, who apportioned out his gifts and blessings to individuals in a way that was harmonious and uplifted the entire worshiping community. There occurred, in his telling, a perfect blending of personal and collective religious experience and practice that created a new Pentecostal community; spiritual unity emerged out of this collective "individual" appropriation of God's grace. From Bartleman's point of view, in the act of worship participants at the Azusa mission supernaturally were knit into one spiritual body, into a worshiping community that was in perfect tune with God and with each other.

At the time of the Azusa Street revival many of the Pentecostal leaders, including Charles Parham, William Seymour, and Bartleman himself, had been drawn to the new doctrine and experience from Holiness ranks. Parham and Seymour simply added the experience of Holy Spirit baptism evidenced by tongues to the Holiness crisis experiences of salvation and sanctification (eradication of inbred sin). Moreover, as historians James Goff and Cecil Robeck point out, Parham and Seymour insisted that only a believer who had experienced first, conversion, and second, sanctification, could be genuinely filled with the Holy Spirit Pentecostal style. Bartleman offered his audiences a dissenting view. Anticipating William Durham's later challenge to the Holiness-Pentecostal community, Bartleman denied that a believer must first have had a second crisis experience (sanctification) before receiving Holy Spirit baptism. Pentecostalism, in his view, was a "new order," a fresh revelation of the Holy Spirit, a "far more mighty revelation of . . . the Holy Ghost" that simply could not be contained in "old jars" or placed in a theological straitjacket. There was no need "to stickle for a 'third experience,'" he wrote. The reality of the experience, Bartleman claimed, was a greater argument than doctrine. Most important, he admonished Pentecostal people to understand that love, as discussed by the apostle Paul in 1 Corinthians 13, was a better evidence of the Christian life than a cleansing (sanctification) experience or even speaking in tongues.[22]

Bartleman also criticized Pentecostals who overemphasized the manifestation of tongues. He frequently warned against giving the Holy Spirit and tongues priority over Jesus. He pled that Jesus be kept at the center of Pentecostal preaching.[23] He further jeopardized his ministry opportunities in Pentecostal churches by taking issue with leaders who dogmatically taught that tongues was the sole initial evidence of having received the Holy Spirit. "To declare that no one has ever had the Holy Ghost, without they have spoken in 'tongues' is an unwarrantable position. It cannot be proven," he boldly wrote in the *Way of Faith* sometime before August 1910. Bartleman further stated, "The manifestation of 'tongues' *may* prove a powerful initial evidence even to the one exercised that the Spirit has come. But that must not be depended on for future, abiding consciousness of His presence."[24]

Excess and dogmatism were Bartleman's major concerns, not speaking in tongues itself, which he believed had pragmatic and spiritual benefits. In a letter to the *Way of Faith*, reprinted in the *Triumphs of Faith*, and in a tract entitled *The Fullness*, Bartleman provided a very early apologetic for the value and functions of the baptism and of tongues speaking. He asserted that tongues attracted outsiders to Pentecostal meetings, proved God was still in the "miracle-working" business, and awed congregations into silent reverence. Messages in tongues that were real spoken languages, he explained, usually were directed to a specific individual in the congregation with a particular need. The Holy Spirit baptism experience itself, he asserted, endued the believer with power to witness to the lost and also subdued and refined the believer's carnal nature, eliminating "religious self-conceit" and nudging the believer toward the goal of "pure spirit."[25]

At one point during his second cross-country preaching trip, Bartleman compared his ministerial style to that of other Pentecostal preachers, and in the process he theologized about the nature of Pentecostal spirituality. Some ministers, he told his readers, specialized in teaching "a definite, instantaneous, epochal work to be realized in the human heart." In contrast, his specialty was to encourage believers continually to go on into a deeper life in the Lord. He warned his readers to avoid the danger always inherent in religious traditions that emphasized "instantaneous works of grace"; specific experiences, even tongues and baptism, tended to become a "fixed, rigid system of finality" and therefore hindered further spiritual progress. To avoid this he urged Pentecostals to develop what he considered the implications of their Pentecostal baptism: growth in spiritual power, simplicity, and unity. Of course, he pointed out, all experiences had to be tested against the Word of God, "our guide and boundary, the declared will of God."[26]

The new order that was Pentecostalism, Bartleman wrote, even demanded a new theology of sermon preparation. Because Pentecostalism was "a fresh realm of the Spirit," an "age of advancement," a work of God different from that of the past or "old order," Bartleman argued, the Spirit operated differently from even in the recent past, shed new light on the Word, and thus affected sermon preparation. "For instance," he wrote, "some time ago we had to spend a week getting a sermon ready for the Sabbath. We would have to read a number of books and work our brains, and be on a strain from Monday morning until Saturday night, and repeat the operation the next week and so on. But we don't have to work that way these days." Instead, Bartleman explained, truth now came largely by revelation. "Perhaps I will be standing before the people, and God will flash a truth into my mind, and the spirit will unfold and develop it, and I will find myself in a whole new realm of thought regarding that subject," he told his listeners at Chicago's Stone Church. "That is more directly the way that God proposes to reveal spiritual truth to His people. That is what it ought to be." Bartleman, however, warned against what he called "wild fireism." He suggested that before a preacher could get sermon material directly from the Lord, he had to spend time in prayerful study of and meditation on the Word. Only then would there be some material for God to work on, to bring to the preacher's remembrance.[27]

Unlike many early Pentecostal leaders, Bartleman went beyond commenting on the historical, spiritual, and doctrinal aspects of the new Pentecostalism. As the historian Cecil M. Robeck has noted, he probably was "the most significant social commentator that early Pentecostalism produced."[28] Bartleman believed Scripture distinguished between the heavenly kingdom of God, of which believers were members and to which they owed allegiance, and the hopelessly fallen and corrupt kingdoms of this world. Christians, morally citizens of heaven, therefore, were not to participate in the affairs of the intrinsically corrupt political state except to criticize government policies on biblically based moral and ethical grounds, vote their consciences at the ballot box, and, more radically, engage in acts of civil disobedience should the state and its leaders act in ways counter to Christian principles. Human governments, Bartleman wrote in the midst of World War I, "are simply rotten" and under a divine curse. He extended this sharply dichotomized view of the political and spiritual worlds to the church. To protect the church from compromising its message, independence, and global nature, Bartleman strongly supported the absolute separation of church and state and even condemned the display of national flags in churches.[29]

Bartleman also shared with other turn-of-the-century populistic social critics a conspiratorial view of the exercise of political power. He believed that an elite of corporate capitalists—the "money gods"—and their political lackeys controlled the American government and enacted public policies to further their selfish economic interests. The "people," in his judgment, received no justice from the nation's economic or political system. Nor were they served by the nation's secular press, which Bartleman also believed was controlled by a government that simply manipulated the public into supporting the corporate agenda.

Moreover, Bartleman vociferously condemned capitalism as an unscriptural economic system. He blamed capitalism and the greed that underlay it for the nation's widening class distinctions, inequitable distribution of wealth and income, artificially contrived high food prices through the market practice of trading commodities futures, and unnecessary poverty and starvation in a land of productive abundance. No fan of communism, Bartleman nevertheless in two essays published in 1930 suggested that at least the spirit of communism was consistent with New Testament economic practice, especially as outlined in Acts 2 and 4, where the Christian community held all things in common. Whether such a New Testament economic paradigm should be applied to a secular society and how it might be implemented he never discussed.[30]

The socially conscious Bartleman failed to address the issue of racism in his voluminous pre–World War I writings, yet in From Plow to Pulpit, his autobiography written in 1924, he revealed his racially progressive views. He unequivocally condemned the structural nature of southern racism and sensitively described how during his first preaching trip to the segregated South he lived with and was cared for by the black folk to whom he ministered. Writing such a narrative in the very racist 1920s, the Pentecostal preacher seemed to endorse a social equality and integration radical for its time. In his articles condemning war, he alluded to how the U.S. government had wronged African Americans and had killed off "about all of our American Indians." He further accused American officials, grafters in his view, of pocketing money earmarked for Indian welfare.[31]

Like many early Pentecostals, Bartleman was a pacifist and, on the basis of Rom. 12:19 and 13:9, Matt. 5:9, Gal. 6:10, 1 Tim. 2:8, James 4:1, and other New Testament scriptures, opposed the shedding of blood for any reason, even during a war conducted under the auspices of a legitimate government. He argued that war was nothing more than "legalized murder" and thus contradicted "the whole Word of God and the Spirit of Jesus Christ." Moreover, he pointed out, war wasted human and economic resources and, most significantly, when engaged in by Christians and so-called Christian nations compromised the Gospel message and hindered evangelism.[32]

During World War I Bartleman bombarded the Pentecostal press with explicit antiwar views. In fact, before departing war-torn Europe in the fall of 1914, he pleaded with Christians, especially Pentecostals, not to participate in the war as soldiers and asked churches in the belligerent nations not to support the war effort. Demonstrating a prodigious knowledge both of Scripture, interpreted through a premillennial and anti-Roman Catholic grid, and early-twentieth-century European and American political and diplomatic history, Bartleman at various times blamed the Great War on the sinfulness of the warring nations; the devil who sought to stop the spread of Pentecostalism; Russian despotism, German militarism, and English imperialism; and the drive for power, profits, and commercial dominance by the belligerent nations' political and economic leaders.[33]

Other Pentecostals shared Bartleman's pacifism, even while they declared their loyalty to the U.S. government and refrained from criticizing American involvement in the war. In contrast, with the best of secular radicals, pacifists, and socialists, Bartleman consistently and vehemently condemned the Woodrow Wilson administration for its war policies, which he viewed as shaped by the capitalist desire for profit. He sharply criticized those Pentecostals who supported the American war effort and, he claimed, even insulted and abused fellow Christians who happened to be pacifists.

Specifically, Bartleman attacked the administration's neutrality policy and war trade as a sham and smokescreen for business to reap enormous profits. "We are being drawn into ruin by the lust for gold, the tyranny of our 'money bags' over us," he wrote. He even accused financier J. Pierpont Morgan of being an English agent in disguise and charged that the American press, controlled by English capital, had poisoned public opinion unfairly against Germany. He characterized America's monetary loans to the allies as "blood money" responsible for "killing innocent wives and children" and was sure such loans in time would drag the United States into the war.[34] Bucking the overwhelming public and administration outcry against Germany for sinking the *Lusitania,* a British passenger liner, on May 7, 1915, Bartleman instead placed blame on the money-hungry American munitions makers who had loaded the ship with American-made weapons. In fact, he accused the United States of hypocritically pleading for peace even while it was responsible for the continuation of the war by supplying the allies arms.

Bartleman attacked military "preparedness" and preachers who supported the program; he even accused capitalists of using the military buildup as a cover to "call out the militia to shoot down laborers who may dare to make just demands for their wages." Long before the U.S. Senate's Nye committee report of the 1930s, Bartleman interpreted American intervention in April 1917 as a response to the nation's munitions makers, merchants, capitalists, and manufacturers. Skirting the edges of wartime-imposed laws defining disloyalty, Bartleman attacked patriotism as the servant of American business and opposed the purchase of war bonds. He also denounced the draft, which he argued violated liberty of conscience and treated "men as mere property of their respective rulers." In a blanket condemnation, he declared the entire war a capitalist war and graphically suggested that in the American flag the stars and stripes be replaced with dollar signs. After the war he condemned the government's treatment of conscientious objectors, especially the large number of Christian prisoners held at Fort Leavenworth, Missouri, and Alcatraz in California, and he caustically called on Pentecostal people to repent for their participation in the war and for their unwillingness to become martyrs, if necessary, for their faith.[35]

Bartleman's social radicalism defied categorization in terms of Progressive Era political taxonomy. Unlike secular social critics and reformers, he offered no reform program but Christian evangelism. "God has prescribed Holy Ghost regeneration, not reformation, for earth's ills," he wrote. "The only cure for war, the liquor habit, the heathen, or any other ill man has fallen heir to through the fall is regeneration."[36]

What might account for Bartleman's failure to move beyond his radical critique of American society and provide the Pentecostal community with a biblically informed radical political agenda? For one thing, given Bartleman's interpretation of the Pentecostal movement as an end-times revival, it is inconceivable that he would have considered switching vocations from evangelist to social reformer. Second, Bartleman had no competence, by background, education, social location, or theological training, to tool out specific reform solutions or a revolutionary plan to transform the American state. Third, Bartleman's extremely pessimistic view of human nature, apart from God, would not allow him to consider human efforts to reform society. And, last, Bartleman's antiorganizational bent no doubt also prevented him from imagining bureaucratic political institutions solving societal problems.

Bartleman provided no hints about what influences might have shaped his uncommon Pentecostal social conscience, other than that he quoted Scripture in support of this or that critique of society. But scores of other Pentecostals and Bible-believing Christians read the same Scripture and failed to arrive at his radical disillusionment with American society. How he read Scripture may have been influenced by at least four life experiences. One, his personal history of poverty, ill health, and family tragedy no doubt sensitized him to the plight of the poor and socially marginal folk. Two, Bartleman as a young Christian had been exposed to the social ministries of Grace Baptist Church. Three, early in his pre-Pentecostal ministerial career, Bartleman held socially progressive views. As a Bible student in Philadelphia, he consciously pursued a ministry among the city's lower and working classes; on his first evangelistic trip through the South, he interacted with black Americans as social equals; in 1899, when he preached in the impoverished Pennsylvania and Delaware coal regions, he noted how the coal industry broke the spirit and backs of the miners.[37] Four, although Bartleman does not seem to have believed himself intellectually or socially disadvantaged via the larger society, he nevertheless believed that God preferred working through the humble and poor folk in society, hence God's choice of the mostly poor black and white believers who prayed at Bonnie Brae to launch the Pentecostal revival.

Conclusion

Bartleman's life and ministry both reflected and helped shape the Pentecostal movement's many spiritual and sociological contours. Like many Pentecostal leaders, his early life was marked by economic hardship, physical sickness, emotional fragility, and a desire for a deeper spiritual experience. Like others who ended up in leadership positions in the new Pentecostalism, Bartleman made the religious pilgrimage from mainstream evangelicalism to the rather permeable Holiness movement to Pentecostalism in 1906. But as a spiritual loner and ideological radical, he contributed to the diversity that characterized pre-1920 Pentecostalism. He did so primarily by pushing to the margins of acceptability the doctrinal and behavioral tendencies inherent in the Holiness traditions and the new Pentecostalism: institutional independence, faith living, a delight in "deeper" spiritual experiences, a heightened expectation of the imminent return of the Lord, a passion for world evangelization, and a belief in the power of Holy Spirit baptism to create a radically new egalitarian Pentecostal community.

Ironically, Frank Bartleman, the Pentecostal lone ranger and social critic, had less impact on the long-term institutional and ideological development of Pentecostalism and the denominational powerbrokers who built the movement than he had on those who have written about Pentecostalism's formative years. Bartleman's history of the Azusa Street revival of 1906 and his descriptions of meetings in other Los Angeles Pentecostal missions served as the blueprint that shaped virtually all subsequent accounts of Pentecostal origins. Therein lay his most significant legacy.[38]

William H. Durham: Years of Creativity, Years of Dissent

Edith L. Blumhofer

In a bustling Chicago neighborhood on sultry summer nights in 1907 and 1908, crowds often milled around the sidewalk outside 943 West North Avenue, unable to squeeze into the modest frame building that stood in the middle of the block. Across the busy avenue, beyond an elevated train line, the expanses of Humboldt Park beckoned. To the east and west stood the modest shops and homes of first- and second-generation Americans from Germany and Scandinavia. Inside 943 West North Avenue, people hung on the words of a commanding preacher named William Howard Durham. That summer, the mayhem inside and out seldom abated. Since Durham's return in March 1907 from a brief visit to Azusa Street in Los Angeles, his small Chicago mission had been in the throes of revival, thronged day and night by the merely curious and the staunchly devout. The devoted believed the mission had become the center of an end-times restoration of "Bible Christianity" in Chicago. The most ardent lived in a state of mind so spiritually charged that they saw a thick haze—like blue smoke—resting over the assembled faithful, a reference to the palpable "shekinah," or "glory," that had once filled the ancient Hebrew temple as a sign of God's presence.[1]

Who was William Durham, and what was happening on North Avenue? In the first decade of American Pentecostal history, Durham had few rivals as a compelling articulator of the meaning of a religious movement more often linked with Los Angeles than with Chicago. An indefatigable evangelist, Durham rarely hinted that his busy life included a wife and children. Nor did he spend time pondering his spiritual formation. Yet Durham's rise

William and Bessie Mae Durham, Los Angeles, January 1906. Courtesy of the Flower Pentecostal Heritage Center, Springfield, Missouri.

to prominence in Pentecostalism can be understood only in the larger context of his life. This also helps clarify the role he helped realize for Chicago as a defining center for American Pentecostalism.

William Howard Durham

William Durham came of hardy English stock. His Durham forebears made their way across the mountains from North Carolina and put down roots in the hills of east central Kentucky soon after the Kentucky Territory became a state. The second child of John and Mary Gordon Durham, William Howard Durham was born on January 10, 1873.[2] He and his three siblings lived with their parents near Brodhead, Kentucky, in the hollows northwest of the Rockcastle County seat of Mt. Vernon. Their father—like his father, William Durham—worked as a laborer, and they lived among a large extended family.

The Durhams were Baptists, and during William's childhood one of them—another William Durham of his father's generation—distinguished himself locally as a preacher. Most of the extended family lived out their lives in Kentucky, but in 1890, at seventeen, William Howard Durham left Rockcastle County for Chicago.

In 1890, Chicago beckoned many young men. The railroad hub of the nation, the city bustled with energy. But Durham soon traveled on. The railroad had also put Tracy, Minnesota, on the map by 1881. Tracy had busy railroad yards and boasted excellent prospects for employment. Durham settled there and discovered a young town where he would ultimately find his life's direction.

Tracy was a focus of the efforts of a group of independent preachers who, in the 1890s, turned the area into a hotbed of revivalistic popular religion. There in 1898 Durham's faith came alive, and there in 1905 he wooed and won his wife.

The World's Faith Missionary Association

Perhaps the best-known itinerant preacher in the area in the 1890s was G. L. Morgan, a resident of nearby Windom. Born in Pennsylvania in 1857, George Lorenzo Morgan migrated to Minnesota in the 1880s and immediately became active in the small Protestant churches that dotted the region. He showed a proclivity for preaching and an inclination to the miraculous. Morgan held forth wherever he could find an audience—in schoolhouses, churches, and, most often, in Scandinavian Free Missions, forerunners of the Evangelical Free Church. Religious experiences, miracles, dreams, and visions fueled Morgan's faith and gave him affinities for the pietism of the most ardent Scandinavian Free Church immigrants.[3]

In the 1890s, Morgan came into contact with a cluster of small institutions that represented the religious vision of their founders, Charles and Minnie Hanley. Married in 1878, Charles and Minnie George Hanley had settled in Shenandoah, a county seat of about four thousand in southwestern Iowa, where Charles published the *Shenandoah Post,* the town's only paper.

A deacon in Shenandoah's Congregational Church, Charles attended prayer meetings run by some he described as "very desirous of being wholly given up to God, and entirely free from everything that would hinder or grieve the Spirit in his workings."[4] Their intense prayer issued in emotional experiences Hanley understood as "the power of God." One such dramatic moment in 1887 prompted Hanley to change his life's course. Fortunately, his wife, Minnie, proved sympathetic. Charles Hanley gave up his newspaper and embarked on a faith venture that came to be known as the World's Faith Missionary Association (WFMA). It soon included a faith home, a Bible training school, a monthly paper, an evangelistic mission in downtown Shenandoah, and an itinerant evangelistic ministry.

After enduring the ridicule of neighbors who found this apparent financial and spiritual recklessness puzzling, the Hanleys slowly regained the goodwill of the community.[5] In 1900, they were circulating some ten thousand copies of their monthly paper, the *Firebrand,* offering an informative mix of reports from affiliated evangelists, general religious news, and inspirational articles.[6] It carried no advertising, secular reading, or "worldly features."

The Hanleys' simple teaching differed from that of other proponents of the "deeper Christian life" more in nuance than in substance. "The work at Shenandoah will go up or down as the Lord sees fit on 'Christ is All and in All,'" the Hanleys would insist in 1907.[7] They spent hours each day in community and personal Bible study and prayer, worked for temperance, prayed for the sick, supported local Chautauquas, and manifested a blend of traditional Protestant and particular Holiness proclivities. Their message, summarized in the January 1901 issue of the *Firebrand* under the title "It Is Finished," departed from conventional American Holiness wisdom in one important way: "Christ died once for all." "Everything was fully done long, long ago . . . If it were necessary for something else to be done, it would not have been a perfect sacrifice. Every soul that sees that perfect, precious offering of the Lamb of God must see that it is sufficient."[8] They focused less on a sanctifying moment than on embracing "Christ as All." Their association credentialed those who wanted to work independently of denominations in evangelism and urban rescue missions.[9]

The WFMA seemed made to order for G. L. Morgan, and he rose through the ranks to become associate director. He recruited for the association and sold subscriptions to its paper wherever he preached. In this context, in Tracy, William Durham not only professed faith but also felt the call to preach. For several years he worked with Morgan, who had taken to calling his followers "Children of God."[10] Locals dubbed them "Morganites."

On February 18, 1902, Durham was ordained by the World's Faith Missionary Association. The nondenominational evangelistic setting he now entered introduced him to people he would later engage in other contexts.[11] The pages of the *Missionary World* (successor to the *Firebrand*) and of local newspapers chart Durham's rise to leadership. The summer of 1902 found him reporting success in Wabasso, Minnesota.[12] In January of 1903, he left Wabasso for meetings at the Congregational Church in Arco, where the local paper reported "very successful" services and where Durham also performed a wedding.[13] His efforts in 1904 included meetings in the Swedish Free Mission Church in Slayton[14] but also saw Durham change his permanent address to 943 West North Avenue in Chicago.[15]

Durham's first recorded visit to Chicago as an evangelist occurred early in 1903 when he spent several months with a group of Norwegian Free Church people who issued a monthly paper, *Folke-Vennen*.[16] His activities in Chicago in 1903 and thereafter focused within a stretch of three blocks, on which stood a Norwegian hub around *Folke-Vennen,* a north side tabernacle of Dowie's Christian Catholic Church, a revivalistic Swedish Baptist church, and an independent mission established by a Swedish postal clerk, Emil Iverson.[17]

Durham generally made time to attend G. L. Morgan's annual summer camp meeting at Lake Shetek, near Tracy, and he often preached at Morgan's Christmas-season conventions in Windom, too.[18] Both gathered the faithful for hundreds of miles. In July 1904, Durham participated in the ordination of the veteran G. L. Morgan, several other men, and a woman to "gospel ministry."[19] Morgan's seventh annual winter convention convened in Windom in December 1904. Here, the newspaper reported, the walls "vibrated because of the shouts and laughter caused by the infilling of the Spirit." Among those in attendance were Bessie Mae Whitmore of Tracy and William Durham of Chicago.[20]

In June 1905, Durham returned again to southwest Minnesota to marry Bessie Mae. The ceremony took place on Wednesday evening, June 14, at the Whitmore home. A WFMA preacher, Charles Croft, officiated in the presence of some twenty-five relatives and friends. An announcement in the *Missionary World* enthused over Durham as "one mightily used in the hands of God for the Salvation of Souls and the upbuilding of believers" and his bride as having "a beautiful Christian character" and a "consecrated life." The two left immediately for Chicago, where they lived for a few days in Durham's mission. They then headed east for a series of meetings in Boston, where Durham had already preached in 1904. They were not "at home" in Chicago until September 1.[21]

Bessie Mae Whitmore had known William Durham for several years before their marriage, and she would now play an important behind-the-scenes role in his ministry. The youngest child of Howard Whitmore and his first wife, Julia, Bessie Mae was born near Sycamore, Illinois, in May 1882. The Whitmores, a farming family, responded to enthusiastic railroad advertising and moved to Tracy in 1891. Howard was both farmer and land agent.[22] Bessie showed musical talent and appeared frequently on grammar and high school programs to sing and recite.[23] Bessie and her mother soon joined Tracy's Methodist Church, but her father, though a professing Christian, did not affiliate with any of Tracy's churches. In 1900, Bessie began teaching school. She also discovered the WFMA. She and Durham shared a host of acquaintances as well as religious socialization.

From Boston the Durhams recapped their energetic efforts during the first three months of their marriage: three thousand miles and seventy-five services across Massachusetts, Ohio, Illinois, Michigan, Minnesota, Wisconsin, and Iowa.[24] In the fall of 1905, after special services in Chicago with their Minnesota evangelist friend, Charles Croft, the Durhams left home again on October 10 for a month evangelizing in Minnesota and a series of meetings in rescue missions in Sioux City and Council Bluffs. Durham wrote of the meetings in Sioux City: "Some fell under His mighty power and Oh how the saints did shout."[25] Minta Loveless, the Council Bluffs pastor's wife, described Durham's directness, a trait people often noted: "Bro. Durham is one that can plow right down through the middle of things and hit sin both in low and high places."[26] Meetings in Homer, Nebraska, and Denver found the Durhams constantly at the altar praying with the sick and repentant. They spent ten days in Colorado Springs in the mission, healing home, and Bible school supervised by George Fink. "Oh how God did work, and all denominational lines were forgotten while we sought the 'Best Gifts,'" Durham reported.[27]

The Christmas season found the Durhams in Los Angeles, where William had a happy reunion with old friends, the Osterbergs.[28] On January 7, 1906, Durham began preaching in a tent on Seventh Street. He baptized converts in the Pacific Ocean.[29] A few weeks later he held special services in the Holiness Church in Monrovia, then visited Phineas Yoakum. On March 1, the Durhams left Los Angeles to return to Colorado Springs for a month of meetings before traveling on to Sioux City. Through all of this travel, living constantly in temporary quarters in other people's homes, Bessie Mae awaited the couple's first child. She was back in Tracy, Minnesota, for the birth on April 13, 1906, of William Howard Durham Jr. By their first wedding anniversary, the Durhams had spent barely seven weeks at their home in Chicago.

The Durhams' return to Chicago coincided with the arrival of the first reports of speaking in tongues in Los Angeles. They had many acquaintances among those now caught up in the revival that since mid-April had rocked a small mission on Azusa Street. Before long, advocates of tongues speech arrived in Chicago on their way to "preach Pentecost" around the world.[30] Among them were people Durham knew through the WFMA—like Lucy Leatherman.[31]

In the summer of 1906, the Durhams had ten days of meetings in Council Bluffs, Iowa.[32] From there, they went on to Colorado to work again with George Fink.[33] In August, William submitted the twenty-five-dollar fee required for life membership in the WFMA.[34] Later in the year, William and Bessie Mae took the baby to Kentucky. William had been away for sixteen years, and the extended family now met Bessie Mae and young William. But they did not remain long. William's heart was in Chicago, where the puzzling challenge of the new Pentecost waited to be resolved. Over the Christmas holiday, the Durhams returned to Minnesota, where William attended Morgan's convention and undoubtedly discussed Azusa Street.[35]

At first, Durham, convinced that speaking in tongues was not the only evidence of Holy Spirit baptism, hesitated to endorse the revival. Another Chicago evangelist with whom Durham had been working, John Sinclair, on the other hand, believed the Pentecostal message.[36] Sinclair's endorsing of Pentecostalism in his mission on West Sixty-third Street first forced Durham to confront the movement's claims.

> I had labored in Chicago for four years, in the missions at 943 West North Ave. and at 328 West 63rd Street, and, as both missions stood for the full Gospel, and were made up of deeply spiritual people, I never doubted that most of them had the same experience I had; and I had believed for years that I had the Holy Ghost. But when the Spirit began to fall in 63rd Street and then in North Avenue Mission, to my surprise, the most spiritual persons were the first to be baptized and speak in tongues, but I said to my wife, "You will see some get just what the rest do, that will not speak in tongues." But, when nearly forty in 63rd Street Mission and some fifteen in North Avenue Mission had received the Holy Spirit and every one of them had spoken in tongues, it made me stop and think, especially as I had never doubted that at least two-thirds of these people had exactly the same experience as I had myself.[37]

Durham and Chicago Pentecostalism

Early in 1907, the Durhams' friends, the Osterbergs, wired train fare and urged Durham to come to Los Angeles and see the revival for himself. This time he left Bessie Mae and young William at home and headed west via Minneapolis and familiar haunts in Minnesota. He reached Los Angeles in February and was surprised to meet H. L. Blake, an acquaintance from the WFMA in Minnesota (whom he had seen in December at Morgan's convention) at the Azusa Street mission.[38] Both men "sought their Pentecosts."[39] Blake spoke in tongues almost immediately but, for Durham, "seeking" entailed nearly three weeks of agonizing until on March 2 something "strange and wonderful and yet glorious" happened:[40] "He worked my whole body, one section at a time, first my arms, then my limbs, then my body, then my head, then my face, then my chin, and finally at 1 A.M. Saturday, March 2, after being under the power for three hours, He finished the work on my vocal organs, and spoke through me in unknown tongues. I arose, perfectly conscious outwardly and inwardly that I was fully baptized in the Holy Ghost."[41]

Durham traveled back to Chicago via Colorado, where he preached for George Fink, and Des Moines, where he bore witness to the new Pentecost in the mission associated with Emma C. Ladd, another WFMA stalwart (and wife of the chief justice of the Iowa Supreme Court). On his arrival in Chicago just in time for Easter 1907, he found the missions on North Avenue and Sixty-third Street primed. At North Avenue, Bessie Mae had helped conduct nightly prayer meetings during her husband's absence. Durham now took a "clear stand" for Holy Spirit baptism manifested by speaking in tongues, and the modest mission could not hold the seekers. He moved his family out and opened their living quarters in the rear of the mission for overflow, but the place proved still too small. Bessie Mae was among the first to speak in tongues. Meetings ran day and night. One participant, C. N. Arensbach, exulted: "Since January 13th we have had meetings every night, and expect to keep them up till Jesus comes." After Durham's return from Azusa Street, Arensbach continued, "it became necessary to seek larger quarters, as the people come from near and far to witness the mighty works of God . . . Thursday is set apart for all day meetings, and Tuesday afternoon for workers' meeting. There has been much interpretation. Hallelujah!"[42]

Amid the hubbub, Bessie Mae was summoned to Tracy where her father died unexpectedly on April 18, 1907, after a bout with pneumonia.[43] But the momentum at the North Avenue Mission left the family no time to linger and mourn. The Durhams' efforts were about to assume global dimensions.

As a result of street meetings and personal interaction, Durham had begun to mentor a few Italian Protestants. Several spoke in tongues and began evangelizing Italian immigrants. This soon spread nationwide and then penetrated Italy and the large Italian population in Brazil. Norwegians and Swedes came to Durham, too. Durham's friend since 1903, Ferdinand Sandgren, an editor of *Folke-Vennen,* now became an elder at the North Avenue Mission. He evangelized on behalf of Pentecostalism among Norwegians nationally and took responsibility for the mission's publishing.[44]

Swedish Baptists brought fresh memories of a 1905 revival that had agitated their ranks in Chicago. They called it the "new movement," and during its heyday, some Swedish Baptists had spoken in tongues.[45] In 1908, the North Avenue Mission, again short of space, established a Swedish-language Pentecostal mission.[46] Through these convinced Swedish Baptists, Durham would again influence the introduction of Pentecostalism in Brazil.[47]

With the North Avenue mission prospering, the Durhams incorporated their efforts. A congregational meeting on September 26, 1907, elected three trustees (the names Jensen, Peterson, and Olsen indicate the Scandinavian lay leadership) and adopted a constitution and by-laws. On December 12, the congregation purchased the mission property for $5,000 and assumed a $3,000 mortgage.[48] The purchase made renovations possible, and Durham added an extension, nearly doubling the seating capacity. In 1908, the congregation installed a baptistery where, in the next two years, Durham immersed 800 people.[49] He began issuing an occasional paper, the *Pentecostal Testimony*, published and distributed free of charge "as the Lord provided." By mid-1912, he had circulated 367,000 copies of the paper and 250,000 tracts. From February 1908, Durham authorized the publication of prophecies given at the mission in the form of tongues and interpretation. These were published as *Heavenly Messages*. Some 30,000 copies circulated.[50]

These busy months of expanding influence for the Durhams were trying times for the Hanleys and the larger WFMA. Some of the WFMA's leading members now advocated speaking in tongues as the "uniform initial evidence" of Spirit baptism. Clara Lum, one-time associate editor of the Hanleys' paper,[51] was now prominent in West Coast Pentecostalism, sending the Hanleys glowing reports of her new endeavors.[52] Lucy Leatherman (who had told the Hanleys of her call to Syria in 1904)[53] now left the States as a Pentecostal missionary to Israel.[54] William Durham uncompromisingly endorsed speaking in tongues.[55] M. L. Ryan spoke in tongues and convened a missionary party bound for Japan and China. Emma Ladd identified her Des Moines city mission work with the Pentecostals. Yet the Hanleys could not endorse "uniform initial evidence." They preferred their longtime motto "Christ Is All, and in All" to making any gift a "test of fellowship" and reprinted approvingly Southern Baptist biblical scholar A. S. Worrell's caution: "In most places where Pentecostal meetings are held, there is an undue importance attached to speaking in tongues . . . The error of this position ought, it seems, to be apparent to all people of sound spiritual discernment . . . To a very great extent, they ignore the vastly more important work of the Spirit in the development of the Christ-life in the Trinity-filled believer."[56]

The situation in Minnesota proved particularly critical for the WFMA. H. L. Blake (who had been with Durham at Azusa Street and had spoken in tongues) backed away from "uniform initial evidence" teaching. He now concurred with those who cautioned that speaking in tongues "kept eyes on the Holy Ghost" instead of on Christ and thus opened the door to excess.[57] G. L. Morgan, on the other hand, temporarily embraced Pentecostal teaching and reminded his following: "The greater the manifestation, the greater the persecution."[58]

Morgan's camp meeting in Fairmont, Minnesota, in July 1907 became a "grand victorious Pentecostal meeting" arousing "the powers of darkness and wicked spirits from high places" as never before. Durham joined Morgan, Blake, and Emma Ladd for the event.[59] It was his last effort under the WFMA banner. Durham had no time to dispute the Hanleys' rejection of tongues as initial evidence. His name simply disappeared without comment from the accounts of camp meetings and itinerant evangelism in association with the WFMA. He now circulated only among those WFMA members who clearly embraced tongues speech. The second half of August 1907 found him at a camp in Colorado Springs with his old WFMA friend George Fink—now a Pentecostal.[60]

As "the work" spread, Durham assumed responsibility for additional Pentecostal meeting points around Chicago. By 1912, the North Avenue Mission had helped form at least thirteen other Chicago Pentecostal congregations.[61] This was Durham's way of dealing with cramped quarters. "God," he reported, did not "let us enlarge our borders." Rather, "ministers and workers come and get their baptism; but in almost every instance they go out to labor in other fields. But still the old home mission is crowded to the doors, and many have been turned away."[62]

A North Avenue Mission street meeting at the corner of Clark Street and Chicago Avenue (an intersection in a neighborhood favored by the city's Persian immigrants) brought Persian Americans to the mission. Almost immediately, some spoke in tongues. In the first few months of 1909, Durham baptized twenty-two Persian men, and three soon set out to evangelize their homeland.[63] A Persian mission in Chicago acknowledged its indebtedness to Durham.

Outreach did not disrupt regular rhythms at North Avenue. The mission gave to the poor, entertained the many visitors who came from a distance, and generously supported foreign missions. Stirring accounts from missionaries passing through Chicago whetted appetites for more.[64] The mission doors were virtually always open; passionate prayer ascended around the clock. The congregation met for scheduled services ten times every week, and sometimes these lasted well into the night. Durham described the services as follows: "Sometimes the services might be said to be conducted in the ordinary way, that is, there will be little or no speaking in tongues, and the pastor will preach a sermon. Again, as soon as we come together, we feel the mighty power of God upon us, and at times it increases till there can be no regular order of service, but all is turned over to the Holy Ghost, who runs things as He wills, and at such times one need not leave the earth to be in heaven."[65]

With constant meetings and a hectic travel schedule, Durham obviously relied on others. Some considered it a privilege to apprentice themselves for a time at this acknowledged "powerhouse" of Pentecostalism. In 1909, for example, Robert Semple and his bride, Aimee Kennedy (later McPherson), arrived from Ontario to spend a year with Durham before setting out as missionaries to China.[66] Durham and Aimee Semple formed a team of note in Pentecostal circles: he uttered long messages in tongues, and she responded instantly with interpretations that seemed so remarkable that they were often published and circulated in Pentecostal papers.[67] Excerpts from interpretations of tongues from the North Avenue Mission frequently appeared in print. Like the following brief excerpts from the *Bridegroom's Messenger,* such interpretations generally used the first person:

> The place of power is low at my feet, and the place of blessing is under the blood. I wait to reveal myself and mighty things, that you have not attained to and beyond all that you know. I am seeking the hearts of men and am using every means to bring them.

> Rest in me and I will give you victory.

> I, the Spirit of liberty and of truth, will speak if you will let me have my way.[68]

EDITH L. BLUMHOFER

134

The Semples were with Durham during a particularly trying year. Amid the constant activities of 1908, Bessie Mae had given birth to a daughter, Ethel Mae. Soon pregnant again, Bessie Mae delivered another daughter, Bessie, on August 8, 1909. Bessie Mae never regained her strength and succumbed at age twenty-seven on August 19, 1909, to complications of childbirth. One can only imagine what she endured during the last month of her life. The Durhams had moved to an apartment above the mission that doubled as Durham's study and the church office. Unabated comings and goings; noisy meetings day and night; the Chicago summer heat; the frequent rumble of the elevated railroad just beyond the front window; two toddlers, aged three and one; and a difficult home birth.

Durham took Bessie Mae's remains home to Tracy for burial. Her death occasioned an emotional and spiritual crisis for her husband. Frazzled by constant religious excitement, physically drained, and mentally exhausted, he now coped with her death by vowing to yield himself as a sacrifice—"to make myself an offering to the whole Pentecostal movement."[69] Two sisters, Gertrude and C. (Clara) Ethel (or Ethyl) Taylor, joined the household, Gertrude as housekeeper, Ethel as Durham's secretary.

Less than a month after Bessie Mae's death, Durham convened a two-week Pentecostal Convention at the North Avenue Mission. People came from near and far. Local "saints" provided housing and food, often in cramped quarters, and September 12–26 the meetings ran day and night.[70] Durham allowed himself no space for grief. On October 1, he and the Semples opened another ten-day convention, this time in Findlay, Ohio.[71]

In January 1910, Durham accompanied the Semples to Canada for their farewell services en route to China. On the way to Toronto, they stopped in London, Ontario, for meetings in a private home. The level of response surprised everyone. In three weeks, they laid the groundwork for one of Canada's most successful Pentecostal churches, London Gospel Temple.[72] (Durham would also influence directly the Pentecostal movement in Ottawa, Toronto, and Winnipeg.)[73] Gertrude Taylor brought Durham's toddler, Ethel, to visit him during his weeks in Canada, where Gertrude also helped in the services.[74]

Just after Durham returned to Chicago, on February 23, 1910, his six-month-old daughter died of pneumonia. Severe weather forced the delay of her burial until April, when Durham brought little Bessie's remains to Tracy to rest beside Bessie Mae. Once again, Durham responded by redoubling his efforts. In the throes of his grief and worn by the intensity of constant revival, he now opted to challenge the way many Pentecostals understood sanctification. What followed permanently altered the contours of North American Pentecostalism.

Durham's Emphases

Many early Pentecostals taught that sanctification was a second definite work of grace, an instantaneous experience of cleansing that followed conversion and preceded Holy Spirit baptism. In the Chicago networks that nurtured early Pentecostalism, the teaching on sanctification was less structured than in Los Angeles, but it tended toward the second work, and that now distressed Durham. He later claimed that since his Spirit baptism, in March of 1907, he had never advocated a crisis experience of sanctification. Now he articulated his alternative under the rubric of "the finished work of Calvary," a phrase he certainly knew from the WFMA. It could be argued that he now harped on that one aspect of the Hanleys' teaching. Unlike the Hanleys or G. L. Morgan (who wrote of "resting in the Finished work of Him who has said 'It is Finished'"),[75] Durham took up the phrase as a battle cry.[76]

If the language of finished work was not new to Durham or the World's Faith Missionary Association, it could also be found in the literature of groups like the Keswick movement that urged holiness but did not stress a second work of grace. Durham most likely knew, too, of the thought of E. W. Kenyon, a Massachusetts evangelist who held tent meetings in Chicago in 1908 and who noted in his publication in 1912 that Durham had adopted *his* views of the "finished work of Calvary."[77] If there is a single formative source, G. L. Morgan and the Hanleys seem more likely than others. It is important to recognize that Durham's writings on sanctification (as well as most of what he published in the *Pentecostal Testimony*) were written in this period of grief, stress, and exhaustion. His personal turmoil, exacerbated by problems in his congregation that may in turn have been aggravated by Durham's personal situation, functioned as the lens through which he viewed his spiritual journey and the challenge of the moment. Much of what he left as written record was influenced by his pent-up grief as well as troubles at the mission in the second half of 1910.

In a nutshell, Durham—who had first devoted his argumentative tendencies to defending speaking in tongues as initial evidence of Spirit baptism—now maintained that the "central truth" of the Gospel was the believer's identification with Christ at conversion and thereafter: "We come to Christ by faith, and it is only by faith that we abide in him . . . As soon as a man believes, he is saved, but it requires just as much faith to keep right with God as it did to get right in the first place."[78] The matter of "keeping right with God" posed the problem. In Durham's view, Holiness people generally thought that it necessitated a second experience. Durham insisted that it did not.

Today it is difficult to understand the furor that followed Durham's throwing down of this gauntlet, especially the mayhem among those who claimed to be fully sanctified. Durham described it as a battle and claimed he found himself the object of accusations and slander.[79] He stubbornly stood his ground. God, he said, had revealed to him that the time had come "to establish in all the earth the simple, primitive Gospel of our Lord and Savior Jesus Christ, and that the Finished Work of Calvary was the central theme, yea, the very germ and life of that gospel."[80] In the end, Durham won his point in many places, and everywhere his views helped shape the core of Pentecostal identity. The finished work of Calvary left a permanent rift in North American Pentecostalism, separating those who sought a "second definite work of grace" from those who advocated progressive sanctification.

Durham held strong convictions about other church matters, too. He strenuously opposed organization beyond the local congregation. He regarded the congregation as the appropriate place for ministerial training and objected to Bible institutes, formal or informal. He cautioned Pentecostals about the idea that only those who received Spirit baptism manifested by tongues were saved; the claim that one received the Holy Spirit at salvation; or the assertion that Spirit baptism constituted "the witness of the Spirit." He deemed it necessary in 1911 to oppose rebaptism in the name of Jesus only: "One who is baptized into the Name of the Father, Son and Holy Spirit is baptized into the Name of Jesus. The words of Jesus are sufficient for me." He resisted with equal adamancy advocates of Triune immersion. He had nothing good to say about Pentecostals who discouraged marriage or who insisted that holy living demanded sexual abstinence within marriage (marital purity).[81]

Durham complained about the worldliness of the contemporary church; the advancing cultural authority of science and education; higher criticism;

and the shortcomings of the Holiness movement. He saw a spiritual and moral crisis looming and insisted that God had begun to "hasten the crisis" by pouring out His Spirit. "God's plan," he believed, "is to produce a type of Christianity that will not only teach and live the truth, but through whom [sic] He can reveal the Christ."[82] "Real Pentecost" entailed persecution: "Those who have the spirit of the world will hate with a murderous hatred those in whom God is working through the power of the Spirit." The battle lines were being drawn "by the revelation of Jesus Christ through the Holy Spirit in God's people and by the works of power which will be wrought in their midst." If God's people (the Pentecostals) would only be faithful to their calling, "when He comes He will find a little company standing against almost unheard of odds, but standing as unmovable as a rock, defending the glorious truths of the Gospel. Great and glorious will be our final victory."[83] With this grandiose sense of purpose and meaning as context for his espousal of spiritual gifts and miracles, Durham galvanized his following.

Los Angeles–Chicago–Los Angeles

In the summer of 1910, Durham preached at a camp meeting in Malvern, Arkansas, where he met an influential circle of southern Pentecostal leaders.[84] Then he traveled to New York City for a three-week convention at Glad Tidings Tabernacle "dealing death to sin and striking terror to everything that savored with compromise."[85] He returned to Chicago for the holidays, spent part of January preaching in Minneapolis, and left Chicago again on February 9 for California. He intended to remain a month in California, to preach at other points on the West Coast, then to spend the summer of 1911 in Europe. Instead, Durham concluded that West Coast Pentecostals needed his message, so through 1911 he identified Los Angeles as his home. He spent a few months contending for the finished work up and down the coast as well as preaching to a congregation he called the Pentecostal Assembly (209 E. Seventh Street) in Los Angeles. His presence in the city—aided by a disruption he caused by preaching the finished work at the Azusa Street Mission—almost immediately proved a magnet for some six hundred adherents who gathered in a spacious hall he leased for a year at $100 per month.[86] He severed his ties to the North Avenue Mission and—as in 1903—used *Folke-Vennen*'s nearby address as his Chicago base. (There is some indication that his problems at North Avenue derived from his loss of control over the exercising of spiritual gifts.)[87]

Although Durham began preaching in Los Angeles in February 1911, he spent part of the spring in Chicago. From June 20 to June 30 he was the announced convener of a "Mass Pentecostal Convention" in Ottawa, Canada.[88] He changed his permanent address to Los Angeles as of August 1, but November found him on the road again, this time in Winnipeg preaching another Pentecostal convention. On Christmas night, he opened a convention in Los Angeles, assisted by friends from Chicago as well as from the West Coast.[89] Sometime in 1911 he moved his family to Los Angeles. The Taylor sisters moved, too. During his busy schedule at the end of 1911 or the beginning of 1912, Durham married Gertrude Taylor. Her sister, Ethel, continued to serve as his secretary.

Meanwhile, from February 1 to February 18, 1912, Durham held meetings in a small mission in Portland, Oregon. On the twenty-fourth, he returned to Chicago and began a series of special services the next night at the Persian mission. A few weeks later, he exulted: "Of all revivals I ever attended or conducted this in actual results has by far exceeded any."[90] He had accomplished his work on the West Coast, he claimed, and was now eager to re-establish his base of operations in Chicago. His goal seems to have been a West Coast ministry hub staffed by associates in Los Angeles and a Chicago hub that he would call home. Sometime that spring, Durham opened yet another mission—another Full Gospel Assembly— at 2623 Florence Avenue, north of the North Avenue Mission. His wife was in Chicago with him. He enthused about powerful meetings and many conversions and Spirit baptisms among the "old and young, black and white, Italians, Persians, Scandinavians, Germans, Indians, Baptists, Methodists and Salvationists who came."[91]

The future appeared promising. Then, during the meetings, he caught a cold that he could not shake. He had been plagued by exhaustion for months, and, though "dynamite" while preaching, would collapse and sleep for twenty-four hours after a service, a friend recalled. After months of physical weakness that he resisted at every turn, he left Chicago in July 1912 "to visit his dear ones" in Los Angeles. By then he was gravely ill with tuberculosis. The day after he arrived in the city, he died at the age of thirty-nine, leaving a pregnant twenty-nine-year-old widow and two young children from his first marriage.

California Pentecostals flocked to Durham's funeral, which was under the direction of the Bresee Brothers Mortuary, owned by the sons of the well-known Holiness evangelist Phineas Bresee. William Durham was laid to rest at Inglewood Cemetery with no marker on his grave.

Gertrude Durham loyally kept the family together. She gave birth to a daughter, Gertrude Harriett, in Los Angeles in February 1913. The family lived in the home Durham had found for them in 1911 on South Denver Avenue, and Gertrude worked in a school cafeteria to help pay expenses until the children were grown.

So What?

In modern Pentecostalism, William Durham's name is associated almost exclusively with the finished work of Calvary. His clear articulation of that view—and his posing it as a battle cry—helped define boundaries within Pentecostalism, but that message in itself was hardly new or original. In retrospect, it is appropriate to credit him with clarifying differences on an important doctrinal point. But a fuller look at his life indicates other valuable contributions and some surprising anomalies.

First, it is sometimes difficult to consider early Pentecostals in the context of places and relationships. The language of the records they left tends to be so spiritually charged, so otherworldly in focus, that it neglects more than it reveals. Early Pentecostals tend to dismiss pre-Pentecostal pasts as sinful or, at best, unfulfilled and to date what was important from their Spirit baptism. Painstaking research can partially reconstruct their pasts, however. Nontraditional and traditional sources enable the retracing of steps, the recovery of names, anniversary dates, and events of significance in the communities in which they lived. Such reconstruction may make the choices of early Pentecostals more or less comprehensible, but they may also help explain what appears to be near fanatical devotion to a cause. For example, I have found the agonies of Durham's personal life in 1909 and 1910 a revealing context in which to consider his contentiousness and drivenness in those years.

Reconstructing the past also yields fascinating—if sometimes indirect—insights into the life of a Pentecostal minister's wife. Bessie Mae Durham stood wholeheartedly with Durham in his ministry, but that loyalty did not make her life easy. And the parents' schedules and lack of family privacy took an enormous toll on the children. When William Howard Durham

Jr. filed for a Social Security number in 1936, he did not know his mother's full maiden name, nor did he know the county of his birth. Bessie Mae's death and William Sr.'s choices had effectively robbed him of his extended family.

Equally important in Durham's story are the networks it reveals. Durham helps bring the World's Faith Missionary Association into focus. This, in turn, offers suggestive insights into the religious lives of ordinary people in the small-town upper Midwest. And the World's Faith Missionary Association amply illustrates that the networks through which Pentecostalism spread in North America were in place well before the movement emerged. These people knew each other and worked together before they embraced the new message.

Durham helped make Chicago a defining center for American Pentecostalism in several ways. First, his strong personality and tireless networking gave him stature around the country. Second, he dealt with specific issues in definitive ways, unwilling to accept what happened simply because it happened. Bothered when he could not explain or comprehend something, he opposed his detractors and specified his reasons. Third, he did what he professed to believe, and he stated persuasively (and in influential Pentecostal arenas) ideas toward which many early Pentecostals seemed predisposed. Fourth, Chicago was already a national hub: Durham gave the Pentecostal movement what it required—an outspoken advocate in the best possible location. Durham also reached out easily to the city's ethnic mix. He and his congregation were working-class people in working-class neighborhoods, content to remain there. Fifth, Durham made extensive use of cheap railroad travel and inexpensive printing. The rails took him wherever people gathered; his publications stayed behind when he moved on. The railroad also brought to Chicago evangelists and missionaries from around the world, and it carried away on the first leg of their journeys people who went from Durham's mission to plant Pentecostal teaching in far-flung places like Brazil, Italy, and Persia. For such reasons, then, Durham helped realize Chicago's potential as a defining center for early Pentecostalism. He showed the movement's promise as an ethnically mixed urban phenomenon.

Along the way, Durham manifested some undesirable traits. He confronted people harshly under the guise of battling for truth. He denounced Pentecostals who hesitated about identifying tongues as *uniform* initial evidence of Spirit baptism, effectively disabling any unity among early Chicago Pentecostals. When some challenged his views, he complained that the whole world turned against him. He employed a metaphor of sacrifice to cover his grief and his emotional neglect of his children. He sometimes exaggerated the scope of his pre-Pentecostal ministry experience or the magnitude of the opposition he faced. He thrived best when he felt most embattled. In the absence of visible foes, he waged war in spiritual realms.

It is intriguing that the Pentecostal denominations that identify with Durham actually reject as much of his message as they endorse. His bold advocacy of initial evidence and the finished work of Calvary went hand in hand with his forceful rejection of the most basic traits of modern Pentecostal denominations. He had no use for denominational organization, college and seminary education for pastors and missionaries, church growth and ministry programs, fund-raising activities, or church entertainment and socials. For him, the true church would always be small and persecuted, and he waxed eloquent about a long-forgotten early hope— Pentecostalism's spiritually transformative role as "the revelation of Christ within his people." Much of modern American Pentecostalism would have no fiercer foe than William Durham.

In the end, the association of Durham's name with Chicago is perhaps most fascinating of all. In Pentecostal lore, Durham's name is inextricably linked to the hallowed North Avenue Mission. To be sure, he took responsibility for that mission, but he spent so much time away from Chicago that it immediately becomes evident that other people played active leadership roles all along. Durham's tenure as Pentecostal leader at North Avenue lasted barely four years. It is doubtful he was actually there for even half that time. Rather, he took over an existing mission, molded it for a time, then walked away when he lost control. Still, when in 1911 he briefly called Los Angeles his home (he was there, too, less than half that time), Chicago tugged at his heart and lured him back. He recognized the city for what it was—a strategic crossroads of an emerging modern America. He died devising a way to return. Chicago, then, was Durham's preferred home address, but all along he worked indefatigably to make a larger world his parish.[92]

EDITH L. BLUMHOFER

Thomas Hampton Gourley: Defining the Boundaries

James R. Goff Jr.

Throughout much of the twentieth century, Pentecostalism sought to impress outsiders. The impulse came from two sources. On the one hand, there loomed a genuine concern for the Great Commission. If Pentecostalism was God's answer for the end time—and Pentecostals have held that tenet in common since the movement's beginnings—then believers should be responsible for getting the message out. Over the years, rapid growth has thus been a mark of pride. Numerical expansion seemed to validate their unique place in God's plan for humanity. On the other hand, the impulsion to gloat over numbers also resulted from a darker side—one that represented Pentecostals' innate inferiority complex. Drawn from poorer working-class stock—or from the "other side of the tracks" as first-generation Pentecostals fondly recalled—adherents joined the fold confident that they, rather than the socially prominent and powerful, were the inheritors of God's prophetic gifts and that they would be instruments in the glorious unfolding of His will in the last days. It was essentially reverse conceit. Those without suddenly became the only ones with abundance. The message functioned as a kind of "neat trick," turning social outcasts into a spiritual elite, and the resulting zeal served the movement well as generations of Pentecostals reversed liabilities into assets and turned criticism into assurance of their spiritual wealth.[1]

Indeed, Pentecostals revealed an immense concern with what the rest of the world thought and, as a result, adherents, especially second-generation ones, charted a course for respectability. They copied the success of other Protestant evangelicals, building denominational structures, educational institutions, and religious presses. They prided themselves on their decorum

143

Thomas Hampton Gourley, circa 1895. Courtesy of Phil Gourley, Thomas Gourley's grandson, Aumsville, Oregon.

and relegated to "wild fire" any Pentecostal who tended to step out of line. The process was not a conscious one nor one that mainstream onlookers readily identified. But steadily after 1910, Pentecostals successfully went about the business of harnessing the energy that had been so chaotic in the dynamic days from Charles Parham's New Year's Day revival in Topeka in 1901 through the first three years of William Seymour's reign at the Los Angeles–based Azusa Street Mission.

There was irony here. Pentecostal leaders recognized that the very power that created their vitality threatened to destroy their fragile organizations, yet they themselves had sprung into existence on the very premise that institutions were dangerous because they threatened the free working of God's Spirit. The result was an uncomfortable coexistence of organizers and organization resisters, with a good sprinkling of those who were arguably both at the same time. No doubt the duality is one reason the charismatic movement was so controversial within the older Pentecostal denominations a couple of generations later and, indeed, why Pentecostalism in general remains such a complex historical subject.

In the midst of the story of denomination building, an independent— even chaotic—spirit endured both inside and outside the fold of the organizations. Unfortunately, the names and activities of key players outside the denominations are less familiar to historians if for no other reason than that they seldom left records or followings sufficient to promote their story. Yet the fact remains that it is the unacculturated who have a story to tell as well, in many ways a story closer to the foundations of Pentecostalism than the neatly packaged narrative of the successful organizers.

In that array of unacculturated spokespersons rests the figure of Thomas Hampton Gourley. Born in Peru, Indiana, in 1862, Gourley's early saga mirrored that of many other Pentecostal pioneers. He moved several times in his youth, owing to his father's at least part-time occupation as a Methodist minister. The family had settled in Pawnee City, Nebraska, by the early 1870s and, after a brief stay, moved on to Farragut, Iowa.[2] Gourley spent his young adulthood involved in several different occupations. By 1885, he worked in Topeka as a well driller; two years later he relocated to nearby Kansas City, Missouri, where he formed a loose partnership with his half brother, Will Hawkins, and the two men tried their hand alternately at carpentry and police work. With other family members, the two even speculated a bit in local real estate. A dramatic change came in 1894 when Gourley was converted under the ministry of his brother-in-law, William Tasker, an ordained minister in the United Brethren Church. Within a year, Gourley served as an itinerant evangelist himself, holding revivals in a series of United Brethren, Congregational, Methodist, and Baptist churches in the Kansas City area.[3]

Family tradition came to believe that Gourley's conversion had been sparked by dire health problems brought on by a severe drinking habit begun when the young man served a three-year stint as a Kansas City police constable beginning in 1890. Reminiscent of Parham and a host of other Pentecostal icons, Gourley claimed dramatic and instant healing from stomach disorders that had come to plague him and believed that the physical relief came alongside his spiritual healing and decision to follow God's leading into the ministry.[4] Late in 1896, following a successful revival in Norton County in western Kansas, he married Effie Masden, a local schoolteacher from Lenora. Soon the newlyweds embarked on an adventure as tent evangelists, spurred no doubt by youth and boundless faith but hindered by the young bride's poor health.[5]

Whatever the circumstances of Gourley's decision to set off on the sawdust trail, several things had become clear by the 1890s. Gourley, heavily influenced by the radical wing of the Holiness movement, steadily distanced himself from the mainstream organizations of his day. His meetings were highly emotional affairs that emphasized the moving of God's Spirit. In addition, he evoked controversy easily, sparking a local upheaval in Lawrence when he brought his tent revival to town in 1897 and local students—Gourley proponents labeled them "hoodlums"—proceeded to destroy the tent.[6]

Gourley's expedition to Lawrence began peacefully enough with local newsmen reporting "a good attendance and [that] interest was great."[7] But as the extended revival continued, the harmonious relationship between Evangelist Gourley and the citizens of Lawrence became badly strained. By late September, spurred in part by the resumption of the academic term at the University of Kansas, tempers over late-night noise resulted in a 10:00 P.M. row that disrupted the prayer meeting and destroyed the tent. Newspapers from nearby Topeka focused on the accusation of hypnotism against Gourley, reporting the attack as a coordinated effort on the part of three hundred "conservative University students and law-abiding citizens . . . to drive the objectionable character from town." The *Topeka Daily*

Capital showed little restraint, describing Gourley as "a 'reformed policeman' of uncouth appearance, dress, and language" with "no personal charms except this power to throw his convert into a cataleptic state." Accusing the evangelist of focusing his efforts on susceptible young girls, the *Daily Capital* reporter then described the tumultuous scene: "The mob gathered quickly and reached the tent just as a great part of the audience had gone and the evangelist had a few persons on the mourners benches completely under his spell. A rush was made on the big tent and when this was completely demolished, his living tent was torn thread from thread and his furniture broken and cooking utensils scattered to the four corners. It is not thought that he will return and general satisfaction is being expressed that the town is rid of him."[8]

But Gourley was not easily displaced. According to subsequent news reports, he continued to face opposition and was forced to move his meetings to the outskirts of the city. Drawing on sympathetic support from the local *Lawrence World,* which blasted both university and city officials, Gourley completed his revival in a local sporting "rink." The debacle devolved quickly into a town-and-gown dispute, with editorials alternately blaming the impotency of the local police force, the students and administration for denying any responsibility, the press for exaggerating the extent of the damage and ill will, and local citizens for their inability to abide by the spirit of the First Amendment.[9] Gourley remained a resident of Lawrence for another two years, moving only after the unexpected death of his wife in July 1899.[10]

Effie Gourley's death created a temporary period of turmoil for her widowed husband. He moved to Kansas City, where he again worked briefly as a carpenter. But Gourley did not abandon the call to preach. He continued to preach in the Kansas-Missouri area for another four years, remarrying in January 1901. He and his new bride, Mary Neff, became parents of a son, John, born in Topeka in July of 1902. By the time their second son, James, was born in May of 1904, the family had relocated to Los Angeles, where Gourley presumably continued his career as an evangelist.[11]

By December 1906, Gourley's whereabouts and activities had become clear. Readers of the "News Section" of the *Seattle Daily Times* were greeted with giant headlines on Sunday, December 2, which proclaimed "WILD NIGHT IN CHURCH OF HOLY ROLLERS!" The paper's description of events seemed astounding even alongside the hyped press other reporters of the day gave to Holiness and Pentecostal assemblies. The highlight of the evening, during which worshipers could be heard—the paper claimed—a full block away, was the firing of a bullet through the glass window of the front of the downtown mission building. No one was hurt, but police officers arrived to investigate and remained on duty to see that no further incidents occurred. Reporters also made much of the inclusion of a "colored female deacon" as one of the principal leaders, though the audience seems to have been predominantly white. Despite the tumultuous welcome, and perhaps because of it, Gourley stayed in Seattle. Within a year he began publishing a religious paper, the *Midnight Cry*, and operating a Bible school from his headquarters mission at 1617 Seventh Avenue.[12]

By now the interest of Pentecostal historians in the little-known Gourley should have been piqued. He was in the Topeka-Kansas City area in January 1901 and in Los Angeles and surrounding towns from 1904 perhaps through the summer of 1906. What part, if any, did he play in the pivotal revivals led by Parham and Seymour, and was the revival in Seattle an extension of either of those revivals? Though Gourley's connection to early Pentecostal development has never been established, his presence in these revival centers suggests an early affiliation. In fact, the maverick preacher met on at least one occasion with the younger Holiness preacher Charles F. Parham. In May of 1899, while Parham operated the Beth-el Healing Home in Topeka, Gourley had accompanied his first wife, Effie, in a short stay in response to her worsening health. Though the meeting had occurred more than a year before Parham's celebrated New Year's Day revival at Stone's Folly, it is likely that Gourley absorbed at least some of Parham's eclectic theology.[13] Indeed, the visit came at a most opportune time. Only two weeks earlier, Parham's *Apostolic Faith* had introduced the idea of glossolalia for missionary purposes. The paper recounted the story of Jennie Glassey, a St. Louis native who had, according to another Holiness periodical, received tongues in answer to prayer and had gone to find her place in the mission field.[14]

Any formal connection Gourley might have been tempted to make with Parham and his fledgling movement, however, was undoubtedly muted by Effie Gourley's death only two months after the stay at the healing home. Nevertheless, circumstances continued to place Gourley alongside the fabled Pentecostal pioneer. Gourley's marriage to Mary Neff in January

1901 also took place in Topeka, certifying his presence in the city at the time of Parham's Bethel Bible School "tongues revival." Given the press the Bethel students generated and Gourley's obvious interest in this type of religious encounter, the event could not have escaped his notice even with the distraction in his personal life.[15]

His presence in the Los Angeles area, of course, also suggests that Gourley may have weighed the merits of early reports from Azusa Street. By 1905, he and his family had apparently located in Temecula, some eighty miles south of Los Angeles. Did Gourley attend any of the early meetings at Azusa, and did the interracial character of Azusa spark his inclusion of a black female in a leadership role in the later Seattle meeting? If so, he left no record of such a visit, and that alone seems evidence enough that he did not make the trip. However, it is likely that he was aware of the revival at least with the first local news reports in April 1906 and saw it as an overall part of God's miraculous workings in the last days. Even so, while Gourley was almost certainly aware of the activities of the Pentecostals, he himself had not yet climbed aboard when he initially journeyed to Seattle. When news reports of his December 1906 Seattle revival appeared, they failed to mention anything about tongues, a fact no reporter worth his salt would have omitted. In contrast, when news of M. L. Ryan's Pentecostal meetings in Salem, Oregon, made the Seattle papers only ten days after the initial reports of Gourley's revival, the theology and practice of glossolalia took center stage in reporters' accounts.[16]

Nevertheless, at some point during the first ten months of 1907, Gourley adopted the Pentecostal theology coming out of the Azusa Street Mission. The contact presumably came through an affiliation with Thomas Junk, an itinerant who traveled from Azusa to Seattle at about the time of Gourley's own arrival in the fall of 1906. Junk reported the Pentecostal progress in the city to William Seymour and others back at the mission in Los Angeles as early as December 1906. Late in the fall of 1907, both Gourley and Junk were affiliated with the same mission on Seventh Avenue.[17]

Though a part of the fold by the midpoint of 1907, Gourley held loose, apparently ambivalent, ties to the emerging Pentecostal revival. While in Seattle, he failed to develop strong friendships with others who were rapidly spreading the Pentecostal message, though he had accepted without question the validity of the charismatic gifts. Always suspicious of the leadership qualifications of others, the divisions that plagued the movement almost from the beginning likely alienated him. The first issues of the *Midnight Cry* loosely tied the paper to Azusa by reporting on other Pentecostal activities on the West Coast that had their genesis in Los Angeles. The inaugural edition noted, with apparent support, the recent departure from Seattle of Ryan and a band of Pentecostal missionaries who had gone to Tokyo, opened a mission, and begun a religious newspaper there. The second issue of the paper also reported on Pentecostal work elsewhere, complete with names and addresses of other missions in the Northwest.[18] Nevertheless, that second paper contained a word of warning that "a great deal of trouble is coming to the 'Apostolic Faith Movement,' on account of the different teachings on divorce and marriage," though the paper did not elaborate except to state its own view that divorce was allowed on the biblical principal of Matt. 19:9, but remarriage was not allowed so long as the initial partner remained alive.[19]

The third issue of the *Midnight Cry,* appearing in February 1908, signaled two momentous changes. William Welch, a mysterious figure whose name had been listed as the correspondence person in the first two offerings, abruptly disappeared without any explanation, and, for the first time, a voice appeared that separated the paper from the dominant theology of Azusa. The role of the paper from the beginning had been vague, with the inaugural issue explaining its goal as both evangelistic and instructive. The theology clearly sympathized with that of Azusa, as with that of Parham's work in the Midwest, noting a firm belief in salvation, healing, sanctification, and the Baptism with the "Holy Ghost and with fire."[20] But with Welch's disappearance came a redefinition of the paper's mission to publish the truth as relates to "the fulfillment of the prophecies pertaining to [Christ's coming] kingdom, and the scriptures showing the day in which we live," along with words that detailed a clear division among the ranks of West Coast Pentecostals.[21]

> Some, who have received what passes current upon the coast for baptism with the Holy Ghost, have written and preached extensivly [*sic*] upon the fire; some ridiculing it, others saying the Holy Ghost was for Christians but the fire for sinners. But remember, when you are teaching Pentecostal Baptism, the fire APPEARED UNTO THEM.

JAMES R. GOFF JR.

150

Acts 2:3. We don't believe they were sinners but a specially prepared people.

So, brethren, don't mistake the Word and warp it to fit your experience and ideas, but having received an anointing, go on and keep seeking God. And we will assure you that, when God puts His seal of fire upon your baptism, it will abide and you will find *yourself* an holy offering unto the Lord before *His* Fire ever touches you.[22]

Given the language and his consistent use of the term *fire* as far back as the 1897 revival in Lawrence, Kansas, Gourley obviously was trying to reconcile his own belief in the baptism of fire—a tenet he no doubt picked up from some of Benjamin Irwin's followers in the Midwest—with the new doctrine of Holy Spirit baptism.[23] While he accepted the validity of glossolalia, he continued to believe that the baptism of fire set Christians apart for service. The same February 1908 issue featured a front-page article entitled "The Baptism with the Holy Ghost and Fire," which sought to explain Gourley's own interpretation of the matter. Noting the "extravagant claims of some" as well as "the absence of the real power claimed" and referring specifically to Los Angeles a year earlier, the evangelist argued that Holy Spirit baptism—and tongues in particular—was not "the enduement with power, spoken of by Jesus." Rather, Gourley argued, "tongues are for a sign and that for a witness and no farther, as we see in this latter day. The baptism is the filling with the Holy Ghost; the gifts or power are the operations of the Spirit, and we have to tarry until we are endued with power. This will never come until all of self is gone and we are willing to be used of God as He will."[24]

Quite frankly, Gourley failed to see in much of Pentecostalism the kind of end-time saintliness he expected. Rather, he feared that religious enthusiasm prompted too many into a chaotic frenzy of missionary zeal. For Gourley, who had been preaching with success since 1895, this uncontrolled passion threatened to discredit God's genuine end-time work. In May 1908, a clear indictment of mainstream Pentecostalism and the leadership squabbles within the movement appeared, noting the ambitions of "Parham, Seymore [*sic*], Ryan and a host of other self styled apostles." The result, Gourley argued, was that Pentecostals were going the way of other denominations, "bringing their sectism in the Pentecostal work, misunderstanding and divisions."[25]

Considering the mysterious disappearance of Welch, it is likely that Gourley, always the most important figure behind the newspaper and the most generous contributor, simply wrestled control of the paper away from whatever cooperative effort had launched it and set it upon its own unique course. The May issue noted a move to 711 Olive Street, a site not far off Seventh Avenue that the paper had earlier praised for the founding of a Salvation Army childcare facility.[26] Ironically, the issue also noted the visit of Frank Bartleman from Los Angeles, concluding cheerily that Bartleman should "come again."[27] While Bartleman's visit established Gourley's continued link with Pentecostalism, he was clearly on the margins of the developing movement. Subsequent issues rarely included names other than Gourley's and decidedly fewer references connected it to Azusa or any other Pentecostal work.[28]

Gourley's denunciation of the evils of organization reflected a consistent paradox that most early Pentecostals shared. Intensely antiauthoritarian, they nevertheless demonstrated a strong tendency toward authoritarianism within their own circles. Though virtually all early Pentecostal writers and speakers officially deplored the sectarian spirit that rallied groups of followers around the charismatic leadership of individuals, in practice most continued that very trend. Indeed, men like Parham decried the sectarianism and denied any personal ambition only to spend the rest of their careers pointing out the important role that they had played in bringing about the true Pentecostal movement.[29] Gourley actually received a letter from Parham while in Seattle, noting in August 1908 that he had "not long ago . . . received a letter from a self-styled projector of the Faith, signed: your Father in the Gospel." Like other Pentecostal leaders, Gourley, however, rejected Parham's claim to authority and urged his readers to allow God to "rub our heads down to their normal size, before we delude very many more soft-headed and fearful-hearted Christians into following men and women."[30]

Yet Gourley proved different from the bulk of leaders who accepted a theology of Pentecostal charismata for the end time. He remained more caustic, separating him and his followers from other Pentecostals as well as from others in the Christian community. With the volatile expansion of Pentecostals along the West Coast during the years after the outbreak at Azusa, he drew his followers inward and avoided contact with others who preached similar doctrine. In early 1909, he left the mission on Seventh Avenue and established his own Pentecostal community at Ballard Beach, just north of Seattle. For the next year, his followers worshiped as a separate band, establishing a tenuous economic relationship with the handful of other residents in the seaside community. Following the New Testament literally, Gourley formed a commune there and, in little more than a year, "built a town of forty-two houses, a canvas walled tabernacle on a float and a fairly substantial schoolhouse for the children of the colony." Ultimately attracting as many as forty-five families and numbering between 150 and 175 residents, Gourley's Ballard Beach commune seemed successful enough to outside reporters who later described the operation to readers of the *Seattle Post-Intelligencer*:

> The men of this colony fished to supply the table and sometimes sold part of their catch or worked at various trades in the city. Their families were housed in shacks, most of which were fairly comfortable and some quite pretentious, with electric lights, gay wall paper and a number of separate rooms. One dining hall served the colony, which was governed by a simple feudal system of which Gourley was the head. All property and money was turned over to the prophet and expended by him for the common good. There was always simple but enough food. Driftwood from the beaches, obtained with Gourley's launch, was sawed into stove lengths at the community sawmill.[31]

Though local businessmen appreciated the business that came from Gourley's community and later praised the evangelist and his flock because "they paid cash for everything or else did without," Gourley ultimately grew concerned about outside influences. Seattle health inspectors had been called on occasion over neighbors' concerns of "alleged unsanitary conditions," and there had also been early complaints about "noisy religious services." Most disturbing to Gourley was the arrival of outside missionaries who attempted vigorously to proselytize from among his flock. As a result, Gourley made an even bolder move. In March of 1911, he abruptly led the band away from the Ballard Beach base and relocated almost seventy miles north on Lopez Island, a twelve-mile-long member of the San Juan chain of islands in the Puget Sound.[32]

The move rested upon his understanding of the nearness of the end, a common belief among Pentecostals then and now, but one that Gourley viewed in a unique way. Like other Pentecostals, he was fascinated with the idea that the dawning of human history's seventh millennium would bring the end time, thus following a divine plan highlighted by a series of sevens—a plan initiated in the seven-day creation explained in Genesis. Equally a part of his eschatology was the belief that the outpouring of charismatic gifts signaled the beginning of the end or, more precisely, the beginning of the last millennium described in Revelation 20. As a result, he bombarded readers with an elaborate sketch of human history outlined on a full-page supplement to the *Midnight Cry*. The supplement included notes inside a set of wheels overlaid with a drawing of the veil inside the Jewish Temple. The notes described the progress of human history and included Gourley's interpretation of a set of visions recorded in Ezekiel, chapters 1 and 10. The parallel article on page 1 included numerical calculations suggesting that the time of Christ's Second Coming must be at hand.[33] Initially Gourley theorized that the Pentecostal outpouring represented the first three and a half years of the tribulation period and thus foreshadowed the final three and a half years of destruction and evil that would follow. As a result, he seems to have believed that the evil period would begin sometime around 1910 or 1911—perhaps an underlying reason for his removal to Lopez Island—and that the end of the tribulation would come at some point over the next few years.[34]

Life on Lopez Island was not completely isolated for Gourley and his band of 150 followers. Though they eventually settled on Hunter's Bay, a remote location, they enjoyed occasional contact with the seven hundred or so settlers who lived in the three other small towns on the island. Colonists practiced marriage and family life as before, but certain functions, particularly meals and work, were ordered by the colony, thus freeing up extra time for Bible study and prayer. A schoolhouse for the younger members of the colony surrounded a communal bakery and dining hall. Private residences were usually tent structures complete with wooden floors and adjacent lean-tos. Workers were oftentimes farmed out to the mainland, where they received food and supplies in lieu of wages, and the colony even ran an occasional ferry service for both passengers and goods coming to the island. In an arrangement secured with the landowner, Gourley apparently used the land rent-free. Though other islanders were no doubt suspicious of the sect, some did frequent the Sunday services and partake of the colonists' hospitality in after-church dinners. Disputes were few, though the colony did have at least one publicized legal problem with relatives after an estate was willed to the colony upon a member's death.[35]

From his remote position in the Lopez Island commune, Gourley moved further and further away from the experience and theology of the bulk of the Pentecostal movement. Even as he did, he remained fervent in the belief that he, not they, understood the full meaning of God's outpouring of end-time gifts and wonders. In fact, in occasional issues of the *Midnight Cry*, he chided Pentecostals for their failure to follow the letter of Acts 2. Denominational ministers were content to teach their followers "to *believe* what Jesus said; but [that] it was not necessary to *do*, or observe it."[36] As a result, true or "full Pentecost" had not yet come. When it did, Gourley assured all who would listen that a radical departure would occur, similar to that which he had inaugurated on Lopez Island.

> When Pentecost fully comes to us . . . we will live as those did to whom the faith was first delivered. We will see people forsake all they have; and all that believe will live together, and have all things common, and no one will call that which he possesses his own. "And all that believed were together, and had all things common;" This is the best evidence in the Bible of belief in eternal life. Here is belief which this so-called 'Pentecost' has not given us. "And sold their possessions and goods, and parted them to all men, as every man had need." Acts 2:44, 45.[37]

World War I enhanced Gourley's belief in the soon coming end, even as the passing of years forced him to adjust his timetable. Like other Pentecostals, he viewed the war with suspicion and expected that it would prompt the outbreak of Armageddon.[38] Yet again, the degree of Gourley's opposition and zeal was unique, leading to his trial for violating the Sedition Act of May 1918. Based on statements he made in a July 28, 1918, sermon at Richardson, a small town located across the island from his colony, Gourley was indicted and brought before a jury in January 1919. Specifically, he was charged on five counts of making seditious remarks and interfering with the sale of liberty bonds and war stamps. Local news reports recounted a packed courtroom trial with as many as twenty-one witnesses alleging that Gourley made the following public statements in addition to "numerous other remarks of a similar nature": "The government is taking our boys and putting them in camps and cantonments and will send them back to us nothing but libertines and gamblers. This war is not fought to make the world a decent place to live in, but in order that the capitalists may make more money. I will not buy Liberty bonds, and I advise you patriots not to do so."[39] The testimony of witnesses proved vague enough that, coupled with Gourley's testimony that his statements were taken out of context, the jury deadlocked and the U.S. district attorney later moved to dismiss the case. Nevertheless, the widely publicized trial combined with growing unrest among the Lopez faithful over food shortages and allegations of fiscal mismanagement to prompt Gourley's decision to leave the island commune and its residents the following year.[40]

After the sedition trial and his decision to leave Lopez, Gourley returned to an earlier theme—the redemption of the body. Not surprisingly, he found his place back among the ranks of the Pentecostals, though again outside the dominant denominational structures. Having cited the redemption doctrine as early as 1908, claiming specifically his amazement that Pentecostals of all people might refuse its validity, Gourley now created a brief furor by proclaiming that a perfect state of health should be attained.[41] Presumably the imminent Second Coming figured into his belief that a person would not face death, though Gourley was later chastised in his obituary by a belittling press as "the man who said he would never die," with no apparent understanding of the theological subtlety involved.[42]

At any rate, the doctrine of perpetual health apparently led Gourley and his family to St. Louis in 1921. At age sixty, he still enjoyed vigorous health and testified that he had not been sick a day in his life since his remarkable healing and conversion back in 1894.[43] In St. Louis, Gourley established a relationship with the Pentecostal mission run by Mother Mary Moise and, for a brief time, served as leader of her mission.[44] This relationship introduced him to J. R. Moseley, an eccentric Pentecostal and former Mercer College professor who sponsored the evangelist's visit to Macon, Georgia, and defended him before the press. In late February 1923, as Moseley and Gourley traveled via train from Macon to St. Louis, tragedy struck. The Dixie Flyer derailed near Calhoun, Georgia, and Gourley and one other passenger perished in the wreck. Less than two months later, Moseley still struggled with the prospects of the evangelist's death, noting that "there was an authority and a sense of Divine presence about him that made him one of the rare men of history."

> I was on the same seat with Mr. Gourley . . . when the train, moving at possibly sixty miles an hour, jumped the track. I prayed, closed my eyes and surrendered to the care of God as a child clings to a father and mother when in danger. When the coach stopped and I opened my eyes; I saw Mr. Gourley's body severed from his head, below the coach, . . . As there was no one I could get to to help who was not being cared for, I went to praying, and the first light that came that seemed like light from God was that Mr. Gourley, whom I had seen and said was a kind of a John-the-Baptist prophet and baptizer for his day, . . . has lost his head as John lost his. It was made very clear to me that it is not in the truest doctrines, even about Christ's blood, death, resurrection, redemption and immortality that we are preserved, but by Christ or God Himself, and that the best that we can do is to believe, to cling to Him, to pray, to love, to obey and to be humble.[45]

Whatever his doubts about perpetual health, years later Moseley remained struck by his own comparison of Gourley to John the Baptist. No longer mentioning the evangelist by name, he nonetheless recalled the tragic event by noting that "when the undertaker came and brought out my friend's head on a platter, it reminded me of the experience of John the Baptist, who prophecied [sic] of the Kingdom nigh at hand that he failed to enter while in the flesh."[46]

Gourley's unusual death brought an abrupt end to any substantial influence he might have established on Pentecostalism in the South and Midwest. The redemption of the body doctrine played only a minor role in the movement in the 1920s, though in various forms it would be revived in years to come.[47] Nevertheless, there is enough to suggest that Gourley served as a minor player in the early spread of Pentecostalism. He embraced the arrival of charismatic signs and wonders and added them to his collection of Holiness doctrines and practices. More important, he represents the degree to which many early leaders refused to conform to the opinions and theological ideology of the larger Pentecostal community. Gourley's continued belief in the immediate dawn of another dramatic restructuring of God's people kept him out of the mainstream of Pentecostal denominations while his communitarian impulse helped define the boundaries of what was not acceptable in those larger organizations. Even after the fears and paranoia of the World War I era conspired to thrust Gourley back into some degree of Pentecostal fellowship, he chose a radical route—espousing a doctrine that seemed destined to disappoint. Though his legacy did not survive as an organization and his tragic death spelled a quick end to what promised to be a larger influence in the Midwest, he remains important as a representation of the degree of division and chaos within early Pentecostalism.[48] Always caustic and unbending, he failed to acculturate his views to those of the growing number of Pentecostal organizations. To the end, he preferred to find God's voice on the extreme edge. It is instructive that Tom Gourley always found a ready audience. Perhaps, on that same edge, historians will find much of the rest of Pentecostalism as well.

Alice E. Luce: A Visionary Victorian

Everett A. Wilson and Ruth Marshall Wilson

When Alice Luce died in October 1955, the term *Hispanic Pentecostalism*—a statement about Anglo-American Protestantism among Latin American cultural Catholics—still seemed an oxymoron. The same year, however, Donald McGavran, with the publication of *The Bridges of God,* laid the groundwork for the church growth movement, whose proponents soon began to draw attention to the Pentecostals' effectiveness in mobilizing marginal populations. The November 2, 1963, issue of *Time* magazine referred to the Hispanic Pentecostals as "the fastest growing church in the hemisphere." Thus, even as Alice Luce was inconspicuously ending her sixty-year ministry, the still largely overlooked movement in which she had invested her organizational efforts was showing signs of extraordinary vitality. In view of her initiative and effectiveness, Luce, who had once been known primarily for her devotional writing, has been identified as one of the architects of the burgeoning Hispanic Pentecostal movement. Without her vision for developing Latin leaders in the Assemblies of God, these districts—the largest Hispanic Pentecostal grouping in the United States—would likely have been less aggressive, institutionally structured, and connected with the Anglo movement than they are today.

The Preparatory Years

Luce spent her early years in the home of an Anglican vicar in Gloucester, England, the eldest of a large family with Huguenot roots. Her father, who had been influenced by Keswick teaching, taught her Greek and Hebrew. Deeply interested in missionary work, the elder Luce supported the Church Missionary Society (CMS), with which his daughter later affiliated. Alice Luce had a conversion experience at age ten and at some point felt called to Christian service. While she never married, her

Alice E. Luce, circa mid-1930s. Courtesy of Latin American Bible Institute, La Puente, California.

buoyant amiability, well-rounded personality, and wide circle of friends reflected a high level of personal fulfillment. She may have received a legacy or had other resources that brought her a measure of financial security. She lived for many years—and eventually died—in her own home in California.

Alice Luce never forsook her English upbringing. Her simple but correct attire, perky hats, grammatical English, sensitive but unaffected manner, and her breadth of perspective all reflected her fortunate origins. After high school she was educated at Cheltenham Ladies College, a normal school, and studied nursing and theology at the London Bible College in preparation for overseas service. She had an aesthetic sense. By the modest standards of her Pentecostal contemporaries, she was considered an accomplished organist, and her home in California was graced with several beautiful mementos she had brought from India. In her declining years, when a friend seemed surprised that she kept her fine china in the cupboard for daily use, Luce's response was, "Of course, that is what it is for."[1] She spoke French, Hindi, and Urdu, and not only learned Spanish in midlife but also sufficiently commanded the language to compose or translate smoothly flowing, grammatically correct articles, books, and lessons by the score.

India

In 1896, at age twenty-three, Alice E. Luce sailed for north India under appointment with the Anglican-sponsored CMS. Her destination was Azimgarh, a city of 19,000 inhabitants located near the sacred city of Benares, now known as Varanasi. As a center of Hindu intellectual and cultic life, the region was rich in tradition, which, to the Anglican missionaries, seemed especially heathen and resistant to their influence. Arriving with a small contingent of British missionaries, Luce stayed in Benares for a year of language study. In July of 1897, just days before Luce began her assignment, the missionary whom she had come to assist at the high school died of cholera.

The new missionary promptly engaged in home meetings in *zenanas,* the section of private homes restricted to women. As for the influence of the missionary community, "the high school has been the means of educating most of the principal men and many of the shopkeepers in the town of Azimgarh and its neighborhood," her supervisor reported, "and these are in consequence more or less friendly to the Mission."[2] The station had not known a male missionary for upwards of twenty years. The tedium, frustrations, and unpleasantness of missionary work may be inferred by the annual entries of the *Proceedings.* The reports for 1898 and 1899 indicated that Luce and her coworkers had prolonged absences from ill health. In 1900 Luce had to leave her work to replace the director of the Benares girls school, who had taken sick. Nevertheless, before leaving for a furlough in England in February 1902, Luce summed up her first four years of service by insisting that "the joy of the Master's service would more than make up for all one could have to give up at home."[3]

In fact, the religious work was disappointingly difficult and slow. Conversions were infrequent and the zenanas were closed to the missionaries during Luce's absence because of rumors that they poisoned the wells. The year following Luce's return, an outbreak of the plague forced the inhabitants of Azimgarh to evacuate the city entirely. When dead mice were found in the teachers' room, the staff took refuge in tents and grass huts and did not resume work again until mid-1904.[4]

In the spring of 1905 Luce was made the acting principal of the Queen

Victoria High School. While the educational oversight was left to another missionary, Luce functioned as the school administrator. Noting the progress achieved during the academic year, the CMS report commented on an accompanying revival. "Nearly every girl in the school received definite blessing" and, at the conclusion of the special spiritual emphasis, some gathered on their own initiative to seek for "yet fuller blessing."[5]

In retrospect, however, Alice Luce looked on her work in India as having limited spiritual effectiveness. "For many years I was teaching both in England and India and more than once I had charge of Normal Schools where we taught Theory of Teaching and Methods of Teaching to the native Christian teachers, whom we were training to work among their own people. I always classed those among my secular subjects and did not connect them with the Bible in any particular way."[6] The most important result of her tenure in India may have been the reformulation of her own view of missionary strategies. She came to recognize the need to prepare Indians themselves to assume positions of leadership and focused to a greater degree on the spiritual development of the people under her influence.

Baptism in the Holy Spirit

In view of the widespread attention given to a series of unusual religious developments in India prior to and during Alice Luce's tenure as a missionary, she could hardly have been indifferent to the possibility of having such a climactic experience herself. Gary McGee has compiled a list of the revivals that for several decades had erupted in India. He also notes that the Welsh revival of 1904 received considerable attention in India. "Through newspapers, booklets, journals, and other missions periodicals, missionaries and Christians of major language groups were enabled to keep abreast of the events."[7] Whether or not Luce was among the missionaries whom McGee described as persons who "lived on the fringes of the missionary community," praying for paranormal phenomena, by her own account she was spiritually aspiring. Luce later related how an Indian woman asked her whether the signs referred to in Mark 16:17–18 were meant for today. "I told her in faith I was sure [that God] did mean them to be fulfilled, and that I was also sure they were being fulfilled even down to the present moment, though I had not then heard of all [Luce's emphasis] of them. It was not long after that when I heard of the Latter-day Outpouring of the Spirit and received it myself."[8]

Judging from the proximity of Azimgarh to the conference sponsored by denominationally unaffiliated missionary Albert Norton in 1910, McGee concludes that Luce probably experienced Holy Spirit baptism at a Pentecostal conference in Fyzabad, North India, in February of that year.[9] Luce later described her climactic experience:

> Never can I forget what the receiving of the Latter-rain outpouring of the Spirit meant to me. I was far away in the north of India, having been there a good many years, and only knowing by hearsay how God was pouring out His Spirit in [the United States] and other western lands. He had been awakening a great hunger and thirst in me for more of Himself, and had been dealing with me in a special way for months. Humbling, searching and breaking me down lower and yet lower at His feet. Then when the Spirit came in fullness as on the Day of Pentecost, it seemed to me as if He took me by the hand and led me into the very heart of God the Father, to show me how He was rejoicing over Jesus, the Son of His love. It was (as is every new step in the Christian life is) a new vision of Jesus; but it was from the point of view of the heart of God, where the Holy Spirit told me I had now come to abide.[10]

Luce later reported that, with increasing accounts of Pentecostal phenomena, defamatory literature appeared over the south of India. "The whole movement was attributed to the devil, and many absurd and ridiculous writings were written by our enemies, which no sane person would believe."[11] Since she quoted in some detail narratives about responses to Pentecostal phenomena, there is reason to suppose that she experienced both the enthusiasm and the opprobrium attached to those events.

Luce left India in 1912 after a critical illness. Accounts attribute her poor health to various causes, but at the time she suffered severe, debilitating fevers.[12] Upon recovering in England, she was lent to the Zenana Bible and Medical Mission (later known as the Bible and Medical Missionary Fellowship), under whose auspices she went to Vancouver, British Columbia, in 1913. She resigned her CMS appointment the following year.

There is room for speculation as to whether poor health was Luce's only concern. In 1914, the last of her sixteen years of service, the CMS *Proceedings* mentioned her resignation without comment, despite the effusive commendation given other CMS missionaries upon their retirement. There can be little doubt, at least, that she had begun to develop new perspectives on evangelism. She later recounted having come across the writings of Roland Allen, the Anglican author of *Missionary Methods, Saint Paul's or Ours* (1912). "When I first went out as a missionary to India, I accepted without hesitation the methods of the board under which I was working, and went on laboring for many years along those lines. Then a book was written, whose author's name I cannot now recall, entitled, *Missionary Methods, Paul's or Ours?* We missionaries all read it, and thought the writer somewhat visionary and impractical; but that book first opened my eyes to the diametrical distinction between our method of working and those of the New Testament."[13]

In view of the comprehensive exposition of missionary methods given by Allen, as well as the time-honored emphases on the establishment of the "indigenous church" by Rufus Anderson (1796–1880), John Nevius (1829–93), and other Protestant missionaries of the preceding decades, Luce hardly needed to devise her own missiology. Prior to reading Allen's work, she appears to have reached a crisis in her own experience that facilitated a radical shift in her thinking. While various motives—disaffection with the progress or conditions of her work, her own maturity, some crisis or disappointment, or the encouragement of friends—may have moved her toward such a conclusion, Luce linked her changing attitude toward the CMS to her own spiritual development.

Some years after being baptized in the Spirit, Luce came to believe that there was such a thing as "doing apostolic work along apostolic lines." Presumably, she accepted Allen's thesis that the New Testament provided an adequate blueprint for modern missionary undertakings. Having developed some disdain for the plodding institutional approaches that had characterized CMS efforts in India, she apparently wished to accelerate and intensify evangelization, a position like that taken by Donald McGavran, who also would serve as a missionary in India. Like Allen previously and McGavran later, Luce saw the formation of self-sufficient congregations and the cultivation of leadership within the community as prescribed biblical principles. "As a humble worker in the great missionary field, there has been a great burden on my heart for months past to learn from our Great Teacher how to more closely pattern my work and methods after His Word, and to reject all plans and ideas that are not His best. To this end I have been studying the life and teaching of Paul, our great model missionary."[14] She further indicated that her previous work had been unduly restricted and vowed not to be "drawn into those denominational methods which have no scriptural warrant, but learning in ever-increasing humility to depend absolutely on the guidance of the Holy Spirit, and let Him work."[15] In apostolic times, Luce noted, those who had established the church, its leaders and pillars, were called to be its first missionaries to the heathen from a Pentecostal church.

After leaving Vancouver, Luce resided for the next three years in California, during which she was associated with Florence Murcutt, a Jewish medical doctor whom she apparently had known previously.[16] Murcutt, who had built a home in Long Beach, California, prior to the outbreak of World War I, was in Vancouver about the time Luce resigned her position with the CMS. The two women went to Texas briefly to consult with Henry Ball, who in 1915 was just beginning the Assemblies of God work among Mexicans along the border.[17] There they were ordained as Assemblies of God ministers. At the time, Murcutt gave her home address as Manhattan Beach, California. During this interval both Luce and Murcutt contributed articles to the *Pentecostal Evangel,* and soon the women began a collaborative effort that occupied the remainder of their careers. At age forty-two, Luce appeared able-bodied, energetic, and determined to evangelize Mexico.

Texas, Mexico, and California

In 1917 Luce worked in Kingsville, Texas, with Henry Ball. Her report in the *Pentecostal Evangel* noted that the Lord had graciously given her the Spanish language, enabling her to preach and teach. In addition to her pastoral and evangelistic work, she functioned as a publicist and fund-raiser. She wrote that she had received funds from the estate of a friend for the construction of a tabernacle building and that Raymond T. Richey's congregation in Houston was also supporting their efforts. In Ball's absence Luce maintained the work in Kingsville and kept the readers of the *Pentecostal Evangel* informed about the progress of his efforts in Matamorros, just across the border from Brownsville.[18]

A major advance in their work occurred when a convert on his own initiative took the message to his family in Los Indios, a border settlement. Luce detailed how this development fueled confidence that the Pentecostal work was dynamic, growing, and hardly dependent on a resident missionary. In the light of these and other successes, Luce saw as her main task the conservation and enhancement of the growing work.[19] Moreover, although she was dependent on Henry Ball for the leadership of the work in south Texas, she had a vision for entering Mexico on her own. "We need your prayers for the Mexican work very specially at this time, for it is a time of change and of development. Do ask that we may be very clearly guided in every step, and that God will make clear what is His best for each one of the workers."[20]

In November 1917, Luce reported working in Monterrey, Mexico. She was accompanied by Florence Murcutt, Sunshine Marshall, and another companion. Despite considerable opposition, she was able to attract an audience.

> The Lord has been opening up the work before us in a truly marvelous manner, sending people to our windows all hours of the day to ask for Gospels or to inquire about the way of salvation, and giving us as many as we could seat at our nightly meetings, with large crowds standing outside the three wide windows, listening most attentively, and taking away Gospels with them. There are some who we believe are really saved, and others are very near; while others again, we hope, will soon begin to seek definitely for the baptism of the Holy Spirit. One young sister who is seeking with all her heart lay under the Spirit's power last Wednesday from 10 a.m. till 6, praising God all the time without a moment's intermission—a thing which would have been utterly impossible to any human power.[21]

But clearly the work was tenuous. Luce was convinced that to be effective her coworkers needed to become proficient in Spanish immediately. Moreover, she lamented in the same report that Mexico was morally decadent and politically corrupt. "Brethren, the Brethren, pray for us! This is a most critical time in the work in this city. The enemy is doing his very utmost to run us out, not only by the outward opposition, but also by his attacks on our bodies through the climate."[22] Reports that a military officer had designs on Sunshine Marshall may have made the women concerned about her safety.

Whatever the reason, the missionaries found it necessary to leave after only a brief time, reportedly at the insistence of the American consul. On their return to Texas, Marshall married Henry Ball and began a lengthy, productive ministry. Luce continued on to the Pacific Coast to take up missionary work among the expatriate Mexicans in Los Angeles. Whether because of having a home on the West Coast, because of a desire to organize her own work, or because the need and opportunities for missionary ministry were as ample in California as in Texas, Luce launched out on her own, largely leaving behind the work undertaken by Henry Ball in Texas, except for providing his school with instructional materials.

Luce and Murcutt quickly settled into the task of promoting the Hispanic work in California. "After visiting the various Mexican assemblies in the northern part of the state in January," Luce wrote, "Sister Murcutt and I retired to Los Angeles, which the Lord seemed clearly to show was to be our headquarters, and where we have over 60,000 Mexicans in this one county alone." In the center of the Mexican quarter, they rented a house with a large hall seating two hundred. Called "La Placita," it eventually became part of the landmark tourist center Olvera Street. "It was in about as dirty and tumbledown a condition as you could imagine, but the Lord has graciously sent us the money (over $1900) that we needed to thoroughly fumigate, clean, whitewash, repair and furnish it."[23] The women shared part of the building with the Prestons, a married couple, and their children, who joined them in their effort to establish a church. Luce hoped to begin a campaign with Francisco Olazábal, a well-educated, former Methodist minister who had recently been brought into the movement as a result of the influence of George and Carrie Judd Montgomery.[24]

The anticipated evangelistic meeting went well, Luce wrote in June, 1918. "Brother Olazábal from San Francisco has been here for a month's special campaign. And God has used his faithful messages to bring the light on Pentecost to many, especially those who had known him here before in the Methodist Episcopal Church when he used to criticize and persecute 'this way.' They began to say, as of old about Saul of Tarsus, 'that he now preacheth the faith which once he destroyed,' and to inquire what had made the change in him."[25] Luce hoped not only for a growing congregation but also for workers who would share her vision and assume the burden for extending the Pentecostal message. "We get good crowds at the open air services," she reported, "but very few follow us into the hall as they are so afraid of being hypnotized or else absolutely careless and gospel-hardened." She was also concerned about proselytizers who influenced her converts. "Pray that the Lord will raise up a real band of overcomers in this wicked city who will be ready to go all the way with Him and who will be kept true to Jesus and the teaching of His Word and not led astray by the many false teachers."[26] According to Clifton Holland, the Oneness doctrine, among Luce's concerns, was preached among the Hispanic Pentecostals in southern California well before Luce arrived.[27] As a result, Luce insisted on appropriate training for converts, all of whom were poten-tial leaders. "The minister whose Bible study is shallow and careless . . . will find that his people will develop a shallow, backboneless Christian char-acter, unstable and unreliable, easily moved about by every wind of false doctrine or error. The minister who takes time to dig into the Word and to study how to make it living and active to his hearers in the power of the Spirit of God will raise up a people rooted and grounded in the faith."[28]

Rather than lamenting the mobility of her migrant parishioners, Luce saw in the Mexicans' patterns of seasonal employment an opportunity to extend the message. "The summer time has been a special opportunity for 'scattering' as the Mexicans of this state move around to the various fruit-picking centers; and in the case of our Christian families we trust it has been true that 'they that were scattered abroad went everywhere preaching the Word.' They certainly have been testifying for Jesus wherever they went, distributing numbers of Spanish tracts and Gospels, and from one place they sent to me for some hymnbooks that they might hold meetings."[29]

When the scattered flock returned to the area the next winter, the Health Department prohibited public meetings because of the raging influenza epidemic of 1918–19. "Our time has been taken up more than ever in visiting the Christians and those seeking salvation, as well as praying for the sick." Already, according to Luce, she had gathered a congregation of about sixty members, all but one of whom had been filled with the Spirit. Despite considerable opposition, she was aware that the fledgling movement was spreading among the network of relatives, friends, and neighbors of the converts. "The light is spreading in many of the villages and Mexican settle-ments within a radius of twenty miles of this city. We are having the joy of receiving calls not only to pray for the sick, but to visit whole families in various places who are anxious about their souls. So we prove once more in joyful certainty that all things work together for good to them that love God."[30]

Luce the Educator

In 1921 Alice Luce published a three-part missionary series in the *Pentecostal Evangel* to promote the indigenous church philosophy set forth by Roland Allen. These policies were adopted by successive Assemblies of God missionary executives, beginning with Noel Perkin (1926–59) and continued by J. Philip Hogan (1960–90) and his successors. Given the subsequent growth of the Assemblies of God worldwide, Luce's exposition of the sovereignty of the Holy Spirit to initiate and develop the church without undue outside influence, control, and resources appeared timely and strategic.

In 1921 Luce and Murcutt went to San Francisco to assist Robert J. Craig in his newly established Glad Tidings Bible Institute (GTBI) in the Fillmore District. There they taught for a year and ministered in Spanish-speaking churches before returning to southern California. "The Lord is giving us much encouragement in the Spanish work here with some very bright conversions," Luce reported.[31] She continued to teach intensive or summer courses at Glad Tidings for several years. The missionaries who went out from GTBI, in large part because of her influence, went dispro-portionately to Latin American countries.

The Hispanic Pentecostal movement within the Assemblies of God lost its strongest voice, Francisco Olazábal, in 1923 when a group of ministers who felt that they were restricted by their affiliation with a primarily Anglo group withdrew to form their own organization. The accounts from the perspective of the seceding churches detail the grievances of the Hispanic pastors, notably the discrimination that they received from the Anglo missionaries and executive officers and the refusal of the Assemblies of God to grant the Mexican pastors autonomy and financial support commensu-rate with that of the Anglos.[32] Whatever her role, Luce's unfolding ministry among Hispanics, and especially her encouragement of Hispanic leader-ship and the affection she received from her colleagues in the Latin churches, speak for themselves. While Demetrio Bazán, who attributed his conversion to Luce, at first joined Olazábal's new organization as the editor of its official publication, he soon resigned to rejoin the Assemblies of God and became the first superintendent of the group's newly created Latin

American District in 1939. The memoirs of Nellie Bazán convey the thinking of other Hispanic pastors that their separation from Olazábal had to do with confidence in the emerging leadership—specifically, uncertainty about the new group's form of organization.[33]

In 1923, Luce, accompanied by Florence Murcutt, returned to her homeland, where the women visited Pentecostal congregations in Wales and spoke at the Whitsuntide Pentecostal Convention at Crosskeys, Monmouthshire.[34] In Sudbrook they recruited three members of a Pentecostal family to attend GTBI in San Francisco. The Williams brothers, Richard and Ralph, entered Glad Tidings in the fall of 1923 and were followed by their sister Olive a year later. When the two men graduated in 1925, they and their wives joined Luce in the establishment of a church and a school in San Diego.[35]

Development of the Hispanic Work

On their return to the United States, Luce and Murcutt reported that the churches were doing well. "The work here [in Los Angeles] seems to be in splendid shape, the mighty power of God falls in every meeting; the assembly has just about trebled in size since I have been away."[36] Similarly, Luce reported sustained growth in San Francisco during the year.

In 1924 two hundred pastors and other workers registered at the Seventh Annual Convention of the Latin American Pentecostal churches held in San Jose, California. The group was multinational, with Puerto Ricans, Mexicans, other Latin Americans, as well as Portuguese, in attendance. Whereas there had been only two organized churches in 1917, forty churches were operating seven years later.[37] At the General Council of the Assemblies of God in San Francisco in 1931, Luce related the development of the work among Spanish-speaking groups, and she continued to be a liaison between the Hispanic and Anglo churches for another quarter century. In 1935 there were two hundred Hispanic ministers on the Assemblies of God roster. By 1939 the number of established churches in the United States had risen to 170, besides 125 in Mexico.[38]

The contribution Luce made to the growth and development of the Hispanic Pentecostal churches can only be inferred. There is no doubting that she remained a primary interpreter of the movement to the denomination by the series of articles she published in the *Pentecostal Evangel*, including "Portions for Whom Nothing Is Prepared" (1922), "The Strangers within Our Gates" (1927), and "Pentecost on the Mexican Border" (1939).[39] While her contribution was only one among many, her influence seems to have been strategic. Soon after her death, the Latin American District, led by Demetrio Bazán, divided in two by forming a new Spanish Eastern District. The growth and development of these churches has continued to the present, with the formation of eight different regional districts throughout the United States and Puerto Rico.

The Latin American Bible Institute

In 1926 Luce began the Latin American Bible Institute (LABI) in San Diego. She also contributed to a school with the same name that Henry Ball started simultaneously in Texas by providing much of its curriculum and educational materials. The two institutions, both of which still operate, have trained hundreds of Hispanic Pentecostal leaders. These alumni include well-known evangelists Robert Fierro, Nicky Cruz, and Sonny Arguizoni (LABI California); and Juan Romero, Demetrio Bazán, and Simón Franco (LABI Texas); as well as a number of other officers of the Latin American Districts of the Assemblies of God. The schools also produced several superintendents of the Mexican Assemblies of God, including Rodolfo Orozco (1930–40), his son Juan C. Orozco (1944–60), and Rubén J. Arévalo (1940–44). In 1935 LABI was moved from San Diego to nearby La Mesa, California, and in 1941, to East Los Angeles. The school moved to its present site in La Puente, California, in 1947. By the 1940s Luce reported seventy graduates from the West Coast school, in addition to several hundred who had completed her correspondence courses.[40] Despite the challenges of developing a school without adequate resources and qualified personnel, LABI continued to produce many men and women who contributed importantly to the movement. Although Luce raised funds for the school and served in an advisory capacity, she remained in the background and encouraged younger men and women to assume places of leadership.

In 1927 Alice Luce and Florence Murcutt constructed a church building in Manhattan Beach, California. They were still pastors of the congregation in 1929 when the remaining debt on the structure was retired. Throughout the 1930s the church remained a center of British culture, as

Englishman Arthur W. Frodsham, older brother of Stanley H. Frodsham, then the editor of the *Pentecostal Evangel,* succeeded Luce and Murcutt as the pastor.[41]

Luce's Later Years

Throughout the 1930s Alice Luce continued to produce materials for publication. In addition to the courses of study she prepared for the Bible institutes, she wrote regularly for the *Luz Apostólica,* the organ of the Latin American District of the Assemblies of God. She also wrote for the *Pentecostal Evangel* and edited the Gospel Publishing House quarterly teachers' manuals for the senior and intermediate classes. In addition, she translated several of her studies from English to Spanish and revised her published books, *The Messenger and His Message, Pictures of Pentecost in the Old Testament,* and *The Little Flock in the Last Days.* Her literary output, had she contributed nothing more, would have been sufficient to have made her an important asset to the early Hispanic Pentecostal work. Nor were her publications whimsical. Her textbook on the geography of the Bible (which she wrote in Spanish as *La Geografía de la Biblia*) was for that era a remarkably sophisticated treatment.

Luce's major publications, her books and strategic articles on Latin America, more than mere promotional pieces, epitomized her views on Christian faith and the Pentecostal experience. Luce saw the work of the Spirit as a grand design, a comprehensive program of human salvation, which in the last days would draw out a select group of spiritually sensitive souls. These believers must be well prepared for the assigned task, as her *The Messenger and His Message* clearly taught, but the impetus of one's ministry was clearly reliance on the Spirit. To participate in this privileged empowering for service, the Pentecostal, like the Old Testament Nazarite, abstained voluntarily from that which was "superfluous, injurious, and a bad example." As a woman's long hair was a symbol of submission to her husband, the long hair of the Nazarite represented his absolute surrender to the will of God, the attitude required of the Pentecostal believer. Luce depicted the Holy Spirit, like wine in the natural realm, as the Christian's source of refreshing. "How important it is for the prospective missionary to learn this lesson before going forth into the dry and barren deserts of heathenism," she insisted. "He must learn not to depend on meetings, on Christian fellowship or on 'earthly props' for his spiritual life; these will all be absent in the mission field, and the only life that will avail him there is that whose springs are in God Himself, feeding on the hidden manna, drinking at the upper springs."[42] While Luce supported expressions of fervor in meetings, she saw in Pentecostalism something more profound. Her *Pictures of Pentecost in the Old Testament* reveals her comprehensive view of the work of the Spirit, of which the New Testament and latter rain outpourings were a fulfillment and a continuation.[43] Already, in 1927, however, Luce detected a spiritual declension among Pentecostals and urged a return to higher levels of commitment. Nevertheless, she believed that the revival had not reached its apex. The movement's greatest impact lay ahead.

Late in their ministries, Luce and Murcutt traveled to Fiji and Australia, then returned to take up residence in Inglewood, California. Murcutt died in 1935, while Luce survived another twenty years. For the remainder of her life she collaborated with several other women to promote the formation of a missionary society for women among the Anglo churches of southern California. In 1947 her article "What Is the Use of Our Women's Missionary Councils?" was published in the *Pentecostal Evangel* to promote the ministry of women nationally.[44] This organization, which spread rapidly throughout the Assemblies of God, intensified the missionary impact of the denomination's churches.

Luce continued her writing and other efforts supportive of the Spanish-speaking work after she celebrated her seventieth birthday in 1943. Agustín (Augie) López, a southern California businessman, recalled holding street meetings with Luce in the early 1950s. He and his sisters would arrive in the family car to take her and her pump organ to a lot in east Los Angeles where they would hold services under an awning. López would play his saxophone, accompanied by his sisters' accordions. The group would sing gospel songs and give brief testimonies and messages. López remembered that passersby would stop to comment on how well the "white-haired lady played the organ."[45]

Early in the 1950s Luce sold her Inglewood home and had a modest house built in Los Angeles, opposite the site of Bethel Temple, an Assemblies of God congregation, where she could walk to meetings. She shared the home with Jovita Bonilla, who had become Luce's assistant and companion, helping her both in maintaining her home and in her work at the Latin American Bible Institute. Before her death she arranged for

Bonilla to occupy the house during her lifetime, after which it would be given to LABI. One day in 1955 Luce called her friends Gordon and Elizabeth Marshall to her home in Los Angeles. The Marshalls, part of the Manhattan Beach congregation, had supported Luce's ministry for many years. Luce, now eighty-three, told them that she had cancer and had purchased a plot at the newly opened Forest Lawn Cemetery in Hollywood Hills. The entry in Elizabeth Marshall's diary that day reads: "We feel like we are losing our mother." On October 27, 1955, two funeral services were conducted at Bethel Temple, Los Angeles—the first, at 8:00 A.M., conducted in Spanish, the other, at 2:00 P.M., conducted in English. The pastor of Bethel Temple, Arne Vick, preached at the afternoon service, with participation by Robert Fierro, Demetrio Bazán, Simón Franco, and other representatives of the Latin American churches.[46]

The Legacy of Alice Luce

By the time of her death, Luce had become a spiritual icon who epitomized competence, character, faith, and dedication. In retrospect, her personal strength appears to have emerged from her idealistic youth and her disciplined life as a missionary. Her hazardous experiences prepared her for leadership and forged a personality that was at the same time practical and visionary, decisive and considerate. If she was composed and reliable, she remained warm and personable, as evidenced by her many friends and devoted followers. But other questions remain, such as what motivated and sustained her? And how did a person of her intellect and gentility find so much common ground with the "disinherited" men and women with whom she associated in the early movement? Obviously a strong personality, she nevertheless must have had many personal struggles, times of reflection, temptations, aspirations, disappointments, and doubts that were sublimated or submerged in religious intensity.

Alice Luce can hardly be portrayed stereotypically. She was quite different from other early Pentecostal women like Maria Woodworth-Etter and Aimee Semple McPherson, who were characterized by a dramatic flair. She was forceful but evidently not officious, at times appearing almost retiring in her desire to remain in the background. Victor De León described her as "the type of person that worked for the Lord, not expecting recognition."[47] Augie Lopez referred to her as a "back-row" person who tried to remain inconspicuous even in a group photograph or by taking a seat in the rear when attending a church service.[48] She was independent in thought and action without being aloof. She mixed unselfconsciously with people of varied social circumstances, appearing as much at home in humble as in comfortable surroundings. Among men and women who had little preparation, she was well read, an effective writer who was aware of the secular world about her. During an era of debate about the inerrancy of the scriptures, she confidently referred to modern or alternative renderings of biblical texts, the Revised Version, the Weymouth New Testament, the Hindi and Spanish versions, and the Hebrew text of the Old Testament. In her writings she cited the Catholic mystic Madame Guyon (1648–1717) and the Baptist missionary to Burma Adoniram Judson (1788–1850) with equal admiration.

However incongruent, Luce, along with several other notable pioneers, helped lay the foundation of one of the movement's most important expressions, its growth among the Spanish-speaking peoples of Mexico, the Southwest, and the Pacific Coast. Her efforts were undertaken during years of hardship and limited results when there was little promise of success and when only a satisfying personal experience, hope of the Second Coming, and the urgency to complete the evangelistic task gave the movement its impulse. Her depth of conviction and clear vision were strategic at a time when for many observers the Pentecostal message of healing, holiness, and hope was often eclipsed by emotional excesses, factionalism, and inadequate resources. Estéban Camarillo, with whom she was associated for several years at LABI, attributes the effectiveness of the Assemblies of God to Luce's early emphasis on congregational autonomy and the training of leaders. He contrasted Luce's approaches to groups with centralized, autocratic leadership. At least more democratically organized groups, unlike those that were based on dominant personalities, were spared some of the problems of succession and the transference of power.[49] But how did a British-born spinster, a long-term Anglican missionary to India, emerge in midlife as a leading figure among early Latin American Pentecostals? An even more fascinating question is how she became so endeared to her followers to be referred to by a Mexican historian as "synonymous with the Latin American people."[50] The answer given by Victor De León is that Luce's motives were transparent. "Though a silent leader, her desire was to create leaders. And this she did very well."[51]

Ultimately, one must conclude that Alice Luce found a place in the hearts of many men and women, both Hispanic and Anglo, who benefited from her quiet competence, gentle firmness, and inspiring faith. While she faced strong opposition in her work, never overcame the limitations faced at the time by women, and was surrounded by competing sectarian factions, she managed to retain her unwavering focus and composed equanimity.

Although she was unique, Alice Luce provides considerable insight into the motivation and intention of early Pentecostals. A part of the revival on three continents for forty-five years, she was both produced by and a producer of the movement. She was an activist, sometimes moving on to a new effort before having completed an earlier project. Moreover, she maintained an extensive network of associates, both English-speaking and Hispanic. She was linked to many of the early Pentecostal leaders, especially those on the West Coast and in Latin America. Her publications reflect the theological foundations on which the movement was built; the esteem she received from her Pentecostal colleagues reveals the role played by select women in this formative period; and her approaches help expose the expectations and strategies of the founding generation. Her references to the entire scope of church history, and especially to Moody, Finney, Wesley, and other revivalists, indicate that at least some first-generation Pentecostals saw themselves as heirs of an ongoing tradition, albeit a revival movement whose tempo was increasing in light of the imminent Second Coming. There can be little doubt about the magnitude of the contribution Luce made to fledgling Pentecostalism—only wonder that the early movement was influenced by such an unlikely figure in such unforeseen ways.

EVERETT A. WILSON AND RUTH MARSHALL WILSON

Francisco Olazábal: Charisma, Power, and Faith Healing in the Borderlands

Gastón Espinosa

A religious revolution is taking place in the Latino community in the United States and Puerto Rico today. Recent studies on Latino religiosity have shattered previously held stereotypes that to be Latino is to be Roman Catholic. In *One Nation under God: Religion in Contemporary Society*, Barry Kosmin and Seymour Lachman found that 66 percent of Latinos now claim Roman Catholic allegiances and 25 percent claim Protestant allegiances.[1] Supporting this seismic shift in Latino religiosity, Andrew Greeley estimates that more than sixty thousand Latinos are leaving the Roman Catholic Church every year in the United States for evangelical/Pentecostal Christianity. He goes on to argue that almost one million U.S. Latinos have "defected" from the Roman Catholic Church to evangelical/Pentecostal Christianity since 1973. He calls this mass defection "an ecclesiastical failure of an unprecedented proportion."[2] Almost all the scholarship on this shift in Latino religiosity has argued that it is a relatively new post-1960 phenomenon. Contrary to popular opinion, this seismic shift began in the late nineteenth and early twentieth centuries. The Latino Pentecostal movement in general and the ministry of Francisco Olazábal (1886–1937) in particular served as one stream in the growth of religious pluralism during the 1920s and 1930s, when the first nationwide mass conversions from Roman Catholicism to Protestantism took place in the United States, Mexico, and Puerto Rico.

Francisco Olazábal was a major catalyst in the shift. He not only contributed to the birth and/or development of at least fourteen denominations by 1937 but also converted tens of thousands of Latinos throughout the United States, Mexico, and Puerto Rico to the Pentecostal

Francisco Olazábal, circa 1927. Courtesy of the Latin American Council of Christian Churches, Brownsville, Texas.

movement during his more than thirty-year ministry. The key to Olazábal's success and rise to national prominence was his healing ministry and his ability to exercise charisma.[3] Olazábal was a Latino Pentecostal charismatic faith healer who used his power of healing to attract an estimated 250,000 Mexicans, Puerto Ricans, Anglo-Americans, Italians, and blacks to his evangelistic services throughout North America and the Latin Caribbean.

Olazábal's life and ministry provides a window into the dynamics of early Pentecostalism. His story demonstrates the struggles that early Latino Pentecostal ministers faced in Anglo-American Pentecostalism, in American society, and among themselves. Perhaps more important, Olazábal's story challenges the unspoken binary interpretation of American religious history and Pentecostalism as essentially a black-and-white story, showing that the Latino Pentecostal movement began much earlier and was much larger and widespread than has been generally believed. Finally, Olazábal's story invites scholars to revise and retell the story of American religions from the periphery, a story of south to north, not just east to west. When the lives of Latino religious leaders like Olazábal are taken seriously, the old paradigm of restricting the story of American religions to U.S. geopolitical borders and boundaries will have to give way to a new paradigm of North American postcolonial religious history.

Birth of Charisma: Olazábal, Catholicism, Methodism, and the Assemblies of God

The Latino Pentecostal movement traces its origins back to the fabled Azusa Street revival in Los Angeles in April 1906. Mexicans like Abundio and Rosa López attended the revival until a conflict between William J. Seymour (1870–1922) and the Mexican contingent led to the de facto expulsion of Mexicans from the mission. This expulsion contributed to the growth of the Latino Pentecostal movement in the Americas. In 1913 the fledgling Latino Pentecostal movement was torn asunder by the Oneness, or Jesus Only, controversy near Los Angeles. This controversy split the Pentecostal world into Trinitarian and Oneness camps, the latter of which denied the classic doctrine of the Trinity and instead posited that Jesus manifested himself as God the Father, God the Son, and God the Holy Spirit. In 1915 H. C. Ball, Rodolfo Orozco, and Alice Luce founded what is now known as the Hispanic Districts of the Assemblies of God, and in 1916 Francisco Llorente and Antonio Castañeda Nava formally organized the Oneness denomination called the Apostolic Assembly of the Faith in Christ Jesus. Almost every indigenous Latino Pentecostal denomination in the United States founded prior to 1960 traces its genealogy one way or another back to one of these two movements. The next major turning point in the history of the Latino Pentecostal movement came in 1917 when a tall Mexican Methodist evangelist named Francisco Olazábal joined the Pentecostal movement.[4]

Francisco Olazábal was born into a traditional pious Catholic family in El Verano, Sinaloa, Mexico, on October 12, 1886. Although little is known about his father, Juan Olazábal (ca. 1851–1901), we do know that Francisco's mother, Refugio Velázquez, was a devout Catholic. She nurtured Francisco in the rich and polyvibrant world of Mexican folk Catholicism. From her he learned to pray the rosary and to the saints, venerate Our Lady of Guadalupe, light colorful prayer candles at their home altar, and honor the local priest. Popular Mexican Catholicism taught that sickness and disease were not caused by chance or microbes but rather by evil spirits and spells cast by witches *(brujas)*, spiritualists, and angry village saints. Olazábal grew up in a setting where the supernatural world was alive and divine healing was an accepted part of everyday life.[5] There is good reason to believe that he heard stories about the famous Mexican folk healers like María Teresa Urrea from his home state of Sinaloa and Don Pedrito Jaramillo from the nearby state of San Luis Postosí.[6]

Francisco Olazábal's spiritual world took a dramatic turn away from popular Mexican Catholicism when in 1898 his mother converted to evangelical Protestantism in Mazatlán, Mexico. She became a lay Methodist evangelist. Refugio took Francisco on her evangelistic journeys throughout the rugged Sierra Madre Mountains of north-central Mexico. Around 1903 Olazábal turned away from his mother's evangelistic ministry when he went through a rebellious streak. He traveled north to visit his relatives in San Francisco, California. Plans to sail the world as a mariner abruptly ended after he rededicated his life to Jesus Christ in 1904 through the evangelistic work of George Montgomery, a member of the Christian and Missionary Alliance. After his rededication, he returned to Mexico.[7]

Once back in Mexico, Olazábal returned to the Methodist Church. He attended the Wesleyan School of Theology in San Luis Potosí, Mexico, from 1908 to 1910. There he came under the influence of the Anglo-American Methodist leader F. A. Onderdonk. During this time Olazábal conducted small-scale evangelistic campaigns in the Mexican states of Durango, San Luis Potosí, Zacatecas, and across the U.S. border in Texas. As the fires of the Mexican Revolution (1910–20) engulfed the nation, hundreds of thousands of Mexicans fled across the U.S. border, including Olazábal, who assumed the pastorate of a small Mexican Methodist church in El Paso, Texas, in 1911.[8]

While in Texas, Olazábal met an Anglo-American Methodist woman who encouraged him to study at the Moody Bible Institute, her alma mater. Following her advice, Olazábal trekked north to Chicago around 1912, where he enrolled. It was here that he developed his English skills and read Bible commentaries, church history, and Charles Finney's *Lectures on Revivals of Religion*. At Moody, Olazábal studied under now-famous evangelical leaders like Reuben A. Torrey and James M. Gray. Torrey taught him that the baptism with the Holy Spirit was a necessary part of the Christian life. However, Torrey differed with Pentecostals (a group he criticized) because he did not believe that tongues was the initial evidence of Holy Spirit baptism and that one had to speak in tongues to prove they had received the baptism.

After Torrey left Moody to pastor the Church of the Open Door in Los Angeles, he asked Olazábal to leave the school and minister to the growing Mexican population in Los Angeles. Olazábal accepted the offer but later ran into conflict with Torrey's teaching that Holy Spirit baptism was a definite experience. Olazábal was not persuaded that the baptism added anything important to the Christian life. After parting with Torrey, Olazábal joined the Spanish-speaking Methodist Episcopal Church in California. In 1914, Olazábal married Macrina Orozco, the daughter of a family of prominent Protestant ministers in Mexico. Two years later, the Methodist Church ordained Olazábal to the ministry.[9]

Methodist Episcopal Church leaders claimed that he was doing "splendid" and "valuable" work in southern California. In one year he raised thousands of dollars to build a new massive mission-style church in 1915 in Pasadena, California. Shortly thereafter Olazábal was transferred north to Sacramento and San Francisco, where he assumed the pastorate of two Spanish Methodist churches.[10]

After moving to San Francisco, Olazábal ran into George and Carrie Montgomery. To Olazábal's surprise, they had become Pentecostals, a group he often criticized from the pulpit. After initially rejecting the Montgomerys' newfound message, he later became persuaded that Holy Spirit baptism was a second definite experience and a necessary part of the Christian life. He also became convinced that divine healing was available to all who asked in faith. Olazábal's belief was put to the test when the Montgomerys and a few other people laid hands on and prayed for his wife, who was suffering from a physical ailment. Olazábal claimed that Macrina was healed as a result of their prayers. Olazábal soon realized that his belief in speaking in tongues, the gifts of the Holy Spirit, and divine healing placed him at odds with the Methodist Church. For this reason, he decided to leave the denomination in order to preach the "full Gospel." In response to Methodist criticism of his newfound beliefs, Olazábal stated, "I was blind, but now I see. You cannot make me believe that there is something wrong in my head now, there is rather something right in my heart . . . I am not going to try and be a bishop in the Methodist church. I would rather be a humble Pentecostal preacher."[11]

Methodists were shocked to hear that one of their most promising young evangelists had defected to the Pentecostals. Vernon McCombs, the superintendent of the Spanish-speaking Methodist work, traveled to San Francisco and spent six hours trying to persuade Olazábal to remain in the Methodist Church, even offering him a yearly salary of two thousand dollars and other bonuses if he would stay. Although he considered the offer, he turned it down because he stated he wanted to be "free" to express himself in ways unacceptable to the Methodist leadership at that time.[12]

In 1917, Olazábal left the Methodist Church and joined the Assemblies of God (AG), from which he received ministerial credentials. A year later, he traveled south to Los Angeles, where he conducted a successful evangelistic campaign for Alice E. Luce, the leader in the Spanish-speaking AG. After the campaign he moved to El Paso and opened a Mexican mission to reach the thousands of immigrants streaming across the U.S.-Mexico border. By 1921 his charismatic personality, ability to heal, and rhetorical gifts led to the conversion of more than four hundred Mexicans along the border.[13]

As Olazábal's popularity continued to grow, he ran into conflict with H. C. Ball and Alice Luce. Reflecting the well-intentioned pious paternalism of their day, Ball and Luce tried to take control of the second convention in Victoria, Texas, and dictate its agenda and outcome. They believed that the Mexican Pentecostals in Texas were incapable of organizing and leading their own district within the AG. Although H. C. Ball denied this, internal documents indicate otherwise. Olazábal and a group of Mexican Pentecostal ministers (some of them from independent Pentecostal churches) found Ball's attitude toward Mexicans unacceptable. Ball and Luce wrote the AG headquarters accusing Olazábal of instigating trouble by calling for a separate Mexican district under Mexican leadership. There was some truth to the charge. Olazábal did attempt to effect reform from within Ball's paternalistic and racialized vision of the Mexican work. As early as 1920, he laid out a new vision for the council and began to push for the creation of a Bible school under Mexican administration. He also argued for indigenous Mexican leadership of the fledgling Mexican AG work. As his frustration with Ball and Luce continued to grow, his power base expanded. He criticized Ball and Luce for not keeping their promise to support the Bible school he later started in his home and for exaggerating the personal success of their work among Mexicans.[14]

The simmering tension erupted into full-blown conflict in the fall of 1922 when Ball told the Mexican leaders at the annual convention that they could not elect a new president of the Latin District Council until the following year. Most believed that Olazábal would be elected over Ball. Interpreting the statement as a tactical political move to thwart his election as president of the council and push him to the margins, Olazábal protested the decision and attempted to seize power by rallying Mexican pastors to his cause. Mexican ministers split over whom to follow. While some, especially those who had joined the Pentecostal movement prior to Ball's work, joined him, those who had converted under Ball's ministry remained loyal to the lean Texan. After six years of ministry in the AG, Olazábal recognized the racialized politics he now faced. With nine cents in his pocket, he resigned from the AG in December 1922. When Olazábal was later asked why he resigned, he responded, "The gringos have control."[15]

Aimee Semple McPherson and the Mexican Billy Sunday

While the controversy raged on, Olazábal encouraged independent Mexican Pentecostal churches and pastors to form a new denomination. While most pastors and churches in the Mexican AG convention decided to remain, others joined Olazábal's new organization. On March 14, 1923, the Interdenominational Mexican Council of Christian Churches was legally incorporated in the state of Texas. A Mexican American Pentecostal denomination was born. Despite the hardships that Olazábal's new denomination faced, by 1924 it counted more than thirty churches in California, Texas, Arizona, New Mexico, Kansas, Illinois, Michigan, Ohio, Indiana, and Mexico.[16]

While Olazábal had conducted evangelistic healing crusades with the Mexican AG prior to 1923, it was not until after the schism that his healing ministry began to take on genuinely national proportions. Olazábal's evangelistic healing ministry was reignited by the alleged healing of the twelve-year-old deaf-and-dumb daughter of Guadalupe Gómez. He had never performed what was, in the minds of his followers, such a "great" and obvious "miracle." Church of God leader Homer Tomlinson, one of Olazábal's closest Anglo-American friends, later stated that "from this new beginning his faith for healing and the salvation of souls seemed to take on new proportions."[17]

Empowered by a newfound confidence in God's ability to heal, throughout the 1920s Olazábal crisscrossed the nation preaching to thousands of Mexicans in migrant farm labor camps, factories, and inner-city barrios. In Los Angeles, his healing campaigns caught the eye of another former AG preacher, Aimee Semple McPherson.

In 1927, the glamorous McPherson was fascinated by the reports she heard from some of her Mexican American parishioners about Olazábal's healing crusades in Los Angeles and Watts. After personally attending his services in Watts, she called Olazábal the "Mexican Billy Sunday," a clear compliment, as Billy Sunday was the most famous and successful evangelist of their day. Shortly after McPherson preached at his campaign in Watts, she invited Olazábal and his two Mexican congregations to her five-thousand-seat Angelus Temple in Los Angeles. Olazábal's churches attended a number of evening services. At one historic meeting in October 1927, McPherson and Olazábal went to the podium, where the theatrical McPherson delivered a sermon entitled "In the Valley of Decision." Olazábal translated her sermon into Spanish. In vintage McPherson style the sermon was dramatized and illustrated by a team of actors with theater props. The Mexican congregation was emotionally moved not only by McPherson's hospitality but also by her public blessing on "our Mexican brethren."[18]

McPherson asked Olazábal and the council to merge with her Foursquare Gospel denomination. Olazábal felt flattered but said the decision to merge had to be decided by the entire council. He later took the idea of a merger to the next national convention, where his Mexican compatriots soundly defeated the proposal. They did not want to submit to Anglo control and, in effect, replace one set of Anglo leaders for another. Olazábal met with McPherson and related the council's decision. McPherson was indignant by what she considered a very generous offer to a Mexican denomination made up of migrant farm laborers, maids, ditch diggers, and the like. She excoriated Olazábal and demanded he return the more than $100 "love offering" she had raised for him at Angelus Temple. Defiant, Olazábal told McPherson that "love offerings" are never returned. Angry, McPherson looked at Olazábal and told him to get out of her office and never return.[19] Sometime after the conflict with Olazábal, she persuaded one of his leaders, Anthony Gamboa, to defect to the Foursquare Gospel and start a rival ministry. This conflict helped give birth to the Foursquare's Spanish-speaking work in the United States.[20]

The symbolic impact of Olazábal preaching on stage with McPherson in Angelus Temple, one of the largest churches in the United States at that time, cannot be overstated. In a day when Mexicans were considered cheap labor and cultural "outsiders," her recognition convinced many of Olazábal's followers that he was indeed "anointed of God."

As word of Olazábal's healing campaigns spread across the United States, he was invited to speak at the Palace Opera House in Chicago. His evangelistic healing campaign attracted more than three thousand a night for several weeks. The traffic in human bodies was so great that police had to be called out to control the crowds.[21]

The Spanish Harlem Revival of 1931

Word of Olazábal's evangelistic healing campaign in Chicago soon spread to New York City. Francisco Paz, a Pentecostal minister, had attended one of Olazábal's healing services in Chicago and asked him to conduct a similar campaign in New York. In the summer of 1931 Olazábal traveled to Spanish Harlem for what would become the most important chapter of his life and the birth of his transnational ministry.

"Probably not less than 100,000 different people have attended the Olazábal meetings in New York City since he inaugurated his meetings in New York in August, 1931," one periodical claimed.[22] Despite the humidity and summer heat, vast throngs of people attended his services at the gigantic Calvary Baptist Church in Brooklyn, the first place Olazábal held his evangelistic services. The large crowds were no accident. Olazábal's people distributed thirty thousand flyers announcing the healing campaign.[23]

Olazábal's healing services blazed with power and emotion. Despite the nail-grinding poverty the Great Depression was wreaking on the Latin American community outside of the church, inside the church people sought spiritual relief to offset their aching bodies and souls. The services were run the same way every night. Olazábal walked onto center stage, led the congregation in a time of rousing singing, preached a twenty-five-minute evangelistic sermon, and then lifted his arms in the air and asked those in the balcony to come down to the altar of the church, repent of their sins, and convert. Thousands answered his call. After the altar call, Olazábal began what many, perhaps most, of the people came for—divine healing. While many turned to a *curandera,* or a spiritualist, for healing, others turned to *El Azteca,* or the mighty Aztec, as Olazábal was referred to by his followers.[24]

Olazábal and his followers claimed that hundreds of people were healed of blindness, tuberculosis, deformity, tumors, heart conditions, rheumatism, deafness, and many other physical ailments and diseases in his 1931 Spanish Harlem campaign. As at the Azusa Street revival in Los Angeles, the "relics" of their former life—rosaries, amulets, canes, and crutches—were thrown into a large pile on stage as a symbol of God's power to transform their weary spirits and broken bodies. The campaign converted thousands to the Pentecostal movement and prompted Olazábal to organize the mother church of his movement, Bethel Temple, in New York City. This church, an enormous former synagogue, had grown from just a handful of members in August 1931 to more than fifteen hundred members by 1932, making it one of the largest churches in New York City. The vast majority of his parishioners were former Catholics, Spiritists, or agnostic socialists.[25]

Thousands of women joined the revival movement because it afforded them the chance to go into the ministry and exercise a prophetic voice. No doubt influenced by women such as his mother, Refugio Olazábal, Carrie Judd Montgomery, and even Alice Luce and Aimee Semple McPherson, Olazábal did allow women to go into the ministry. Although he did not ordain women to the pastoral role, he and the council did grant them the right to preach from the pulpit and organize, pastor, and administer churches, and serve as evangelists and missionaries. However, women were not normally allowed to serve communion, perform baptisms, or conduct weddings without a male elder or pastor present. Despite these limitations, the council produced a number of famous pastors such as María Jiménez, who pastored very large churches in both Chicago and El Paso, and evangelists such as María Teresa Sapia, Leoncia Rosado Rosseau, and Julie and Matilde Vargas. Rosado Rosseau went on to cofound the Damascus Christian Church and Matilde Vargas to conduct evangelistic services in the Latino community across the United States.[26]

Word of Olazábal's healing services spread rapidly not only through Depression-era Spanish Harlem but also through New York's Italian and Anglo-American boroughs. Soon a growing number of Italians and Anglos began attending regularly. The number of non-Spanish speakers attending Olazábal's services was so large that he began holding English-language services on Monday nights and Italian-language services on Thursday evenings and Sunday mornings. Olazábal also regularly ministered in black Pentecostal churches in Harlem and throughout New York City. His ministry had now crossed linguistic and racial boundaries in a day when the Ku Klux Klan, white superiority, and racial segregation shaped the racial and social imagination of a large segment of Anglo-American society.[27]

After Homer Tomlinson, pastor of Jamaica Tabernacle Church of God, heard about the "miracles" taking place at Brooklyn Temple, he invited Olazábal to conduct evangelistic healing services in his Anglo-American Jamaica Tabernacle Church. Surprised by the offer and eager to make connections with Anglo Pentecostal leaders in New York, Olazábal accepted. For weeks he conducted meetings at Jamaica Tabernacle. Tomlinson proclaimed the campaign an "overwhelming success," as more than eight hundred people were converted. Tomlinson also claimed that "hundreds were healed," including a twenty-four-year-old cripple who had been paralyzed since his youth.[28]

Olazábal and His Critics

Olazábal had his critics. When prominent Anglo Pentecostal leaders like Robert A. Brown and J. R. Kline asked J. R. Flower and H. C. Ball about

Olazábal, they were told that he vilified the Assemblies of God and had "done a great injustice to the work of the Lord." Ball also claimed that his evangelistic work "soon goes to pieces" when his campaigns were over. A few Mexican pastors left the council and accused Olazábal of being heavy-handed. Others accused him of authoritarianism and of practicing favoritism. Still others complained that he was too lenient with pastors who had fallen "into sin" or had compromised their Christian testimony.[29] Many of the complaints were all too true. Despite the large crowds that attended the campaigns, the churches he organized after the campaigns were often a fraction of the size. Olazábal's ministry style could be authoritarian at times, especially by today's standards. There were instances where he assigned ministers to churches in a part of the country where the minister did not want to serve. He would also publicly criticize a church congregation that did not support its minister. In a day when divorce was grounds for immediate dismissal in the ministry, Olazábal made exceptions. There were instances when he allowed people who had gone through a divorce to continue their ministry but only if their spouse had been the one who had committed adultery and/or abandoned the family.[30]

Olazábal was also accused of not healing everyone he prayed for. He openly acknowledged this fact. In fact, Frank Olazábal Jr. estimates that only 80 percent of those prayed for received healing. Puerto Ricans like Roberto Domínguez and one Anglo-American member of Homer Tomlinson's congregation claimed that, despite Olazábal's prayers for healing, they had not been healed. Olazábal responded to these charges by stating that it was God's prerogative to heal. He was simply a vessel through which God manifested his healing power, nothing more. From a critical reading of the healing testimonies published in the *Christian Messenger* magazine, it is clear that a majority of those who claimed healing were women. Furthermore, most of the "healings" were for minor ailments, although a number of people did claim to be healed of more chronic ailments like tuberculosis, cancer, tumors, blindness, deafness, and terminal diseases. Most doctors would probably categorize many of the alleged cures as examples of psychosomatic cures brought about by the power of positive suggestion. The fact that the Latino community has a long tradition of folk healing and that most people could not afford a doctor may also help explain his appeal to thousands across the United States, Mexico, and Puerto Rico.[31]

Puerto Rico "Para Cristo": The Mexican Billy Sunday in Puerto Rico

Despite protests from critics and cynics, news of Olazábal's healing crusades quickly spread to Puerto Rico. Soon invitations began to pour in from the island inviting the Mexican faith healer to hold campaigns in San Juan and Ponce. He responded to one such invitation by the Defenders of the Faith denomination, and in 1934 he conducted the first mass island-wide evangelistic healing crusade in Puerto Rican history. He held services in tents, churches, civic auditoriums, and sports arenas. *El Mundo,* the largest newspaper on the island, dubbed Olazábal the "Mexican Billy Sunday" and claimed that he converted twenty thousand people to the Pentecostal movement throughout the island.[32]

Olazábal returned to New York City from Puerto Rico like a triumphant Caesar in the eyes of his Spanish-speaking followers. He quickly realized that the key to his success there was his ability to garner the interdenominational support of Protestant leaders across the island. While at first some denominations opposed his work, by the end of his Puerto Rican campaign, most had been won over by the overwhelmingly positive response of both the press and the masses. Many Protestant ministers, such as Daniel Echevarria (Baptist) and Carlos Sepúlveda (Presbyterian), decided to join Olazábal's Latin American Council of Christian Churches.

In 1936, Francisco Olazábal stood at the height of his popularity. Letters were arriving from all over the United States, Latin America, and Europe asking him to conduct evangelistic campaigns. Olazábal began sketching plans to conduct evangelistic-healing services in Spain, Argentina, Venezuela, and Ecuador. In the mid-1930s, the mainline Protestant *Christian Herald* magazine and the conservative Protestant *Sunday School Times* published flattering articles on his ministry. Writing for the *Christian Herald,* Spencer Duryee described Olazábal as "The Great Aztec" whose transnational ministry was "one of the most startling stories . . . in modern religious history." He went on to compare Olazábal to the Apostle Paul, John Wesley, David Livingstone, and William Booth. Still others, like McPherson and the Puerto Rican poet Luís Villaronga, compared him to the famous evangelist Billy Sunday.[33]

Although Pentecostal in creed, ritual, and practice, Olazábal recognized that his ecumenical evangelistic healing message transcended denominational borders and boundaries. Rather than push his brand of Christianity on people, he would simply invite them to receive Holy Spirit baptism and spiritual gifts when they were ready. While the private Olazábal often said that speaking in tongues was the key to his healing ministry, publicly he stated that he was not Pentecostal, at least not the stereotypical Pentecostal; he was simply "a Christian." This kind of ecumenical-sounding discourse attracted the attention of influential mainline Protestant leaders like Robert E. Speer, who agreed publicly to support Olazábal's next Puerto Rican campaign in the spring of 1936.[34]

Olazábal's ministry took a dramatic turn in 1936. Just days before he was to leave for his second campaign in Puerto Rico, he received devastating news: Speer had decided to withdraw his support. Shocked and disheartened, Olazábal asked his trusted friend Homer Tomlinson why. "Tongues," Tomlinson quietly said. Speer had telephoned Tomlinson and stated that he had just learned that Olazábal "belonged to the 'tongues' people" and therefore had to back out immediately.[35]

Disappointed but not devastated by the loss of Speer's support, Olazábal arrived in Puerto Rico in the spring of 1936 ready to repeat his 1934 campaign. Yet the setback with Speer was nothing compared to what he would experience on the island. Roman Catholic leaders looked at Olazábal as farmers look at an oncoming plague. They used their influence with the newspapers to persuade them not to announce his campaign or arrival on the island. Some accused him of pocketing two thousand dollars from his first campaign in 1934. Still other religious leaders even distributed literature denouncing him as "a stealer of the sheep of the widow." More devastating, however, was the opposition he faced from his Pentecostal and evangelical colleagues, who were threatened by his growing popularity on the island. They, too, tried to shut him down. Everywhere he turned to secure facilities or the once plentiful local support, he was denied. Jealousy and fear of Olazábal's growing movement in Puerto Rico along with his own independent and headstrong style prompted the otherwise warring Catholic, Protestant, and rival Pentecostals to oppose him.

Despite Olazábal's interdenominational focus and cooperation, his movement counted almost half a dozen churches on the island in 1936. It appears that he did not pocket the two thousand dollars but instead had given most of it to another pastor to organize a church for the Defenders of the Faith. Despite the difficulties he now faced, he continued to hold evangelistic services. In the capital city of San Juan, Olazábal was forced to meet outside the city limits on a racetrack. In Ponce he was denied regular meeting places and had to conduct his meetings at the docks. Frustrated at every turn, he wired his wife in New York and asked her to send his large evangelistic tent to the island to protect the visitors from the drenching tropical rain and scorching sun.[36]

The lack of support from Speer, opposition from the Catholic Church, and criticism from his former Protestant supporters was more than Olazábal could handle. Even before his tent arrived on the island, he boarded a ship and steamed home for New York City, arriving unannounced and without fanfare. According to one report, there on the porch of his home, in front of his close friend Homer Tomlinson, Olazábal wept. With tears streaming down his face he confided to Tomlinson that he had never been so discouraged in his entire life. Rejection by the Anglo establishment was hard enough, but to find his fellow Latino Protestant leaders also aligned against him really bothered him.[37]

The 1936 *Puerto Rico Para Cristo* campaign marked a sharp turning point in Olazábal's vision. Prior to that campaign he saw his healing ministry as bridging the racial and denominational divides that diced up American Protestantism. He now realized that such bridging would be difficult, if not impossible. Now that the influential Speer knew he was "a tongues speaker," he realized that interdenominational support would be virtually impossible to win from mainline Protestant denominations. His dream of an interdenominational, transnational, and multiracial ministry was frustrated by forces seemingly beyond his control.

Pentecostal-Roman Catholic Tensions in the Southwest

Although Olazábal's pride and image had been tarnished, he left New York later to begin a new campaign in El Paso, Texas, the place he had begun his transborder ministry in the United States twenty-five years earlier in 1911. Upon his arrival he found María Teresa Sapia of Puerto Rico, and his own daughter, Martha, preparing for his arrival. Olazábal at first had free rein in El Paso, as Catholic leaders were unaware of his arrival. Wasting no time, he secured the enormous city auditorium for his healing services. Thousands of Mexicans poured into the meetings. As with charismatic healers before him, Olazábal's message of hope, healing, and spiritual transformation attracted the masses.[38]

Once Catholic leaders in El Paso found out about Olazábal's campaign, several attempted to shut him down. Eyewitnesses claimed that the Catholic Church sent spies into Olazábal's meeting, where they stood in line to have themselves prayed for so they could call him a "fake." The "spies" were reportedly discovered and asked to leave. Father Lourdes F. Costa of El Paso also began publicly to attack Olazábal in the El Paso newspapers by challenging his claim to heal. Olazábal wrote back with an equally sharp letter stating that the reason people left the Catholic Church was that it lacked real transformative power.[39] Despite the attempts to silence Olazábal, he claimed that more than three thousand Mexicans were converted and scores of new churches were founded as a result of the 1936 El Paso campaign.[40]

Healing Southern White Bodies: Mexicans and Southern Pentecostalism

No sooner had the El Paso campaign ended than Olazábal and his son Frank Jr. headed for Cleveland, Tennessee. Olazábal realized that if he was ever going to have an international and multiracial ministry he needed major financial support and the freedom to travel unrestrained by the cares of administering the council. He was tired and took a second look at the Anglo-American–based Tomlinson Church of God (TCOG), which had asked him to join their movement a few years earlier. He realized that, while he may not have been able to win the support of mainline Protestants like Robert E. Speer, he still could win the support of the TCOG.

Re-energized from his recent crusade in El Paso, Olazábal attended the 1936 TCOG Annual Assembly in Cleveland, Tennessee. On September 10, 1936, before an audience of six thousand white southerners, the somewhat reluctant Olazábal placed his hand on a Bible and swore allegiance to the TCOG. While no formal legal documents had been signed, it was a symbolic gesture of what both he and the TCOG considered an inevitable union. The TCOG was electrified. In one fell swoop they had added an estimated 150 churches, fifty thousand people, and Francisco Olazábal. At least so they thought.[41]

"Hundreds Seek Faith Healing" at the TCOG convention, read the headline of the *Chattanooga Times* on September 12, 1936. "More than 700 persons were anointed with oil and prayed for . . . in the annual healing service here tonight before a packed audience that overflowed into three surrounding blocks," the reporter went on to claim. When asked if he was a healer, Olazábal replied by stating, "The only thing I know is I am a believer in Jesus . . . [and] that he is the same yesterday, today, and forever."[42] The *Cleveland Daily Banner* claimed hundreds of people came "under the spell of Rev. Francisco Olazábal."[43] The response of this southern white crowd to Olazábal was overwhelmingly positive. Despite his Spanish accent, or perhaps because of it, thousands of white southerners streamed forward to be healed by the tall Mexican evangelist. Tomlinson claimed that Olazábal prayed for more than fifteen hundred people at the 1936 annual convention. Olazábal made such an impact at the 1936 convention that hundreds of letters continued to pour into the TCOG headquarters for the next two years requesting that Olazábal pray for them.[44]

Olazábal's psychologically devastating setback in Puerto Rico had been softened by his recent campaigns in El Paso and Cleveland. Triumphant in the eyes of his own Spanish-speaking followers, he returned to New York City. He had entered the Anglo-American world and had taken center stage. His life and ministry was the embodiment and dream of countless other Latinos living in the shadow of Jim Crow America in the 1930s.

Reignited by his recent campaigns in El Paso and Cleveland, Olazábal confidently led two thousand Latinos in a planned march down New York's Fifth Avenue. Standing six abreast, shouting, "praising God," and singing, they boldly waved colorful banners, much as Pentecostal and evangelical Christians do today in the International March for Jesus. They gathered at the plaza at the end of Fifth Avenue and 110th Street for a rally. The parade was a powerful symbol that Olazábal and the Latino Pentecostal movement were here to stay.[45]

"A Great Oak Has Fallen upon the Mountain": The Death of Charisma

"Rev. F. Olazábal . . . Dies of Injuries Suffered in Auto Accident" read the *New York Times* obituary on June 12, 1937.[46] Francisco Olazábal was dead. On June 1, near Alice Springs, Texas, on his way to an ordination service in Mexico, his car skidded off the slippery blacktop surface and overturned. Although critically injured, he was taken to a hospital where he appeared to recover. Then, on June 9, 1937, Olazábal died from internal hemorrhaging. He seemed to know that death was imminent and reportedly dictated a message to his followers. In it he admonished them to continue the work he had started and to keep the Holy Spirit at the center of their ministry. In the minds of his followers, a giant of the faith had fallen.

Olazábal's death shocked his followers. On hearing the news some said many of his closest friends and followers fainted.[47] In a scene reminiscent of presidents and other national figures, Olazábal's body was placed in a two-thousand-dollar gas-vapor-filled casket and taken for public display in his great temple in the heart of Spanish Harlem for three days. Some estimate that not fewer than fifty thousand Puerto Ricans, Anglo-Americans, and blacks paid their last respects over the three-day period. Homer Tomlinson eulogized Olazábal before thousands by stating that "a mighty man of God has fallen in the midst of his labors." "A great oak has fallen upon the mountain." Those who had been healed by the once "mighty Aztec" now looked on in disbelief. On the last day of the memorial, there was a procession of an estimated twenty thousand people who walked alongside the hearse that contained the body of the dead apostle to Latinos. From New York City his body was taken for display to Chicago, then to El Paso, and finally to Los Angeles. In East Los Angeles, the place he called home, thousands of Mexicans, blacks, and Anglos came from across the Southwest and Mexico to pay their last respects to the Mexican apostle. His body was laid to rest in Evergreen Cemetery, not far from that of William J. Seymour.[48]

With Olazábal's death, the leadership of the council was up for grabs— at least in the minds of the Puerto Rican contingent. Without Olazábal's charisma to hold it together, the movement fragmented along ethnic and regional lines. Miguel Guillén, a Mexican American and the new president, was reportedly insensitive to Puerto Ricans and thus proved unable to rein in the Puerto Rican nationalism surfacing in the council. Members balked at Guillén's ascendancy to the presidency. Many of the Puerto Ricans were tired of feeling like second-class citizens in the council and resented the "Mexican American" leadership, which the city-wise Puerto Ricans considered generally ignorant and inferior. A number of key Puerto Ricans and a few Mexican leaders split the council into warring factions, each championing its own leader. By 1938 the council leadership was in complete disarray and was fighting for its very existence. While everyone preached unity, fragmentation and rebellion spread. As with the schism in 1923, hundreds were confused and not sure which way to turn or whom to follow.

The first schism took place in February 1938, with Gilberto Díaz breaking away from the council in Chicago. In the fall of 1938, Carlos Sepúlveda, Felipe Sabater, and Frank Hernández did the same in New York City. In 1939, Sepúlveda founded the Assembly of Christian Churches in New York. No sooner had the Sepúlveda crisis ended than another erupted when Olazábal's wife, Macrina, decided to leave the council in 1942. The last major schism prior to 1950 took place in 1947, when Alejandro Leal of Texas broke away with ten churches to found his own denomination. These schisms took their toll on the council and almost destroyed the movement.[49]

The fragmentation of the council made the union between the Latin American Council of Christian Churches and the TCOG impossible. Despite the internal conflict going on in the council, the TCOG continued to move toward consummation of the union. Despite generous overtures, there was a general sentiment in the council, from Miguel Guillén on down, that the TCOG really wanted Olazábal and numbers, not rank-and-file Mexicans, Puerto Ricans, and other Latinos. This fact, along with the infighting within the council, killed any major movement toward union with the TCOG. Tomlinson's dream of a "grand union" between the two denominations went up in flames.[50]

The Significance and Legacy of Francisco Olazábal

Francisco Olazábal left a lasting mark on North American Latino Christianity. No single Latino religious leader has shaped the history and development of the early Latino Pentecostal movement in North America and the Latin Caribbean as he did. Called the "Apostle Paul to the Latin Americans," Olazábal contributed to the origins of at least fourteen denominations.[51] By the time of his death in 1937, he claimed 150 churches and fifty thousand followers throughout North America and the Latin Caribbean. Although these numbers are high, even if he attracted half this many it would make the council one of the largest Latino Protestant denominations in North America and the fourth largest Pentecostal denomination in the United States in 1937.[52]

Olazábal was a Latino Pentecostal prophet whose popularity can be attributed to his ability to exercise charisma. After trying to transform the Mexican Assemblies of God from within, Olazábal was pushed to the margins, where he attempted to take control of the movement. The fact that he stood up against Anglo-American leaders and seized control over his own life and movement in Jim Crow America was remarkable in the 1920s and 1930s and not lost on his followers, who called him the "mighty Aztec" or *El Azteca*. His authority was not dependent solely upon Anglo-American approval but reportedly came directly from God. He was the Protestant version of the famous Catholic folk healers El Niño Fidencio, Don Pedrito Jaramillo, and María Teresa Urrea. His ministry tapped into the tremendous emphasis on healing in Latino spirituality already in place in Latino Catholic culture and religiosity. Although his healing ministry was spurred by his experience of speaking in tongues, it did not fully blossom until after he had broken away from the AG. His healing ministry, along with his emphasis on church planting, women in ministry, personal evangelism, citywide crusades, and mass-marketing techniques, help explain his ability to attract the masses. All of these factors helped give birth to one of the first completely indigenous transnational Latino organizations in North America and the Latin Caribbean.

Olazábal's prophetic rejection of Anglo-American racism and pious paternalism created a message that would rise again in another Pentecostal leader during the Chicano movement (1965–75): Reies López Tijerina.[53] Ironically, after Olazábal's death his vision of Christianity was institutionalized and routinized by his followers who demanded stricter adherence to the letter of Pentecostal doctrine than had Olazábal himself. This transition from charismatic prophet to institutionalization created a period of tremendous instability and led to the fragmentation of the council into a number of smaller denominations or councils *(concilios)* and scores of independent churches that exist to this day throughout the United States, Mexico, and Puerto Rico. It is precisely this tendency to produce charismatic prophetic leaders who split off from existing denominations to form their own that has kept the Pentecostal movement constantly fragmenting and spreading almost one hundred years after it first erupted onto the stage of world history.

Despite Olazábal's impact on American religious history and Pentecostalism, scholars have overlooked his story. Yet he is important because his story demonstrates that the Latino Pentecostal movement began much earlier and was much larger and more indigenous, independent, diverse, and transnational than previously believed. His story also shatters the biracial view of early Pentecostalism as essentially a black-and-white story and demonstrates that the present growth of Pentecostalism in the Latino community actually traces its roots back to the early twentieth century, not the 1960s and 1970s as is often asserted. Francisco Olazábal's legacy is evident in the thousands of churches throughout North America and the Latin Caribbean that in one way or another trace their spiritual genealogy back to *El Azteca*.

Evangelists Maria Woodworth-Etter and Watt Walker, circa 1920. Courtesy of the
Flower Pentecostal Heritage Center, Springfield, Missouri.

Maria B. Woodworth-Etter: Prophet of Equality

Wayne E. Warner

It was an unusual scene in Louisville, Kentucky, that summer in 1888. And to many in the city the scene was downright shameful. Here was a white woman from the North trying to mix the races in an evangelistic meeting under a big tent. Allowing a woman to preach was bad enough, some groused, but she was preaching to blacks and laying her hands on their heads in healing prayers. It was a pretty simple decision for white residents: they would stay home if the evangelist had no more respect for southern culture than to try to mix the races. "I told them God made the whole human family of one blood," the evangelist countered as she refused to consider a racial ban. In this apparent impasse, Kentuckians faced two of the most controversial issues to test the consciousness of the nineteenth- and twentieth-century Christian church in America: how the church viewed women in ministry and racial integration.

As one of the leading preachers of the period, Maria B. Woodworth-Etter (1844–1924) stood in the vanguard on both issues. By her very presence behind the mass evangelism pulpit between 1880 until her death in 1924, she promoted and encouraged women to enter the ministry. And when she spoke to women about considering God's call, they listened—during a period in which few women were in the pulpit and suffragists were crusading for women's basic rights, such as casting ballots in national elections. As a result, during her lifetime Etter arguably opened as many or more doors for women to preach than any other person. And throughout her nearly forty-five years on the "sawdust trail," she vigorously defended the equal rights of all races to worship together. Her impact in this latter area is more difficult to document than her importance in promoting women in ministry. But because her outspoken positive views on the racial issue as early as the 1880s are hard to ignore, the second part of this chapter will focus on this age-old American problem.

Women in the Pulpit

If God calls a woman to preach the gospel, and His blessings are upon her, "in confirming His Word with signs following," whose right is it to question her right to preach the gospel, pastor a church, or lead a movement under God?

—*Edith Mae Pennington*

Struggling for Acceptance

When one considers the public opportunities for women in the nineteenth century, the conclusion seems evident that women carved out their own breaks or they did not come. Having a woman elected to public office or appointed as a corporate CEO was unknown. Though their legal rights were almost nonexistent and most did not live long enough to vote in national elections following the ratification of the Nineteenth Amendment, a few women pushed ahead. Today we recognize trailblazing women like Clara Barton, founder of the American Red Cross; Fannie Crosby, hymn writer; Mary Baker Eddy, founder of Christian Science; Julia Ward Howe, composer of the *Battle Hymn of the Republic;* Susan B. Anthony, feminist leader; Frances Willard, educator; and Maria Mitchell, discoverer of a comet in 1848.

Men held a stranglehold on the pulpit, and few women could break that grip. Society dictated that women belonged in the home. Churches agreed and added their own interpretation of Scripture that forbade a woman from usurping authority over men. Preaching and ministering, in their thinking, did just that in 1929. A strong voice for fundamentalism, Presbyterian pastor Clarence Macartney noted that "when the apostle speaks of false teachers leading off 'silly women,' he has a very modern sound. From Eve down to Mrs. Eddy, women have played a sad part in the spread of anti-Christian doctrines, and that under the guise of Christian teachings."[1]

The restrictions against women preachers were built into the infrastructure of the church. And Macartney in the twentieth century, like others in the nineteenth, offered constant reminders that the kingdom would be better served if women were listening to sermons rather than trying to preach them. Frances Willard's nineteenth-century dream still seems a long shot for would-be women preachers. She predicted that "the time will come when these gates of Gospel Grace shall stand open night and day, while woman's heavenly ministries shall find their central home within God's house." Several nineteenth-century publications supported women's rights in the ministry, including Phoebe Palmer's *Promise of the Father* and Catherine Booth's *Female Ministry: Or, Woman's Rights to Preach the Gospel.* These writers acted as a burr under the saddle and helped prepare women and the church to accept the inevitable.

A Call to Preach

After the Assemblies of God was organized in Hot Springs, Arkansas, in 1914, women's rights became an issue. Women could be evangelists or missionaries and could develop other specialized ministries. They could speak at the annual general council business sessions but could not vote until 1920; they could not officially serve churches as pastors until 1935. E. N. Bell, one of the leaders of the Assemblies of God during its first nine years, delivered notice from his editorial position in 1915 that he would exert his influence at an upcoming general council that the body would not waste time discussing women's rights. He called it "beating the bushes around about small and non-essential matters."[2]

As slow as the Assemblies of God was in giving women more freedom, the group was ahead of the times and most denominations. If women faced so many hurdles trying to enter the ministry and being successful, we might wonder what motivated them to untie the apron strings and strike out on rickety trains, bounce from one town to another, and fight the elements to set up tents or clean out abandoned store buildings—especially when few of them had a guarantee that people would be interested enough to participate. The motivational key that most, if not all, felt was their divine call. Any number of women preachers, as well as men, began their life stories by telling of dramatic calls from God that kept them from doing anything else with a clear conscience.

When Etter objected to a divine call on her life because she lacked a formal education, she said Jesus spoke, "Go, and I will be with you." She replied in a dialogue not unlike Isaiah's. "Lord, I will go. Where shall I go?"

Jesus answered, she wrote, "Go here, go there, wherever souls are perishing."[3] She told a St. Louis reporter in 1890 that during her call she saw a vision of the Bible on the wall of her room; the Holy Ghost as a dove, the "Lord seemed like a great ball of fire"; and she added that the Lord talked to her frequently, "the same as other persons do."[4] It appears that the more drama one experienced in connection with a call—often in conjunction with Holy Spirit baptism or another crisis experience—the more inclined one was to enter the ministry. Taking a cue from the apostle Paul's experience while he was on the Damascus Road (Acts 9), Etter had her own dramatics: bright clouds, weightlessness, liquid fire, and angels all around in the fire and glory. During the rest of her life she would look back to that day as the moment when she received both her call and Holy Spirit baptism. And she added that it was through the power of the Holy Spirit that she was able to stand before hundreds of thousands of people "proclaiming the unsearchable riches of Christ."[5]

Other women preachers experienced their own dramatic calls.

Florence "Mother" Crawford's call did not match Etter's fireworks, but it seemed unique in its own way. She said that God spoke to her on a dance floor in 1906. Not knowing the voice of God, she confessed, she continued dancing—an activity she would later condemn as sinful. Then the voice boomed into her spirit, "Daughter, give me thine heart." The next three days and nights became a time of crying out to God for this Etter contemporary. She testified later that God led her to the Azusa Street Mission—where she was baptized in the Holy Spirit and surrendered to a preaching call. That surrender led her up the Pacific Coast, where she founded the Apostolic Faith, Portland.[6]

Another Etter contemporary evangelist was the flamboyant Aimee Semple McPherson, founder of the International Church of the Foursquare Gospel. Her call to preach came in 1915 after she had returned from China, where she had buried her missionary husband, Robert Semple. Following her marriage to Harold McPherson she told of a near deathbed experience in which God reminded her that He had called her: "Preach the Word!" she heard Him say. "I have called thee, and ordained thee!" She believed it was either die or answer the call. "I made my decision and gasped out the words, 'Yes—Lord—I'll—go!'"[7]

Kathryn Kuhlman compared her calling to her dramatic conversion at a small Methodist church in Concordia, Missouri, in 1921 when she was fourteen years old. A woman's place, she would argue, is where God puts her. "For me it is in this ministry. This is my place because God put me here."[8] Responding to that summons, she gained notoriety as an evangelist for twenty years but had—to her lifelong sorrow—moved out of the will of God. She had married Burroughs A. Waltrip Sr., another evangelist, who had left his wife and two sons in Texas. Kuhlman said many times that she knew the relationship was wrong. One day in Los Angeles she went for a walk. It was not long before she saw a street sign: DEAD END. Immediately she knew the sign illustrated her life. Here she surrendered her life anew and made a decision to give up Waltrip. "I can take you to the street," she would often say sobbing, "the street where Kathryn Kuhlman died." It was a new call for her remaining thirty years of ministry.[9]

An informative parallel marks the crisis moments in the experiences of the three best-known women evangelists of the twentieth century—Etter, McPherson, and Kuhlman. They had traded earlier calls for marriage—all three of which ended in divorce—and then responded positively to what they described as God's persistent and urgent summoning.

A Closer Look at an Ohio Farmer's Wife

In 1880 Etter, a thirty-five-year-old Ohio farmer's wife, accepted the challenge to break through the heavy restrictions men had used to protect the pulpit as their own domain. Her life's career description was outlined in a 1912 published sermon, "Women's Privilege in the Gospel." The preaching dream for Maria Underwood began as a thirteen-year-old new convert in her Disciples of Christ Church in Lisbon, Ohio. "I heard the voice of Jesus calling me to go out in the highways and hedges and gather in the lost sheep," she wrote for her 1894 autobiography. But she was also a realist. She had never heard of women ministering in public except as missionaries. She reasoned that the only opportunity to fulfill her calling would come if she ever married, and then she could minister with her husband.

But it was not until Etter was thirty-five, married, and had given birth to six children that her calling began to press upon her again. She studied prominent female characters of the Bible. "The more I investigated," she wrote later, "the more I found to condemn me . . . I had one talent, which was hidden away."[10] But her husband, P. H. Woodworth—whose intelligence was often questioned by newspaper writers—was smart enough to know he belonged behind a plow, not a pulpit. Furthermore, he questioned his wife's sanity for ever thinking that anyone would listen to her preach. The surprising results from her preaching in their home area of eastern Ohio, south of Youngstown, apparently opened her husband's eyes. In about eighteen months he saw his wife conduct nine revival meetings, organize two churches (one with seventy members), organize a Sunday school of about a hundred members, preach in twenty-two meetinghouses and four school houses, and deliver two hundred sermons.

Philo Woodworth did finally yield to his wife's pleas to go with her into an itinerant ministry—she as the preacher and he as the manager of the tent and food sales for worshipers drawn to the protracted meetings throughout the Midwest. Newspaper stories suggest that Philo could have used a crash course in public relations, as he repeatedly embarrassed the ministry. Despite Philo Woodworth's adverse part, Etter continued to draw huge crowds and was pleased with the fruit. "God blessed my labors," she beamed, "in this short time with more glorious results than I had expected to see in years, or perhaps in a lifetime of labor."[11]

In 1880 Etter led her small party to western Ohio, where she met with immediate success in evangelism. Although she held credentials with the Winebrenner Churches of God, her initial ministry involved eight separate denominations. It was only the beginning of nearly forty-five years that she would labor coast to coast in Holiness- and Pentecostal-flavored churches, in the open air, in roller skating rinks, in courthouses, and under the canvas big top. Etter attracted thousands in memorable meetings throughout the Midwest in the 1880s.

But not everything turned up rosy. Because of her practice of sending converts careening into trances when they received the power of the Holy Spirit, Etter was roundly criticized wherever she went. An Anderson, Indiana, reporter called her the "great paralyzer" because of the trances. The assessments from ministers in Kokomo, Indiana, were more explicit. After telling a newspaper reporter that he did not accept any of Etter's antics, Elder E. L. Frazier said, "I have not witnessed the like since I attended the meetings of the poor black slave in Kentucky thirty years ago."[12] A Father Lordemann said he believed Etter's meetings "are a reproach and a disgrace to the religion of God."[13] On the other side of the ledger, a medical doctor, well known for his unbelief, repented and became one of Etter's best advertisements in Pendleton, Indiana. This Dr. Troy testified a year later that he had been healed of diabetes and had given up his medical practice for the ministry. He could number more than a hundred converts. "I am 58 years old," he shouted to an enthusiastic camp meeting crowd in 1886, "and the last year has been the happiest of my life."[14]

The *Cincinnati Enquirer* reported from Etter's 1885 Hartford City meeting that a sixty-two-year-old lawyer by the name of John Cantwell was an unbeliever until he saw Etter go into a trance. "He broke down and began to weep," Etter said. "We all got down on our knees . . . the first time [he] had ever bowed before the living God." Cantwell's testimony jolted another attorney, Elisha Pearce, and he joined his colleague at the once despised mourners' bench. For sixty-two years, Cantwell said, he had served Satan but was now converted and had come to "the great fountain of everlasting life, drank at its sacred shrine," and was redeemed.[15] Stories like the ones Troy and Cantwell told catapulted Etter into one of the more popular evangelists and miracle workers of the late nineteenth century. And her reputation carried her into the twentieth century as one of the icons of the Pentecostal movement.[16]

Beginning with her five-month 1912 campaign in Dallas, Etter found herself in demand throughout the Pentecostal movement until her death a dozen years later at the age of eighty. Her books, recounting her exploits from coast to coast and containing her sermons, were standard fare for Pentecostal publishing houses and were promoted in their periodicals.

Reaching the Pinnacle of Success

For evangelists to reach success, they must find acceptance with the people they are trying to reach. Being a woman made that goal even more elusive. Having the support of the media, local pastors, and the communities at large certainly helped, but finding a supportive congregation was essential. Even though local newspapers, pastors, police, and medical professionals often came down hard on Etter, she could smile because their criticism had little effect on the thousands who filled her tents during the heyday years. In many cities such criticism actually publicized the meetings and attracted people who had not known of the circuslike crusades.

In her first revival campaign—which was in her husband's hometown in eastern Ohio—Etter dealt with doubts and apprehensions. But she gained the assurance she needed to preach to the relatives who gathered out of curiosity for her first sermon. If God had called her, she reasoned, he would provide the words and the power to reach any congregation. She approached that first pulpit with little preparation except prayer. As she arose to speak, the prophet Isaiah's words to King Hezekiah came to her: "Set thine house in order; for thou shalt die, and not live." She could always look back on this service as proof that God had called her and that the wide-eyed congregation believed her calling was authentic. As she began to speak, the "man-fearing" spirit left. "We continued the meeting a few days," she wrote, "and 20 claimed to be converted."[17]

Just as not every would-be evangelist would strike success so quickly, neither would all of Etter's meetings in the next forty-five years run as smoothly as this one. Acceptance in any given town was often slow. Officials arrested her in at least three cities, charging her with obtaining money under false pretenses, practicing medicine without a license, and disturbing the peace. Angry citizens often intimidated Etter and her coworkers and even threatened their lives. During Etter's 1889–90 tent campaign in Oakland, California, supporters of her ministry built a protective wall around the back of the platform because of death threats from the vigilante group White Caps. A few months later a mob surrounded the eight-thousand-seat tent in the infamous hoodlum-infested Kerry Patch area of St. Louis, throwing rocks and shouting insults in an attempt to halt the meetings. Etter recalled that dangerous period in her 1894 book *Life, Work and Experience of Maria Beulah Woodworth:* "Men stood on the seats with hats on; cigars and pipes in their mouths . . . They would shoot off fire crackers, and when we sang, they sang louder; when we prayed, they clapped their hands and cheered us. They had pistols and clubs, and were ready to kill us, and tear down the tent . . . It looked like surrender or death."[18]

Also during the St. Louis meeting, two doctors tried to have Etter committed as insane because worshipers under the tent—including Etter— were going into trances. The *Weekly Medical Review* branded Etter's tactics as hypnotism and the leadership as possibly fools or knaves. As can be expected, the controversy gave newspapers plenty of copy to fill their columns and stirred up more interest among the citizens of St. Louis. But Etter came up with an unlikely ally. In defending her rights and criticizing the doctors—and the medical profession in general—the *St. Louis Republic* fired off harsh language in its editorial "Quackery and Emotional Religion." "Ordinarily this may be treated as a jest," the editorial stated, "but when the effort to obtain free advertising takes the form of cowardly annoyances to a defenseless woman, who, however ignorant and unconventional she may be, is certainly trying to do what good she can, it deserves the unqualified condemnation of all who love fair play."[19] Etter's followers cheered a major newspaper coming to their leader's aid but no doubt resented the same writer describing her as ignorant and unconventional.

Was she insane and dangerous? The case was dropped when the judge stated he had no jurisdiction to order Etter subjected to evaluations. Based on reports in early twentieth-century Pentecostal publications, most editors viewed Etter as perfectly sane and a prophetess for the hour. One reservation should be noted from an oral history interview with David Lee Floyd. This early Arkansas preacher admitted misgivings about women preachers but attended Etter's meetings in Hot Springs, Arkansas, during the summer and fall of 1913. Supporting the meetings were E. N. Bell, D. C. O. Opperman, and Howard Goss—three of the men who called for the organization of the Assemblies of God in the same city a few months later. When asked what these three leaders thought about Etter, Floyd hesitated for a moment and then answered that they supported her but cautioned others about "giving her too much authority."[20]

One prominent Pentecostal who had no qualms about recognizing a woman's call to preach or giving Etter too much authority was Robert J. Craig, who along with his wife, Mary, founded Glad Tidings Temple, San Francisco, and what became Bethany College of the Assemblies of God. Craig urged ministers in 1916 to use Etter's life and ministry as an example. "If the Pentecostal ministry would study her life and count on God, expecting the supernatural to be revealed in each meeting, what a mighty agency ours would be in the hands of God."[21] Craig gave credit for the early growth of his big-city evangelistic center to Etter and to Aimee Semple McPherson's 1917 and 1919 crusades. Etter's meetings, especially, he called "a turning point" in the work, as numbers of stalwarts joined the effort.[22] Other ministers would join Craig in ignoring gender and describing Etter as a turning-point, Bible-quoting, Holy Ghost evangelist.

Throughout her long ministry, Etter established a strong base of support. Ministers invited her to conduct meetings; editors of Christian publications publicized her meetings; those who attended her meetings bought her books and gave financially. Early Pentecostal Howard Goss described Etter as a great warrior and an ideal evangelist. "She never seemed to tire," he wrote. "Nothing daunted or shook her faith . . . With a faint smile on her face, her right hand slightly upraised, she would calmly and gladly, I think, have walked into a den of lions for Jesus."[23] Even today Etter enjoys uncritical acceptance from many charismatics and Pentecostals. Evangelists Benny Hinn and Kenneth Hagin quote her, often with legends that grow with the repeating. The late David duPlessis enthusiastically told me, "Her books were marvelous. Years ago I used to read her books often for the wonderful inspiration they provided."[24]

Opponents met Etter and her entourage from coast to coast, however— like the St. Louis medical doctors, critical newspaper editors, and officials who ordered her arrest in Massachusetts, Nebraska, and California. The trances and prayers for the sick infuriated them to the point where they took aim at Etter and fired broadsides. Others opposed her because she was a woman and in their opinion did not belong in the pulpit. Had Etter been any weaker, she would have backed away from the opposition and returned to the Ohio farm. But the feisty and confident evangelist took the hits and stayed on course.[25]

Encouraging Other Women

In her 1894 autobiography Etter reviewed fourteen years of itinerant evangelism and marveled at how she had been able to—in a sense—clone herself. "Ever since I started in the work, God has been raising up men and women by hundreds who have gone out as ministers and evangelists." And she added that letters poured in from them, reporting their "trials and triumphs"—a frequently used phrase for Etter. They looked to her as "a mother for advice."[26] With the difficulty women encountered trying to answer a call to preach, perhaps the most encouraging counsel would come from a trailblazer and role model. Etter provided that for countless women, including the most famous of all, Aimee Semple McPherson.

McPherson had gained notoriety by the end of World War I as a result of preaching on the East Coast and in the Midwest, and from her initial efforts in publishing the *Bridal Call* magazine. In October 1918, now twenty-eight years of age, she rolled her big Oldsmobile touring "Gospel Car" from the east toward Los Angeles, where she would find her place in the sun—and the center of controversy—for the remaining twenty-six years of her life. But she had an important stop in Indianapolis. For years she had longed to meet the old veteran sawdust trail preacher, Etter, who had just opened her tabernacle five months earlier. "I have longed to hear her preach and be at her meetings," McPherson wrote in her diary. "Tomorrow Mrs. Etter's tabernacle will be open and I will have the desire of my heart. Glory!"[27] Etter was seventy-four at the time and still preaching campaigns even though she had established a local church in Indianapolis. But now one could almost feel the changing of the guard. A new generation was ready to blaze trails and gain even more notoriety than Etter had managed in nearly forty years of preaching.

Etter knew what it was to have men set up roadblocks in her efforts to preach. And she knew other women faced the same treatment. She believed some were misusing the apostle Paul's statement that women were to remain silent in the church and learn from their husbands at home (1 Cor. 14:34). It did not forbid women to preach or lead, she argued. And she asked, "What will those do who have no husbands? Do you suppose they will remain in ignorance and be lost?" A tinge of ridicule came through when she added, "If some women had to depend on their husbands for knowledge, they would die in ignorance."[28]

She tried to convince the opposition that the scriptures gave clearance for women to enter the ministry. Her sermon "Women's Rights in the Gospel" argued that women in the Old and New Testaments were called of God. Priscilla and Phoebe, who ministered with Paul, were two of her examples. Paul commended Pheobe to the church at Rome (Rom. 16:1). "This shows that [Pheobe] had authority to do business in the churches," Etter argued, "and that she had been successful in winning souls to Christ."[29] As for her own credentials, she wrote that she was ordained an elder with the Churches of God (Winebrenner), in September 1884, "with authority to administer the ordinances and to solemnize matrimony." So forget the opposition, Etter advised women who felt a call to preach. "It is hightime for women to let their lights shine; to bring out their talents that have been hidden away rusting, and use them for the glory of God."[30]

Carrie Judd Montgomery, an early Pentecostal evangelist, editor, and faith home founder in Oakland, cooperated in Etter's 1889–90 meetings in the Bay Area.[31] In her 1936 autobiography, *Under His Wings,* Montgomery recalled meeting many people through the years who were converted and blessed in that campaign. One woman in particular told Montgomery that the "arrow of conviction fastened on her heart" and she finally yielded to God's call and later operated a "soul-saving" mission for many years. Many other women responded to Etter's emotional pleas beginning in the 1880s. Now more than a century later she is still a role model for women who respond when they read her challenges in reprinted sermons and books.[32]

Racial Views and Practices

Some of the wealthy citizens said that they liked the meetings [Louisville, August 1888], would help support them, but they would not do anything if we let the negroes come. Ministers and professing Christians said the same. They said all evangelists that had been in the city could do no good until they drove the negroes away. I told them God made the whole human family of one blood. Christ had died for all . . . I thank God we had no desire to drive them away, but felt glad to have the privilege of leading them to Christ.

—*Maria Beulah Woodworth-Etter*

A Ninety-Day Integrated Southern Crusade

Etter had been on the sawdust trail for eight years when she felt led to conduct evangelistic meetings in "one of the wickedest cities in the world," Louisville, Kentucky—even though she did not know a person there. Not only would she receive stiff opposition from those who disagreed with her evangelism style, she would also have the challenge of trying to mix the races in a southern city—nearly seventy years before the integration crisis at Little Rock's Central High School. Despite heavy rains that inundated Etter's tent in August 1888, the crowds began to build with many responding to her call to the mourners' bench. Soon the tent was filled, and hundreds stood outside hoping that those inside would leave so they could get closer to the action. Though she had earlier ministered for a month in Memphis—and "worked some with the colored people of that city"—there is no indication in her books that she tried to integrate the meetings. She does report that African Americans in Memphis accepted her message like children and were converted "all over the house, while I was talking."[33]

Now, during the summer of 1888, she would learn that mixing the races would not win friends among Louisville's white community. With a deep sense of wrong being done to an entire race, Etter wrote that the southern whites were so prejudiced that integrating church services would create strong opposition. The whites would stay at home if blacks were permitted to come. It would take a miracle and human ingenuity to keep both races under one tent. So Etter introduced a compromise: she put black worshipers in one corner of the tent.

"Some of the wealthy citizens said that they liked the meetings," Etter wrote about her dilemma, "would help support them, but they would not do anything if we let the negroes come."[34] What shocked and provoked Etter was that ministers and professing Christians ranked among the prejudiced. She held a different set of values and experiences. She had seen first-hand racial discrimination as a child in Lisbon, Ohio, where an underground railroad operated for the fleeing southern slaves. She chose to support the underdog. Beginning in her earliest meetings in the North, she welcomed blacks and conducted services in black churches. She also featured blacks in her meetings as soloists. But now she was on the southern banks of the Ohio River in Louisville. Geographically, Lisbon is less than four hundred miles from Louisville. Culturally, in 1888 it was a million miles away.

"I told them God made the whole human family of one blood," she wrote in 1894. "Christ died for all. Christ said, 'Go preach my gospel to all nations, to every creature.'" And she asked a penetrating question for these nineteenth-century white believers in Louisville: "Can we obey God and drive the hungry souls away?" When a delegation came to talk her out of allowing blacks to attend, she said that God told her to go where he sent her "without respect to person or place." Etter held her ground on personal convictions, fearing that the Holy Spirit would leave if she drove blacks away. And her steadfastness paid off. "God came in such wonderful power, it was not long till they seemed to forget the color. The altar was filled with seekers." But the irony was that white people were on one side and black people were on the other.[35]

Hundreds of blacks were converted in these Louisville meetings that ran for three months. But the reality of southern culture determined her final act in the city: she organized two missions—one for whites and one for blacks. About the black mission, Etter wrote that the people had done a good work for the Master. "I believe the work will go on till the trumpet sounds, and we shall meet them with the sheaves they have gathered for the

Lord."[36] Though the Louisville integration experiment lasted but ninety days, Etter left the "wicked" city with a good feeling. Blacks were given equal opportunity to participate in the services and respond to her altar calls, and she was pleased that she could help them start a church.[37]

Racial Equality from Start to Finish

From her earliest ministry beginning in 1880 until her death in 1924, Etter's racial views and practices remained consistent. Unafraid, she promoted her unity theme, and who was she to turn anyone away? In the North, she faced few problems with her views and practices under the tent. It was in the South, as in Louisville, that she ran into conflicts. Black participation began as early as her 1885 Hartford City, Indiana, meeting, where she used a black barber, Ananias Frazier, as her soloist. During her Springfield, Illinois, campaign in 1888–89, a black woman soloist ministered.

Newspaper reporters—North and South—often noticed the number of blacks in attendance. One of the accounts citing considerable black participation came from the 1889–90 Oakland campaign. The *Oakland Tribune* wrote that black people were Etter's most earnest adherents. When an Oakland minister wrote a letter to the editor calling Etter a "pious fraud," D. E. Johnson, pastor of the local African Methodist Episcopal church, reacted quickly. Etter had been opposed by the devil, saloonkeepers, and some ministers, Johnson wrote, "yet draws greater audiences than any minister in town without the aid of a fine choir and organ."[38] Later Etter invited him to pray the prayer of dedication for her new eight-thousand-seat tent in Oakland. Another black minister, J. E. Currin, also responded to considerable criticism aimed at Etter during the Oakland meeting, defending her calling from Acts 1:5–8 and 2:4.

Twenty-two years after the Oakland meeting, leaders of the World-Wide Camp Meeting in Los Angeles invited Etter as the main speaker in a 1913 gathering that attracted some two hundred ministers and hundreds of laypeople. Among the influential Pentecostal ministers in attendance was Garfield T. Haywood, a well-known black leader and another strong Etter supporter. In his Indianapolis paper, Haywood wrote that many were healed through "the instrumentality of His humble servant, Sister Etter, whose simple faith brought deliverance to many." And he added that on one occasion people were healed as Etter "raised her hands toward heaven, while she was leaving the tent."[39] Haywood's daughter, Rollie Ellis of Indianapolis, told me that her parents used to take her to the Woodworth-Etter tabernacle. She would never forget the collection of crutches, canes, and wheelchairs displayed in the church—silent testimonies of people who had been healed.

From time to time after the turn of the twentieth century, Etter returned to the South and Southwest with her salvation-healing campaigns—stopping in Dallas, Houston, and San Antonio, Texas; Hot Springs, Arkansas; Memphis, Tennessee; Meridian, Mississippi; Warrior, Alabama; Atlanta, Georgia; London and Louisville, Kentucky; Tampa, Florida; and places in between. Because of the outstanding success of her first Atlanta meeting, Etter returned in 1914. But it also was a place where the race question resurfaced.

In the 1914 Atlanta meeting a few black ministers dared to attend, sitting alone in the back. It was permitted, but then word circulated in the black community that God was moving in old-time power. Soon black Atlantans had crowded the church, and Etter had a major problem on her hands. Finally the executive committee for the Etter meetings in Atlanta—apparently with Etter's blessing—decided on a compromise. Blacks could attend but not in large numbers, a policy that would give whites a better chance for seats. That ruling did not stop blacks from seeking out Etter's ministry. At the close of the meetings they would stand outside hoping that she would stop and pray for them. Etter also addressed the problem by taking her crusades one night a week to blacks in some of the biggest churches in Atlanta, creating an overwhelming response. First, they knew that in Etter they had a friend. Second, her message of salvation, spiritual power, and healing struck a responsive chord. When it came time to pray for the sick, Etter discovered it was almost impossible to hold back the rush toward the front. Many fell to the floor in the traditional Etter trance—which she called the "slain of the Lord."[40]

African Americans in Atlanta were not the only minority to receive personal attention from Etter. As the 1920 Etter tornado gathered momentum in Sioux City, Iowa, the excitement attracted several Native Americans from the nearby Hochunk-Winnebago reservation. Because many of the Indians were unable to attend the Sioux City meetings, ninety-three of them signed a petition inviting Etter to their reservation. Etter initially agreed to conduct meetings for a day or two, but the response was so overwhelming that she stayed more than a week. A lawyer who was president of the Indian Societies of the United States told Etter that he and another prominent Indian had hated each other but that, as a result of the meetings, they now loved each other. A young Indian man appeared at Etter's Omaha meetings six weeks later and told of the successful Winnebago meeting and that God had called him to become a minister so he could return to his people on the reservation. He added, "I shall go back there and preach the word of God." Etter wrote, "As a result of my work [in Winnebago], I feel quite an interest in them and shall never cease to pray for them."[41]

Martin Luther King Jr., during the civil rights struggle of the 1950s and 1960s, declared the Sunday morning worship service "the most segregated hour of Christian America." When Etter opened her tabernacle in Indianapolis in 1918, however, King's declaration would not have applied. Everyone was welcome, as can be seen in a congregational photo showing a crowded tabernacle—with a sprinkling of African Americans seated side by side with whites. And the Hochunk-Winnebago tribe also kept in contact with Etter. Some of these Native Americans who became acquainted with Etter in Nebraska traveled to her tabernacle in Indianapolis for salvation and healing. Another indication of openness was a favorite evangelist she engaged to travel with her party and to preach occasionally at the tabernacle. Her followers would never forget the Native American Watt Walker—especially when the popular speaker was decked out in his leather, silver, beads, and headdress.

Summary

The women and children began to wear cleaner clothes, and came with their bonnets on, and left their dirty aprons at home. The men shaved and combed, and came with their families. They said the meeting was doing good; that their wives and children were getting more tidy and keeping their homes cleaner.

—Maria B. Woodworth-Etter

Throughout her long forty-five-year ministry, Maria B. Woodworth-

Etter saw the need for a two-pronged overhauling of the Christian church and American society. Preaching a "gospel of power," she argued, was the antidote for both. She promoted and defended women in the ministry and maintained an open-door policy for rich as well as poor, Caucasians as well as minorities, society's elite as well as the disinherited, and the educated as well as the uneducated.

A St. Louis newspaper reported in 1890 that many drunkards had signed Etter's "abstainer's" pledge. Etter said of that meeting, "Many of the best citizens came to the meetings and were astonished at the great victory we had gained over the rough element, and the good order attained."[42] And with the same Holiness-charismatic-Pentecostal brand of Christianity, she cut a wide swath from coast to coast in her challenge to social and religious mores. A. H. Argue, a revered early Pentecostal evangelist, described Etter's 1913 meeting in Chicago as the "mightiest visitation from God of these latter days." One of the admonitions that set Etter apart from other Pentecostals and fundamentalists of the day demonstrated an open-door policy for all people: "Don't denounce churches. Don't denounce the Catholics. Catholics won't come in for fear you will denounce them. I never mention Catholics." Show them and the "formalists" the real Gospel, she added, and they will "want to get alive."[43]

Etter's followers then and even now revere this Ohio farmer's wife turned evangelist. Her converts and others whose faith she strengthened cannot be numbered. But the cost was high. Countless thugs from California to Massachusetts and from Washington to Florida scrambled for an opportunity to disrupt her Gospel meetings. Seemingly they operated a network that spread the word from city to city that Etter was on the way. They loved nothing better than a rock-throwing, tent-shaking brawl.

One might wonder about the often violent reaction. Perhaps Etter's unconventional tent meetings as opposed to religious services held in established churches is one answer. When a gang of youth with nothing but time on their hands saw a huge tent being erected, they were naturally interested. When they learned that the meetings were conducted by outsiders, they no doubt became territorial—and in some cases violent. Ministers not in her camp, which was the majority, and reporters, who sharpened their pencils and wit at Etter's expense, viewed her racial practices, spiritual trances, and female ministry as divisive and unwanted in their communities.

When the *St. Louis Republic* writer called Etter a "defenseless woman" in

1890, Etter herself was the first to disagree. She then voiced her personal faith in God with her favorite Bible verses: "Not by might, nor by power, but by my Spirit, saith the Lord of hosts" (Zech. 4:6), and "For by thee I have run through a troop; and by my God have I leaped over a wall" (Ps. 18:29). An absolute conviction about her call and the needy people lined up to hear her message would be more than enough to keep her going to the next Kerry Patch, the next rained-soaked tent, the next band of ruffians, the next troop to run through, or the next wall to leap. But always with the assurance that the battle belonged to the Lord of hosts.[44]

Builders

Florence Crawford, circa 1915. Courtesy of the Apostolic Faith Church, Portland, Oregon

Florence Crawford: Apostolic Faith Pioneer

Cecil M. Robeck Jr.

> I happen to be . . . the first white woman that received the baptism of the Holy Ghost in this Latter Rain Gospel in the City of Los Angeles, and I have seen a few things from that day to this, and don't you never doubt it. . . . I have seen the great God of Israel protect this Latter Rain Gospel and hold it steady . . . and He is going to pilot a few through to the pearly gates, on the old lines. . . . I want to tell you, I would rather have that old Word of God in my heart, and know it was there, and would meet all the Goliaths and the demons of hell that come up against this wonderful truth, that would rob us and steal away some of the fundamental truths of this old Bible. There is a few of us today that could go to the stake . . . but we will never lower the standard of that old Gospel.

Like many early leaders in the Pentecostal movement, Florence Louise Crawford was convinced that her position was the only true one. The "old Gospel" she preached was rooted in the Bible and founded along "old lines." Though this "Latter Rain Gospel" was offered to many, only "a few" would grasp its meaning, the few who would be willing to go to the stake for the sake of that Gospel, the same few whom God would eventually pilot through the pearly gates.[1]

When Florence Crawford died in 1936, "the few" included three thousand persons who attended her funeral and a line of cars that extended nearly three miles between the Woodstock campground, where the funeral was held, and the Rose City Cemetery in Portland, Oregon.[2] The few also included thousands of believers in hundreds of churches in the United States, Scandinavia, India, and especially in Africa. It is her unique and successful ministry, built on restlessness and experimentation, that this chapter seeks to explore.

Years of Preparation

Crawford was a pioneer who operated in a bastion of male privilege, the clerical world. She claimed to be the first white woman to receive Holy Spirit baptism in the Azusa Street Mission in Los Angeles in 1906 and was, from the beginning, fully aware of the significance of her own role in the spread of that revival around the world.[3] The fellowship of churches she founded ultimately became known as the Apostolic Faith Mission (Portland, Oregon). Affectionately called "Mother" by her followers, Crawford participated in the church with maternal passion and conviction. Moreover, during most of her ministry (1907–36), she remained a single parent, rearing two children.

Crawford came by her pioneer spirit legitimately. As children, her parents, Oscar Reed and Mary Lehnherr Reed Brown, had each traversed the Oregon Trail with their parents in a covered wagon pulled by ox teams.[4] In Oregon, her maternal grandfather settled the region now referred to as Myrtle Point, while her paternal grandfather, an Illinois doctor, established the first gristmill in the Umpqua region of western Oregon. Florence Louise Reed, one of ten siblings, was born to the Reeds on September 1, 1872, and was reared in this largely agricultural area.[5]

Like many who pioneered the rough-and-tumble Pacific Northwest, the Reeds did not embrace the Christian faith that was then embraced by much of the nation. The Reeds were products of the Enlightenment. They were socially connected free thinkers who entertained other like-minded pioneers in southwestern Oregon. Their library highlighted the writings of Thomas Paine and Robert Green Ingersoll.[6] Crawford frequently recalled that her parents read the works of these men aloud in much the way that the Bible was read in the homes of others. Their home served as a gathering place where the Reeds hosted famous free-thought speakers. And in the end, she labeled them infidels.[7]

Reared in a cauldron of free thought, Crawford had her own ideas regarding God. Once as a child, she later recalled, she sneaked off to a nearby camp meeting where she heard the gospel message and was deeply touched through the singing of "Oh, the Bleeding Lamb."[8] On another occasion, when a "noted infidel" gave a lecture in her home, he asked her to sing. She agreed to do so if she could pick the song. Her choice was "Jesus, Lover of My Soul." Her song brought tears to the eyes of a number of those present, an event she contended effectively cut the heart out of the lecturer's message.[9] Not yet a Christian herself, Crawford evinced at a young age a spiritual sensitivity that would flourish in adulthood.

As did other early Pentecostal leaders, Crawford seems to have endured her share of childhood illnesses. She attributed her poor eyesight and need for glasses to spinal meningitis, which she claimed to have contracted three times. As a young teenager, she was thrown from a carriage and landed on a stump, injuring her back. Bedridden for weeks, the injury sustained in the fall required that she wear a "surgical support" for eleven years.[10] Owing to her poor health, Crawford moved to the Los Angeles area by 1890, where she lived for a time in a "tent house."[11] Since she came to California as a young woman no more than eighteen years of age, it is probable that she came with one of her brothers. The most likely candidate is C. C. Reed, a man who, in 1906, made his living as a tailor in Highland Park, California.[12]

Even in Los Angeles, Crawford's illness persisted—to the point where she described herself as "a physical wreck." Her lungs were badly infected, apparently from tuberculosis, and she suffered extensively from a chronic cough and hemorrhages.[13] She sought medical help in Los Angeles and in San Bernardino,[14] where she took up residence on a farm in the Menefee Valley, near what is now Hemet.[15] There she met with little relief. "I took the Scott's Emulsion, I used the egg and wine, the doctors tried their skill and they failed, I was nothing but skin and bones."[16] Still, she recovered enough to lead a busy life. She married and gave birth to two children, Raymond Robert (1891) and Mildred (1897).

The details surrounding Crawford's religious awakening are vague. Most likely, her conversion occurred in Los Angeles around 1900. According to her often repeated testimony, as a young woman she ran in circles that frequented the theater, hosted card parties, and engaged in ballroom dancing. It was while she was on the dance floor that she believed God first addressed her with the words "Daughter, give *me* thine heart." She heard them three times in the midst of her dance and immediately concluded that God had spoken them. This incident led her to seek out an unnamed friend who prayed with and for her and led her to make a confession of faith.[17]

In all likelihood, this divine encounter was only the tip of the iceberg in what lay behind her conversion. Her desire to be part of the southern California social scene would surely have led her to frequent churches from time to time. Her husband, Frank Mortimer Crawford, was reportedly a Congregationalist and was not antagonistic to the church.[18] When Florence Crawford was converted, she sought counsel first from a Methodist minister. She informed him that she wanted to be baptized. Though she became a member of First Methodist Church, she later stated that she had disagreed with the minister over the mode of baptism he suggested (he promised a baptism by sprinkling and she wanted one by immersion). Quickly she rose to become a class leader.[19] Her ability to argue a mode of baptism so early in her Christian life, however, suggests that she possessed strong religious convictions before she met with the pastor.[20]

Following her conversion, Crawford threw herself into her church and rescue work. She also became something of a church hopper, worshiping with the Methodists, the Presbyterians, the Christian Alliance at the Gospel Tabernacle Church, and Joseph Smale's First New Testament Church. Her pastors at the Gospel Tabernacle included the Rev. W. C. Stevens, a former Presbyterian pastor who had served as a member of the founding board for Occidental College but who joined A. B. Simpson's Christian Alliance around the turn of the century, and the Rev. J. H. Ballard.[21]

Crawford involved herself in a variety of community projects, related no doubt to her participation in the Methodist Church, and in the Women's Christian Temperance Union (WCTU). In 1905, the WCTU held a national convention in Los Angeles. The *Los Angeles Express* noted that a "Mrs. Crawford" was among those who met the delegates at the Southern Pacific station as the delegates arrived from around the country.[22] The following year, she attended the county convention of the WCTU as a delegate from Highland Park, where she lived with her family.[23]

Rescue work appealed deeply to Florence Crawford long before she preached the "Latter Rain Gospel." Regarding this period in her life she later wrote, "many a time when I was just miserable and wretched and couldn't hardly crawl around, I would go up to the old county jail in the city of Los Angeles."[24] Through her rescue work, she met a variety of people. She personally knew the sheriff, and many of the detectives, policemen, and ministers in Los Angeles.[25] She often visited what she called the "old prisons and the slums" and worked with the juvenile court.[26] She gave frequent public appeals in various Los Angeles pulpits and the city's clubs for aid to the rescue work.[27] Because of her work with the WCTU and her concern for the young people of her day, she joined the local chapter of the National Congress of Mothers, founded in 1897 and now known as the Parent-Teacher Association (PTA).[28]

Active as she was, though, Crawford remained restless.

> Every evangelist that came to that city I would have an interview with him, if it were possible. And it nearly always was and I would tell him of that hunger in my heart; and he would ask me a few questions and I would answer them. I could tell him that once I loved the things of the world, the fine clothes, fine carriages. (We had no automobiles.) But I said, "it is all gone, and I am giving my time in the slums and jails and caring for the sick and dying." And all he said was, "you couldn't have any more." I was only justified by faith, but God had given me a good dose of it, I am here to tell you.[29]

She was unsatisfied merely with her "justification." She wanted more. She claimed that she was searching for sanctification, but these ministers told her that she was already sanctified. She was convinced that they were wrong, for she said, "I knew that the fire of God had never fallen on the altar of my heart."[30]

During this period of searching, a revival raged in Wales. The papers and pulpits of Los Angeles covered this event. Among those who visited Wales to observe the revival firsthand and meet its leader, Evan Roberts, was the Rev. Joseph Smale, pastor of First Baptist Church.[31] Smale returned in June 1905, determined to bring the revival to Los Angeles.[32] He established a number of home prayer meetings and conducted a series of meetings that lasted three months. Board members at First Baptist Church objected and Smale resigned. By September 24, 1905, Smale had leased space at Burbank Hall and organized the First New Testament Church.[33]

Crawford attended Smale's First New Testament Church from time to time.[34] When later she described the events of that period to her own followers, she remembered, "The young men in the First Methodist church were holding all night prayer meetings"—an unprecedented activity in Los

Angeles. To her, it illustrated how deeply the people of that day sensed their own spiritual need. "God was laying it on the hearts of the people to pray for the outpouring of the Spirit."[35]

In April 1906 a woman with whom Crawford was acquainted, but whom she had not seen for a number of years, called at her home. This woman told Crawford that she would find what she was seeking at the Azusa Street Mission.[36] Following her first service there, Crawford called aside someone, probably Pastor William J. Seymour, and said, "Brother, God Almighty brought me into this place, and I want you to tell me where I stand." He allegedly responded, "Sister, you have got a wonderful case of salvation, but you need to be sanctified." She knelt and prayed. She returned home and continued to pray for several days. At 5 P.M. the next Friday, she claimed to be sanctified. "And just a week from that day, at five o'clock, sitting in my seat [at the Azusa Street Mission], the Holy Ghost came down from Heaven and fell upon my life, and baptized me with the Holy Ghost and fire, spoke through me in another language."[37]

The next day, Crawford took her daughter, Mildred, to a dentist for a tooth extraction. The dentist informed Crawford that, because of complications suffered from diphtheria, her daughter would need surgery to aid her breathing. Crawford sought medical help for her daughter, but before any surgery was performed she decided to pray. She argued the case with God, saying, "God, if you could take this woman, who never spoke another language in all her life, and make her speak in the Chinese language, You can heal this child." Mildred slept through the night, and her mother later testified that she was healed from that moment. Crawford's son, Raymond, had been watching and he asked his mother if God could not heal her as well. She thought about his challenge to her and then concluded that the "doctors had failed." Once again she prayed. This time she promised God that she would preach the Gospel if God would heal her. She removed her brace of eleven years and never wore it again. She believed she had been healed.[38]

Crawford's experience at the Azusa Street Mission convinced her that the worshipers there had the answers for which she had been searching. They recognized, in turn, the gifts that she brought to them. Her rescue work, involvement in the National Congress of Mothers, and public speaking skills made her valuable to the unfolding work of the mission. Throughout the summer, Crawford integrated herself into the meetings at

Azusa Street and into what might be called the inner circle of leaders who set mission policy.

In September, Crawford's vision for the potential that the message of Azusa Street held for others took a new form. William F. Manley, founder of the Household of God and now serving as the pastor of a congregation in Oakland, California, attended meetings at Azusa Street in August 1906. He offered to host those who would bring this message to Oakland. M. L. Ryan, then leading a small mission in Salem, Oregon, did the same. Crawford was ready and willing to go.

Crawford approached her "overseer," most assuredly Pastor Seymour, about the possibility of her going to Portland: "he didn't see how I could go, he didn't think it was the thing for me to go." She prevailed upon him, arguing that, if God had called her, God would make it possible for her to go and would show Seymour that she was to go. "Very well," he reportedly acquiesced.[39]

Entrusted with the task of overseeing the opening of new works throughout California in the name of the Apostolic Faith Mission, Crawford prepared to leave. By late November, the mission had produced new stationery under the name "The Pacific Apostolic Faith Movement," and featured prominently on the letterhead was "Florence Crawford, State Director."[40]

Her traveling expenses covered, Crawford left Highland Park and with it her husband and son. Taking her daughter, Mildred, with her, she headed north on an extended evangelistic tour.[41] G. W. Evans, his wife, May Evans, and William F. Manley accompanied her to Oakland, California, where they held a series of meetings for the Household of God.[42] Within days they reported hundreds at the altar. Sixty-five people received Holy Spirit baptism, among them Manley and a Portuguese evangelist, Adolf Rosa, from the Cape Verde Islands. Others were sanctified or converted. A series of short meetings turned into a five-week session.[43]

In the meantime, M. L. Ryan anxiously awaited Crawford's arrival in Salem, Oregon. In early October, Ryan announced to the local press in Salem that he expected a group from the Azusa Street Mission to arrive shortly. Even the *Los Angeles Express* carried the news of their upcoming meetings in Salem. A list of evangelists Ryan expected included G. W. and May Evans; Thomas Junk and his wife, who were ultimately bound for China as missionaries; Florence Crawford; and two African American women, Ophelia Wiley and Lulu Miller. Ryan's expectations were high, but he predicted that when this group arrived in Salem they would all face persecution.[44] By the following month, however, the group had still not arrived. Ryan, who published a newspaper called *Apostolic Light,* ran a letter from Clara Lum in Los Angeles. She reported that the group had left Los Angeles and was in Oakland, but held out the promise that "the Lord [was] showing her wonderful things about the work in the north."[45] The saints in Salem had to be encouraged.

Ophelia Wiley arrived by Sunday, November 15, when she took part in services.[46] Someone had marred the meetings earlier by throwing a rock through the window.[47] Meanwhile, a reporter for the local paper described their "tongues" as "the silly talk of the superstitious."[48] Someone sympathetic to Ryan wrote an anonymous letter to the editor, complaining about the biased reporting of the papers.[49] Tensions grew but Crawford remained absent. She finally arrived about December 15.[50]

Crawford's presence in Salem during the month of December was anything but tranquil. There she engaged in the practice of writing in tongues. This practice had marked the beginnings of the Apostolic Faith movement in Topeka, Kansas, but was ultimately rejected at the Azusa Street Mission in Los Angeles.[51] Practitioners believed that since the Spirit enabled one to speak in tongues it should also be possible to write in tongues.

The local news found this story worth carrying. Ryan declared Jesus to be left-handed, since Ryan, who was normally right-handed, was able to write in tongues only with his left hand. Reporters called Crawford Ryan's "nearest rival in this new specialty" and reported that she could write in seven or eight languages. Despite such coverage, Crawford and others reported that good results came from the meetings.[52]

On December 29, 1906, Florence and Mildred Crawford traveled to Portland, Oregon, arriving at noon. Their host was an African American pastor, John F. Glasco, at St. John's Gospel Mission at 235 Second Street, a congregation in decline.[53] Glasco's family had visited the Salem mission during Crawford's time there and had invited her to come to their church upon arrival in Portland. At 3:00 P.M., services began in a blacksmith's shop, now turned church. The neighbors were furious. Already reputed as a noisy congregation, complaints filed by neighbors against the church were quickly compounded with Crawford's arrival. Readers of Portland's *Evening Telegram* were informed that the mission *required* that "the men hug and fondle the women." Participants were said to clean "the filth from the dirty floor of their chapel by rolling around in it to save brooom [sic] expense." The meetings were interracial, and outsiders who disapproved of the ease with which the races mingled accused the congregation of mistreating Crawford's daughter.[54]

Neighbors complained that they were losing business because of these "ignorant and feeble-minded persons." The anger expressed by neighbors can be measured by the speed and extent to which the community became involved. Within forty-eight hours of Crawford's arrival the mayor of Portland, Police Chief Gritzmacher, Judge Frazer of the juvenile court, and Lola Baldwin of the Travelers' Aid Society had joined forces to investigate the meetings. Stories of the Salem meetings that had run in the Portland papers had put the city on the defensive. Crawford had been in town only two nights when Judge Frazer issued a citation for mistreatment. Two probation officers delivered it to Crawford on New Year's Eve.[55]

The previous evening, Mildred had received her Holy Spirit baptism and spoken in tongues in the meetings at St. John's Gospel Mission.[56] The fact that she was only nine made her the center of attention. The stage was set for a showdown with the juvenile court authorities. With only one day to prepare, Crawford was summoned to appear before Judge Frazer in the juvenile court at 4:00 P.M. on January 2. In the meantime, the *Evening Telegram* kept the pressure on the embattled evangelist by publishing various charges against her.

The paper claimed Crawford had placed her daughter under some hypnotic spell. She had not provided for the "proper care and treatment" of her daughter, now nicknamed the "bride of the Lord," and had allowed Mildred to become the "chief attraction" to the "fantastic orgies" of blacks and whites. The free mixing of these Christians across racial lines scandalized the town. The paper even reported that the court might take Mildred away from her mother. Crowds of Portland residents made a beeline to the mission, raising an enormous commotion. Finding it impossible to conduct her services without interruption, Crawford reportedly flew into "a rage."[57]

When Crawford appeared before Judge Frazer, Captain Bailey served as the primary witness against her. The testimony against Crawford suggested that nine-year-old Mildred was "not being properly cared for and that she was allowed to indulge in the improper practices of the hysterical cult, mingling with negroes and whites of both sexes." Judge Frazer ordered

Crawford not to allow Mildred to attend the evening meetings. Furthermore, she was to enroll Mildred in school by January 4 or leave town. A "recalcitrant" Crawford grudgingly agreed. "The laws of man would for a time triumph over the will of God," she grumbled.[58]

By the next day, Mildred Crawford had caught a cold. As a result, Florence Crawford did not accede to the judge's order on January 4. Mr. White, the probation officer, immediately reported the girl's truancy to Judge Frazer, who empowered White to investigate further. The *Evening Telegram* reported that the officer "found the child in bed with the room full of fanatics of both sexes and colors." Crawford informed White of her daughter's cold and her plan to send Mildred back to their home in Los Angeles.[59] Crawford's reasons seemed to satisfy White. For three more days Crawford ministered in Glasco's mission. From December 29 through January 8, thirty-eight people received Holy Spirit baptism.[60] On January 8, Crawford left Portland, stopping off in Santa Rosa and Oakland before arriving in Los Angeles.[61]

After a short stay with her family in Highland Park, Crawford left her children in the care of her husband. On March 19, 1907, she returned to the road. She went first to Oakland, where she held meetings with standing room only. She "appointed deacons according to the word" and visited the work in San Francisco. The jails, hospitals, and soldiers' camps at the Presidio were "thrown open to us," she wrote. Even the chaplain received his "Pentecost."[62] Next she went to Santa Rosa, where several were baptized in the Spirit, and the Baptist church dismissed services to allow the congregation to attend one of her meetings.[63] Crawford then traveled south to San Jose, where she held a further week of meetings. She reported that seventeen new converts were baptized in the Spirit, and others received their sanctification and Spirit baptism. Three men were "set apart as deacons, and five women were appointed to look after the young converts." She visited the works in Oakland and San Francisco once again. Her stay in the Bay Area lasted seven weeks. Finally, she moved on to Portland, arriving again at Glasco's church on Friday, May 3. The following Sunday, eight people were baptized in the Spirit.[64] She would stay in Portland until July.

On June 1, 1907, while Sister Crawford was in Portland, the Azusa Street Mission began its Los Angeles camp meeting. Crawford was summoned home in July to care for Mildred, who had broken her arm. A proponent of divine healing, Crawford's husband, Frank, had at first refused medical attention for their daughter. Only when city officials and an Episcopal minister, alerted to the problem by concerned neighbors, threatened Crawford with prosecution did he acquiesce and allow his daughter's arm to be set.[65]

Moreover, just a week after Crawford's return, William C. Trotter, superintendent of the Union Rescue Mission in Los Angeles, announced to the board of the mission that he had received Holy Spirit baptism and spoken in tongues. While the Los Angeles press made big news of the story, the Pentecostal community rejoiced at Trotter's willingness to testify publicly that he had cast his lot with theirs.[66] Though Trotter had been a very successful superintendent of Los Angeles' rescue work, the board immediately declared his position vacant. They would not tolerate a tongues speaker. The movement had its first high-profile "martyr." Crawford had undoubtedly worked with Trotter when she was active in rescue work in Los Angeles. Nevertheless, Crawford and Trotter must have discussed his future at the camp meeting. Three weeks later the papers reported that he planned to go to San Francisco to work for the Apostolic Faith.[67]

The camp meeting ended Saturday, August 31. As things returned to normal, Crawford worked with the Azusa Street Mission but kept her ties with the other Apostolic Faith missions throughout California and Oregon. By late fall, she had again traveled north. She held a meeting in Santa Barbara sometime in early September and was pelted in the head by a whiskey bottle thrown her direction as she knelt in prayer at the altar. She accepted these marks of "martyrdom" and informed Azusa Street that she rejoiced to be able to bear in her body the marks of Christ.[68] She continued up the coast, finally returning to Portland with Mildred. There, Will Trotter, his wife, Bertha, and their two daughters, whom they named Florence and Mildred, as well as others from the Los Angeles area, soon joined her. Trotter quickly became Florence Crawford's chief lieutenant in the Portland work. He continued in that capacity for nearly a decade.[69]

In November 1907, Crawford led a group of associates that included Mildred, Trotter, James R. Conlee, and a Sister Neal on a trip to Winnipeg, Canada, where they participated in a Pentecostal convention.[70] From Winnipeg, they traveled to Toronto and back to Minneapolis–St. Paul. While Crawford was in Minneapolis "searching for clear direction as to where to go next," she reached the conclusion that God was directing her to return to Portland to establish a permanent, independent work.[71]

The Formation of the Apostolic Faith (Portland, Oregon)

It is difficult to assess everything that transpired during this period, in large part because of Florence Crawford's silence. Her reports back to the Azusa Street Mission all but ended in January 1908. She had returned to Portland. She testified to her love for Jesus and her pleasure at having had the opportunity to sit under the exposition of the scriptures offered by Pastor William J. Seymour at the Azusa Street Mission. Through her subsequent years, Crawford would look back repeatedly at Azusa Street with a great deal of fondness as *the* source of the modern Pentecostal revival and the work that had enabled her to begin the Apostolic Faith Mission in Portland, Oregon. In January 1908, the *Apostolic Faith* (Los Angeles) printed its last extant report on the work in Portland. It noted that a mission had opened there at 224 Madison Street.[72]

Loyce Carver, general overseer of the Apostolic Faith Mission from 1965 until the mid-1990s, stated that upon Crawford's return to Portland, Pastor Glasco turned his own work at Second and Main Street over to her. Crawford accepted his gift on the condition that the church would no longer take offerings. The congregation would learn to depend upon faith.[73] With many friends in Los Angeles, Crawford and Trotter set to work. Crawford and Clara Lum, editor of the *Apostolic Faith* (Los Angeles), remained close. Trotter had a wider circle of friends throughout the larger evangelical community. He continued rescue work in Portland in the name of the Apostolic Faith movement, maintaining an especially close relationship with Lyman Stewart, founder of the Union Oil Company, cofounder of the Union Rescue Mission of Los Angeles, and, later with his brother, the financier of *The Fundamentals,* a twelve-volume series of books that would become the backbone to the modern fundamentalist movement.[74]

More difficult to piece together are events surrounding the separation of Florence and Frank Crawford. What is clear is that the two did not share the belief that Florence Crawford had been called to minister in Portland. Frank Crawford stayed in Highland Park and continued work as a real estate developer and builder while his wife pioneered a new ministry. While the family has remained silent on the issue, others have not.

The nature of marriage had long been a topic of discussion among the Apostolic Faith people in Los Angeles as well as in Portland. Questions arose as to whether one could leave a spouse in order to enter ministry as a result of a divine call, and whether or not sexual relations within the marriage were to be reserved for purposes of procreation only. In September 1906, the local press reported that the talk of desertion for the sake of pursuing the truth or entering into ministry was all too common at the Azusa Street Mission.[75] The *Apostolic Faith* (Los Angeles) ran several articles on the subject, some perhaps inspired by Florence Crawford.[76]

Whether the marriage issue or her decision to move permanently to Portland was what ultimately separated Florence Crawford from further cooperation with Seymour after 1907 remains uncertain. Once she had moved to Portland, however, she assumed that the center of the revival had moved north with her. She built a base of power that incorporated the Apostolic Faith works in Oakland and San Francisco and even a mission in Los Angeles, all of which had been founded by people serving under the auspices of the Azusa Street Mission.

On May 13, 1908, ties were severed further when William J. Seymour married Jennie Evans Moore. For reasons yet unclear, the wedding proved too much for Clara Lum, who moved the *Apostolic Faith* to Portland.[77] This provided Crawford with a paper in which she could communicate to her own followers. It came ready-made with mailing lists of sympathetic people. Yet Crawford's acceptance of this paper and its lists in service to the Apostolic Faith Mission (Portland, Oregon) inevitably led to conflict with William J. Seymour and his followers, as well as with a few of her own.

With her position now more or less secure, Crawford set about building a network of churches throughout the Northwest and around the world. In Portland, she and Trotter drew on their rescue work experience. They began to reach out to the people of the streets, the jails, and the docks that speckled the banks of the Columbia and Willamette Rivers. During the summer of 1908, Crawford's son, Raymond, joined her in Portland. That fall he became a convert, and by 1910 he was ordained to assist her in the work.[78]

From the beginnings of the work in Portland, Oregon, summer camp meetings played an important part. By 1908, camp meetings were held on the edge of Portland at Mount Tabor. These meetings provided Crawford with a platform from which to gather recruits. There she trained ministers new to the movement and preached, taught, prayed for healings, and generally held court.

Crawford assumed her responsibilities with a strong sense of direction. She led the movement from her Apostolic Faith Mission on the corner of Front and Burnside. Trotter, and soon others, were moved about at her discretion, trouble-shooting, establishing new works, serving in various pastoral capacities, and evangelizing. At least one independent account provides a strong element of realism to the situation. Ned Caswell, an itinerant printer and member of the Peniel Mission, traveled regularly between Los Angeles and Seattle visiting various missions. His journal, recorded between 1908 and 1910, documents a struggling mission fluctuating between success and failure.

His first reference to the Apostolic Faith Mission in Portland came on September 27, 1908. It was anything but flattering: "I looked in at the Apostolic Faith in the afternoon, good attendance and the usual demonstrations. I understand Mrs. Crawford is in charge and Trotter there; with more or less 'popery' (Lee). Miss Black Dress from Azusa St. is there. I think of Isaiah's keen vision when he said, 'The heart is deceitful above all things and desperately wicked.' The devil and the flesh are deceiving many."[79]

The following week his assessment was more sympathetic. "I heard Trotter at the Apostolic Faith one night," he wrote, and "he did the best I ever heard him—John 3. Mrs. Crawford looks well. Their meetings are well attended. Quite a number of touring 'preachers' come this way—and the usual nuisances."[80]

Over the next several weeks, Caswell frequented the Apostolic Faith Mission. "Trotter and Mrs. Crawford *et. al.*, were out in a gospel wagon today doing some good preaching. Their mission is prosperous," he wrote on October 11. On October 18, he noted simply that he attended the Sunday evening service and, on October 25, "Trotter, Mrs. C., etc., held a fine gospel wagon meeting on Second & Burnside this afternoon."[81]

Caswell was also attentive to the difficulty of the work that Crawford and her associates were undertaking. On December 13, 1908, he observed, "At the 'tongues' mission I saw Mr. & Mrs. Moore, Trotter, Crawford, etc. They seem somewhat run down, and I get the idea finances are not as easy as formerly."[82]

Shortly after the New Year, Caswell returned to California, and he visited the Apostolic Faith Mission again on February 21. "Fair weather. I was over to Oakland today, at the [Salvation] Army in the afternoon and at 'Azusa' even[ing]. Saw Harry Smith's mother. The Muirs have the [Salvation Army] corps now. The Apostolic Faith holds forth on Tenth street. I found Bowman and his wife and got a blessing through them. B[owman] has been laid up with rheumatism. Mrs. Crawford arrived while I was there and will be there a week or so. She looks fine. They had a good house."[83] An entry a week later, February 28, however, registered some disgust with Crawford's leadership style: "Fair and warm. I was in Oakland again today. Sister Crawford was at the A[postolic]F[aith] P.M., also Lee and his wife. It seems they have to give up their all tomorrow. The papers have been roasting them and others have been persecuting them. Mrs. Crawford seems to be Lording it worse than ever. The usual friction was manifest. Lee has a nice-looking wife. Bowman has applied for the union and worked two nights on the *Tribune*. He is suffering reproach now, of course. The young Irish girl was there."[84]

Trotter ministered in Portland, then in Seattle, and later in San Francisco. But as the senior member of Crawford's pastoral staff, Trotter performed critical duties, especially with those on the margins of society. What is interesting, however, is that while Trotter and Crawford seem to have had a good working relationship with one another, neither of them ever mentioned the other in any of their writings. Trotter's correspondence with Lyman Stewart, however, reveals a strong friendship between these two men—Trotter apprised Stewart of the work while Stewart sent support. Letters chronicled Trotter's travels, conversions, efforts at tract distribution, and attendance at the Portland mission.[85]

Letters also reveal Trotter's personal perspective on the ongoing work in Portland. He clearly believed the work manifested Jesus' promise that His followers would do "greater works" than Jesus had accomplished among them. "I believe you are glad to know that very many poor helpless men and women are being reached and saved in our work," wrote Trotter. "Last night's service was wonderful beyond expression,—when I gave the altar call they flocked up to the front and bowed on their knees until the long bench was filled and they knelt all over the room and many were blessedly saved, and best of all they are standing and going on to know the Lord."[86]

Trotter worked from the "gospel wagon" as well as in the hospitals, jail, and even the "rock-pile." By late July, he applied to Lyman Stewart for more copies of the Gospel of John. The three thousand he had from Ralph Smith of the Bible House had been distributed. In October, Stewart would again fill a similar request. Indeed, support from Lyman Stewart proved to be both sustained and substantial.[87]

By Christmas Eve, Trotter reported to Stewart that there were eight hundred in attendance at the Apostolic Faith Mission, noting that, at one service during that week, 150 had come to the altar for prayer.[88] Conditions continued to improve according to Caswell. The Apostolic Faith Mission had "doubled the size of their hall." "'Bro. Tom [Hezmalhalch]' 'preached' this morning and Mrs. Crawford looked fat and comfortable. Big congregation. I didn't see Trotter. He was there P.M., same as ever. Bro. John [G.] Lake 'preached' P.M."[89] The following week Caswell observed, "At the Apostolic Faith tonight Trotter gave a great testimony. Mrs. Crawford was there. There must have been over four hundred people, maybe many more. The churches were crowded and many turned away."[90]

Throughout the 1910s, the situation of the Apostolic Faith Mission (Portland, Oregon) improved. The letters from Trotter to Stewart provide a window into those times. Each paints a glowing account of the mission's growth yet offers some insight into the intensity of the work that Crawford and Trotter undertook. Because he traveled extensively for Crawford, Trotter's letters also document events in Crawford's Seattle, Oakland, and Los Angeles missions.

During these years, the work also met a number of challenges. The work at the Azusa Street Mission in Los Angeles was devastated by an attempted coup while Pastor Seymour was on an extended trip in 1911. William H. Durham, a pastor from Chicago, came to Los Angeles intent upon transforming the mission's theology. He claimed that the mission's teaching on sanctification, a teaching that Crawford continued to proclaim, was wrong. Convinced that he could change her mind, Durham begged Crawford, "Just give me one meeting; all I want is one meeting." She refused him categorically, saying, "You will never get your foot inside of a meeting that I have got anything to do with, not even your foot will ever step inside of my place."[91] She was adamant about her theological position. She would not stray from her original understanding of sanctification as a second work of grace. Her experience had been too hard sought.

Conclusion

In 1913, the Worldwide Apostolic Faith Campmeeting convened in the Arroyo Seco on the site of the original Azusa Street Campmeeting of 1907. Some of the people who had led the camp meeting in 1907 were once again involved. But neither the Apostolic Faith Mission on Azusa Street nor the Apostolic Faith Mission (Portland, Oregon) was a sponsor of the meeting. Trotter, who was working at Crawford's Los Angeles mission at the time, was concerned that Lyman Stewart be clear on that point. The Apostolic

Faith (Portland, Oregon) and, by clear implication, his own ministry had nothing to do with that camp meeting.[92] In spite of his concern to distance his work from the camp meeting at the time, Trotter ultimately came to accept the "New Issue" or "Jesus' Name" theology that found a hearing at that event. This development would ultimately lead to a schism between him and Crawford in the mid-1910s.

About 1914, fundamentalist preacher Henry Allen "Harry" Ironside issued a scurrilous attack on Pentecostalism. Disgusted with what he called the "marked insubjection and Scripture-defying attitude" taken by Pentecostal women, he used the Apostolic Faith Mission of Portland, Oregon, as the principal example of what he considered to be wrong with Pentecostalism. He claimed that the *Apostolic Faith* (Portland, Oregon), like the movement as a whole, assiduously avoided mentioning "Jesus as Lord" or "God as Father." He claimed to have visited Crawford's missions in San Francisco and in Portland, Oregon. "We could scarcely believe such scenes were possible outside a lunatic asylum," he wrote, "and even there the keepers would not permit such goings-on." While such charges leveled against Crawford's work by a man of Ironside's reputation were designed to bring her work into disrepute, they undoubtedly helped distinguish early Pentecostals from their fundamentalist counterparts, thus, in a sense, strengthening their position.[93]

Florence Crawford, clearly the matriarch of the mission, seemed to take criticism in stride. Her discipline was severe, however, and those who questioned it were summarily forbidden to attend the church.[94] In 1919, one of the ministers of the Apostolic Faith Mission, Fred Hornshuh, attended the summer camp meeting, where much of the business of the church was conducted. He had a meeting with Crawford regarding some of his concerns, allegedly over her leadership style. The meeting must have been extremely difficult for both of them, and in the end Hornshuh was dismissed. In keeping with her concern for the purity of the Apostolic Faith Mission, Crawford instructed others to shun Hornshuh. While the majority of those who were under her care supported her, a few did not. Opponents met in August 1919, and by November they had incorporated the Bible Standard Mission.[95]

Perhaps it is predictable that "Mother" Crawford's "few" would splinter. Still, she managed in a male-dominated world to establish a ministry that continues to work effectively today.[96]

Bishop G. T. Haywood, circa 1920. Courtesy of the Flower Pentecostal Heritage Center, Springfield, Missouri.

G. T. Haywood: Religion for Urban Realities

David Bundy

Scholars of American religion have usually interpreted the rise and early development of Pentecostalism according to a classical urban-rural paradigm. That theory is essentially as follows. During a period of migration from the rural countryside of America, displaced workers faced a diverse environment hostile to the values that had nurtured their lives and spirituality. This hostility made them long for the old-time religion and the old-fashioned values of their pre-urban experience. In a burst of antiurban religious sentiment Pentecostalism arose to fulfill that longing. It is a standard interpretation for both black and white Pentecostalism in American religious culture.

There is reason for questioning that thesis. One case stands out. Garfield Thomas Haywood (1880–1931), elected the first general secretary (1919) and then the first presiding bishop of the Pentecostal Assemblies of the World (PAW) in 1924, established an ecclesiastical and theological tradition that continues to influence Pentecostalism around the world. Few African American theologians of the first half of the twentieth century have influenced more people than the quiet, determined man, G. T. Haywood, from Indianapolis.

While some expressions of Pentecostalism may be understood as a negative response to urban migration, Haywood understood Pentecostalism as an urban religious tradition that celebrated and depended on the structures of urban life.

The Social Formation of G. T. Haywood to 1908

Few details about Haywood are known between his birth in 1880 and his conversion to Pentecostalism sometime before May 1908.[1] He was born in Greencastle, Indiana, about thirty miles west of Indianapolis, where his father worked as a laborer in local factories. He attended public school in the city and for two years attended the prestigious Shortridge High School, a nationally significant institution that focused on the arts and crafts and literature. There Haywood received an education that shaped his writing and artistic abilities.

After leaving school, Haywood earned part of his income as a writer and cartoonist on the staff of two African American newspapers in Indianapolis, the *Freedman* and the *Recorder*. These periodicals followed carefully the issues posed by institutionalized discrimination and racial politics through the nation. His cartoons reflected that concern with racial issues. The tone of the papers and of the cartoons was proudly African American and reflected a refined understanding of turn-of-the-century American racism. Although Haywood's cartoons are signed, his articles, as most articles in these periodicals, do not reveal their authorship.

Haywood's family had experienced much of the racism reflected in the newspapers. His parents, Benjamin and Penny Ann Haywood, following the pattern of migration of African Americans to the North, left North Carolina for a small city in Indiana. Garfield, their third child, was born on the second stage of that migration. They left Greencastle for the larger city because racial attitudes and discriminatory employment practices there made it difficult to establish a stable economic base for the family. Church was important to the family. As a young adult, Haywood served as Sunday school superintendent in both Baptist and Methodist churches in Indianapolis. The immigration of African Americans into Indianapolis led to increased fear and racial polarization. Shortly after Haywood left Shortridge High School, the school closed its doors to African Americans, a segregation that would not be challenged for decades.

The Early Development of Pentecostalism in Indianapolis, 1906–1908

The context of Haywood's experience is the early development of Pentecostalism in Indianapolis. It is within this milieu that his theology, values, and program must be understood. Pentecostalism began quietly enough in Indianapolis in 1906, but that quiet was short-lived. Soon there were investigative reporters from the *Indianapolis Star* assigned to provide daily press coverage, investigations by the police and the mayor's office, high-profile divorces, and many converts. The excitement caused by the development of Pentecostalism was unprecedented in Indianapolis religious history, with scrutiny from the city establishment paralleled only by the experience of the tradition in Los Angeles. It is against this backdrop that one must understand the early ministry of Haywood.

The national and then international movement was defined through a periodical created to spread the ideas and provide news of the new religious movement. In September 1906 the first issue of the Los Angeles–based *Apostolic Faith* proclaimed "Pentecost Has Come."[2] Early fascicles of the *Apostolic Faith* reported "Pentecostal experiences" in cities around the world. Indianapolis was first mentioned in January 1907.[3] Glenn A. Cook reported that he had arrived in Indianapolis from Azusa Street about January 15. He found a group of people "seeking the baptism" at a Christian Missionary and Alliance congregation at the corner of East Street and Massachusetts Avenue.

This congregation had been formed under the leadership of George N. Eldridge, formerly a minister in the Methodist Episcopal Church. Eldridge had been defrocked after thirty years for preaching the traditional Holiness Methodist staples of sanctification and healing. Several in the congregation had been members at the prestigious Meridian Street Methodist Episcopal Church, from which George D. Watson had been defrocked for preaching the Methodist doctrines of sanctification and healing in independent camp meetings. Among them were Charles and Mary Reynolds, who had given Watson sanctuary when he was locked out of his home and church by his wife and district superintendent. Their daughter, Alice, remembered that Watson stayed in his room and prayed until "the toes of his shoes turned permanently upward." Two years earlier Mary Reynolds had experienced healing at a Church of God (Anderson) camp meeting in Anderson, Indiana. The story was reported in both the *Indianapolis Journal* and the *New York Times*.[4]

The Pentecostals were forced to leave the Christian and Missionary Alliance Church, and in late January the *Indianapolis Morning Star* discovered them at the "Pentecostal Tabernacle" located at the intersection of Senate Avenue and St. Clair Streets, a modest lower-middle-class area, finding a group of "twenty women and men worked to a pitch of religious fervor." Cook prayed with and for the people seeking a "new religious language." The informant reported that Cook could interpret his own "language but was not conversant with those of his converts."[5] A few weeks later, on March 7, 1907, Cook wrote to the *Apostolic Faith* that the congregation was meeting at 1111 1/2 Shelby Street in Fountain Square, about two miles from downtown near a recently disbanded Dowie Center, but on a streetcar line.[6] In early April, the group relocated to Murphy Hall, the former Spiritualist Temple, at the corner of New York and Alabama Streets.[7] This downtown location, which facilitated African American involvement, was across the street from the Young Men's Holiness Association of C. W. Ruth (a founder of the Church of the Nazarene) and within a block of the national headquarters of the Pentecost Bands, founded by Free Methodist Vivian Dake after the model of maverick Methodist Episcopal missionary William Taylor.[8]

Most of Glenn Cook's converts were working-class persons. Some were at least middle class. Many were second- or third-generation city dwellers as the census records and city directories reveal. The Reynolds family is illustrative. Charles Reynolds was a successful real-estate agent. His daughter, Alice, was a graduate of Shortridge High School when she was converted, and she later studied at Butler University. Her husband, Joseph R. Flower, was the son of the manager of Indiana Seed Company and an intern at the prominent McKinney firm. Sarah Cripe owned a restaurant near Murphy Hall. Mrs. Tom Oddy was the wife of a wealthy broker, co-owner of the firm Cooper and Oddy. Louise Rodenberg was a schoolteacher. S. B. Osborn and family had moved to Indianapolis from Chicago to serve as pastor of the Zionist congregation in the city. The social profiles of early converts suggest adherents from nearly every social level in the city. It was certainly not the religion of "the disinherited" in terms of social position or financial resources. For most of these people, life in the city had been quite good. The problem with these observations is obvious. Only a handful (about seventy-five) of the several hundred early converts have been identified by name.

Pentecostal communities in Indianapolis were determinedly interracial during the first decades. It was regularly noted in city newspapers that within Pentecostal meetings there was a blurring of the color line. Worship was open to all without respect to race. Black men and women led white men and women in worship and counseled them. This caused extensive comment and persecution.

A defining moment was the visit of William Seymour to Indianapolis in 1907. Seymour, arguably the founder of Pentecostalism, had long-standing ties to Indianapolis. City directories indicate he moved to the city in 1895, apparently directly from Louisiana. He worked as a waiter in three prominent restaurants: "the old Bates House," the Denison Hotel, and the Grand Hotel. He lived at 127 1/2 Indiana Avenue and then at 309 Bird Street in African American sections of the city. Claims about church participation are difficult to substantiate. His rented rooms were near an African American Baptist chapel served by another Seymour, probably a relative, a connection that might explain his employment at prestigious hotels. Oral sources among African American members of the PAW testify that he joined a church with a committed multiracial tradition, the Evening Light Saints, the early name for what is now the Church of God (Anderson). He left Indianapolis in late 1899 or early 1900 for Cincinnati, where, according to those same sources, he attended God's Bible School off and on for perhaps as long as two years. He apparently moved to Houston in 1905 and then to Los Angeles in early 1906. None of the connections to religious institutions in Indianapolis and Cincinnati can be verified in published or archival sources.

No mention of race is found in early Indianapolis Pentecostal publications. Clergy and visiting pastors are not identified as to race. However, the local newspapers recorded strife with the city over the issue, not among the Pentecostals but between the local populace and the Pentecostals. For example, Ernest Lloyd, an African American, was an active leader of the Indianapolis Apostolic Faith Mission. On Saturday, May 4, 1907, he was the cause of a near riot in Murphy (Spiritualist) Hall. "Under the 'power'" he apparently attempted to perform an exorcism on Naomi Groves, a twelve-year-old Caucasian girl. The loud prayers, her weeping, and the sight of him holding her head between his hands while he prayed aroused racist passions among several visitors, and the *Indianapolis Star* further inflamed the city with the headline, "Negro Bluk Beats Demon out of Girl."[9] The Pentecostals quietly put Lloyd on a late train out of the city to prevent physical harm. Glenn Cook attempted unsuccessfully to restore calm. Peace did not return until six policemen were stationed to stand at the back of the hall.

William J. Seymour was invited to Indianapolis by Sarah Cripe, the restaurant owner described by the *Star* as the "Bluk's Patron Saint."[10] She had provided home and food and $8,000 cash for the Pentecostal evangelists who were too busy evangelizing to hold regular jobs. She commented on Seymour: "He is a negro, but he is the discoverer of this great faith . . . this wonderful negro is coming right here to be with us." The *Star* noted that Pentecostal "enthusiasm has died down temporarily, awaiting the arrival of a negro who is regarded as the originator of the scheme."[11]

Seymour arrived in Indianapolis on a Sunday evening in late May 1907. W. H. Cummings and family and Jennie Moore, all African Americans, accompanied him. The racist inclinations of the reporter for the *Star* came to the fore in narrating the appearance of Seymour at the Apostolic Faith. The reporter wrote that "preceded by the sound of negro laughter, heavy footsteps on the stairway . . . and the opening of a passageway down the aisle, the much looked for leader of the Bluks strode into the midst of his faithful followers." To the horror of the reporter, Cook "threw both arms around his neck and kissed him." Temporary accommodation was found, "the white members of the flock being eager to do some part in entertaining the negro leader and the Cummings family." The newspaper also provided a careful description of Seymour: "This leader of the sect stands full six feet in height. He wears a rubber collar, decorated by no sign of necktie. Adorning his mouth is one massive gold tooth, flanked by rows of other teeth, perfectly straight and white. The beard that he wears could be called a flowing one if it was longer. It flows, what there is of it. His voice is like the roaring of a cannon and of all his most striking characteristics, he has but one eye."[12]

The presence of the persuasive Seymour provoked more than one social crisis in Indianapolis. The most celebrated case was that of Mr. and Mrs. Tom Oddy. Mr. Oddy was a prominent broker. His wife had for some weeks attended the Apostolic Faith Mission, but when she accepted the blessing from Seymour, "she dropped humbly on her knees before the negro and he seized her hand and prayed in stentorian tones." The *Star* quoted Mrs. Oddy: "this brother is a man of God. And after all, we should not hesitate to associate spiritually with negroes. In the great beyond the negroes and whites will be together." She made it clear that her new spiritual relationships at the Apostolic Faith Mission superseded her allegiance to her estranged husband. Mrs. Oddy, the *Star* informed its readers, "threw aside all restraint at the meeting yesterday (4 June) afternoon. She played the organ, sang and prayed. At the end of the service, Mrs. Oddy and W. G. Cummings, a negro sang a duet."[13]

The day after this story broke (June 5) Seymour left Indianapolis for a preaching engagement. The *Star* noted the departure: "Negro Bluk 'Blows.' Why? Husband May Know."[14] It was clear that other prominent white women had similar familial problems because of their enthusiasm for the ministry and spiritual leadership of Seymour. This was clearly more than Tom Oddy could tolerate, and, on June 6, 1907, the *Star* reported that he had asked his wife for a divorce.[15]

The publicity about the divorce and Pentecostal liturgy attracted both the curious and the protesters. By June 10, it was necessary to divide the crowd to avoid public disorder. Seymour conducted a meeting for African Americans downstairs in Murphy (Spiritualist) Hall, and Cook simultaneously conducted one upstairs for European Americans. African American participation grew rapidly owing to the presence of Seymour. According to the *Star,* "The gain in numbers of negro attendance was noticeable, and the familiarity with which the colored members of the flock were greeted was noticeable. In the center of the front row sat Frank Cummings, negro interpreter, a white man on one side of him and a white girl on the other. . . . Miss Alice Reynolds, a former student at Shortridge High School, and Frank Cummings, negro conversed long and earnestly about something that was interesting to both, ending with a hearty laugh, provoked by a remark of the young negro."[16]

The *Star* commented on two other issues. First, in an effort to discredit Pentecostal claims, it was suggested that glossolalia was nothing more than "the patois of the creole negroes of the gulf coast, which is a peculiar Afro-American corruption of English, French and Spanish with an occasional term from some African language."[17] Second, the *Star* observed that during foot-washing ceremonies in the worship of the Apostolic Faith Mission, participants were divided by sex but not by race. The men and women stood with their backs to each other, but no other distinctions were made. After the foot-washing service, the *Star* noted, "affection was displayed in a lavish way . . . White women threw their arms about the dusky necks of negresses and went through performances that would put to shame the most accomplished 'park spooning.'"[18]

The press, husbands, and police found the intense interaction of whites, especially the women, with the blacks offensive. The *Star* reported that police surveillance was increased. Public pressure was intense to deal with this explosive situation, but police reports commissioned by Mayor Bookwalter found nothing actionable.[19]

It is unclear when the African American presence at Murphy Hall ceased or came to be such small numbers that they did not merit mention; it is uncertain when meetings there were discontinued. One piece of evidence holds interest. The periodical *Pentecost* was edited by J. Roswell Flower in Indianapolis from August 1908 to February 1909. This paper, which eventually became a founding periodical of the Assemblies of God, does not mention African Americans, either as a group or as individuals. No African American names are mentioned in the publication. No articles are by African Americans, and, despite the news from around the world and the emphasis on missions to Africa, the African American Pentecostal churches in Indianapolis are never mentioned, not even in the address lists. Given the composition and social-class level of African American participation in early Indianapolis Pentecostalism from the extensive and detailed articles in the *Star*, this was clearly a conscious decision on the part of Flower. The interracial experiment among most influential Indianapolis European American Pentecostals had come to an end. In this context, African American Pentecostals in Indianapolis began to create a new reality.

Creating a Multiracial Pentecostal Congregation, 1908–1913

The existing racial climate provided the context for the development of another Pentecostal congregation in Indianapolis that also got its start from a Pentecostal emissary from Azusa Street in Los Angeles. The church founder, Henry Prentiss, left less of a trail than Cook and Seymour. He arrived in Indianapolis in 1907 and began a congregation in the African American area of downtown Indianapolis. The press ignored him. There is no indication that he participated in the meetings conducted by Seymour and Cook. And he did not receive the respect and adulation of European American Pentecostals given to the other arrivals from California. He began his work in a small, somewhat dilapidated storefront. In February 1909 Prentiss decided, for unknown reasons, to leave his congregation of thirteen persons (including Haywood, Haywood's wife, and other relatives, most of whom appear to have been converts from the Bethel AME

Church) to the pastoral care of Haywood. Haywood had been converted through the efforts of Prentiss and mentored in pastoral skills.

It is doubtful Haywood attended the Pentecostal meetings in Murphy Hall, but he would have known of them from newspaper accounts. African American newspapers of the city do not mention the early Pentecostal revival. After Haywood's conversion, he appears to have severed his relationship with those publications, although it is uncertain how he earned his livelihood. It is doubtful that the small congregation, apparently composed primarily of relatives, could have supported a pastor. The Indianapolis African American newspapers were interested in the social status of African Americans and were little different in their social values, except with regard to racial questions, from the European American papers of the period. Haywood also resigned from the African American secret society the Knights of Pythias.

That first congregation, although located on West Michigan Street in the African American community, appears to have been multiracial from the beginning. The building seated about twenty-eight persons. The members were regularly pelted with rotten fruit, eggs, and stones on their way to church, not because they were Pentecostal (that name was widely used by the Holiness groups in Indianapolis) but because of the intimate multiracial interaction and participation of whites and blacks in worship. Despite the persecution, the congregation met every night of the week and soon more secure facilities were needed. In 1908 the thirteen members moved to the corner of Michigan and Minerva Streets, to a facility that seated seventy-five. Despite a leaky roof and the unwanted attention of hooligans, attendance increased, and the congregation boarded up the windows and met behind locked doors.[20]

The next moves, to larger buildings at better locations, facilitated the transformation of the community into a growing church with its own publication. In February 1909, the congregation moved to a facility beside a railroad track at Lafayette Street and Twelfth Street. A few months later, the congregation found a more suitable 150-seat building at the corner of Missouri and Twelfth Streets.[21] At that location, Haywood began publishing the periodical *Voice in the Wilderness* in 1910. Designed for national circulation, it was printed by his brother Benjamin Haywood. It was advertised as a monthly but later the letterhead stated, "published as the Lord provides." How often that occurred remains unclear. Only a few issues have been discovered.

The earliest extant issue of *Voice in the Wilderness* is the second, published in Indianapolis in July 1910. The masthead affirmed holiness, an eschatological focus, and Christian unity: "This is the Lord's paper, published for that 'Oneness' amidst God's saints throughout the land, as our Lord prayed in John 17:11, 21 and 22."[22] It published a piece entitled "Message in Tongues Interpreted" that included many of Haywood's key themes: simplicity of faith, the availability of gifts of the Spirit, humility of the believer, praise for victory over the powers of darkness, and "victory comes only in trusting." Of course, the article was not signed. Haywood also discussed the problem of divorce and made it clear that remarriage after divorce was forbidden, even if the couple remarried before "one is saved and baptized with the Holy Ghost."[23] Another article includes a letter from a reader in Findlay, Ohio, another center for early Midwest Pentecostalism, urging persons to seek sanctification, or holiness.[24]

The periodical increased the visibility of the congregation. A convention was announced for July 1911 and advertised nationally. The building at Missouri and Twelfth Streets was too small to entertain the anticipated crowds. The Peniel Mission (Holiness) was rented from the owner, initially for a month, and the congregation moved their benches to this new location at the edge of downtown near the original location of the first Indianapolis Pentecostal congregation at Eleventh and Senate. It is not known how many persons attended that first "Apostolic Convention," but Haywood decided to stay in the larger building and in 1915 purchased the facility for five thousand dollars. The building seated about six hundred persons. In November 1911, the congregation numbered fifty.[25] By 1913, it numbered more than four hundred.

The convention and publication contributed significantly to the development of Haywood into a nationally significant Pentecostal leader. From 1910 to 1913, Haywood was in demand as revival leader and preacher throughout the United States and Canada. His stature as writer and speaker were fueled by an avid intellectual curiosity. He read widely, continuing habits developed before his Pentecostal days. While many early Pentecostal preachers cautioned against reading beyond the Bible, Haywood's sermons and essays were laced with literary allusions from a wide variety of sources.

Developing an Institutional and Theological Identity, 1913–1919

By 1913 it was clear that individual Pentecostal congregations were severely limited in their ability to deal with larger national and international concerns. The periodicals had served to hold them together and provide for a level of communication, but now a more distinct institutional and theological identity was needed. Haywood was an important figure in the process that provided that identity.

Four primary factors led to the changes that swept through Pentecostal ranks in 1913 and 1914: (1) the response of the larger culture to Pentecostal multiracial activities; (2) racism within Pentecostal ranks (despite the Pentecostal value against racism); (3) the need for free transportation on the railroads; and (4) the threats to Pentecostal pacifism by the draft laws. African American and European American clergy traveling and ministering together were frequently harassed and sometimes even imprisoned. C. H. Mason's Church of God in Christ was able to offer a solution to the transportation and military service problems. It did not, however, resolve the racial problems. Mason was arrested several times for traveling with European American Pentecostal clergy.[26] Pentecostals were experiencing the difficulties inherent in the efforts of minority groups with marginal social status to change dominant cultural structures and social practices. Few Pentecostal pastors had the charisma and personal strength of Haywood, who was able to lead a multiracial congregation and develop nationally significant conventions.

Something was needed to provide larger-scale organizational security. Between June 15 and June 22, 1913, a "Convention and Campmeeting" was held at "Gibeah Bible School in Plainfield, Indiana, to form the Pentecostal Assemblies of Indiana and the Central States."[27] The gathering was called by D. Wesley Myland, director of the Gibeah Bible School, and Flower. The delegates were exclusively European American.

G. T. Haywood was invited to attend one afternoon and to give the keynote address. It is unclear why he was invited. One could conjure reasons: he published a successful periodical, had developed the largest Pentecostal congregation in the state of Indiana, and was an accomplished speaker. It is also possible that he did not stay because of decisions about the racial composition of the proposed organization. In any case, Haywood spoke to the assembled on John 21:16, "Feed My Sheep," arguing that competent pastoral leadership for the emerging Pentecostal congregations was necessary to consolidate the work of the evangelists. Haywood's sermon articulated clearly the agenda of the conference leaders. A committee was chosen to "confer together and . . . arrange an order of procedure for definite and systematic service in uniting and developing the work."[28] African Americans, including Haywood, were not included in the proposed organization. The processes of establishing racially separate structures for Pentecostalism had begun in earnest. For the rest of his life, Haywood would fight against this destruction of the early Pentecostal vision of overcoming racial division.

On a national level, things moved quickly. Flower became the dominant force in the establishment of the Assemblies of God, USA, in 1914. *The Pentecostal Evangel* became the official organ of the new denomination. G. T. Haywood, according to some sources, attended the Hot Springs, Arkansas, constitutional meeting of the Assemblies of God. He does not appear in the official photograph, and there is no evidence that he signed the protocol or was invited to do so. There is no doubt that he returned to Indianapolis more isolated from other Pentecostals in both the North and South.

Shortly after the formation of the Assemblies of God and the exclusion of African Americans from the fellowship, Glenn Cook returned to Indianapolis with a new Pentecostal vision: "Oneness," or non-Trinitarian theology. Oneness Pentecostals observed that when new believers were reported baptized in Acts, baptism was done not with a Trinitarian formula but "in the name of Jesus." Many Pentecostals rejected the popular American religious understanding of Trinity as tri-theism. Most of the multiracial and African American churches in the North followed Haywood's lead in accepting the "new issue," as the teaching was called. Most Indianapolis Pentecostals accepted the "Jesus Only" doctrine. Hundreds were rebaptized using a non-Trinitarian baptismal formula. The determined effort of Flower was a major force in keeping the national Assemblies of God from joining the new wave. This conflict over doctrine and liturgy permanently divided Pentecostalism. The gap between the all-white Assemblies of God and the other churches intensified, now also because there was often a doctrinal distinction, especially in the North and Midwest.

Excluded from the Assemblies of God, but still a northern church, Haywood and his congregation found collegiality in the PAW. The details of the founding of the PAW are lost in obscurity, but it certainly began in

Los Angeles, and there is some evidence that the organizational history can be traced back to a meeting in 1907. It is also clear that that meeting was called to coordinate evangelistic efforts, not to establish an organization. It next surfaced in Portland, Oregon, under the leadership of J. J. Frazee. Haywood suggested that he was involved with the PAW as early as 1911.[29] The Indianapolis summer conventions were not advertised as PAW conventions from 1913 to 1916, but they were later recognized as such in PAW sources. As far as can be ascertained, Haywood did not attend the annual meeting of the PAW called by Frazee in Portland, Oregon, on January 29, 1917, nor did he attend the meeting at Eureka Springs, Arkansas, in October 1918. Delegates at this meeting reached no agreement on forming an organization but deferred decisions until a meeting could be held in Indianapolis.

A few days later Haywood began advertising a meeting for January 17–27, 1919, in Indianapolis. At that meeting, Haywood and others drafted a constitution. Haywood was elected general secretary of the new organization.[30] The next "annual" meeting took place in October 1919. This was a tour de force for Haywood. He rented Tomlinson Hall, a major conference center seating about three thousand persons. The extant photograph of the meeting reveals the hall with raised dais; the ceiling draped with red, white, and blue bunting; and a crowd about evenly mixed with black and white participants proudly seated before the banner "Annual Meeting of the Pentecostal Assemblies of the World."[31] Haywood and his congregation had come a long way from the threatened and culturally isolated community of thirteen believers across town.

From 1919 onward, the history of the PAW and Haywood were linked. He was elected to various offices and helped the denomination survive with dignity the separation of the southern and most northern European American clergy. He and the Indianapolis congregation provided funds and leadership for the establishment of new congregations around the country. Haywood's protégés became the first wave of national leadership for the PAW after the European American exodus from the PAW in 1924 to form churches that eventually became the major constitutive elements of the United Pentecostal Church.

The national role energized the Indianapolis congregation and it grew rapidly. By 1919, the facility at Eleventh and Senate Streets was too small. A second story was added to include a large sanctuary designed to seat 1,100. In 1924 this site allowed no room for growth. Essential to the congregation's attractiveness was its social vision and theological sophistication. Haywood and the congregation criticized the growing racism in Indiana both by the example of its corporate life and by the quiet daring of its pastor. Haywood continually defied the racially defined social limits of the city. He built a house north of the area generally lived in by African Americans. He purchased an Overland Touring Car in 1923 at a time when few African Americans had good quality automobiles. Despite opposition and threats to its members' interracial fraternization, the church grew. It was thoroughly multiracial during the years that the Klan dominated Indiana political and social life.

During 1924, perhaps the year of the Klan's greatest influence in Indiana, Haywood dared to break yet another taboo. In Indianapolis, the area north of Fall Creek was off-limits for African Americans. It was carved into small self-governing enclaves for the wealthier European Americans. Haywood purchased a number of vacant lots used primarily as a dump. The city refused to allow construction of a building that looked like a church, since it was assumed that any African American enterprise north of Fall Creek would fail. A compromise was reached. The building was designed on the outside as a school building so that it could be renovated by the city in the event the church was closed. Haywood drew the architectural plans, they were accepted by the city, and members of the congregation constructed the building. In November 1924 the congregation moved into its new 1,500-seat quarters. The church, Christ Temple Apostolic, had a national theological and institutional identity.

Defining the New Reality, 1920–1931

Haywood served the fledgling PAW as administrator, theologian, composer, and mission executive. He traveled widely both in North America and beyond. As an administrator he made nearly every significant decision about the development of the PAW during this period. A stream of at least thirteen books and more than a hundred hymns poured from his pen. These books provided an informed Oneness Pentecostal theological voice and established the trajectories of the tradition on important theoretical issues. In addition, there were tracts, prophecy charts, and paintings on the walls of the Christ Temple Apostolic. He wrote hundreds of articles and "notices" for *Voice in the Wilderness* and other Pentecostal periodicals.

He was the founding editor of the PAW denominational periodical, *Christian Outlook*, as well as congregational periodicals.

Haywood decided that the PAW should have an organized mission program. His congregation became the primary sustainer of the project that sent missionaries to Liberia, South Africa, India, Japan, Egypt, the Caribbean, and China. African Americans were among the missionaries at most locations.[32] The new reality of the PAW did not evolve without problems. Racism led to the separation of the majority of the European American clergy to form separate denominations. Pressure came from inside and outside the white clerical ranks. The other problems were to some degree administrative. Haywood basically administered the denomination as he did his church. He kept studying and evolving in his positions. Though he expected his protégés and congregation to follow his lead, they did not always do so. Some were unable to accept his travel to Palestine in 1927. Few African American ministers made the trip to Israel. White big-steeple pastors, not African American pastors, normally undertook this type of excursion with their exploits chronicled by the local newspapers. As in other instances, Haywood broke that color line, but at a cost to his relationships with the less fortunate of his own congregation. Others questioned his use of a movie camera. Pentecostals sometimes saw movie cameras (and the movie industry) as sinful. Haywood rejected the idea that a particular technical development had independent moral status. He filmed widely, and the resulting films were shown in the churches.

Two larger issues proved problematic: divorce/remarriage and the role of women in ministry. Haywood had argued in 1910 on the basis of biblical texts that remarriage after divorce constituted adultery and could not be tolerated. Then his nephew, who had been involved in a messy divorce and remarried, came to church, was "baptized in the Holy Spirit," and experienced glossolalia.[33] Blood and spiritual gifts proved more powerful than traditional biblical arguments. Haywood wrote a book to make the argument that "our former views on the subject were wrong." He wrote to "prove that persons who are divorced and remarried before they were filled with the Holy Spirit are forgiven of their past."[34] Haywood also encouraged women to serve as preachers. For some, this contradicted the Bible.

These issues, combined with unfounded accusations about his administration of the PAW mission program funded largely by his

Indianapolis congregation, became major points of contention between Haywood and dissenters to his leadership. At the 1930 convention he was attacked by East Coast PAW bishops led by Bishop Grimes.[35] Haywood returned to Indianapolis with his influence somewhat diminished. He was also sick, probably with a heart condition aggravated by the stress. Despite that illness, he departed in January 1931 for Jamaica to visit PAW missions there and to preach. He also took the most modern and compact movie camera available.

When he returned to Indianapolis, he was often too ill to preach. He died on April 11, 1931. His funeral elicited an outpouring of grief and was covered by the national press, white and black. His opponents in the PAW converged on Indianapolis to pay homage and to struggle to control his legacy.

Urban Religion

From its earliest development in Indiana, Pentecostalism did not seek refuge in the rural areas. The major center was Indianapolis. In the city, Pentecostals could experiment with more freedom to establish new paradigms of ecclesial and social interaction. The ecclesial experimentation included a rejection of traditional structures and liturgy and experimentation with both. Adherents soon discovered limits in that context, but were still more free than they would have been in smaller cities or rural areas. Likewise, most of the leadership for the new tradition did not come immediately from the rural areas but emerged from at least second-generation city dwellers who had successfully negotiated the urban situation. This was true for African American and European American Pentecostals. Indeed, they celebrated realities of the urban landscape, including the resultant linguistic, cultural, and racial diversity and interaction.

A primary element of ecclesial experimentation related to architecture. Conventional lore holds that Pentecostalism began in a stable in Los Angeles. In Indianapolis, the early buildings were a small warehouse, a small store, and a former Spiritualist temple. Little was done to change the buildings. Signage was simple and inconspicuous. The primary concerns were functionality and security. The individual was the real temple of God and the congregation assembled was the church. Haywood was happy to build his church to look like a school if that would enable the church to accomplish its mission.

Haywood and other Pentecostal leaders celebrated the availability of transportation and other technologies as gifts of God to help them fulfill their mission. They were aware of the significance of Indianapolis as a transportation hub. They reported that there were more interurban lines connecting to Indianapolis than to any other city and that only Los Angeles could compete with the urban rail system that made most sites within forty miles quickly accessible. At a time when most churches were dependent on congregational members being within walking distance of the church, Pentecostals, from the beginning, located on rail lines. Every Pentecostal church name recorded during the early period indicated its location either in the city grid or on the transportation network. Haywood's leadership was enhanced because two of his brothers were printers. They enabled Haywood to become one of the most prolifically published of the early North American Pentecostal theologians. The original press remains an important relic of the congregation of Christ Temple Apostolic.

The use of urban/rural metaphors and allusion in early Indianapolis Pentecostal publications is revelatory. There are no instances in which rural situations or values were cited as authoritative or glorified. Instead there was a continual reporting on the work of the Holy Spirit in cities around the world. That "work" was understood to provide the means by which the limitations imposed upon normal human agency could be transcended by powers and abilities bestowed as gracious gifts of God. The ultimate purpose of the gifts was for the spreading of the Gospel to "the ends of the earth." As a fringe benefit, the spirituality of the individual could be transformed.

These data indicate that early Pentecostalism in Indianapolis as well as the ministry of Haywood and the resultant PAW cannot be satisfactorily interpreted as in the usual urban/rural paradigm. Instead, it can be argued that Pentecostalism came onto the Indianapolis scene as a tradition that celebrated and depended on modernity as expressed in the urban. The participants about whom we can know economic details were reasonably well off and secure. Racial diversity was celebrated and relativized. Linguistic and cultural diversity were applauded and understood as positive tools for the mission. Liturgical innovations provided a context in which the religious leadership of women and blacks even over white males could be warranted.[36]

Charles H. Mason, circa 1920. Courtesy of the Flower Pentecostal Heritage Center, Springfield, Missouri.

Charles Harrison Mason: The Interracial Impulse of Early Pentecostalism

David D. Daniels

A little more than a decade after the advent of the Azusa Street revival, with its experiment in interracial worship and organization, Charles Harrison Mason and the Church of God in Christ (COGIC) redoubled their commitment to the interracial impulse in Pentecostalism. In 1917 COGIC published its interracial commitments in its church manual in a section entitled "equal in power and authority":

> Many denominations have made distinctions between their colored and white members. Some advised electing colored officials to preside over colored assemblies, while others have refused to elevate any colored elder to the episcopacy or any other office corresponding to it having equal power with white bishops. This has led to many misunderstandings and has caused the organizing of many separate colored denominations. The Church of God in Christ recognizes the fact that all believers are one in Christ Jesus and all its members have equal rights. Its Overseers, both colored and white, have equal power and authority in the church.[1]

In this statement Mason and COGIC expressed their firm commitment to racial equality. Here is a public statement in which COGIC intentionally embodied an interracial impulse and understood itself as making a political and moral statement against racism and segregation by erecting a denominational structure that reflected the oneness in Christ Jesus shared by black and white Christians. The document promoted racial equality, stating that the denomination's "Overseers, both colored and white, have equal power and authority in the church." Mason led the COGIC experiment with three distinct interracial organizational structures as an effort to demonstrate the possibility of a racially inclusive denomination during an era when most religious bodies were racially homogenous or segregated internally. Thus Mason and COGIC surpassed the rhetoric of racial equality and the practice of racially mixed worship by erecting an interracial denominational structure and creating an interracial leadership. COGIC's structure attracted white clergy and congregations that joined a predominantly black religious group in an era when segregation defined American Christianity and society.[2]

Mason's contribution to the interracial impulse within Pentecostalism and American Protestantism remains an understudied topic of American religious history. He is best known as the founder of COGIC, a denomination now classified by C. Eric Lincoln and Lawrence Mamiya as one of the seven major historic black churches. COGIC ranks as the largest black Pentecostal denomination in the United States; according to some studies, it is the largest of all Pentecostal denominations in the country. Currently, while its worldwide membership is smaller than other international Pentecostal denominations, COGIC congregations exist on every continent.[3]

During the first twenty-five years of Mason's leadership within COGIC, the group experimented with three distinct interracial organizational arrangements. These experiments, or interracial polities, included a race-specific clergy fellowship, an interracial structure, and a white minority conference. While COGIC attracted and organized white congregations during its first twenty-five years, most white Pentecostal denominations resisted making the interracial impulse a constitutive element of early Pentecostalism. These denominations conformed their racial structures to the Protestant racial arrangement of segregation practiced in the United States. Mason countered this trend through his efforts to overcome racial prejudice and institutional racism by erecting a racially inclusive organization. What were the dimensions of the interracial impulse that Mason promoted in COGIC? What were the sources of the impulse that shaped him?

Recently the scholarly community and the general Pentecostal readership have been involved in the debate over the existence of a racially integrated period of early Pentecostalism. How does the interracial impulse within COGIC fit into this debate? The debate spans the continuum from the nonexistence of integration to an identifiable interracial era. Those who seek to correct the myth of the interracial era ask questions about periodization: How long did this designated period last? Were the alleged interracial interactions of the Azusa Street revival mere anomalies? Others recognize an integrated period, focus upon the Apostolic Faith Mission (Los Angeles), but limit the period to 1906–8 and 1911, the time when some blacks and whites did worship together. Those who argue for an identifiable integration era stress the interracial interactions that shaped Pentecostalism after the Azusa Street revival within local congregations in various cities and denominations such as COGIC and the Pentecostal Assemblies of the World. Interestingly, the COGIC interracial experiment extended from 1910 to 1933.

Mason joined the ranks of early black and white Pentecostal leaders who campaigned to make the interracial vision of the Azusa Street revival constitutive of Pentecostalism. His commitment to integration, though, was not merely a by-product of his encounter with the revival, but was shaped by his pre-Pentecostal religious affiliations. He intersected with various African American Protestant movements of the late nineteenth century that participated in the construction of early Pentecostalism. Two movements in particular framed the interracial impulse: the black Holiness movement and the black restorationist movement.

The Making of Mason as an Interracial Leader

Like other black Pentecostal pioneers, Charles Harrison Mason was the child of slaves and grew up in the racially segregated plantation communities of southern black sharecroppers and tenant farmers. While his childhood years intersected with the Reconstruction era and its cast of high-profile African American politicians and community leaders, he lived his teenage years and came to adulthood during the turbulence of the white backlash against African American racial progress. Mason, a native of Tennessee, was born near Bartlett (later annexed by Memphis) on September 8, 1862, to Jerry and Eliza Mason and lived until 1961. His mother served as his tutor and model in the Christian faith, being a "woman of great faith," a praying woman marked by a "gift of prayer." Jerry Mason, a Civil War veteran, died after the war. Subsequently, Eliza married John Nelson. By 1876, the family had relocated to Plumersville, Arkansas.

Mason, reared in the Baptist tradition of his parents and stepfather, possessed a piety marked by dreams and visions, a characteristic of slave religion.[4]

Mason experienced Christian conversion in 1880 at age seventeen. His stepbrother, I. S. Nelson, who served as pastor of the Mount Olive Missionary Baptist Church, baptized him later that year. Mason expressed a keen interest in spirituality. He exhibited a strong commitment to prayer, and during revivals "he would labor night and day for the salvation of souls," singing and praying with people seeking conversion at the altar. In 1893 Mason received his license to preach.[5]

Within the Baptist churches of Mason's youth, there existed heated debates about the character of the partnerships between black and white Baptists. Three main parties arose. One party espoused racial equality between black and white Baptists and joined interracial endeavors as well as denominational entities marked by racial equality. Another camp accepted interracial cooperation marked more by white paternalism than racial equality. The third camp promoted religious separatism and rejected white paternalism, only entering selective interracial partnerships committed to racial equality. They preferred that African American Baptists experience self-determination rather than promote interracialism. Each camp was open to interactions with white Baptists, but the debate was over the ethical prerequisites that determined the parameters of race relations; these prerequisites predicted which camp would more likely partner with northern rather than southern Baptists. Central to the debate were the moral terms that would structure interracial cooperation. This debate helped established the framework of racial politics for young Mason's world.[6]

Mason's interest in spirituality kindled his attraction to the Holiness movement. His Holiness experience followed the trajectory of the larger black Holiness history of the late nineteenth century, which bracketed the white Holiness discussion of sanctification as an eradication or suppression of sin. In 1893 Mason received the sanctification experience in Arkansas, an experience that came through his reading of the scriptures. The primary text for him was Jesus' prayer for the disciples' sanctification in John 17:17. Sanctification for Mason combined freedom and separation from sin with the presence of power in ministry. Mason's description of power in ministry resembled the understanding that others called the anointing, the capacity in preaching to be a channel of God, to draw people to God, to initiate a revival and make conversions happen at an accelerated pace. The Holiness message for Mason called people to delight in God: praising God, relishing praying, hearing God speak through Scripture, absenting oneself from frivolity. This delight in God came in sanctification. For Mason, the biblical preaching of holiness convicted people of sin and "convinced them that sin was destroying them, their churches and all that they possessed," in addition to being the "cause of all their sickness and disease."[7]

Mason encountered Holiness teaching through his association with William Christian, a black former Baptist who founded the Church of the Living God (Christian Workers for Fellowship) in 1888 near Wrightsville, Arkansas. Christian focused his Holiness teaching on living a holy life, explaining that the biblical mandate was simply to do right and live right. He led an independent black restorationist movement and sought to popularize the teachings of Alexander Campbell: rejecting denominationalism and aiming to teach only the simple message of Christ, disavowing unscriptural titles of churches, such as Baptist and Methodist, and embracing the New Testament church as the model. Christian also preached sanctification as living a clean life. By 1900 the denomination included nearly ninety congregations in eleven states.[8]

Central to the interracial impulse that Mason fostered was a rejection of the racial prejudice that served as a cardinal principle of Christian's message. Christian introduced Mason to a theology of polygenesis that undercut myths of European racial superiority and African racial inferiority. Inverting the dominant polygenesis theory that claims a superiority of Europeans, Christian contended that the biblical creation story was only an account of the origins of one race, the African, and that God also created two other races, Asian and European, on prior occasions. Thus the people covered in Scripture are mainly Africans, along with Jesus. Within the racial politics of the era, Christian's reading of the scriptures challenged the biblical interpretation of the Hamitic curse that purported to defend black inferiority by reinterpreting the curse as an intra-African, not interracial, affair. Thus Christian debunked black inferiority without making claims to black racial superiority. According to one account, Mason associated with Christian until 1895. While retaining his Baptist credentials, he fellowshipped with Christian's group during the early 1890s.[9]

Around 1890 Mason married Alice Saxton. Their marriage ended in separation by 1893 because Alice objected to his entry into the ministry. They remained separated until her death in 1905. After his estranged wife's death, Mason married Leila Washington. Together they had eight children.[10]

To prepare himself educationally for ordained ministry, Mason enrolled in and graduated from the Minister's Institute of Arkansas Baptist College in Little Rock, an institution that advocated black leadership and racial equality. Earning the diploma fulfilled a goal that he had set for himself. Prior to enrolling in the Minister's Institute, he had matriculated into the college division of Arkansas Baptist College in 1893. However, in three months he withdrew from the college and transferred to the institute to receive a ministerial education.[11]

The Interracial Impulse of the Black and White Holiness Movement

While the black Holiness movement of the nineteenth century that Mason joined in 1893 arose during the antebellum era, it developed institutional structures only in the post–Civil War era with the founding in 1869 of the first black Holiness denomination, the Zion Union Apostolic Church. Until the late 1870s the black Holiness movement was predominantly a phenomenon among the various black Methodist congregations between North Carolina and New York and also in Missouri. At these black-sponsored Holiness meetings, whites regularly attended as speakers and participants. The speakers included national white Holiness leaders such as John Inskip and William McDonald. During the late 1870s the black Holiness movement expanded beyond black Methodism and entered black Baptist and independent religious circles in Michigan, South Carolina, and the mid-South region. The black Holiness movement of the late nineteenth century exhibited a strong interracial impulse that envisioned blacks and whites cooperating as equals in the church and society.[12]

In 1895 Mason joined three other Holiness Baptist ministers, Charles Price Jones, John A. Jeter, and Walter Pleasant, in establishing the black Holiness movement in the mid-South. They sponsored regional Holiness conventions from 1896 to the early 1900s that were noted for their racially mixed audiences. According to Jones, at their conventions were "blacks and whites" committed to "seeking God together." The most prominent white person to attend these conventions was Joanna Patterson Moore, the first missionary sponsored by the Baptist Women's Home Missionary Society. Initially, the black Holiness movement in the mid-South served as a renewal movement among black Baptist congregations. The movement attracted leading black Baptists within the region such as Virginia Broughton and Charles Lewis Fisher. Virginia Broughton, the first black female graduate of a southern college (Fisk), served as a Baptist missionary and an author; Charles Lewis Fisher, valedictorian of Morgan Park Baptist Seminary (Illinois), was a college professor and author. The Holiness fellowship of Jones and Mason became well known through their fellowship's publication, *Truth,* as well as the books and hymns that Jones wrote. Yet by 1899 black Baptist associations and state conventions in Mississippi and Arkansas began disfellowshipping Holiness Baptist clergy from their memberships because of the Holiness critique of denominationalism that was interpreted as anti-Baptist. By the time Mason went to Los Angeles to attend the Azusa Street revival, the Holiness movement that he assisted in founding had expanded to fifty-eight congregations within six states of the wider mid-South region: Alabama, Arkansas, Louisiana, Mississippi, Tennessee, and Kentucky. Almost 80 percent of the congregations were within Mississippi and Arkansas, with the vast majority being in Mississippi.[13]

The interracial impulse within the black Holiness movement had a similar expression among white Holiness networks. There were reports of racially mixed events in which African American Holiness leaders from historic black denominations such as the African Methodist Episcopal Church (AME) and the African Methodist Episcopal Church Zion (AMEZ) were speakers and participants. These leaders included AME evangelist Amanda Berry Smith, AMEZ evangelist Julia Foote, AME Bishop Abraham Grant, AMEZ Bishop Alexander Walters, Charles Price Jones, healing teacher Elizabeth Mix, evangelist Susan Fogg, songwriter Thoro Harris, evangelist Emma J. Ray, and others. There existed biracial fellowships such as Daniel Warner's Church of God and Benjamin Irwin's Fire-Baptized Holiness Church. Various ministries and fellowships welcomed African American participation: Joanna Patterson Moore and her ministry in Nashville; J. O. McClurkan and the Pentecostal Alliance, with headquarters in Nashville; the Southern California and Arizona Holiness Association, with offices in Los Angeles; Martin Wells Knapp and God's Bible School and Missionary Training Home, in Cincinnati; and Albert Simpson, along with the Christian and Missionary Alliance.[14]

Theological affirmations and rhetorical strategies also undergirded the interracial impulse. Various white as well as black Holiness leaders such as Thomas Doty, Amanda Berry Smith, Enoch Edwin Byrum, and J. O. McClurkan published critiques of racism within Holiness publications. Thus, from Pennsylvania and Missouri in the 1870s to Mississippi, Tennessee, and Illinois in the 1890s and early 1900s, there were black and white Holiness leaders who seemingly promoted the interracial impulse.[15]

The black and white Holiness movements exhibited an interracial impulse during the late nineteenth century in different ways. The most pervasive model within the black and white Holiness movements was the practice of racially mixed meetings, either as a result of the participants or speakers. Seemingly, this was the only expression of the interracial impulse within the black Holiness movement because white clergy and congregations refrained from joining black Holiness fellowships. A second model reflected the practice of predominantly white Holiness clergy associations accepting blacks as members but denying them opportunities to serve as national officers on equal standing with whites. A third, but rare, model included one African American within the white national leadership of the predominantly white Holiness fellowship.

The Azusa Street Revival, Mason, and the Early COGIC

The Apostolic Faith Mission exhibited an interracial impulse in its earliest services on Bonnie Brae and at 312 Azusa Street expressed by sectors within the black and white Holiness movements. The mission for a short time included blacks and whites in leadership as well as among the membership. The racial composition of the mission was recognized early by sympathetic and critical commentators of the Azusa Street revival. Historian Cecil Robeck tracked the transformation of the revival from a small all-black meeting in February 1906 to a black revival with a few whites in April 1906, and then to three hundred whites and about twenty-five blacks by September 1906. He ascertained that while the official membership was integrated, albeit predominantly black, whites held a disproportionate number of leadership positions. The interracial impulse of the Azusa Street revival had two periods of high visibility, periods where the revival attracted a racially diverse audience, 1906–8 and 1911. In Robeck's assessment: "Clearly, Seymour may be credited with providing the vision of a truly 'color-blind' congregation. His was a radical experiment that ultimately failed because of the inability of whites to allow for a sustained role for black leadership."[16]

David J. Young and John A. Jeter, two other leaders from his Holiness fellowship, traveled with Mason to Los Angeles in order to attend the Azusa Street revival in 1907. Each of them testified to receiving the baptism of the Holy Spirit at the revival. Mason had heard about the revival sponsored by the Apostolic Faith Mission (Los Angeles) from William T. and Dovie Simmons, two acquaintances who resided in Texas. William Simmons wrote to Mason and others about the revival that he and his wife attended during early 1906. While initially the experience eluded William, Dovie Simmons did receive the experience; William received Holy Spirit baptism a few years later.[17]

Besides whites integrating a previously all-black revival, what was astonishing about the Azusa Street revival were the conversions that occurred in the racial consciousness of whites such as Frank Bartleman, Gaston B. Cashwell, and others. These were individuals who admitted to being prejudiced but who experienced a conversion in racial consciousness that led them not only to reject prejudice and willingly associate with blacks, but also to educate their networks about integration. In the words of Anglican vicar A. A. Boddy, "white pastors went back to the South and reported to the members of their congregations that they had been together with Negroes, that they had prayed in one spirit and received the same blessings as they." Mason's encounter with the interracial impulse at the Azusa Street revival was a familiar aspect of his religious life and possibly reinforced the authenticity of the Pentecostal experience proposed by William Seymour.[18]

Although seminal, the interracial impulse was contested within early Pentecostalism. Prominent black and white Pentecostal leaders campaigned to make the interracial vision of the Azusa Street revival and of many emerging congregations and fellowships constitutive of Pentecostalism. Black Holiness congregations in Los Angeles, Portland, Memphis, Indianapolis, and New York City were the originating sites for the introduction of Pentecostalism. These cities and sites witnessed congregations that practiced integrated worship as modeled by the Azusa Street revival.[19]

Mason's embrace of the Pentecostal message and experience, though, led to the fracturing of his Holiness fellowship. Mason led a small group of clergy that reorganized COGIC into a Pentecostal fellowship. The majority of the Holiness fellowship, though, remained under the leadership of

Charles Price Jones. The debate between Jones and Mason on the Pentecostal message and experience centered on whether speaking in tongues in Acts referred to a recognizable language or an unknown language, reflecting the wider discussion among Pentecostals and others about glossolalia. Jones rejected the notion that an unknown language could fit the Pentecost event. Mason disagreed with Jones and argued for the biblical basis of his own interpretation. This theological difference led to the separation of Mason's group from Jones's.[20]

Mason and the COGIC Interracial Experiment before 1914

Mason's commitment to the interracial vision was evident in his readily admitting three white fellowships to join COGIC between 1910 and 1913. The additions transformed COGIC into a racially inclusive network of fellowships. This Pentecostal experiment in institutionalized integration consisted of three sectors: (1) the predominantly African American fellowship led by Mason, the official head of COGIC; (2) a group of white Pentecostals led by Howard Goss and later Mack Pinson and H. G. Rodgers; and (3) a smaller group of white Pentecostals led by Leonard P. Adams. Significantly, Pinson, Rodgers, and Adams knew each other, having previously participated in a Holiness fellowship led by J. O. McClurkan. Since McClurkan's group included blacks, Pinson, Rodgers, and Adams might have been predisposed to working with Mason after their Pentecostal experiences.[21]

Howard A. Goss entered a relationship with Mason seemingly around 1910. Goss had previously worked with Charles Parham and had defected from Parham's fellowship in 1907 along with some other midwestern clergy. Goss used the title "The Church of God in Christ and in unity with the Apostolic Faith Movement." Pinson and Rodgers entered the relationship before 1913 with their Pentecostal clergy fellowship based in Dothan, Alabama, which they had organized in 1909 along with D. J. Dubose and J. W. Ledbetter. Pinson's fellowship initially used the name Church of God. At least by 1913, the Pinson and Goss groups had merged with COGIC, while Adams remained distinct within Mason's fellowship. By late 1913, the five leaders had crafted "The Call" for the 1914 Hot Springs meeting, the founding gathering of the Assemblies of God, which listed the following names on the roster of the Churches of God in Christ: M. M. Pinson, A. P. Collins, H. A. Goss, D. C. O. Opperman, and E. N. Bell.

H. G. Rodgers, Pinson's associate, was also on the roster of 352 Pentecostal leaders in COGIC. Mason attended the Hot Springs meeting and bestowed his blessing on the newly constituted Assemblies of God.[22]

Leonard P. Adams formed a separate white fellowship and entered a relationship with COGIC by 1910 and began holding annual conferences around 1911. Adams and Mason had both established Holiness congregations in Memphis during the early 1900s, but they never crossed race lines to worship together. It was the Pentecostal experience that brought the congregations into a relationship. Adams had invited Gaston B. Cashwell to preach at his Memphis congregation in 1907. Cashwell arrived on May 8, 1907, and, accompanied by H. G. Rodgers and M. M. Pinson, conducted a revival in which Adams received the Pentecostal experience. Adams began organizing a congregation in Memphis during 1906. Cashwell later preached to Mason's congregation. Adams joined COGIC with his white fellowship around 1910 and began holding annual conventions by 1911. After the departure of the white COGIC fellowship associated with Goss into the Assemblies, Adams's fellowship remained the only white COGIC fellowship until 1917. The roster of COGIC overseers included Adams in a 1917 list. Adams's Memphis congregation, Grace and Truth, continued under his leadership until 1919 when he resigned. The congregation called H. E. Shoettley, a white COGIC pastor from Toledo, Ohio. By 1923, Grace and Truth, along with other congregations associated with Adams's COGIC fellowship, joined the Assemblies of God.[23]

A critical issue is this: how do we define the relationship between these white clergy and Mason prior to 1914? While historians like Ithiel Clemmons identified this time as an interracial period within COGIC, historians like Vinson Synan interpreted the relationship as "purely, nominal, extending only to ministerial credentials." Synan further noted that "most of the white ministers preferred to gather informally in 'state camp meetings' where their ecclesiastical affairs could be discussed freely without reference to Mason or any other church officials." When Synan and others make their assessment of the relationship, to what are they comparing Mason's organization?[24]

First, how was COGIC as an organization best characterized between 1910 and 1914? Polity issues were at the core of COGIC's identity. Before Mason introduced Pentecostalism to COGIC, the fellowship had debated the form of its organizational structure. By 1906, Jones advocated a structure in which the congregations and clergy could join and the fellowship would ultimately hold the rights to the property. Mason proposed that the organization define itself as a fellowship of clergy, with the property belonging to the congregation. Basically, the fellowship consisted of three networks of clergy: Charles Price Jones's, Charles Harrison Mason's, and Charles Gray's. While Gray's network extended throughout central Tennessee, Jones's and Mason's overlapped geographically. The three largest states within the membership were Arkansas, Mississippi, and Tennessee. Each held separate state assemblies. In addition, the fellowship sponsored a regional convention. Each state overseer possessed the authority to admit ordained ministers into the state assembly and national fellowship; they also signed the ordination papers of new ministers. While Charles Price Jones served as the elected leader of the fellowship, he functioned more as a general moderator than a president or presiding bishop. Thus COGIC under Mason's leadership would later grant the different white networks a similar type of arrangement practiced by COGIC during its Holiness phase.[25]

Mason and the COGIC Interracial Experiment after 1914

Adams's fellowship remained the sole white group within COGIC after the formation of the Assemblies of God in 1914. In 1916 a new group of white congregations joined COGIC, creating a second white fellowship. This group of congregations became identified as the "White Branch of the Church of God in Christ" as well as the "Western Department." They recognized Memphis and Los Angeles as their headquarters. These congregations were located in California, Washington, Oregon, Nevada, Utah, Arizona, New Mexico, and Texas. William B. Holt occupied the office of the general superintendent of the White COGIC branch.[26]

Mason attracted white support within and outside of COGIC. In 1916 he led a large camp meeting for whites in Nashville. In 1919 he preached to a large mixed audience in Little Rock. Within COGIC, Holt emerged as the most prominent white COGIC leader. Between 1916 and 1933 he held various national offices within the denomination. Holt crossed racial lines, ministering among whites, blacks, and Hispanics. When Holt joined COGIC, he was designated the overseer for the new group of white congregations as well as the head of COGIC's Spanish missions. By 1925, Holt assumed the office of general secretary and later the national field secretary of the denomination. Born in 1880, he was a native of Fort Worth, Texas. He relocated to California by 1901 and was converted at a Baptist school during that year. Later he received the Holiness experience at a camp meeting in Downey, California. In 1903 he associated with a Holiness fellowship, the Pentecostal Church of the Nazarene, receiving a ministerial license; later he matriculated into the Nazarene Bible College. He received the Pentecostal experience in 1914.[27]

Holt and his other white colleagues identified with Mason's interracial impulse. As well as affirming racial equality, Holt espoused social equality between the races. Holt publicly violated the racial etiquette of southern segregationists by greeting Mason and other black clergy with a holy kiss as well as hugging them, engaging in a "shocking display of interracial intimacy." Such intimate interracial behavior was reminiscent of blacks and whites embracing each other at the Azusa Street revival.[28]

The pacifist activities of COGIC and Mason during World War I attracted accusations that some of the white COGIC members were German agents or sympathizers. The anomaly of white clergy and congregations in a predominantly black denomination seemed best justified by the idea that some of these whites were recruiting blacks within COGIC to support the German cause and challenge military involvement of the United States. The historian Theodore Kornweibel Jr., however, judged these accusations to be false. COGIC's interracial impulse defined its rejection of the military draft and its campaign for conscientious objector status for draft-age male members. Mason reportedly characterized World War I in racial terms. He interpreted the possible defeat of the United States as divine judgment for racial discrimination against African Americans. Mason based his pacifism on the New Testament aversion to "war in all its various forms." Nevertheless, to counter charges of treason, Mason permitted his followers to buy war bonds and pledge their allegiance to the country and the president.[29]

COGIC approved and published its 1917 manual within the racial and geopolitical context of the period. The document clearly identified Mason as the chief overseer of the organization who presided at the official meeting of the racially diverse group of general overseers, including Adams and Holt. Included in the publication were pictures of the key black and white COGIC leaders, offering a visual representation of the interracial complexion of COGIC leadership. The document codified COGIC's policy of integration against the backdrop of racial discrimination and segregation. It juxtaposed the COGIC polity of racial inclusion over against the segregationist polity of other U.S. denominations. The statement presented two polities of racial subordination rejected by COGIC: an executive leadership system of racial subordination wherein whites supervised blacks, and an executive leadership system wherein blacks supervised blacks, albeit within a hierarchy controlled by whites. The document identified these racial polities as a primary reason for the collapse of the interracial moment within American Protestantism and the formation of "many separate colored denominations." In opposing racial inequality in leadership, COGIC erected a structure that conferred "equal power and authority" to its black and white leaders. Such an achievement demonstrated the deliberative and prophetic stance of COGIC interracialism.[30]

Until 1924 COGIC defined the boundaries of its jurisdictions geographically, often aligning them with state boundaries. To accommodate white congregations and clergy, COGIC introduced in 1924 a racial jurisdiction for the white membership that overlapped with the established boundaries of the existing jurisdictions. The white COGIC clergy and congregations were located in seven states: Arkansas, California, Illinois, Indiana, Iowa, Massachusetts, and Michigan. Included in the ministerial list were four women evangelistic helpers. The formation of the national jurisdiction did attract new whites into COGIC, such as August Feick and the Indianapolis congregation of Maria Woodworth-Etter that he assumed as pastor after her death in 1924. Thomas O'Reilly occupied the office of the overseer for the white COGIC community in Michigan, and Feick joined William B. Holt in the position of general superintendent of "The White Churches of God in Christ," a body incorporated in February of 1924.[31]

The new national interracial COGIC structure seemingly progressed until it was undermined by internal crises. In 1928 Thomas O'Reilly was removed as overseer in Michigan because of teaching a doctrine alien to COGIC; the minutes did not record the issues of the doctrinal dispute. William B. Holt, though, supported the removal. During the general assembly in 1931, two questions were raised regarding the interracial experiment within COGIC. The first issue related to the separation of the white COGIC congregations into a national jurisdiction with a white overseer. The question was whether there should be "a white overseer over white

DAVID D. DANIELS

people of Church of God in Christ." The second issue regarded interracial worship: "whether white and colored should worship together or be separated." The two issues were prompted by previous interracial COGIC congregations separating racially to constitute new white congregations for the white COGIC jurisdiction. In Mason's reply, he articulated his support of voluntary racial separation by whites on a practical ground, ethical principle, and biblical precedent. The practical issue related to the common good of the congregation. Mason contended that "when conditions became such that a separation is for the peace and welfare of the congregation," the separation was justified; the ethical principle advocated freedom of association. He stated that "if it [separation] is desired by the whites for their freedom it is alright." Mason also noted the biblical precedent of the early church having distinct missionary strategies based on race. He surmised that, "as St. Paul was sent to the Gentiles and St. Peter to the Jews," it was appropriate for blacks and whites to have different leaders. However, Mason demanded that a notion of civility prevail, and he denounced what he identified as "the Spirit of division through strife."[32]

In 1933, August Feick resigned as pastor of his Indianapolis congregation. The congregation withdrew from COGIC and joined the Assemblies of God under the pastorate of Thomas Paino Sr. During the same year, William B. Holt was unseated from his national office as field secretary. The grounds for dismissal were unclear. However, he responded to the change in the political situation by sending an angry letter outlining his displeasure as well as denouncing what he deemed as racial prejudice and discrimination. In the letter he mentioned a conspiracy against him. He considered himself to have been dealt with unfairly and accused the denomination of failing "to bestow proper honor upon him." The council summoned Holt and interviewed him about his accusations. To clarify the larger issues of the interracial COGIC experiment, guidelines were established regarding "how white ministers and members are dealt with in the Church of God in Christ."[33]

The COGIC experiment with an interracial structure ended in failure after almost twenty-five years. The last fifteen years of this experiment appear to have revolved around the relationship between Mason and Holt. However, even with Holt's leadership among whites, COGIC had difficulty retaining white congregations for more than a decade. The reasons for the retention problem could range from congregational crises related to transitions in pastoral leadership such as in Adams's congregation, Grace and Truth, to leadership crises within the white hierarchy such as the O'Reilly controversy, to structural issues within COGIC itself.

Conclusion

Mason presided over COGIC after it was reorganized into a Pentecostal denomination until 1961, serving as its ecclesial leader for fifty-four years during an era of growth into a national and international organization. Mason guided the interracial impulse of COGIC that had its origin in the black and white Holiness movement. This impulse shaped Mason's leadership as well as the blacks and whites he led in erecting the three distinct structures of racial inclusion. Though COGIC as an integrated denomination of black and white congregations and leaders failed after twenty-five years, white clergy and members remained present in COGIC history throughout the twentieth century and into the twenty-first century. What is significant about the first twenty-five years of the COGIC experiment of racial inclusion is the intentional organizational endeavors that COGIC sponsored to foster the interracial impulse, setting COGIC within a small class of American denominations that rejected segregationism and practiced interracialism. When it is recalled that COGIC was a southern-based, predominantly African American–led denomination, the phenomenon of white congregations joining COGIC makes the organization even more rare in American religious history and its experiment of racial equality a radical moment in American history.[34]

DAVID D. DANIELS

Carrie Judd Montgomery: The Little General

Jeannette Storms

"Clara, I will get up now."
This statement, uttered in faith by a frail teenager, initiated a miracle of healing that resulted in a ministry that spanned sixty-six years. A religious and theological entrepreneur, Carrie Judd Montgomery made a significant contribution to the Holiness, faith-healing, and Pentecostal movements. A quiet but persuasive communicator, Montgomery used her writing abilities and spiritual authority to influence and introduce scores of people to a deeper life in Christ and ministered healing to the sick and suffering. In contrast to the religious climate of her day, she took a bold stand against sectarianism and endeavored to be an agent of ecumenical unity.

In 1880 Montgomery documented the testimony of her healing in *The Prayer of Faith* and the next year started the publication of a monthly journal, *Triumphs of Faith*, that featured articles by influential evangelicals such as A. J. Gordon, Andrew Murray, and A. B. Simpson.[1] In addition to her writing abilities, Montgomery's preaching and teaching career initially took her across denominational lines into Presbyterian, Episcopal, Baptist, Holiness, and Alliance churches and conventions and eventually around the world after her experience of Pentecostal fullness.[2] Although she came from a proper and deeply religious family, both Carrie and her wealthy stockbroker husband, George S. Montgomery, burned with a zeal to help the disenfranchised and started an array of institutions aimed at rescuing the fallen, caring for the orphaned, and providing a place for healing and restoration. With an Episcopal heritage, unique interpretation

George and Carrie Montgomery with their daughter, Faith, circa 1905. Courtesy of Beth Herrstrom, Oakland, California.

of Spirit baptism, interdenominational ministry, and ecumenical focus, she could be regarded as a forerunner of the charismatic movement.

Faith's Foundations

On April 8, 1858, when Orvan and Emily Judd held their newborn daughter, Caroline Frances, little did they realize that she was destined to become "one of the best known women in America."[3] Orvan K. Judd graduated from Union College in Schenectady, New York, and later studied law but was never successful in practice since he often sought to bring reconciliation as soon as possible without prolonged litigation. His most important job, though, was the formation of his children. Seeing Carrie's keen intellect, he arranged for her to begin Latin studies at age nine and later French studies. Emily Sweetland Judd, who had composed and published some poetry before marriage, spotted Carrie's aptitude in writing and encouraged her. When Carrie was fifteen, Emily introduced her to David Grey, editor of the *Buffalo Courier*, who shortly thereafter published her first work—a poem entitled "Clouds." At seventeen, she entered Buffalo Normal School, where she embarked on a four-year classical course of study to become a teacher.

Carrie's spirituality was shaped through regular church attendance, observance of prayer before meals, and family worship times. When she was eleven, on one occasion her mother reproved Frank, her brother, for something that Carrie had also done. This incident pricked Carrie's conscience, prompting her to pray and receive God's grace. In 1869, Bishop Arthur Cleveland Coxe confirmed her in the Episcopal Church. The early deaths of two siblings and the protracted illness of her father deepened her development spiritually by causing her to reflect more deeply on the meaning of life and eternity. Yet she did not isolate herself or become depressed; instead, she stayed busy by teaching Sunday school classes, ministering to the poor, and working in the temperance movement.

In 1873, Carrie Judd took a brief respite from school to accompany her brother, Charlie, to a sanitarium, Home on the Hillside, directed by Dr. James C. Johnson. She assisted the director's wife with the editing of their *Health Magazine* and other office tasks. This experience gave her useful insight for her future role as editor of her own journal, *Triumphs of Faith*, and provided a valuable model for her future faith-healing home.

Although the Judds were devout churchgoers who began each day with family worship, Carrie characterized them as "quite reserved . . . in speaking about spiritual truths with their children" and matters such as "answered prayer and healing (were) largely unknown." Even though she was a confirmed Christian, Carrie recalled an inner spiritual void that prompted her to cry out, "O, God, if there is such a God as the Bible tells about . . . reveal Thyself to me so that I will never doubt again." As she approached seventeen, a spiritual struggle erupted between her longing for more of God and her unwillingness to give all to Him—especially her writing talent! Finally, in desperation, she cried out, "O, Lord, I am going to hold it tight in my clasped hands, but if Thou MUST have it, tear my hands apart."[4]

Faith's Awakening

In the winter of 1876, Carrie slipped on an icy sidewalk and sustained a serious back injury. Complications set in when she contracted spinal fever, which deteriorated into hyperesthesia. Her physical condition made it impossible for her to read or write and created anxiety because of the financial burden that it placed on her family. Her nerves were so sensitive that she had to be isolated in a darkened room since the least noise was "unendurable." It was "a nightmare of horror." As she grew increasingly weak, her condition was declared terminal.

During this time, her father spotted a small item in the newspaper describing the healing of Elizabeth Mix, an African American lay minister from Wolcottville, Connecticut. At Carrie's prompting, her sister, Eva, wrote to Mix and requested prayer. Mix replied by referring to James 5:15 as the basis for trusting God for physical healing and challenged her "to lay aside all medicine" and "lean wholly upon God and His promises." Mix set a definite time for prayer and exhorted her to "pray for yourself, and pray believing, and then *act faith*. It makes no difference how you feel, but get right out of bed and begin to walk by faith."

On February 26, 1879, at the appointed time of three o'clock in the afternoon, Mix and her friends in Connecticut prayed. At the same hour, Carrie and her family gathered for prayer in Buffalo, New York. While family members prayed downstairs, she requested her nurse to read from the Bible. She reported later, "Suddenly some words she was reading arrested my attention; they seemed to be illuminated . . . in such a way as to create a new faith within me." Without even praying, Carrie "quietly and without excitement" declared, "Clara, I will get up now." For the first time in more than two years, Carrie turned over and raised up, then swung her feet over the side of the bed and began walking to a chair. At the time of her healing, she also received an impartation of the Holy Spirit, which she called "the baptism of the Holy Spirit," and made a commitment to share her testimony with others whenever she had an opportunity.[5]

As news of Judd's healing spread, the *Buffalo Commercial Advertiser* picked up the story and published an article entitled "A Modern Miracle" on October 30, 1879. The account drew national and international attention. A deluge of letters resulted, and many sought her out—both skeptics and sincere seekers. In response to these letters and inquiries, Judd wrote the small book, *The Prayer of Faith* (1880). In it, she gave her testimony and then articulated some basic scriptural teaching on faith healing. In London, the small volume received a warm reception and attracted the attention of W. E. Boardman and the editor of the *Christian Herald.* It was later translated and published in German, French, Swedish, and Dutch.[6]

Because of the reception that *The Prayer of Faith* received, her brother, Charlie, challenged her to begin the publication of a monthly magazine that would "give instruction from the Word of God and testimonies to the Lord's wonder-working power." In January of 1881, Judd began publishing her monthly journal, *Triumphs of Faith,* which she personally edited without interruption until her death in 1946.[7] It usually contained an editorial by Judd and featured articles by a variety of leading evangelicals on topics that focused on the higher Christian life and divine healing. Robert L. Stanton's series, "Gospel Parallelisms: Illustrated in the Healing of Body and Soul," appeared in 1883 and represented one of the first in-depth teachings on the subject of healing in the atonement, which understood Christ's finished work on the cross as being effective not only for salvation but also for healing of the body.[8] From the first, *Triumphs of Faith* contained a perceptible stream of references to missions and missionaries, with items tracking faith-healing homes and their ministries internationally.[9]

In 1880 Judd began a Thursday evening "faith-meeting" at her parents' home in Buffalo. Describing these meetings as interdenominational in character, she remarked that "the Lord manifested Himself in our midst by pouring out upon us spiritual blessing, and also in healing the sick."[10] As the "faith sanctuary" meetings flourished, Judd realized the need to expand this ministry by developing a faith home. A two-story house in the vicinity of her family's home was rented at 323 Fargo Avenue, Buffalo, New York. On April 3, 1882, Faith-Rest Cottage opened its doors with "informal consecration and thanksgiving services" and provided a place where the sick or weary could come for a time of spiritual renewal with Bible studies being taught daily and prayers offered for the sick. Fashioned after the faith principle modeled by George Muller and Charles Cullis, the ministry was entirely supported by "voluntary contributions." In December of 1884, Judd reported, "Many have been blessedly healed in this little Home, and life-long invalids have gone forth strong in the Master's strength to work for Him."[11]

After the news of her miraculous healing broke in 1880, Judd received many invitations to share her testimony in a wide variety of settings. In

1883, she took a trip to New York, where she met A. B. Simpson, who showed her a copy of his monthly magazine containing a reprint of her first editorial, "Faith's Reckonings." Later, Simpson invited Judd to "assist permanently in his work," but she declined, sensing that God wanted her to continue the faith ministry that she had initiated. Simpson opened many doors of opportunity for Judd to minister publicly, and they frequently shared the platform at conventions. In 1885 she received a personal invitation from W. E. Boardman to attend and teach at the First International Conference on Healing and Holiness in London, England.[12] Personal glimpses from her journal reveal the extent of her ministry that crossed denominational and racial lines. In May of 1889, Judd recounted a trip to Virginia where she ministered with Quakers and among whites and "coloreds." She mentioned being ostracized from certain churches that had a prejudice "first against women preachers and second against nigger preachers" (that is, those who preached among African Americans).[13]

When the Christian Alliance was organized in 1887 at Old Orchard, Maine, Carrie F. Judd was appointed the first recording secretary. Because the "attitude" of this new movement was more "spiritual" than "organic," Judd did not view her identification with this body as being in conflict with her Anglican heritage or affiliation. In February of 1888, *Triumphs of Faith* contained a copy of the "Constitution and Principles" of the Christian Alliance in which its stated "attitude" was articulated as, "It shall be, not an ecclesiastical body, but a fraternal union of believers, in cordial harmony with Evangelical Christian of every name." From 1888 to 1891, her journal contained a monthly news item called "The Work and Workers" that traced the movements of different leaders in the alliance and also carried notices about conventions and camp meetings. After her marriage to George S. Montgomery and her move to the West Coast, she continued to work closely with the Christian Alliance, even after induction into the Salvation Army. After her personal Pentecost, Judd proved influential in spreading the Pentecostal message among members of the alliance and saw many receive the fullness of the Spirit.[14]

Through her book *The Prayer of Faith*, Judd made a popular contribution to the faith-healing movement and the development of the doctrine of divine healing. In many respects, her initial views on healing echoed those voiced by Charles Cullis in his book *Faith Cures* (1879), which interpreted James 5:14–15 ("And the prayer of faith will heal the sick") as normative and applicable to believers of all ages. Her first editorial in *Triumphs of Faith*, "Faith's Reckonings," articulated the view that actualizing faith functioned solely upon the basis of God's Word and operated outside feelings or circumstances. She wrote, "We always find ourselves acting upon what we really believe, and just as far as we *act faith*, so far shall we be expressing our belief in God's faithfulness. It is not necessary to feel some particular emotion in our hearts, but to *act* as though we believe what we *profess* to believe."

Even though the evangelistic model of healing as expressed in the ministries of persons such as Maria Woodworth-Etter, Aimee Semple McPherson, or (later) Kathryn Kuhlman has been popularized, another mode of healing, namely, the pastoral model of healing, has functioned quietly and effectively in various segments of the church. Judd employed this method in bringing healing to people through biblically centered instruction coupled with the prayer of faith and the laying on of hands. Through Faith-Rest Cottage and later the Home of Peace, Judd provided a place where the sick and suffering could find rest and spiritual renewal in a pastoral model of healing.[15]

While her writings on healing in the 1880s centered on actualizing faith, she did not personally write about healing in the atonement. However, she did offer a thought-provoking insight about the sacramental aspect of healing by speaking "of that wondrous means of grace and strength, the Sacrament of the Lord's Supper . . . I believe that if we will accept *all* that He offers us in that holy and mystical body, of which we spiritually partake, we may find renewed physical life as well as spiritual."[16] She also focused on the holistic aspect of faith healing with the view that its effects transcended the physical and spilled over into the dimensions of soul and spirit. A survey of editorials published in this first phase of ministry revealed a primary focus on the higher Christian life with faith healing being treated in a secondary way. This reflected her belief in an experience subsequent to salvation, popularly known as Holy Spirit baptism, which ushered the believer into a deeper dimension of spirituality and empowerment for victorious Christian living.

Faith's Adventures

In June of 1889, Judd traveled to Cook County, Illinois, to speak at the Summer Convocation of Christian Workers. George S. Montgomery, a successful businessman from the West Coast, attended the camp meeting and invited Carrie Judd and Elizabeth Sisson (another convention speaker) to San Francisco to minister in various meetings.[17] Little did Judd realize that it was a divine appointment or that she would share the next forty-six years with him.

A Scot, George Simpson Montgomery was born on January 14, 1851, in Tyrone County, Ireland, and immigrated to America in 1866. By 1880 he had amassed his first fortune through gold mining in Mexico but later lost it through a day of wild trading on the Pacific Stock Exchange. Returning to the gold mines in Mazatlan, Mexico, he recouped his fortune. By 1888, he was back in San Francisco, where he was listed in the *San Francisco Blue Book* and held membership in the Bohemian Club, indulging himself in "one continued round of worldly business and pleasure," but such a lifestyle took its toll. On September 29, 1888, he set sail for Japan on the S.S. *Gaelic* hoping to regain his health. During the voyage, the spirit of God confronted him in his stateroom and made it clear that "God was calling for the *last* time." He later recalled that he responded by falling to his knees and confessing his sins and need of a savior.

When his ship docked in San Francisco harbor on December 22, 1888, Montgomery disembarked a spiritually changed person, but his health continued to deteriorate. Shortly thereafter, Dr. George Smith, a physician, influenced Montgomery to attend a healing meeting being conducted by Alexander Dowie in Oakland. Through Smith's intervention and persuasion, Dowie visited Montgomery and prayed for him personally. Later Montgomery testified, "I had no special manifestation at the time . . . The next morning I realized the new life which had been imparted, and felt as though I could run like a boy . . . I was not only healed of Diabetes, but also of chronic rheumatism."[18] After this, Montgomery was a changed person with one goal—to glorify God through his life and business abilities. His real estate holdings became a great blessing, not only to the ministry that he and Carrie shared but also to other Christian organizations that he endowed with large amounts of property.[19]

Before Christmas of 1889, George and Carrie announced their engagement. C. F. Wrigley, rector of St. Mary's Episcopal Church, and A. B. Simpson united them in marriage on May 14, 1890, in a quiet yet joyful ceremony at her parents' home. In August, they arrived in California after an extended trip through the Midwest and various western points of interest. In San Francisco, they settled into their new apartment and quickly became involved in ministry, with Carrie preaching at various churches and conducting meetings in their home while George provided financial and moral support for the fledgling ministry.[20]

A variety of pioneering ventures filled the decade of the 1890s. In September of 1890, the People's Mission opened as an outreach to those in desperate spiritual need in San Francisco. During the first nine days of its operation, Carrie Montgomery reported, "We praise God that souls have been saved nearly every night since the Mission opened, thirty or more in nine days." A home for "street girls" opened soon thereafter. On Thanksgiving Day of 1891, George and Carrie enlisted in the Salvation Army. The January 1892 edition of her journal contained a photo of Carrie in her uniform and expressed their joint commitment to "identify with the Salvation Army." Later William Booth made them "honorary officers, a non-commissioned status that allowed George to keep his businesses."

In the meantime, George had taken Carrie and her mother to Park Place in the Oakland hills, where he built a home for his family as well as one for Carrie's mother, who had come to live with them. On May 25, 1891, the Montgomerys' only child, Faith, was born. She soon became the delight of her mother and the object of her father's undivided attention. Later that year, more than a hundred friends gathered to dedicate this property as the site for a new temperance town known as "Beulah" (later Beulah Heights). The Montgomerys envisioned that it would be a "city populated by the redeemed . . . a City of Refuge for many oppressed and helpless ones."[21]

In the summer of 1892, George took Carrie and baby Faith to a virgin redwood tract known as Cazadero—formerly used by the Bohemian Club. In October, accompanied by Mr. and Mrs. Lawrence Greenwood and B. Fay Mills, the Montgomerys took another excursion to Cazadero, where "we drove to a most beautiful natural auditorium formed by a circle of immense redwood trees." There they sang and worshiped the Lord, "after which we sank on our knees on the velvety sod and offered prayer and praise to our adorable Redeemer." From this experience, Carrie received a desire "to organize a permanent camp-ground . . . as a free resort for all of God's children." In July of 1893, the first Undenominational Union Camp Meeting was held there and continued annually almost without interruption until 1918. After the Montgomerys' Pentecostal experience, the name was changed to World-Wide Pentecostal Camp Meeting. In 1914, Smith

Wigglesworth and George T. Studd were the featured speakers.[22]

In the fall of 1892, Major Kyle dedicated a Salvation Army Rescue Home at Beulah that opened its door to fallen girls who needed "a refuge from the storm." In April 1893, Carrie Montgomery reported that "most of the girls of the Rescue Home have been gloriously saved; their testimonies and prayers are full of power and rejoicing." She described the conversion of one who "was completely enslaved by the morphine habit" and of a Jewish girl who, though resistant at first, was "gloriously saved" and filled with joy "at finding the Messiah."[23]

On April 20, 1892, ground had been broken for a new faith home that would house the ministry of Carrie's former Faith-Rest Cottage. As the foundation was being laid by the workmen, "a pure, snow-white dove suddenly appeared" and circled directly over George Montgomery's head. Owing to this incident, George suggested the new faith home be named the Home of Peace. At the dedication service on November 7, 1893, Mannie Payne Ferguson read a poem entitled "The Home of Peace" that described the mission of the new home as an "oasis . . . a nest for birds of broken wing . . . a place where storms . . . cease . . . and captives . . . find release." Initially the Home of Peace functioned as a faith-healing home but later expanded its ministry to become a place of rest and recuperation for missionaries journeying to and from various mission fields. From 1894 to 1898, it housed a missionary training center (known as Shalom Training Center) under the direction of Mr. and Mrs. H. C. Wardell, which provided biblical and theological training for persons preparing to be missionaries or Christian workers.[24]

In 1894 Carrie referred to the "needs of orphaned and abandoned children." Beulah Orphanage opened its doors in the summer of 1895 and initially housed thirty children between the ages of four to fourteen. In 1902, she reported that there were "three different homes under the one Orphanage. Sunshine Home is for the older children, the Bird's Nest for children from three to seven years of age, and the Rose Bud Home is for little babies." According to reports, a revival swept through the orphanage in 1907 that affected many of the children spiritually.[25]

In October of 1895, a reporter from the *Oakland Enquirer* visited the complex of ministries initiated by the Montgomerys and described "Beulah, in the Hills, the Salvation Retreat." His report detailed a multifaceted ministry composed of an "undenominational religious training school," a new orphanage, a home for workers of the Salvation Army (where Catherine Booth was to speak), and a home for fallen girls. The Montgomerys were innovative and gifted at initiating ministries, facilitating and administering them, and then giving them away to others. To the Salvation Army, they donated the People's Mission in San Francisco and the Home for Fallen Girls in Oakland. George Montgomery donated land to Mills College in Oakland and provided a lot to establish the first Home for Aged and Infirm Colored People in the state of California in 1895. However, the two ministries that Carrie Montgomery sustained long term were the *Triumphs of Faith,* which remained in circulation from 1881 until 1970, and her flagship ministry, the Home of Peace. In 2000, the Home of Peace continued to minister interdenominationally as a Christian bed-and-breakfast and as a logistical service for missionaries from more than a hundred organizations.[26]

Prominent themes in the *Triumphs of Faith* during the decade of the 1890s related to holiness, prayer, and the higher Christian life, with A. B. Simpson and Andrew Murray being prime contributors. Articles by William Booth and members of his family, as well as ones by Hannah Whitall Smith and Jesse Penn-Lewis, reveal Carrie Montgomery's connection to the Salvation Army and the Keswick movement. In the 1890s a fuller development of the doctrine of divine healing was articulated in it. Whereas in the 1880s she had relied on others to write about healing in the atonement, in April of 1892 she asserted, "We shall find the Gospel of Healing running like a golden thread all through the Bible . . . because God has made such abundant provision for our healing in the atonement of our Lord Jesus Christ."[27] In this phase, she affirmed the place and importance of praise and personal testimony in the retention of healing by publishing the small book *The Life of Praise.* However, the faith motif was still the primary focus of her writing on the subject of healing. As the decade of the 1890s drew to a close, there was an increased emphasis on holiness but one clothed in Pentecostal imagery with prayer themes surfacing frequently.[28]

Faith's Empowerment

On April 18, 1906, while fires burned out of control in San Francisco owing to a killer earthquake, the headlines of the *Los Angeles Daily Times* announced another kind of quake on Azusa Street, where Pentecostal phenomena had broken denominational, racial, and gender barriers.

Montgomery's coverage of Azusa and the ensuing revival was low-key. As a woman with an Anglican background who was refined and dignified, she maintained a cautious but open attitude. The first mention of the Azusa revival occurred in her journal in December 1906, when she published a letter by Frank Bartleman. The comments preceding the letter revealed that George Montgomery had attended the meetings "and was thoroughly convinced . . . that God was mightily working to bring His people to a place of increased power for service." Carrie Montgomery was also impressed by positive reports that she had received from Pandita Ramabai and other missionaries about the worldwide impact of the movement. Finally, when one of the workers at Beulah Heights received the "fullness of the Spirit, with the sign of speaking in tongues," she paid close attention, observing that this worker's life now revealed a greater anointing as well as a deeper relationship with God.[29]

On June 29, 1908, Carrie Judd Montgomery received her personal Pentecost by faith quietly in the home of a friend in Cleveland, Ohio. Seven days later, she spoke in tongues while visiting in the home of another friend in Chicago. She recorded that, as she tried to sing a song, "some of the words would stick in my throat. In a few moments I uttered a few scattered words in an unknown tongue and then burst into a language that came pouring out . . . For nearly two hours I spoke and sang in unknown tongues . . . Some of the tunes were beautiful and most Oriental." Harriette Shimer, a missionary of the Society of Friends in China, reported her amazement at hearing her sing and speak in a number of different Chinese dialects.[30]

Immediately upon her return to the West Coast, Montgomery became an open advocate of the Pentecostal experience. The October 1908 issue of her journal announced "Pentecostal Meetings at Beulah" and invited "those who are . . . hungering and thirsting for the baptism of the Holy Spirit" to come for special prayer. A testimony by S. R. Break, taken from the April 1909 edition of her magazine, revealed her paradigm in leading seekers into the Pentecostal experience.

> In the latter part of August, 1908, in a simple prayer meeting in an upper room of Mrs. Montgomery's home at Beulah, California . . . definite prayer was offered and hands laid upon me for the Pentecostal fullness . . . I accepted in simple faith, standing on the Word of God . . . On the 10th day a number of us met again in the same room . . .

> While in prayer the desire to speak in a new tongue came upon me and . . . by a very definite act of faith [I] yielded that member to Him and commenced to sing with my natural powers, when, quietly, peacefully, I felt . . . the Holy Spirit's quickening and found myself singing in a new tongue the wonderful works of God. Prayer came in tongues also and clear interpretation with it for different persons, and passages of scripture.[31]

From her personal experience and writings, it appears that she did not initially view Pentecostal fullness and speaking in tongues as synonymous, nor was speaking in tongues viewed as the initial evidence that one had received Holy Spirit baptism.

One of the difficulties that Montgomery experienced in embracing "pentecostal fullness" owed to her understanding of her healing in 1879. "At the time of my miraculous healing . . . I was made conscious of the Holy Spirit's work in revealing Jesus in and to me . . . This experience I have always referred to as the baptism of the Holy Ghost . . . I was not to depreciate His precious work . . . but to follow on to receive the fullness of the same Spirit."[32] Her theological response to "pentecostal fullness" was articulated in her journal more than three years later in the form of two articles, "Sanctification and the Baptism of the Holy Spirit" and "The Remnant of the Oil."[33] In these articles she delineated a three-stage process consisting of salvation, sanctification, and Holy Spirit baptism, with faith as the only condition for receiving them. Montgomery did not mention tongues as "the initial evidence." From her own experience, she believed that, at the moment when she received the fullness of the Holy Spirit by an act of faith, it was hers, though she did not speak in tongues until seven days later. By believing in a three-stage process, she closely reflected the doctrinal position of those from a Holiness heritage who embraced Spirit baptism but retained the doctrine of sanctification. Furthermore, by making faith the only condition for this experience, she became a forerunner of the charismatic movement of the 1960s and 1970s, since she viewed tongues as a likely consequence of Spirit baptism but not as the initial evidence.

From 1908 onward, influential Pentecostal leaders such as A. A. Boddy and Smith Wigglesworth were hosted regularly at the Home of Peace and participated in camp meetings sponsored by the Montgomerys. *Triumphs of Faith* carried testimonies of various persons who had received Holy Spirit baptism, as well as instructive articles about it, while still including articles on the doctrines of holiness and divine healing.[34] Montgomery also wrote and published books and tracts that emphasized the themes of faith, healing, and Holy Spirit baptism.

In December of 1908, her journal contained a news item about the closing of Beulah Orphanage, so that she "might be more used in the exposition of the word of God." The Montgomerys were now free to pursue the dream of a lifetime—an around-the-world missionary trip. On January 23, 1909, they sailed for Honolulu on the S.S. *Manchuria.* Throughout 1909, *Triumphs of Faith* carried month-by-month news of their travels and missionary ventures—in Hawaii, Japan, China, India, and finally England. In England, they visited the Pentecostal Conference in Sunderland hosted by A. A. Boddy and were introduced to a number of Pentecostal leaders from different parts of Europe and the United Kingdom.[35]

After docking in New York on July 3, Carrie Montgomery embarked on a busy round of speaking engagements that included A. B. Simpson's Tabernacle and Marie Burgess's Forty-second Street Mission. She spoke at the Christian and Missionary Alliance (an amalgamation of the Christian Alliance and the Evangelical Missionary Alliance) convention in Nyack and at an Alliance church in Boston. At the Old Orchard convention in Maine, A. B. Simpson scheduled her to teach every evening and gave her complete "liberty in Bible teaching about the Holy Spirit's Fullness." On the return journey to California, the Montgomerys stopped off at two more Alliance camp meetings in the Midwest, at which "the Lord gave us a precious ministry of praying for many who were hungry for the baptism of the Holy Spirit." In these meetings, they were joined by Mr. and Mrs. D. W. Kerr and Pastor John Salmon, who had also received Pentecostal fullness.[36]

After this international trip, Montgomery engaged in an active itinerant ministry traveling to the East and frequently visiting Los Angeles and other places on the West Coast. She also personally edited her monthly magazine and managed the Home of Peace. She influenced many in the Alliance and other denominations to embrace the experience of Holy Spirit baptism. In 1918, A. B. Simpson invited her to speak at the Gospel Tabernacle in New York City, where she "told . . . the great things God had done for me, not only in body but also in mind and spirit through the incoming of the Pentecostal fullness of the blessed Holy Ghost."[37]

During this period, Montgomery also devised new ways of reaching out to her neighborhood and the city of Oakland. In 1910, she started an inter-denominational divine-healing meeting on Monday afternoons at a hall in downtown Oakland that continued for twenty-five years. Using the biblical method of laying hands on the sick and praying for them, she saw many healed and transformed spiritually. This new evangelistic and healing outreach was in addition to her regular Tuesday afternoon meetings at Beulah Chapel that consisted of prayer, Bible teaching, and testimonies. In 1913, a "Union Missionary Prayer Meeting" was instituted on the first Thursday of each month and was devoted exclusively to intercession for world evangelization and missionary prayer requests. In February of 1914, Montgomery noted some of the results of these prayer times: "On our February All-Day Missionary Prayer meeting . . . our Beulah Chapel was filled, and there was a most blessed spirit of intercession for the mission-aries . . . The spirit of worship was marvelously manifested . . . Many broke out in heavenly singing, in new tongues . . . A number have been baptized with the Holy Spirit, and many dear ones . . . received the Comforter in Pentecostal fullness."[38]

As a person who had received Holy Spirit baptism in midlife after a fulfilling and respected ministry, Montgomery brought a steadying voice of maturity to the fledgling Pentecostal movement. On January 11, 1914, she officially identified with the movement and received her "Credentials," or "Certificate of Ordination and Unity," from the Church of God in Christ as a "missionary" and "evangelist." Formed in Meridian, Mississippi, in June of 1913, this loosely organized, predominantly white association evolved into the Assemblies of God in April of 1914 at Hot Springs, Arkansas. Montgomery is therefore regarded as a charter member of the Assemblies of God since her membership in the association predated the official organization of the denomination. In her application for ordina-tion with the Assemblies of God on November 30, 1917, she affirmed that she was engaged in ministry as the pastor of Beulah Chapel and also served as an evangelist and part-time missionary in Mexico.[39] For years she had joined her husband in his missionary ventures in Mexico. After receiving Holy Spirit baptism, the Montgomerys increased their missionary outreach to Hispanics, leading many to Christian faith and facilitating them in ministry. The founding of the Latin American Council of Christian Churches was an indirect result of these endeavors.[40]

Though her theological understanding of Spirit baptism took three years to formulate, Carrie Montgomery's personal response was immediate. Her editorial, "Christ's Quickening Life for the Mortal Body," in August of 1908 articulated a topic that became a major theme for the rest of her life. In it, she described the ecstasy of being overwhelmed by the Holy Spirit. She spoke of the holism and materiality of such an experience, including personality integration and physical healing day by day through the renewal of the Holy Spirit. In addition, she embraced signs and wonders as a way of validating the proclaimed Word of God and the means of creating inroads to the unchurched. In terms of divine healing, her primary focus continued to be the themes of faith, healing in the atonement, and the prayer of faith (James 5:14–15), but she developed more fully the topics of spiritual warfare along with the conditions for and hindrances to healing. As a result of her Pentecostal experience, Montgomery found herself empowered to pursue a greater preaching and teaching ministry with heightened involvement in world missions.[41]

Faith's Fragrance

The decade of the 1920s marked a transition between Montgomery's vibrant years as an evangelical entrepreneur and theological groundbreaker to a respected voice in evangelical and Pentecostal circles whose experience and wisdom contributed valuable perspective and direction. While maintaining an active writing and speaking ministry, she became a steadying influence to the young Pentecostal movement. She provided a voice of maturity and acted as a bridge between evangelicals with a Holiness heritage and the more radical and often misunderstood Pentecostals. Through her Monday divine-healing meetings, many were changed and healed. Concerned about the lack of "harmony among the Lord's children in Oakland," Montgomery desired to facilitate an ecumenical meeting that would "unite all these dear ones in His own love." In 1910, she revealed her deep commitment to ecumenism by observing, "The communion of the saints in Christ's love is the most important thing. It is absolutely vital. Without it you can have no assurance of your continued welfare of soul or body."[42] In this sense, she might be regarded as a charismatic, since all of her life, both before and after her Spirit baptism, she moved across denominational lines and had a deep commitment to unity in the body of Christ.

With the death of her husband, George, on September 6, 1930, Montgomery's health and vitality gradually waned. However, in 1931, at age seventy-three, she traveled coast to coast with her secretary, Elizabeth Wood, preached in various cities, and edited *Triumphs of Faith*. The Depression in the 1930s brought a time of testing for her faith principles, but God proved faithful by continuing to provide financially for the Home of Peace. As the years progressed, the home focused increasingly on assisting missionaries going to and from the field by providing lodging and logistical services. At age seventy-eight, Montgomery authored her last book, *Under His Wings*, an autobiography describing her life and ministry. By that time, her daughter and son-in-law, Merrill Berry, were assisting her in ministry at the Home of Peace while looking after the family's lumbering business in Cazadero and the gold mines in Mexico.[43] As the only survivor of the faith-healing movement who lived to see the beginnings of a fresh wave of divine healing and revival through the ministries of persons such as Oral Roberts and William Branham, Montgomery acted as an important organic link to the faith-healing movement of the late nineteenth century.[44] She died on July 26, 1946. At a memorial service honoring her at the Alliance Tabernacle in Oakland, J. Narver Gortner described the role that she had played in leading many from mainline denominations into the experience of Holy Spirit baptism. On August 17, 1947, the *Pentecostal Evangel* carried the news of her death and mentioned her miraculous healing and Pentecostal baptism. It noted that "soon after the Assemblies of God fellowship was formed, Mrs. Montgomery became affiliated and has been one of our ministers ever since."[45]

Carrie Judd Montgomery's life and theology revealed a high degree of consistency, stability, and continuity, yet she was able to embrace dramatic changes as fresh winds of renewal moved across the church. In her personal life, she was a quiet and unassuming person who, nevertheless, brought healing to thousands through sound biblical teaching, one-on-one personal ministry, and a quiet and unobtrusive manner when praying for the needy. Observers reported that when she entered a room she was the immediate focus of attention and took charge in a quiet, gracious, and unassuming way. Perhaps she was most fond of the nickname "Little General," which her husband, George, had lovingly given her. Reflecting on this name, her grandson, Loren Berry, stated, "Although she was very short and slight, she had a commanding presence which came from the anointing and presence of God in her life."[46] As a general of God, She acted as a spokesperson who stood at the forefront of the Holiness, faith-healing, and Pentecostal movements through her identification with the Christian and Missionary Alliance, Salvation Army, and Assemblies of God. As an entrepreneur, she pioneered a variety of ministries and was able to make critical paradigm shifts to embrace change and re-create ministry structures that were responsive to the times. As a person of compassion she led many to faith in Christ and imparted healing and spiritual empowerment for a more holistic and integrated life.[47]

Antonio Castañeda Nava: Charisma, Culture, and *Caudillismo*

Daniel Ramirez

Afterwards they transported me to a white building and carried me inside where a man was seated in a chair (I was unable to see his face as my faculties were very weak). He asked me, "Did you drink the water?" I answered, "Yes, I drank." "Now go and preach the gospel, and do not fear, for I will be with you."

—Antonio C. Nava

Antonio Castañeda Nava's account of his 1918 ministerial calling, like that of other prophets, resonates with the themes one expects of those who claim or are ascribed charismatic authority: disquiet of the soul, visitation or transportation by heavenly beings, the loss of normal sensory faculties, raw elements (fire, water, earth) as metaphors, obedience, and commissioning. The locus of enunciation also matters. Framed thus, the testimony and career of an immigrant farmworker preacher—like those of African American washerwomen in the Azusa Street revival a decade earlier—invite a reexamination of the struggle of subordinated people against unequal arrangements of social, economic, and ecclesiastical power in early-twentieth-century America. Their long-overdue study also represents an opportunity to rectify the ultimate inequities in the field of American religious history: caricature, dismissal, and erasure. Finally, as with the other apostles of early U.S. Latino Pentecostalism (Juan Lugo and Francisco Olazábal), the portraiture of Nava as movement builder may offer insights

289

Antonio Castañeda Nava, presiding bishop, Apostolic Assembly of the Faith in Christ Jesus, circa 1964. Courtesy of Bernice Nava Ares, Modesto, California.

into the current phenomenon of religious change that is sweeping Latin America and Latino communities in the United States.

The recovered voice of Antonio Nava does not merely cry in the regional wilderness. Nava derived great meaning from experiences and ties south of the U.S.-Mexico border, drawing upon these to buttress the position of his own ethnic religious community in its negotiation with more powerful institutions and actors in the United States. For example, the contemporaneous consolidation of Mexico's tumultuous revolution (1910–20) into an institutional regime (1929), a process that allowed for a period of stability and growth in that country, may have inspired Nava's own commitment to the routinization of charismatic authority. The denomination he helped establish in the United States was incorporated one year after the founding of the Institutional Revolutionary Party in Mexico. The growth and development of Latino apostolicism (Oneness Pentecostalism), then, can be traced through the several stages of Antonio Nava's career: from charismatic prophet to cultural champion to visionary *caudillo* (strongman).[1]

Biographical Sketch

Born October 4, 1892, to Simón and Roberta Nava of Nazas, Durango, Mexico, Antonio Nava sought to enlist in the insurrectionary forces at the start of the Mexican Revolution. His father's firm opposition and the restive youth's desire to save face with peers prompted Nava to seek paternal blessing in 1915 for travel northward instead. He secured employment in the cotton fields of California's Imperial Valley. Fellow farmworker Marcial de la Cruz was instrumental in Nava's conversion to Oneness Pentecostalism in 1916. Nava began his ministry in 1918, evangelizing and pastoring in Yuma, Arizona, and the border towns of Calexico, California, and Mexicali, Baja California. Along with colleagues de la Cruz, Francisco Llorente, Felipe Rivas, José Ortega, and others, Nava shepherded the growth and consolidation of the apostolic movement in the southwestern United States, Mexico, and Central and South America.

The Latino apostolic movement traces its roots to the historic 1906–9 Azusa Street revival in Los Angeles, a cradle of modern worldwide Pentecostalism. Nava and others gathered the embers of the Azusa revival and transformed them into a full-blown religious movement notable for its cultural and ecclesial autonomy. As had been the case at Azusa, early Mexican converts and preachers received a measure of support from African American leaders. The first credentials obtained by the evangelists arrived under the aegis of Bishop Garfield T. Haywood's Indianapolis-based Pentecostal Assemblies of the World (PAW). In 1930 Nava severed the loose ties with the PAW and incorporated the Iglesia de la Fé Apostólica Pentecostés as the Apostolic Assembly of the Faith in Christ Jesus. From

1933 to 1944, Nava and his Mexican counterpart, Felipe Rivas, engineered the exchange of territorial jurisdictions (trading Texas for Baja California to align with national boundaries) and formalized ecclesial ties between the Apostolic Assembly and the Iglesia Apostólica de la Fé en Cristo Jesús in Mexico. In the same period Nava published *Himnos de consolación,* modern Protestantism's first original Spanish-language hymnal, a compilation made up almost entirely of indigenous hymnody composed by Latino authors such as de la Cruz and Nava himself.[2]

Firm ties to Mexican referents notwithstanding, Nava's rise to leadership in the United States would not have occurred without a successful negotiation with the native Mexican American community, many of whom gathered under his decades-long pastorate in east Los Angeles. Nava's marriage in 1933 to Arizona native Dolores Ochoa exemplified the endurance of cultural affinities almost a century after the United States' occupation of Mexico's northern territories. Her bilingual abilities allowed her to broker Nava's relationship with the wider English-speaking world. Both the Los Angeles *Times* and *La Opinión* (the city's premiere Spanish-language newspaper) provided a daily window on local and national events.

Nava served as presiding bishop of the Apostolic Assembly until 1950, when he was succeeded by Benjamin Cantú of Texas' Rio Grande Valley. Nava returned to presidential office in 1963 and relinquished the leadership in 1966 to Efraín Valverde of Salinas, California. Thereafter, he served in an advisory capacity to the denomination as an honorary bishop. After the death of his wife in 1982, Nava settled in the apostolic retirement home in National City, California, eventually taking up residence in Union City, California. In 1985, together with fellow patriarchs Rivas and Ortega, he undertook a valedictory tour of the denomination's northern California region. In 1992 the Apostolic Assembly celebrated the centenary of Nava's birth. The San Diego event was marked by several civic and legislative tributes in Nava's honor, including recognition from U.S. President George Bush and proclamations authored by several congressional, legislative, and municipal authorities. In 1994, the Apostolic Assembly established the Antonio Castañeda Nava Trust as the church's charitable agency for the support of retired ministers, widows and orphans, educational scholarships, and disaster relief.

Nava lived in good health past his centenary year, eschewing even minimal medical attention throughout his busy career. The onset of health problems in his final three years culminated in his death of natural causes at the age of 106 on August 1, 1999, in his Union City, California, home. The Apostolic Assembly and Iglesia Apostólica interred their copatriarch (a designation shared with Rivas of Mexico) on August 10 in San Jose, California. At the time of his death, Nava was survived by eight children, twenty-two grandchildren, twenty-five great-grandchildren, and one great-great-grandchild.

Today, with six hundred churches in forty states, missionary affiliates in eighteen countries, and allied denominations in five countries, including the larger Iglesia Apostólica in Mexico, the Apostolic Assembly represents a flagship denomination within the broader Mexican and Mexican American Protestant movement. The Latino apostolic community of North and Central America is estimated at well over half a million adherents and sympathizers. When expanded to include sectarian offshoots like the Guadalajara-based Luz del Mundo (Light of the World) church, apostolicism may constitute roughly one-half of Mexican/Chicano Pentecostalism, a significantly higher ratio than the Oneness members of either white or black counterparts in the United States.

Caricature vs. Portraiture: Charisma and Mysticism in the Assertion of Power

It would be fruitful to recall the metanarrative set in place a few decades ago by students of Pentecostalism, namely the one that spoke of social and economic deprivation, psychosocial stress, and stunted liberation. Take, for example, Swiss sociologist Lalive d'Epinay's description of Chilean Pentecostal churches as religious replicas of hacienda society on "social strike" and uselessly disengaged in apolitical, albeit urban, enclaves from meaningful societal and political participation.[3] Set against the heady possibilities of socialism, the opiate of Pentecostalism threatened to stymie proletarian projects of economic and political liberation throughout the hemisphere. Subsequent events in Chile, especially the co-optation of Protestant church leadership by Augusto Pinochet in the wake of his 1973 overthrow of the democratically elected regime of Salvador Allende, seemed to confirm d'Epinay's dire warning.

Closer to home, writing one decade after d'Epinay, Robert Mapes

Anderson constructed the following sociological template for his subjects, early American Pentecostal leaders:

> The composite picture of the Pentecostal leader that emerges from our analysis is that of a comparatively young man of humble rural-agrarian origins. Often a victim of physical as well as cultural and economic deprivation, he nevertheless managed to secure a smattering of advanced education of relatively low quality. Peculiarly subject to the loss or estrangement of those closest to him, his primary relationships deeply tinged with melancholy, cut loose from his roots in the soil, highly mobile and unstable in residence, occupation and religious affiliation, hovering uncertainly between working class and middle class life, he sought a resolution of the anxieties stemming from his social experiences, not by clinging to the faith of his fathers but by the intensification of the pietistic, emotional, and world-rejecting elements of that faith.[4]

This essay does not take issue with d'Epinay or Anderson's descriptions of mobility and marginality. An expansive American imperial and capitalist project took laborer Juan Lugo from one newly acquired territory (Puerto Rico) to another (Hawaii) at the turn of the twentieth century to join the proletarian mix of Chinese, Japanese, Filipino, and natives on the island's plantations. Revolutionary upheaval in Mexico uprooted Antonio Nava and one million of his compatriots in the early twentieth century (another million perished in the conflict).

I argue, rather, that these historical subjects possessed the insouciance to believe that their words and deeds carried cosmic significance. Though the exigencies of civil war at home and an expansive agricultural capitalism may have pushed and pulled him to *el Norte,* for Nava, the leading of the Holy Spirit strengthened his resolve to imagine and carve out an alternative landscape that transcended geographical borders. His subsequent mobility represented more than that of a pliable unit of proletarian labor. Nava's geographical mobility mirrored his theological creativity. First and foremost, it was Nava's charismatic authority as a preacher, mystic, and healer that won his following. When he spoke, contemporary accounts allege, folks listened . . . and followed, even into transgressive heterodox territory.

Recent immigrants and native minorities enmeshed in the net of labor discipline lack the same access to the spoken and written word enjoyed by English-speaking elites. Small wonder, then, that a sector of the "disinherited" (Anderson's term) of American and global society (400 million by one recent estimate)[5] has opted to upend the rules of the sociolinguistic game and to speak in the tongues of angels instead. In this, they have joined a long tradition of babblers and mystics. What for the heirs of the European Enlightenment may represent nothing more than psycholinguistic babble and noise (morphemes wildly tossed together in syntactical disarray), for many speakers signifies a discourse about transcendent goodness, human connectedness, and power relations set aright (especially when that discourse is wedded to material solidarity among the poor). Their articulation of the ineffable interpellates powerful men and systems with claims to justice.

A singular definition of mysticism eludes us, although for typological purposes some would argue, with Louis Dupré, for a "family resemblance" between experiences of God or ultimate reality through other-than-normal sense experience and ratiocination.[6] Ecstasy, the placing of one "outside of oneself in a state of exaltation" or "the seizure of one's body by a spirit and the seizure of man by divinity,"[7] would seem to overlap with mystical experience. As an open-ended category of religious experience, mysticism may include practices as varied as Vedantic Hinduism's search for primal unity ("that one thing, breathless, breathed by its own nature") spoken of in the Creation Song, and Brahman ("a single, abstractly conceived Absolute"),[8] Zen Buddhism's path to emptiness and enlightenment (Nirvana), and St. Paul's vision on the Road to Damascus (Acts 9).

With notable exceptions, most Christian mystics would be of the theistic variety, positing a separation between creature and Creator. Within a Christian genealogy of mysticism, Origen's image of the soul as housing the divine Word, Gregory of Nyssa's mystical night of love, Augustine's ecstatic (Trinitarian) union of the soul, the creation-bounded love mysticism of St. Francis of Assisi, Teresa of Avila's interior mansions, and John of the Cross's dark night of the soul can all find echo in the testimony of a Mexican immigrant who arrived in Los Angeles in 1916 in the aftermath of the Azusa Street revival:

I refused to enter the temple, but at his [Marcial de la Cruz's] insistence I relented, and, much to my surprise, as I entered the place I felt touched by the power of the Lord, and after ten minutes or so I was filled with the power of the Holy Spirit, speaking in other tongues as the Spirit gave me to speak. In all my prior life I had never felt such a thing . . . Oh, unforgettable moment when I experienced the Power of God manifested in my being! By means of the warmth of the Holy Spirit, that immediately subdued my passions, I felt a new life in all my being. This change was effected through the love of the Lord who controlled my soul. My heart was enlightened to love others with the perfect love that is God's. When we left to go home it seemed that Nature had been transformed, and when I heard music in the streets, my heart was saddened, for I wished that all could feel what I was feeling.[9]

Such rapture and melancholy would have suited German theologian Friedrich Schleiermacher just fine, were it not for Antonio Nava's subsequent insistence on passing out tracts and proselytizing aggressively among his compatriots in the U.S. Southwest and Mexico, on articulating doctrinal distinctives, and on establishing a Pentecostal denomination several years later.[10] Not for this intrepid prophet the hushed blush of romantic religion. Also, beyond a Wesleyan warming of the heart, Nava's subsequent vocational vision came wrapped in revolutionary motifs. The 1918 episode, whose conclusion opened this essay, reportedly began with Nava in prayer and meditation:

A vision came upon me in which I was taken by a power away from that place. I felt my body to be the same, but since I was praying, I could not tell if my body was able to react until that power carried me to a very different place, where a sun shone—not like the sun we know, but similar to the moon—and sat me upon on a rock that seemed beautiful to me. At that point a great thirst came over me, and I had no way to slake it. Then I saw to the side of the rock a well in which the water was visible about three meters down. I felt a desire to move and drink that water, but I had no faculties to do so. Then there appeared to me two men in military dress, who asked me if I was thirsty. I responded that I was. They lifted me, and I went to drink the water, as there was a way to descend into the well. The water I drank was truly very sweet.[11]

The epiphany left Nava in a state of anxiety for the next several days as he tended to his tasks as the ranch's sole hand and delivered tracts in the nearby town. Marcial de la Cruz brought along a minister to confirm his (de la Cruz's) ready interpretation of Nava's calling. The visitor (an Anglo) had inquired after Nava, to whom he was supposed to reiterate—in quintessentially Pentecostal style—the urgent vocational message: "I've come with the purpose to deliver the message the Lord gave me for you. He has called you to preach His Word and to preach it right away. I have now fulfilled my mission, and may the Lord bless you and may you obey that which the Lord has commanded." The messenger and de la Cruz conducted Nava's ordination the following Sunday.[12]

While subsequent denominational historiography has glossed over it, Nava's may be the first account of Pentecostal ministerial calling wherein the celestial messengers were garbed in military dress. The would-be revolutionary was finally able to answer the call to arms, albeit this time in the army of the Lord. Nava would go on to display some of the characteristics of the military chieftains, *caudillos*, he had admired as a youth. At once benevolent and despotic, Mexico's Revolutionary strongmen (for example, Pancho Villa, Emiliano Zapata, Venustiano Carranza) commanded deep personal loyalty from their troops and compatriots. Nava would exemplify the former attribute. An unimpeachable integrity and a notable lack of pecuniary motives would also endear him to his colleagues and followers. Thus, at the beginning of his career, Nava more closely resembled the charismatic leader described by sociologist Max Weber: "Charisma knows only inner determination and inner restraint. The holder of charisma seizes the task that is adequate for him and demands obedience and a following by virtue of his mission. His success determines whether he finds them. His charismatic claim breaks down if his mission is not recognized by those to whom he feels he has been sent."[13]

Nava's subsequent ministry was marked by a series of encounters in which he deployed charismatic authority, either as a preacher or a healer. In 1919, he and Ramón Ocampo, a young convert from Zacatecas,

Mexico, left to evangelize in Yuma, Arizona, where Nava's sister lived. Her reported healing from cancer brought several leading families from the Mexican Methodist and Baptist churches (including two elders of the latter, Bernardo Hernandez and Jesus Torres) into the apostolic fold in early 1920. Nava and Ocampo left Yuma in May of 1920 to establish a church in Calexico, on the U.S.-Mexico border. Again, the first recruits were members of the Mexican Methodist church. From this base the evangelists planted two churches in 1921 on the Mexican side of the border, in Mexicali and Colonia Zaragoza, which were joined that year by a third one in Santa Rosalía. Ensconced in this liminal zone, Nava settled in for a relatively prolonged period of pastoral work, until 1928. Forays into Mexico earned the ire of the local Caballeros de Colón (Knights of Columbus), at whose hands Nava claimed to face down several death threats. Stints in the Mexicali jail (with songwriter Elvira Herrera, one of the converted Methodists) merely provided opportunities for more successful evangelism.

Nava's zeal for sharing the "Jesus' name revelation" with ostensibly Protestant church folks quickly drew the ire of Trinitarian Pentecostal and mainline ministers.[14] In fact, by the end of the 1920s, the entire Latino Pentecostal movement in southern California and Arizona seemed to have embraced the heterodox belief in radical monotheism and Jesus' name baptism. Or so it seemed at least to one of Nava's competitors, Assemblies of God missionary Alice Luce, whose dispatches on the Hispanic work (printed in the Assemblies' *Pentecostal Evangel*) lamented the wholesale defection being fomented by "many false teachers."[15] Indeed, it seems that Nava may have eclipsed Assemblies pastor M. M. Pinson among Mexicans in Calexico, on which the *Evangel* reported in late 1919.[16] A month earlier, the *Evangel* had informed its readers of the contested and ever shifting turf among Mexicans in the Southwest.

> In Arizona the work has had more to hinder its growth than in Texas, New Mexico or Colorado. In Texas thus far we have had no new-issue whatsoever, but not so for Arizona. And it seems that after they have entered and split up an assembly that they and the outsiders become so hardened to the gospel appeal as to not be touched. We only have in Arizona one mission, in Pirtleville. Bro. Floyd Howard is in charge. He is a good, capable worker. Bro. Howard also works among the

Mexicans in Bisbee and Douglas in Arizona and in Agua Prieta, Sonora, Mexico.[17]

Luce, who may have been dispatched to California to shore up orthodox belief among Mexican Pentecostals, felt ultimately that the best defense against heresy (and spiritism, the other impediment to church growth) was sound pedagogy and Anglo supervision, both of which she attempted to implement in the Bible institute she founded in San Diego in 1926.[18] Her San Antonio–based counterpart, H. C. Ball, longtime superintendent of the Assemblies' Hispanic work, echoed her concerns to the readers of the *Evangel.* "We need more American missionaries. I have, in the past two years, trained several Mexican workers, but while they are excellent workers, they need American oversight. Let us unite in prayer and faith that we shall see several more missionaries here on the field."[19]

Over against mainline censure (including a debate with two Mexican colleagues in the Imperial Valley) and Anglo paternalism,[20] Nava countered that Latino Protestants had spent only a brief time in the mainline anteroom, had experienced only the fuzziest notion of an *evangélico* identity, and remained, given the scarcity of clergy, essentially sheep without shepherds.[21] Sensitive to the laity's clamor for doctrinal instruction, Nava searched for other tools to shore up his community's position. He discovered a valuable resource in *The Bridegroom's Songs,* a hymnal compiled by PAW leader Garfield T. Haywood and sent to his far-flung network of correspondents. Nava welcomed pianist Luis Herrera's rendition of Haywood's composition, "Baptized into the Body," which Herrera had discovered in the newly arrived booklet. Within a few days the young pastor returned with a freely translated hymn—with Haywood's melody intact but the quick 4/4 tempo slowed—to teach the eager flock.[22] Nava's original Spanish lyrics rendered "El Nombre del Mesías" (The Name of the Messiah) into the doctrinal anthem of Latino apostolicism throughout the hemisphere. Nava's theological creativity can be seen in the textual reworking below (a close ethnomusicological analysis also would reveal musical and cultural reworkings):

"Baptized into the Body" Garfield T. Haywood	"El Nombre del Mesias" Antonio C. Nava	
Haywood	**Nava (Spanish original)**	**Nava (English translation)**

Haywood	Nava (Spanish original)	Nava (English translation)
1st verse		
Have you been baptized into the Body?	La señal que fue desde el principio	The sign that has since the beginning
Baptized with the Holy Ghost	Dada a la humanidad	To humankind been given
There is but one way to enter in it	Príncipe de Paz será su nombre	He shall be called Prince of Peace
Just as they did on Pentecost	Por toda la eternidad	For all eternity
chorus		
Are you in the Church triumphant?	Es el nombre que era oculto	'Tis the name that was hidden
Are you in the Savior's Bride?	Que no era revelado	That was not revealed
Come and be baptized into the Body	Jesucristo, este es su nombre	Jesus Christ, this is his name
And forevermore abide.	En el debeís ser bautizado	Into which you must be baptized
2nd verse		
There is but on Church, Bride or Body	Fué Mesías grande y verdadero	He was the great and true Messiah
And into it we're all baptized	Que a la tierra decendió	Who descended to earth
By the one, true, promised Holy Spirit	Trajo a las gentes luz y vida	He brought light and life to the nations
Tho' by the world we're all despised	Mas el mundo no creyó	But the world did not believe
3rd verse		
Every creed has claim'd to be the Body	Hay un solo nombre dado al mundo	There's but one Name given the world
But the "plumb-line" proved untrue	Por el cual se salvará	By which it may be saved
All their dreams by God determined	Ese nombre da virtud y gracia	That Name gives power and grace
To bring His Son's True Bride to view	Y el que cree salvo será	And he who believes shall be saved
4th verse		
Many thought they were in the Body	O, hermano, sabes tú que Cristo	Oh, brother, do you know that Christ
'Till the Holy Ghost had come	Te podrá salvar a tí	Is able to save you?
When the Word of God opened to them	Ven a El renaciendo de nuevo	Come to him and be born again
They entered in, and yet there's room	Y pondrá Su Espíritu en tí	And He will place his Spirit within[23]

Nava's appropriation of Haywood's music mirrored their relationship, under which the PAW provided sponsorship in the form of licenses and literature but left its "Mexican representatives" free to organize as they saw fit. Haywood's stature as one of the preeminent apologists for Oneness Pentecostalism and his assumption of leadership of the PAW had placed Indianapolis at the center of the multiracial dissident movement. Although neither Llorente nor Nava ever traveled to Indianapolis or any other Oneness stronghold outside of the Southwest, Haywood affirmed their connection in at least one swing through southern California.[24] Whatever their formal arrangements with the PAW, for at least the first decade and a half of growth Latino apostolics negotiated their place as newcomers on the half-century-old Latino Protestant block by forging strategic alliances with other marginalized groups on the religious and social periphery. Put differently, Nava found in African American heterodox hymnody a pliable "defensive, counter-ideological, symbolic expression"[25] to employ on behalf of his community's identity, continuity, and autonomy.[26] And when strengthened, this autonomy of necessity bred creativity. Such fecund and strategic agency and subaltern solidarity eludes the analyses of both d'Epinay and Anderson.

Nava's charismatic strongmanship required one more test, this time in his country of origin. In spite of his leadership duties in the United States, Nava returned to his homeland in early 1928 to evangelize his ailing parents.[27] While there, he made contact with the spiritual progeny of Romana Carbajal de Valenzuela, another refugee from the revolution, whose 1914 return to Villa Aldama, Chihuahua, from Los Angeles had helped usher in the Pentecostal revival in Mexico (that country's oldest autochthonous Pentecostal denominations derive from these origins). While visiting believers in several northern cities, Nava discovered a kindred spirit in young Felipe Rivas of Torreón, Coahuila. After the departure of Miguel Garcia (Rivas's mentor and the founding matriarch's nephew whom Nava had welcomed in the Imperial Valley in 1923), the Iglesia Cristiana Espiritual had fractured into a chaotic free-for-all, complete with long-bearded, tunic-and-sandal-wearing prophets Saul and Silas, whom Nava claimed to have bested in a contest over divine authority. (Nava and a companion, a barber, took up a dare to cut and shave the prophets' hair and emerged unscathed from the promised celestial conflagration.) The Iglesia Cristiana Espiritual ultimately disfellowshipped the Rivas family for their friendship with the émigré preacher from *el Norte*. The expulsion pushed Rivas into closer collaboration with Nava. The personal bonds were soon fleshed out in more institutional ways.

While buttressing Rivas's leadership, Nava received word to return to California to lead the demoralized U.S. church upon Pastor General Francisco Llorente's sudden demise in late 1928. The journey took several months and included a forced stay over in Chihuahua, where the governor was in postrevolutionary rebellion against the consolidating revolutionary federal regime. The intrepid evangelist ascribed the train stoppages and derailments to a higher cause: "I tried to take maximum advantage of the time, since I was not sure how long my visit would last. As soon as the governmental problem was resolved, I would continue my journey. We had already arranged our immigration documents, but this revolution detained us, maybe since the Lord willed it so, and I (now) understand that the Lord wanted us to testify in that place."[28]

The remainder of the borderlands trip, through El Paso, Lordsburg, Phoenix, Yuma, and Calexico-Mexicali, allowed Nava to reacquaint himself with the troubled flock and provide nurture in the wake of two significant defections. His election as president at the fifth convention, held at the end of 1929 in Indio, California, proved a foregone conclusion. (Nava may have been summoned back from Mexico as the compromise choice between two polarized camps.) He also persuaded his colleagues that the loose alliance with the recently splintered and now predominantly African American PAW was inadequate to the developing needs of the growing Chicano/Mexican apostolic movement. Immediately upon the 1930 incorporation in California, Nava directed Secretary Bernardo Hernández to dispatch credentials and notarized letters of deputation to Rivas and Rivas's new assistant, José Ortega, another returned immigrant who had embraced the movement in 1923 in San Juan Bautista (northern California) and had been mentored by Nava in Calexico.[29]

In retrospect, the incorporation and Nava's leadership may have saved the movement. Francisco Llorente's growing cultural and linguistic ambivalence (widowed, Llorente had remarried, this time to an *americana*) caused many of his colleagues to suspect their leader of a drift toward Anglo evangelicalism. By contrast, Nava's monolingual leadership (in eight decades of U.S. residency, Nava's duties and itinerary permitted little time for learning English, this in spite of several autodidactic attempts) stymied any early assimilationist trends and stamped the movement with a Mexican character for the next two decades. The revitalized ethnicity reinforced ecclesiastical and cultural autonomy. Upon taking the helm, Nava successfully implemented his and others' vision for strategic growth and expansion. (Like many pioneer Pentecostals, Llorente distrusted denominational organization and development and had only reluctantly acceded to his colleagues' moves in that direction.) The incorporation and binational consolidation occurred in time for the economic devastation of the Great Depression and its political fallout (massive repatriation) and strengthened

Latino apostolicism for a later reencounter on more equal footing with white and black Oneness Pentecostalism after World War II. The development of close fraternal ties with apostolics in Mexico resulted in formal alliances,[30] joint constitutions (drafted from 1937 to 1944), and structures to facilitate the easy exchange of liturgical, missionary and financial resources, and personnel (both clergy and lay) back and forth across the border,[31] the latter in quiet and subversive contravention of explicit U.S. immigration law.

Nothing short of an explosion in musical and cultural production ensued after incorporation. Set against the grim backdrop of economic recession and political persecution, apostolic hymnody blossomed into such a large corpus that Nava's first compilation effort in the early 1930s, *Himnos de consolacion*,[32] contained more than two hundred hymns, the vast majority of these of original apostolic composition. A concurrent compilation effort by Maclovio Gaxiola in Mexico, *Himnos de suprema alabanza*,[33] gathered more than 160 hymns, again, the vast majority organic to the movement. Even after accounting for a significant number of simultaneously published hymns, the overall number of published original hymns by the early 1940s can be conservatively estimated at three hundred. This embarrassment of riches throws into sharp relief the stark situation in the mainline churches, whose hymnody apostolics were grateful to inherit—especially the more pietistic and devotional ones—but found meager in number, culturally inadequate in style, and problematic in doctrinal content (for example, the several Trinitarian doxologies of mainline liturgy). Apostolic and Pentecostal composers wedded perennial Mexican poetic themes (for example, pilgrimage) to popular musical genres (for example, *corrido* ballads, *huapango* rhythms, *norteño* polkas, and *bolero* romances) and produced a sonic and corporeal experience that resonated in the community's ears, hearts, and bodies. The charismatic *caudillo* and his evangelistic and musical collaborators (including women) transferred much of their attributed power to the liturgical sphere and invested music and performance with a culturally relevant and spiritually effective dimension.

Routinized Charisma

The 1944 constitution provided yet another opportunity for Nava and his colleagues to articulate a visionary blueprint for sustained growth and to move beyond shortsighted, albeit tempting, patterns of capricious chieftaincy. Whereas other Latino Pentecostal denominations had foundered or fractured around questions of leadership succession (usually upon a founder's death), Nava and his colleagues put in place provisions that would ensure continuity—namely, regular four-year elected terms at the executive level. A theocratic, episcopal form of government was wedded to a synodical one; diocesan bishops were to be elected by majority votes of the district's pastors, and national executives by the majority vote of pastors assembled in general convention. The Apostolic Assembly and Iglesia Apostólica granted each other veto power over proposed constitutional changes. Visiting delegations from the sister church were to supervise the host denomination's national elections, thereby adding yet another layer of accountability against episcopal caprice.

The provisions for regular episcopal and executive succession and later for term limits (two four-year terms in a single executive or episcopal position) may reflect the persistent cultural affinities of the U.S. members of the binational constitutional drafting and revision committees. Such regular accountability reflects as much the hard-won legacy of Mexican liberal and revolutionary thought (the cry "Effective Suffrage! No Re-Election!" had summoned the nation to arms against longstanding dictator Porfirio Díaz in 1910) as it does polity models borrowed from U.S. Protestantism.

When Nava opted to step down from the presidency in favor of the younger Cantú in 1950, the investiture of the latter as new presiding bishop was accomplished through the transference of charisma from the man to the office. Photos capturing the solemn moment leave little doubt as to the meaning of the transference of power. Phrases like *la honorable Mesa Directiva* (the honorable Board of Directors) and *nuestra amada Asamblea* (our beloved Assembly) became commonplace in pulpit discourse, serving as both powerful signifiers and rhetorical flourishes. Max Weber's description of charismatic succession seems apt: "The most important example is the transmission or confirmation of priestly charisma by means of anointment, consecration and coronation. The character *indelebilis* signifies the inherent separation of the powers of the charismatic office from those of the person of the priest."[34]

The system of succession set in place endured well beyond Cantú's tenure. Indeed, under its provisions, he removed himself from office in 1963. Nava assumed the presidency for the remainder of Cantú's term and transferred leadership to Efraín Valverde upon the latter's election in 1966. Again, the import of the moment was captured faithfully by ubiquitous cameras.

The Valverde administration (1966–70) tested the durability of the constitution. Relations began to unravel between Valverde and the other executive board members and between Valverde and his counterparts in Mexico, former colleagues of the immigrant bishop. A showdown ensued. A skilled populist and charismatic *caudillo* in his own right, Valverde may very well have gained the sympathies of the majority of the pastorate and laity with his long list of grievances.[35] In a series of contested maneuvers, both sides appealed to the constitution and, ultimately, to the California courts in search of the upper hand.

Nava joined the other leaders in denying Valverde the presidency for a second term. He served on a committee of remonstrance, seeking to rein in the recalcitrant leader. In the end, the courts decided in favor of the board of directors. Valverde relinquished the church property in Salinas, California (where he had been pastor and diocesan bishop), and left to form the Apostolic Church of Jesus Christ International, taking a small but notable number of pastors and members (including Nava relatives) with him.[36] While the episode ranks among the most wrenching in the denomination's history, in the end, the constitution and the strategic support of the Mexican (Iglesia Apostólica) leadership, together with Nava's prestige, kept the church largely intact. Routinized charisma had replaced definitively its more autocratic counterpart. And, in line with Max Weber's analysis, the change did not occur without a struggle.

Ironically, Nava's divestiture of presidential prerogatives years earlier strengthened his steadying hand throughout the protracted conflict. In the end, Nava and others had taken the movement from raw charismatic mode to institutionalized rationality and controlled, routinized charisma. In that process, they had also succeeded in fostering a fecund consciousness of cultural and ecclesial autonomy and in bequeathing a legacy of transborder solidarity to their spiritual progeny. Thus, for the span of a few decades at least, the charismatic *caudillo*, in concert with others, had held off the seemingly inevitable process of assimilation and co-optation in Protestant America, a process that continues to bedevil all ethnic (and mainstream) churches. Today, Latino apostolic missionaries traverse the hemisphere and globe, answerable only to other Latinos back home. As many Apostolic

Assembly pastors negotiate the choppy linguistic waters in search of an adequate pastoral and liturgical method for intergenerational and increasingly multiethnic congregations, they can build upon a firm foundation of identity forged by Nava and others.

In his final decades of retirement and seclusion, Antonio Nava was accorded near iconic status within the movement, one variously guarded or wielded by others jockeying for political and theological position. His increasingly silent presence—in a front pew, a platform seat, or a wheelchair—continued to grace many conclaves, where young children would be taken to touch the hand of the symbol. Visitors to the San Francisco Bay area would schedule time to visit the ailing patriarch. As all his sensory faculties faded, he became blissfully oblivious to the drastic changes occurring in the rationalized structure he had bequeathed to younger men, especially the unraveling of close fraternal ties with the Iglesia Apostólica of Mexico and within the Apostolic Assembly's very own constituency. In the end, sectors of the denomination continued to succumb to and reflect—as ethnic communities are wont to do when threatened by more recently arrived immigrants or seduced by upward mobility and political strategists—the social divisions of class and citizenship status. As it loosed its anchoring ties to its sister church, the Apostolic Assembly began to mimic the harsher sectarianism of Anglo Oneness Pentecostalism. The Iglesia Apostólica, by contrast, operating within a vastly different context of hegemonic Catholicism, continued to assume leadership within Mexican Protestantism and to invite dialogue with fellow evangélicos. The churches' unique vocation for ministry to sojourners also has played itself out in newly overlapping jurisdictions. Northward-bound migrants now are encouraged to seek out fellowship in a growing network of Iglesia Apostólica congregations within the United States. The Apostolic Assembly has reciprocated with aggressive incursions into Mexico. Both churches have recruited dissident clergy on the other's home turf, thereby exacerbating the troubled relations.

A popular apocryphal story made its way into church lore during Nava's final decades: God had assured the patriarch that he would live to see the rapture, the touchstone event in premillennial eschatology in which the faithful are physically caught up to Heaven to avoid the Tribulation period. Thus occasional bulletins on Nava's good or precarious health prompted folks to take stock of their behavior. A final, spontaneous utterance on

February 20, 1999, during his penultimate visit to a hospital was dutifully transcribed by his children and carried immediately through cyberspace across the globe. The patriarch struggled through the fog of slurred speech to utter once more a prophetic vision of the state of human and divine affairs.

> Brethren: This is our final convention. We need to be united, and prepared. We need to be in one accord so that all things may be done from better, to best. Let us move forward. There are millions of souls who do not know of Jesus Christ because there is no one to preach to them. Let us go forth! Christ will give us the victory in all things; there is no better way but through Christ, Satan is defeated! According to prophecy, this is not a time for us to be seated. I have been studying, and we probably have no time left but to move ahead in the Name of Jesus. My God, lift me up. My bones are very heavy, and I cannot rise up, but You are my help. I need to rise up and tell others that You are at heaven's door. The prophecies have been fulfilled. Glory to God! Unto Your Name shall we give all the honor and Glory, and praise forever. Glory to God! [with both hands raised, repeating— *transcribers' note*] Glory to God! Glory to God![37]

The summons resonated widely and eerily (depending on the hearer's state of mind) throughout the movement. The charismatic *caudillo* had come full circle. His speech, though slowed by age, still forced many to pay heed lest the source be more than terrestrial. At Nava's funeral, the Apostolic Assembly's presiding bishop applied a soothing hermeneutic to the belief that Antonio Nava would live to see the rapture, comparing it to the apostle Paul's own hopeful conviction. The Pauline parallel suggests another one. If Pentecostals venerated saints, Antonio Castañeda Nava would loom large in the pantheon.[38]

Bishop Ida Robinson, circa 1930. Courtesy of Minerva R. Bell, Mount Sinai Holy Church of America, Teaneck, New Jersey.

Ida B. Robinson: The Mother as Symbolic Presence

Harold Dean Trulear

The African American religious community is a corporate prophetic witness. That is, at its core it affirms a worldview that stands in critical contradistinction to the prevailing worldview of the United States, one that is characterized by the dehumanization of people of color, notably African Americans. The distinction is prophetic because it makes the claim that the majoritarian culture is held accountable for its racism and dehumanization in light of the standards of love, justice, and equality that are part and parcel of its self-understanding. This witness is not reducible to harangues against racism, but is set against the backdrop of a creative impulse that affirms and ultimately acts to define the humanity of all persons.

The African American tradition affirms life as the central reality of what it means to be human. This life is not just walking and talking, eating and sleeping, breathing and sensing, but it is the real notion that we discover our true selves in the context of our relationships with God and other human beings, and the quality of life is experienced in this same context of relatedness.[1] In a word, the African American religious tradition boldly proclaims that black people are human; they are alive and they are somebody, even if this world says they are not, because God has said so. That somebodiness, constantly under assault under the hegemony of American racism, must constantly be affirmed in order to maintain some semblance of wholeness for members of the African American religious community.

While this life-affirming tradition is manifested in rituals and relationships, symbols and structures, its most visible embodiment is in the lives of people. This is not to deny the reality of institutional life, but rather to seek to find the human element to that life and critically evaluate the models drawn from such an investigation with an eye toward developing some form of liberating praxis, some continuation of the prophetic witness that does not lapse into rhetoricism, irresponsibility, or demagoguery.

Such a life belonged to Ida B. Robinson, an important if underrecognized figure in African American religious leadership during the first half of the twentieth century. Robinson, who founded the Mount Sinai Holy Church of America in 1924 and served its Mother church—Mount Olive Holy Temple—in Philadelphia from 1919 until her death in 1946, is an important figure not only because she led a denomination that grew to 124 churches during her tenure, but also because as an African American female religious leader she represents a symbolic presence in the black tradition that was a central element in affirming life and humanity in the black community. I choose to call this presence "mother," affirming the careful work of Cheryl Townsend Gilkes in documenting the significance of this term in the black church and community.[2]

Contending for a primarily familial understanding of African American community relationships, Gilkes demonstrates that the role of mother in the African American community, while rooted in biologically determined relationships between mothers (as well as other senior women in the extended family) and children, transcends those relationships to include the centers of power that women have occupied in the neighborhood, town, religious, civic, and social organization. Hence, women's roles of authority in all institutional and community life are informed by the role of mothering. Leadership in churches is no exception, and the pastoral performance of black women such as Ida B. Robinson can be interpreted in this light. As such, her career embodies the symbol of mother, and we would expect to find that she guided her congregation using mothering sensibilities drawn from the historic roles of church and community mothers in the African American community. This essay explores the symbolic function of Ida B. Robinson's role as mother to her church. I will argue that, in mothering her churches, Ida B. Robinson created, modeled, and nurtured a sense of life—defined in her tradition as love and holiness—for her congregations. Suggested throughout the essay will be implications for contemporary religious leadership.

To call the mother a symbol in the black church and community is at once to lift it to an abstraction that can be appropriated as a point of reference for the behavior of the group and also to embody behavioral norms in a way that keeps the abstraction from being either reified or mystified. As a point of reference, it signals ways of being in the world. It indicates to all who participate in this symbol system that there are norms of belief and practice that are part of the community consensus. As an embodiment, it recognizes that the way(s) of being in the world indicated by the symbol are always historically and sociologically contextualized. This notion of context is no small matter in the African American religious community, for the lot of the oppressed always involves the struggle between affirming tradition and a sense of rootedness, on the one hand, and openness to creativity (that is, the Spirit) and relevance, on the other. This is what C. Eric Lincoln had in mind when he wrote, "Religion alone has the ability to address itself to what is new and evocative while retaining the assurances of what is settled and traditional—appearing at once to change with changing institutions and to persist through change unaffected by any history but its own."[3]

African American symbolism must, therefore, be dynamic, able to hold tradition and relevance in creative tension, not so new as to be ahistorical and not so temporally specific as not to embrace current realities. It must fit Victor Turner's description of symbols as "dynamic entities, not static cognitive signs . . . patterned by events and informed by the passions of human intercourse, in friendship, sexuality, and politics."[4] The creative use of such symbolism has enabled African Americans to "change with changing institutions" in the historic shift from the primary relationships and intimacy of rural southern living to the secondary relationships and impersonality of urban northern life and "persist through change" by maintaining a strong sense of tradition commonly called the "black religious experience."[5]

Symbols and their attendant rituals still function to move the masses of African Americans. However, one can question the extent to which contemporary modes of symbolism are faithful to the creative and critical impulses mentioned above. If creativity is the capacity to be in touch with and cooperate with meaningful life, if it celebrates the self and offers justice to the other, then we are in need of finding symbols that are consistent with such creativity. If critical capacity implies careful attention to the reality of oppression and the construction of a worldview or philosophy that stands as an alternative to the dehumanization of African American people, then black symbolizing will reflect this reality. Such creative and critical capacities challenge contemporary images emerging from popular music and professional sports, as well as pulpits and politicians. The mothering symbol is such an enduring image, creative and critical, that it deserves attention amidst the clamor of competing symbols.

It is therefore important to explore the roles of African American women as mothers, not so much in the familial sense, but rather as representatives of a tradition of relating and nurturing that served not only as a survival strategy but also as a model for a quality of life deemed ordained of God, and in prophetic contrast to the modes of dehumanization offered by hostile surroundings. For these women, who have labored under the weight of racism, sexism, and classism both within and without the church, the function of the mother symbol as an agent of humanization is crucial. Beyond that, their response to human oppression should serve as instructive to those African American leaders and thinkers who seek to discern a contemporary path for combating present ills. This is the genius of the mother symbol in the black church and community and, for purposes of giving flesh to the symbol in ways that both honor creativity and tradition, we turn our attention to the life and ministry of Ida B. Robinson and her role as mother to her church and community.

Born in Hazelhurst, Georgia, in 1891, Ida B. Robinson spent most of her childhood in Pensacola, Florida. She migrated to Philadelphia in 1917. Her sister had come to Philadelphia some years earlier to find work and had invited Ida and her husband of eight years, Oliver, to join her. While in Pensacola, young Ida established herself as a bright, industrious child, helping her family financially by securing work as a cook during her teen years. She was converted at a street meeting of a local Pentecostal church and began a ministry of prayer and preaching in area homes. Her mother recognized early in Ida's life that she had "innate leadership qualit(ies)" and the community viewed her as one possessed of strong "native intelligence."[6]

Upon her arrival in Philadelphia, she continued her ministry in local homes. She soon joined a small Holiness mission served by a man named Benjamin Smith. The mission, located at Seventeenth and South Streets, was in the heart of the black section of Philadelphia. Her preaching and singing attracted a considerable following, and soon she rivaled Smith in popularity among members of the church community. Seeking to avoid conflict, yet committed to developing her own ministry, she left the mission in 1919 and was appointed pastor of the Mount Olive Holy Church at 505

South Eleventh Street. This was no small appointment, for the next year Mount Olive was part of the founding Holy Convocation of the Northern District of the United Holy Church of America, one of the largest Pentecostal denominations in the black community. Mount Olive had been founded in 1909, and by 1922 "there were thirty-five ministers listed under the heading Mount Olive Holy Church, Philadelphia, Pa., 22 Licencates [sic] and 23 Missionaries."[7]

As her reputation as a preacher grew, she began to accompany the leadership of the United Holy Church in evangelistic campaigns. She often shared the pulpit with G. J. Branch, one of the first bishops of the denomination. In the words of longtime confidant Bishop Mary Jackson, Sister Ida was considered a "Gospel Preacher, prime time speaker," and "crowd gatherer."[8] Bishop Henry Lee Fisher ordained her publicly—and it was the irony of her "public ordination" that set the stage for her separation from the United Holy Church.

In 1924 great concern emerged among the women of the United Holy Church. The whole of the church readily acknowledged their gifts as preachers and leaders; however, they found ordination increasingly difficult to achieve. Those ordinations that were conferred upon women were soon to be done in private ceremonies. Some men in leadership positions questioned the biblical legitimacy of women as pastors. It seemed as if opportunities for women in ministry would be drastically reduced. In the midst of the growing turmoil, Ida B. Robinson was in a period of prayer and fasting. She reported great pains within her body as if she were in labor.[9] During this time, God spoke to her and told her to "Come out on Mt. Sinai" and "loose the women."[10] She interpreted this as a sign that God would have her begin a church movement, not a denomination in the strictest sense, but a confederation of churches that would provide opportunities for women to exercise leadership.

Consistent with her United Holy Church background she called for a Holy Convocation, a week of meetings that would organize these churches into a recognizable whole. Initially the invitation was extended to churches still within the United Holy Church (UHC) to have a dual affiliation with Mount Sinai, but, by the 1925 convocation, Robinson's Mount Sinai Holy Church of America was legally established as an entity unto itself. While there were some UHC churches among the seventeen churches in attendance, it was as an independent body that Sister Robinson's churches met. The first meeting was held Wednesday morning, September 23, at the newly purchased church building at 2122 Oxford Street in Philadelphia, "with songs of praise to God and one hour prayer." Following this, Elder Robinson reportedly read from Psalm 85, owing to a vision the night before illustrating the tenth and eleventh verses ("Mercy and truth are met together; righteousness and peace have kissed each other. Truth shall spring out of the earth; and righteousness shall look down from heaven").[11] The meeting continued with words of celebration concerning the recently acquired charter. Representatives from the legal and finance professions who had helped Sister Robinson acquire the charter noted how impressed they were with her words and actions. While acknowledging that "this is a lot of power to give to a woman," they moved to grant her the charter.[12]

The number of churches in Mount Sinai grew rapidly. Some were existing churches that affiliated with the movement. Others, like the Rose of Sharon Holy Church of Fruitland, Maryland, were begun by Bishop Robinson herself. According to handwritten accounts by Mary Jackson, Bishop Robinson would finance the start of a church with her own funds and then have Sister Jackson keep a ledger of payments made by the church back to the Bishop. The records of the Fruitland church, for example, show Bishop Robinson laying out $700 for the initial construction of the edifice in 1924 and the church making payments back to Mount Sinai in amounts ranging from $10 to $179. The payments made back to the church would then be invested in the starting of new churches. This process would be repeated and it would yield the birthing of new churches.

Mount Sinai took the process of church "birthing" seriously. The concept of church birthing, in contrast to church building, is consistent with the mother symbol of Ida B. Robinson and also with the notion of life affirmed in the black religious tradition. Even before she began Mount Sinai, Sister Ida testified that God had shown her all the "great churches being born" in the city through her, and that people would come from "the North, South, East and West."[13] She continued to rehearse this vision before the people and the metaphor has survived to the present. The emphasis on the birthing of churches is in the creation of life, as opposed to the development of an institution or structure. When she started a church, she was creating a family. In birthing churches, Bishop Robinson made a claim for a certain quality of life to be maintained in the churches. In a real sense, the birthing metaphor used for the beginning of churches was consistent with the image used to describe the initiation of the Christian life. Church membership was not a matter of institutional affiliation, rather it was the creation of a new life for the individual. Simply put, to be at Mount Sinai was to be born into a new family. Some churches even "borrowed" the invitational hymn of the Church of God in Christ, singing after every sermon:

> This is the church of Mt. Sinai
> Oh you can't join it
> You've got to be born in
> This is the church of Mt. Sinai.

Bishop Robinson took seriously the birthing metaphor, which led her to be concerned with the issue of quality of life. By rooting her religious leadership in the mother symbol she avoided the tendency to reduce church leadership to organizational management or institutional maintenance. She believed that leaders must care about persons, with specific attention given to the development of mature individuals in both the personal and communal spheres. Such nurture assumes a goal for human development, a concept of the good person and healthy community that is the end of the maturation process. Hence, Bishop Robinson's ministry placed a premium on both nurture as a signal function of religious leadership and a clearly articulated vision of the good life for both individual and community.

Ida B. Robinson's ministry of nurture took three primary forms, the modeling of moral virtue through the nurture of quality—even familial like—relationships, the visibility of work, and the teaching of wisdom.[14] I will use these categories again here with a slightly different emphasis and with newly discovered data that will further illumine their interpretation. Assumed in all three categories will be the fact that is asserted in the first, namely that love and holiness constitute the primary understanding of the good life for individual and community.

The life that is born must be nurtured. During a time when African Americans were beset by the emerging problems created by rapid urbanization and shifting patterns of rural life, Mount Sinai was affirming and nurturing life, presenting to its members a sense of their somebodiness. While the world was becoming increasingly impersonal, Bishop Robinson, through her mothering, was building relationships that affirmed the personhood of her members and created and sustained life. Urban single family dwellings were converted into crowded multifamily dwellings, and great numbers of people were jammed into the emerging ghettos of north Philadelphia and Harlem, leading to a need for residents to feel individually affirmed and cared for. Recent migrants from the South sought to recapture a sense of the intimacy and support they once knew in rural life. Under such conditions, Bishop Robinson's Mount Olive Church in Philadelphia and Bethel Holy Church in New York offered contexts where such intimacy could occur and thus nurture the members into a sense of the good life. As mother, Robinson's leadership would be the moral emblem of that life.

As the emblem of moral virtue, the black mother offers an alternative way of being in an unfriendly, dehumanizing world. Her life says that moral living is possible, even when social and personal circumstances indicate otherwise. Mother Robinson and her followers offered love to those who felt the estrangement and alienation of urban life and a standard of holiness to those facing the erosion of the institutional support of personal piety that accompanies structural differentiation and urbanization. The model of the standard of holiness is most evident in the Mount Sinai movement. Mirroring the sentiment of the United Holy Church from which it came, Mount Sinai has taught that "holiness," in addition to glossolalia, is evidence of the presence of the power of the Holy Ghost in the life of the believer.[15] For Bishop Robinson and her followers, holiness was to be manifested in certain acts of personal piety and rehearsed the idea that one's character was to be a reflection of the presence of God in the world. Bishop Robinson regularly preached from the text "holiness, without which no man shall see the Lord" (Heb. 12:14b).[16] She often preached and taught from 1 Pet. 1:14–16: "As obedient children, not fashioning yourselves according to the former lusts in your ignorance; but as He which hath called you is holy, so be ye holy in all manner of conversation; because it is written, Be ye holy; for I am holy."

Holiness teaching served as a strong measure of community discipline and control. Mount Sinai was particularly concerned with standards governing divorce and remarriage (forbidden), manner of dress, and issues of "self-indulgence," such as restrictions on the consumption of alcohol, use of tobacco and narcotics, and attendance at dances, movies, and cabarets. However, the holiness standard was not limited to issues of personal piety. In the *Mt. Sinai Manual,* the denomination's handbook for polity, doctrine, and conduct, there is also the following admonition regarding war and military service: "We believe that the shedding of human blood or the taking of human life is contrary to the word of God. This belief makes us adverse to war in all its forms. In times of war, when laws are passed requiring induction into the Armed Forces, we submit to the provisions thereof because of the teaching of Romans 13:1 . . . Our members are instructed to accept induction into the Armed Forces only as Partial Conscientious Objectors . . . not to submit to the bearing of arms in any manner."[17] The manual goes on to state that fidelity to scriptures that call believers "peacemakers" (Matt. 5:9), challenge them to love their enemies (Matt. 5:44), and warn that those who "kill with the sword must be killed with the sword"(Rev. 13:10) support holiness standards in the matter of war and arms bearing.

Ida B. Robinson lived this principle before her congregation. In fact, when World War II broke out, she incurred attention from the Federal Bureau of Investigation for publicly stating that she had "nothing against the Japanese." Making her more suspect was the fact that her church secretary was a German woman, married to an Italian man named Campione. Faithful workers at Mount Olive, Sister Campione was ultimately ordained an elder, and Brother Campione was often recalled as one of the more demonstrative saints when "the Spirit got a hold of him." This nonracist vision for Christian community reflected the holiness standard and made war with other persons problematic.[18]

Holiness also involved a nonsexist vision. The affirmation of women's right to preach was put forth as an ethical issue in the Mount Sinai tradition. In order to be holy, one had to accept the right of women to preach. In 1934 Lillian Sparks of the St. Matthew's Holy Church of Pensacola, Florida, wrote a poem on the subject. The subtitle reads "Composed from our Bishop's Sermon." In it, Sparks asserted that the day of judgment was coming for those who refused to acknowledge the equality of women in ministry:

> You'll wish you had let women alone When they were trying to teach.
> You'll be sorry you tried to hold them down When God told them to preach.
> Come, dear brothers, let us journey, Side by side and hand in hand;

Does not the Bible plainly tell you Woman shall co-ordinate the
man?
The hand that rocks the cradle, Will rule the world you know;
So lift the standard high for God, Wherever you may go.[19]

The use of the word *standard* is important. It indicates that this is a
moral issue. On page 41 of the *Mt. Sinai Manual* the word *standard* is
defined as applying to "any authoritative rule, principle or measure used to
determine the quality, the value or the degree of a thing." Mount Sinai has
"a standard of holiness that promotes principles by which to live." Although
the affirmation of women in ministry does not appear in the list of standards that ensues, the use of the term in the poem comes across as a clear
appeal to the style of moral authority represented by a standard.

This is not to say that such social stances overshadowed the issues of
personal piety that are normally associated with holiness standards. Yet,
even in that realm, Bishop Robinson added a different dimension to the
standards that reflected the role of a mother with responsibility for moral
nurture. One outstanding example is that of the dress codes for men that
emerged in the 1920s and 1930s. Consistent with most holiness traditions,
Mount Sinai had a strict dress code for women. Women were not to wear
jewelry or braid their hair. They often appeared in long black dresses with
white lace cuffs and collar. In church, the head was always to be covered.
At one point, the women came to Bishop Robinson, complaining that standards for holy dress were being applied only to women and that there was
no corresponding standard for men. Bishop responded by asking the men
of Mount Sinai to accept the standard of not wearing a necktie as a symbol
of submission to the desire of the women and a mark of holiness. The men
complied, and began to wear either a collar bar on their shirts or no neck-
wear at all. One longtime member of the movement recalled that, in all his
sixty-odd years in life, he never saw his father with a necktie. After the
passing of Bishop Robinson, the standard was rescinded, but many men
continued the practice well into the 1980s.[20]

Love was the second primary dimension of the moral life modeled by
Mother Robinson. In 1984, Elder Lillian Bagley, a charter member of the
movement, recalled being attracted to "those women in white blouses and
black skirts" who were "so full of love." She singled out Sister Mary Jackson,
later a presiding bishop of the denomination, as a primary example of the

love ethic in Mount Sinai.[21] The image conveyed by Bagley and others suggests a community of women working, praying, traveling together in mutual support and encouragement, with Bishop Robinson as the leader. They met together regularly, in homes and at church. Bishop Robinson often had people visiting and even residing in her home for various stretches. They prayed together and studied together and supported one another with testimonies and words of encouragement.

One person who has been profoundly touched by the community of women was the adopted daughter of Bishop Robinson, also named Ida. Bishop Robinson's brother had difficulty caring for his nine children; when it was announced that he and his family were expecting a tenth child, Bishop arranged to adopt the child and rear it as her own. This daughter is now the bishop of the Greater Mount Zion Pentecostal Church of America, headquartered in Brooklyn, New York.[22] She recalls the women gathering at the Robinson home to discuss the affairs of the church and world. Often she would hide under the table to try to listen to what the women were saying. As the discussion progressed, the time would come to pray. Everyone in the house would stop what they were doing and pray together. "If you had knees," offered the junior Bishop Robinson, "you were old enough to pray."[23]

In the second dimension of the mother symbol, the visibility of work, I refer to the ability of the mother to create the space in which the children learn to imitate her behavior and ultimately perform the same tasks that she does. While verbally teaching the principles of holiness and love are important, these concepts must be modeled and made visible in order for followers to understand how these are modes of being in the world. Certainly, the open door policy at the home of Bishop Robinson is one such example. However, so was the structure of ministerial relations within Mount Sinai. New preachers were encouraged to develop their gifts through the many opportunities they had to preach in Mount Sinai. There were services virtually every evening, with afternoon services on Tuesdays and Thursdays. Sometimes there would be opportunities for two or three sermonettes in a given service, all under the watchful eye of Bishop Robinson or an associate. Of course, Bishop modeled her preaching and teaching styles for her charges on a regular basis, often preaching Sunday morning and evening, and at least two nights a week, including Friday night, which was Young People's Night. She would move up and down the aisles of Mount Olive, alternating between preaching, teaching, and singing. Sometimes she would minister for two or three hours. As she moved about the church, she would personally greet members, a practice that increased her visibility through the ritual of presence. She would intersperse her speaking and singing with "How are my children, tonight?" and, for the young people, "How are my grandchildren?"[24] In this way she ritualized her closeness and availability to members, modeling love and personal concern for them. Additionally, she set a tone for a style of personal leadership that she anticipated would be replicated by other leaders and continued by her successors.

When she traveled on evangelistic tours, Ida B. Robinson always took a group of ministers with her. They learned their "way of being" by watching her in her work. One aide recalls how they admired her missionary zeal. Once on a tour of the South, the bus carrying Bishop Robinson's entourage broke down. While repairs were being made, she turned to an assistant and cried, "Hand me a tambourine." She immediately began to sing and play her tambourine, standing up on a chair until she had drawn a crowd. Bishop preached "right out there in the woods" until several souls came forward to confess Christ as Savior.[25]

It was on such a preaching sojourn that Robinson ultimately died. While touring the South with the Word on her lips and her aides by her side, Bishop passed in April of 1946 in Winter Haven, Florida. Her vice president, Elmira Jeffries, succeeded her, and expanded the church's ministry to the elderly. Bishop Mary Jackson, who had more formal education than Robinson, and had therefore been given the responsibility of reading texts and books to her, succeeded Jeffries upon her death in 1964.[26] Bishop Jackson served until retirement in 1981 at the age of a hundred, when she was succeeded by Bishop Amy Bell Stevens. Amy Stevens was Bishop Robinson's personal nurse, and she was called "Jackrabbit" for her faithful, timely service. She was at Bishop's bedside at the time of her death and governs today with the mantle of Ida B. Robinson squarely on her shoulders, occupying the symbolic mothering role modeled by her mentor.

This type of succession of leadership cannot be adequately captured by purely political categories. What is crucial from our standpoint is that each succeeding leader had access to Ida B. Robinson's life and work. Not only do the presiding bishops evidence the strong connection to Bishop Robinson, but a host of bishops, pastors, elders, and evangelists trace their contemporary ministries to following the lead of Ida B. Robinson, and they point to access to her life in the home, in ritual, and in church life and work as the ground of their succession. Contemporary leadership that is not accessible would seem to suffer precisely at the point of self-replication (birthing) and leadership development (nurture). This is not to eschew models of leadership based upon professionally defined categories, nor to minimize the role of administration and procedure in contemporary black leadership. Indeed, such a manner of succession might even preclude qualified leaders from occupying positions in the church in favor of those "better connected." But Robinson believed in organization. And her practice was to delegate the administrative work to trusted aides (Mary Jackson, Elder Gilliard Jackson, and others) whom she then nurtured and supported in her mothering presence. Her aides had access to her, and she developed them and administered Mount Sinai through delegation and nurture.

Finally, we consider Ida B. Robinson, the mother, as teacher of wisdom. By wisdom, I refer to the capacity to develop a frame of reference from which to view the world, as well as the critical faculties to analyze and negotiate its complexities. Through teaching, the mother provides the fundamental lens through which her children view the world. Mothers help their children order and interpret their life experience in such a way that the world is given an appearance of manageability. This teaching is not mere cognitive exercise but involves the love and intimacy described in our discussion of holiness. The loving relationship becomes the context within which the children learn to negotiate problems and process the pain of life. The loving mother works to have the children adopt her perspective, see the world as she sees it, and persevere as she has persevered.

Teaching was a central part of Ida B. Robinson's ministry. She had a relatively well-developed educational program that included traditional Sunday school instruction, as well as special weekly training for all teachers. Bishop Robinson performed the role of teacher during her Tuesday and Thursday evening services, where her sermons were primarily instructional in character. She was especially known for teaching on holiness, which is consistent with the notion that mothers teach their children how to negotiate the world. But she also was required to teach in the area of women in ministry, given the controversial nature of the practice during her day.[27] This was a complex problem for Mount Sinai in that the Sanctified Church, consistent with the conservative strand of the African American church, has long been a "Bible-based" church, asserting that all belief and practice must have a scriptural reference.[28] As such, Mount Sinai would need to have a strong appeal to Scripture in order to justify its promotion of women in positions of religious leadership.

Bishop Robinson based her theology of equality between the sexes on a literal, chronological reading of Genesis 1 and 2. In those chapters, she taught, there are two distinct acts of God that must be understood in order to see God's plan for the equality of the sexes. In Gen. 1:26 and 27, God created male and female in his image. This created being was subsequently formed into the man Adam in Gen. 2:7. Adam, as created male/female being in the image of God, was then given dominion over the earth. After this, God formed the woman, later called Eve, from the man. But her created essence was in existence from the beginning; therefore, all promises and privileges given by God to Adam applied to Eve as well. Elder Thelma Richey, one of Bishop Robinson's former aides, points back to her mentor's teaching, saying, "Therefore her name is really Eve Adam, because she came right out of the man."[29]

Mary, the mother of Jesus, was another symbol of appeal for Bishop Robinson's teaching on women's ministry. "If Mary can carry the Word of God in her womb, why can't I carry the Word of God on my lips?"[30] Similarly, she appealed to the example of the women who witnessed the empty tomb of Jesus as grounds for the right of women to preach; after all, they were the first to declare the resurrection. Bishop Amy Stevens recalled that, at each Easter Sunday sunrise service, Bishop Robinson would lead the congregation in singing:

> Didn't those women run,
> Didn't those women run,
> They ran the good news to spread.
> The angel had told them to go
> For Jesus had gone on before.
> "He is risen just as he said."[31]

Bishop Robinson was not only a strong teacher; she also envisioned Mount Sinai as a teaching church and her followers as lovers of learning. While some have criticized the black Pentecostal tradition as "anti-intellectual," Bishop Robinson, much like her contemporaries, made provision for educational growth and achievement by organizing a school.[32] The Mount Sinai Holy School contained instruction at both the elementary and high school level, in such subjects as English, arithmetic, geography, American and European history, hygiene, music, art, and Holy Bible. Manual training and domestic science were also available. The school was governed by attendance laws of the Philadelphia School District, "with an officer in attendance who visits the school weekly." The expectation was that pupils would follow rules of holiness and discipline, and that "any pupil having finished the elementary and High School courses of Mt. Sinai Holiness School will be able to enter college, and their Certificate will be recognized by any good Standard School."[33]

Mount Sinai also provided the context for nurturing women and men in the teaching profession. There were a good number of educators in her churches and many young people were inspired by her leadership to enter teaching as a vocation. In 1934, Sister M. E. Wood of Pensacola, Florida, asked, "What [Can] a Christian Teacher Do for Negro America?" in Mount Sinai's newspaper, the *Latter Day Messenger*. Giving credit for her spiritual direction to her mother, friends, and Bishop Robinson, she wrote that "the only hope of the future (Negro) race is to have real leaders, real preachers, especially real teachers . . . The Negro teacher who is working for the betterment of the race must work from a principle, to build a character whom the nation will adore." They are "instruments in God's hands . . . willing to throw off the world and throw the energy of their young lives into the service of the race . . . [putting] on the whole armor of God."[34]

These dual foci of the teaching functions of mothering—that is, direct instruction and creating educational opportunities—present themselves as important resources for contemporary black leadership. Those who lead must train their followers in the ability to think creatively, to analyze issues critically, and to construct practical solutions to complex contemporary problems. They must become actively involved in the enterprise of teaching, letting people know that they are responsible for certain principles, not the least of which is the development of a conceptual framework within which to negotiate the world. Community organizing, participation in the political process, and other forms of public activism must create the space for learning opportunities, allowing and even encouraging the people they serve to become empowered through wisdom. Black mothering has at its core the goal of enabling children to develop this type of wisdom. Bishop Robinson contributed to its institutionalization through her pastoral and episcopal ministry.

The mothering symbol is not the only one available as a construct for the ideational and practical empowerment of African American leadership. Yet its historicity calls for investigation, its complexity mandates analysis, and its efficacy pleads for imitation. Ida B. Robinson represents a host of African American women who self-consciously participated in this symbolization process, both using it as a guide for their own self-image and actions and contributing to its meaning through the externalization of their behavior. More of their stories need to be shared, studied, compared, and critiqued in order to assess the meaning of their lives, for the purpose of accurately recording the historical record and to expose the exemplary and didactic function of history and hagiography in the African American community. This is the politic of the African American story; it is the story told by our mothers.[35]

George Floyd Taylor: Conflicts and Crowns

Vinson Synan

On Sunday morning, April 14, 1901, young George Floyd Taylor of Magnolia, North Carolina, was torn between attending three of the churches in town. A seeker for spiritual truth, he finally decided to attend all three. He wrote in his diary, "I went to Baptist Sunday School, to Pentecostal Holiness preaching and to the Methodist Episcopal prayer meeting." Later in the day he "studied Latin, algebra, Ciciro [*sic*] for entry into the University of North Carolina." Two years later, when Taylor finally cast his lot with the Pentecostal Holiness Church, southern Pentecostalism gained one of its most innovative and energetic leaders. In the years to come, Taylor would distinguish himself as a brilliant writer, theologian, educator, and churchman despite physical handicaps that might have discouraged a lesser man.[1]

Taylor was born in Duplin County, North Carolina, near the town of Magnolia, on August 10, 1881. It was apparent at his birth that young George would be crippled for life. Although it is not known what the medical name for his difficulty was, those who knew him well have described his condition as palsy or palsylike. He himself said that he was "born under bodily infirmities" and was "unable to move about well." In fact, he later said, "I am told that when I was born I was dead. After being rubbed with warm water for one hour, I began to breathe . . . nobody thought that I would ever live."[2] As he grew up, this condition made it difficult for Taylor to walk well or to do anything that required muscular coordination. A sample of his handwriting shows the great difficulty he experienced in writing, and because of this he early learned to use the

325

George Floyd Taylor, circa 1907. Courtesy of International Pentecostal Holiness Church Archives and Research Center, Oklahoma City, Oklahoma.

typewriter, although whenever he could, he dictated his writings directly to a secretary. Because of his congenital handicap, George was set aside at first by his family without much hope of his ever achieving a great deal. He was not sent to school until he was ten years old. In a short time, however, he exhibited great intellectual powers and an indomitable will that overshadowed his infirmity. Joseph Campbell stated that "his physical handicap in some sense perhaps drove him to excel in fields of mental activity. His inquiring, meditative mind reveled in the opportunity to be studious even early in life."[3]

As a seeker for a deeper Christian life, Taylor also visited the Universalist church in Magnolia before joining the Baptist church. There he complained about a lack of warmth or spiritual help beyond discussions on the proper modes of water baptism. At thirteen, he finally left the Baptists to join the Magnolia Methodist Church. There he found the warmth and spirituality that he longed for. For several years, this congregation had been involved in the Holiness movement that had been sweeping many Methodist churches around the nation for decades.

In the fall of 1901, twenty-year-old George Floyd Taylor enrolled at the University of North Carolina and made it through the year with the help of his family, friends, and a loan fund at the university. Taylor wrote, "During that year I spent only five cents more than I had to spend, and that was for parched peanuts." He planned to take a B.A. degree and then go to a seminary for three more years to earn his B.D. degree. After his education he envisioned himself as "an ordinary Methodist preacher" sailing down "an easy road through life."[4]

A. B. Crumpler and the Pentecostal Holiness Church

Taylor's life was radically changed, however, five weeks after leaving the university when he attended a Holiness revival meeting in the Methodist Church of Magnolia led by Abner Blackmon Crumpler of Clinton, North Carolina. Since 1896, Crumpler had made news with his highly charged Holiness revivals where he called for Methodists to return to their Wesleyan roots by seeking the second blessing of entire sanctification. In his loud and boisterous sermons, Crumpler explained the doctrine of sanctification, which he pointed out could be received "in an instant by simple faith." Afterward, the recipient would live a life of perfect holiness with complete victory over sin. Following Wesley, he called the second blessing "perfect love," "Christian perfection," or the "baptism in the Holy Spirit."

Taylor had heard Crumpler before, in 1897, when Crumpler's North Carolina Holiness Association convened in the Magnolia Methodist Episcopal Church. In this meeting Taylor's future wife, Ella Brown, received her sanctification experience. Although he was entranced by Crumpler's theology and stentorian preaching style, Taylor was repelled by the noisy worship that accompanied his preaching. Taylor later recalled that "people would laugh, holler, scream, jump, dance, run, slap their hands, and praise the Lord." Others would fall into trances that might last for hours. Although he was attracted by the lively preaching and praise, Taylor felt uneasy with some of the unrestrained manifestations of these Holiness Methodists. Yet, he said, "great was the revival that had come to the little town of Magnolia."[5]

Crumpler had left Clinton, North Carolina, in the late 1880s to seek his fortunes in Missouri. He soon joined a local Methodist church and felt called to the Methodist ministry. In 1890, he attended a Methodist District Conference and was sanctified under the ministry of Beverly Carradine, one of the premier Holiness preachers of the day. By 1896, Crumpler decided to bring the Holiness message to the people of the Tarheel State. His preaching in eastern North Carolina ignited revivals that featured noisy demonstrations typical of "shouting Methodists." The major attraction, however, was Crumpler's claim that he had not committed a single sin since his sanctification experience in 1890. This led to much discussion and debate wherever he preached. Taylor described the reaction of a local "no-hell-ite" acquaintance who would " get so mad over the thing that he would wiggle in his seat, rise, take off his hat, walk the yard, and charge that he wanted an opportunity to tell that preacher that he committed a sin every time he said such a thing."[6]

In time Crumpler's ministry attracted enough support to form the North Carolina Holiness Association in Magnolia in 1897 with himself as president. From this base, he conducted further meetings across the state. To advance his cause, Crumpler sent regular reports to two important Holiness periodicals, J. M. Pike's *Way of Faith* in Columbia, South Carolina, and George D. Watson's *Living Words* in Pittsburgh. Later, in 1900, Crumpler began publication of his own biweekly magazine, *The Holiness Advocate*. His attacks on religious coldness and worldliness soon included his own Methodist Church, which by 1897 was moving to curtail the Holiness movement within its ranks. In the 1898 general conference, the Methodist Episcopal Church, South, passed "Rule 301," which forbade evangelists to hold meetings in local Methodist charges without the permission of the local pastor.[7]

In the summer of 1898, Crumpler tested the rule by holding a tent meeting near Elizabeth City, North Carolina, without the approval of the pastor. When he was criticized for this infraction, he left the Methodist

Church in November of 1898 to form a new group in Goldsboro that was informally called the Pentecostal Holiness Church, the first local church to bear the name. In 1899, Crumpler rejoined the Methodists hoping to overturn the detested Rule 301 but to no avail. After holding another Holiness meeting in Stedman, North Carolina, he was hauled into a Methodist ecclesiastical court to be tried for holding a meeting without pastoral approval. Although he was acquitted, Crumpler once again left the Methodist Church and began the task of creating a new denomination, which was organized in Fayetteville, North Carolina, in 1901 and named the Holiness Church of North Carolina. While all this was going on, a local Pentecostal Holiness church was organized in Magnolia in November of 1900. Although Taylor attended the organizational meeting, he did not feel disposed to join at that time.[8]

At this point Taylor was struggling with a call to preach. The problem was whether he should enter into the Methodist ministry or cast his lot with Crumpler's new Holiness Church. For months he also struggled over his quest for entire sanctification. This period came to an end on July 3, 1902, when he "received a definite witness that I was wholly sanctified." During this time of seeking he had to overcome distractions from some who claimed ecstatic experiences such as "falling under the power" or "seeing Jesus' face on the wall." Because he had felt no unusual emotions when he received the second blessing, he came to the conclusion that "feeling was not the ground of legitimate experience."[9]

A few months after receiving the coveted sanctification experience, Taylor finally decided to join Crumpler's Holiness Church. The day he joined the church on March 8, 1903, he was licensed to preach. "For Taylor, it was far better to venture into an uncertain financial future and remain faithful in the 'battle' for truth than to compromise one's beliefs in order to gain a guaranteed 'easy road through life.'"[10]

As a minister, Taylor began a course of reading that was deeply to affect his ministry. In 1903 at the nearby Falcon camp meeting, he listened to the preaching of George D. Watson, the famous Holiness teacher who carefully explained that the "baptism in the Holy Spirit" was not received at the time of sanctification but formed a further work of the Spirit. According to Watson this was the difference between "emptying" and "filling." Taylor said that this revelation "revolutionized" his ministry with "new light."[11] Another writer who caught Taylor's attention was J. A. Seiss, the Lutheran author of *The Apocalypse, Miracle in Stone, The Great Pyramid of Egypt,* and *The Gospel in the Stars.* Following Seiss, Taylor became a staunch believer in the premillennial rapture of the church and even went so far as to name one of his sons Seiss Taylor.

Other teachings affecting Taylor included the popular theme of divine healing "as in the atonement" taught by such evangelical luminaries as A. J. Gordon and A. B. Simpson. Soon Taylor came to believe that all sickness was caused by demons and that the only cure was healing in answer to prayer. He soon joined the large number of divine healers who taught that it was better to "trust the Lord for your body" than to resort to doctors and medicine. These ideas were developed in Taylor's first book, *The Devil,* which appeared in 1906. Here he explained that "the Devil fills the air with all manner of diseases" that "hold to the body as a leach on a tree." "Insanity," he said, "was caused by demons which lodge in the brain, from there they work on the nerves." The only answer lay in divine healing in answer to prayer.[12]

Holiness Education

After joining the Holiness Church, Taylor found it impossible to return to the University of North Carolina the following year because of financial reasons. Indeed, he was not to return and finish his college work at the university until a quarter of a century later when he was nearly fifty years of age. One major result of Taylor's year at the university was the birth of a consuming vision for Holiness education, an idea that dominated him until his death. During his stay at Chapel Hill, he reported that "neither the students nor the professors ridiculed those who wanted to serve God so far as I knew. Yet I was constantly surrounded by those who were worldly, and my ears had to listen continually to jokes, foolishness and filth. It was during this time that the idea of a holiness school, or a school free from such influences, was born in my mind."[13]

In 1903, Taylor had his first opportunity to implement his educational vision when the Holiness community near Rose Hill, North Carolina, united with him in opening the Bethel Holiness School. So, on October 12, 1903, the twenty-two-year-old preacher founded his first school. Of his experiences there, he said, "I taught there for four years. We built a dormitory for the third year of the school. When we closed the fourth year, I had a hundred students in school."[14]

Gaston Barnabas Cashwell and the Pentecostal Experience

In January 1907, G. F. Taylor's life and ministry were radically changed by another transforming spiritual experience—the Pentecostal baptism with the Holy Ghost, with the initial evidence of speaking with other tongues. Along with thousands of other Holiness people in the South, Taylor had read glowing accounts in the pages of the *Way of Faith* about the 1906 Pentecostal outbreak at the Azusa Street Mission in Los Angeles led by the African American pastor William J. Seymour. Many of these articles were written by Frank Bartleman, the primary chronicler of the events in Los Angeles. As interest in the new movement spread, Crumpler also printed reports in the *Holiness Advocate*. Taylor, who already believed in "progressive theology,"[15] was strongly attracted to the new tongues experience since he already agreed with George Watson that Holy Spirit baptism was separate from the sanctification experience. Like many others, Taylor was fascinated with the news from Los Angeles.

> Many of us were much interested in the California revival, but we did not think of its interfering with our doctrine. We took it as a great outpouring of the Spirit in addition to what we had already received or as a revival in perfect harmony with our doctrines, just as we are praying for a revival today (1921). We never thought of the holiness people fighting it, or that it would set any of them aside; but thought that we would have a gracious revival in our midst, in perfect harmony with our doctrines, with the speaking in tongues as a gift of the Spirit. So we were praying earnestly for it to come.[16]

By the fall of 1906, a preacher of the Holiness Church of North Carolina, G. B. Cashwell of Dunn, North Carolina, made the trek to Los Angeles to receive his "personal Pentecost." There he overcame his racial prejudices and asked Seymour to pray for him to speak in tongues. After a vivid experience in which he claimed to have spoken "in the German language," Cashwell returned to North Carolina to spread the Pentecostal fire on the East Coast. His first meeting began in December in the Dunn Holiness Church. By January 1907 he rented a three-story tobacco warehouse in Dunn by the railroad tracks, and for most of the month people came from all over the South to hear from the Pentecostal "apostle." Most of the ministers in Crumpler's infant denomination went to Dunn and were soon speaking in tongues. Other ministers from J. H. King's Fire-Baptized Holiness Church also came to Dunn, as well as preachers from the Free Will Baptist churches of North Carolina. The Dunn revival attracted Taylor like a magnet.[17]

Before he could enter into the tongues experience, however, Taylor had to overcome two obstacles. One was the attitude of Crumpler, his ecclesiastical superior. On Christmas night of 1906, Taylor spent the night in Crumpler's home, where his leader declared, "if Cashwell was teaching the speaking in tongues as the evidence of the baptism in the Holy Spirit, he was going to oppose it." The other problem was that Crumpler had long testified that he had received Holy Spirit baptism at the time of his sanctification experience. Despite all this, Taylor began a time of prayer and Bible study to clarify his own theological understanding. "With my heart open to God, I began to search the Word: and to the surprise of my heart, I found in the teaching of the Word that all who receive the Baptism of the Holy Ghost speak with tongues as the Spirit gives utterance. So I gladly yielded my former views and accepted new light on the Word."[18]

Taylor's Pentecostal experience came on January 15, 1907, in the home of a pastor friend, where he remembered that, "five minutes after seeing the first person who had his Pentecost, the Holy Ghost was talking with my tongue."[19] From that point onward, Taylor became a major leader of the new Pentecostal faction in the church, which quickly grew to claim a majority of the preachers. While this was happening, Crumpler made a point of preaching in a revival meeting in Florida while Cashwell's meeting continued in Dunn. In his absence, most of Crumpler's preachers ignored his warnings, went to Dunn, and received the tongues experience. With the winning of Taylor, Cashwell gained an able ally who would join him in "conflict and battle" during the next year.

True to his word, Crumpler sternly opposed the new movement that threatened to engulf his church. The battle lines were now drawn between Crumpler and Cashwell with his new ally G. F. Taylor. For months the struggle raged on the pages of Crumpler's *Holiness Advocate* over the tongues question. Despite his opposition, Crumpler allowed the Pentecostals to publish their testimonies in the paper. A strange situation developed when Crumpler denounced the new movement while letters in the same issue accused Crumpler, and others who resisted the movement, of teaching "the doctrine of Satan."[20] In a short time, Crumpler's opposition to the Pentecostal tide caused so many people to cancel their subscriptions to the *Holiness Advocate* that the paper folded. During 1907 Taylor reported that, "in spite of conflict, the revival swept on in mighty power, and the Pentecostal folk kept gaining ground."[21]

Reports came from all over the South of unusual revivals in the wake of the Dunn meeting. Taylor later described the situation:

> What did our preachers and people do about it? They went to Dunn by the dozens, went down for the baptism with all the earnestness they could command, and were soon happy [in] the experience, speaking in tongues, singing in tongues, writing in tongues, shouting, leaping, dancing, and praising God. They returned to their respective homes to scatter the fire. Great Pentecostal revivals broke out in practically all the churches. Some preachers and some of the laymen held back, but the majority went right into the experience. A great revival had come, and no one was able to stop it.[22]

As the revival continued, it became clear that the new southern Pentecostals were now separating Holy Spirit baptism from the second blessing experience of entire sanctification, thus making it a third blessing. Also, in the excitement over the tongues experience, many people began to use the word *Pentecostal* to describe not only their experience but also their church.

With his church rapidly becoming Pentecostalized, and without a paper to control its spread, the future looked grim for Crumpler and the few preachers and laymen who resisted the revival. By the time of the annual conference in La Grange, North Carolina, in November 1907, the lines had been drawn for a confrontation between Crumpler and the Pentecostal faction whom he labeled "fanatics" and "Cashwell's jabbering followers." Leading the Pentecostals were Cashwell, Taylor, and the vice president of the Holiness Church, A. H. Butler. When Crumpler called for a committee to examine preachers "on points of doctrine," the Pentecostals, sensing a majority, enthusiastically voted in the affirmative. Crumpler thereupon declared his own motion "out of order." Taylor reported that, although "no one hesitated to declare their position," there were "no harsh words spoken." To prove the point, the conference reelected Crumpler to lead the church for another year despite his opposition to the revival.[23]

In the ensuing year the Pentecostal tide continued to swell throughout the South. Cashwell traveled to Memphis and Birmingham to spread the movement into new areas. He also began publication of a new pro-Pentecostal magazine in Atlanta that he named *The Bridegroom's Messenger.* In September of 1907, Taylor had written a new book-length defense of the Pentecostal movement with the title *The Spirit and the Bride.* To bolster his position, Taylor asked his friend Joseph H. King to write the introduction to the book. King, who served as general overseer of the Fire-Baptized Holiness Church, had become head of the little Holiness denomination when the church's founder, Benjamin Hardin Irwin, fell into "open and gross sin." Irwin, one of the most radical of the Holiness preachers, had taught several "baptisms" after sanctification that he called baptisms of "fire," "dynamite," "lyddite," and "oxidite." In 1907, after receiving the tongues-attested baptism, King renounced Irwin's teachings as "fanaticism and extravagance." In King, Taylor found a true friend and ally.[24]

To explain the new Pentecostal phenomenon, Taylor and King harked back to Old Testament prophecies, especially the latter rain promise found in Joel 2. Taylor explained his theory as follows: "The early rain began on the day of Pentecost, and the first manifestation was speaking with other tongues as the Spirit gave utterance, and then followed the healing of the sick, casting out devils, etc. So it would only be natural to expect that in the latter rain Pentecost should be repeated and followed by the same manifestations."[25]

The Spirit and the Bride also called for "dismissing all theories" and "taking the Scriptures just as they are." Here Taylor articulated a new view that later was widely accepted among Pentecostals—that is, that speaking in tongues was the necessary sign for inclusion in the Bride of Christ at the Second Coming. He also made distinctions between the Wesleyan experience of sanctification and the new tongues-attested Holy Spirit baptism. Taylor not only practiced what he preached; he went beyond most other Pentecostals in manifesting spiritual gifts. In fact, for some months afterward, Taylor became widely known for possessing the gift of interpreting spoken and written messages in tongues. People from all over the United States would send him copies of "grapholalia," which he would return with written interpretations. On one occasion a preacher gave an entire sermon in tongues, which Taylor interpreted. After only two years of such intensive charismatic activity, however, Taylor ceased to exercise the gifts of tongues and interpretation and often wondered if he had thereby "quenched the Spirit."[26]

Written in the heat of battle, *The Spirit and the Bride* served as a doctrinal tract for the showdown between Crumpler and the Pentecostals in the following conference that convened in Dunn in November 1908. Without the *Holiness Advocate*, Crumpler was not able to communicate the time or the place of the convention. When asked about this situation by one of his preachers, he replied, "the tongues folk could have their convention when and where they liked, But the Holiness Church would have theirs in Dunn in November." He further suggested that there be a separation.[27]

When the conference convened in Dunn, the result of the struggle was a foregone conclusion. Although the convention again elected Crumpler as president by acclamation, it was apparent that he had lost the battle. The question was settled once and for all when Crumpler walked out of the meeting and the life of the church he had founded. He took with him only two of the fifteen churches and a few "scattered" preachers and laymen. Most of these ultimately followed Crumpler back into the Methodist Church.[28]

The Pentecostals quickly elected a new tongue-speaking president, A. H. Butler, and, with Cashwell as committee chairman, amended the articles of faith. These were changed to read as follows: "on receiving the baptism with the Holy Ghost we have the same evidence which followed in Acts 2nd, 10th, and 19th chapters, to wit: The speaking with other tongues as the Spirit gives utterance."[29] Since Taylor had played a leading part in all these struggles, he, at only twenty years of age, became the prime theologian of the new church. To affirm its Pentecostal identity, the group in 1909 changed its name from the Holiness Church of North Carolina back to the Pentecostal Holiness Church, the name that had been used at the inception of the church.

During these months of conflict, Taylor continued to serve as principal of the Bethel Holiness School at Rose Hill. Although the Pentecostals won most of the church, Taylor could not win over the leaders of his own congregation and school community. When the struggle ended, the Holiness people at the Bethel School rejected the new Pentecostal teaching, forcing Taylor to leave owing to the "tremendous opposition" to this new experience.

No sooner had Taylor left Bethel than he received a call to superintend the Falcon Holiness School in the nearby camp meeting town of Falcon, North Carolina. A vacancy was open there because the previous principal had refused to accept the new Pentecostal experience. At Falcon, Taylor headed the school from 1907 to 1916 with the exception of one year when J. H. King served as principal.

In the years after 1908, a groundswell arose in the Pentecostal Holiness Church and the Fire-Baptized Holiness Church to merge since both groups now taught identical doctrines. Taylor took a lead in persuading the leaders of the Pentecostal Holiness Church to enter into merger negotiations. His respect for J. H. King helped Taylor favor the cause of uniting the two bodies. By 1909 there was no discernible opposition to merger in either church. In the annual conference of 1909 the Pentecostal Holiness Church appointed a committee of three to contact the Fire-Baptized Holiness Church. Taylor was one of the three. After some months of debate and negotiation, the two churches adopted a "Basis of Union" and were merged in the octagon-shaped tabernacle in Falcon on January 30, 1911. Taylor was one of the major architects of the merger.[30]

Sunday School Literature

During these Falcon years, G. F. Taylor founded the Sunday school literature enterprise of the Pentecostal Holiness Church. Commenting on the Sunday school materials available before his work, he said, "a [Holiness] literature was not to be found in the field. The best literature that we knew to get . . . failed to make the spiritual applications that were in the lessons. When many of us received the Baptism of the Spirit in 1907, this impression took a new hold on me. I received dozens of letters from all parts of the country, asking me if I knew of any Sunday school literature in harmony with our doctrines. I had to reply that I knew of no such literature. I felt like something had to be done."[31]

In 1913 Taylor began publishing a full line of distinctive Pentecostal Sunday school materials. He continued this enterprise as a private business until 1929 when he sold it to the Pentecostal Holiness Church with the proviso that all future profits would be given to the cause of education in the church. He also was the founder and first manager of the Pentecostal Holiness Publishing House.

In addition to owning the Sunday school literature business, Taylor also wrote all the quarterlies that he published. His secretary, Francis Huggins, gave this account of his methods of writing: "Mr. Taylor dictated the Sunday school lessons to his secretary, who took them down directly on the typewriter. He was a genius in his field. He dictated the lessons on the level of the beginner, then a little advanced on the primary level, and gradually advanced to the deep truths of the Bible quarterly."[32] Taylor estimated that in the year 1922 about thirty thousand students used his literature. In this work, he proved to be an adept businessman. For many years the profits from the Sunday school literature business formed his sole source of income. As a matter of fact, in later years Taylor supported much of the church's educational program out of his own pocket.

The year 1913 also marked the high point of Taylor's career as a churchman. In the General Conference of the Pentecostal Holiness Church, which convened in Toccoa, Georgia, Taylor was elected general superintendent, the highest office in the church. At the time, he was seen as the only candidate who could hold the newly merged church together. He held this position for four years, from 1913 to 1917. At the same time, he headed the Falcon Holiness School and continued writing and publishing Sunday school literature.

Taylor's major challenge as general superintendent was the eruption of a "gifts movement" in the Virginia Conference in 1916 that threatened to decimate the church in that part of the state. At first the most visible manifested gifts were prophecy, healing, and the discerning of Spirits. These gifts had been fading from the life of the church since the heady days of the first Pentecostal revivals. The revival centered in Roanoke under the leadership of conference superintendent E. D. Reeves, who pronounced the movement to be "of God." The revival soon exhibited unusual phenomena that attracted throngs of followers. Reeves reported scenes in which speakers would identify specific illnesses in persons unknown to them. And in many cases the sick "were miraculously healed instantly before the eyes of large congregations." Some preachers were able "to reveal secret sins to visitors which led even the most skeptical to repentance." People often "began to shake violently or demonstrate other involuntary responses to the working of the Holy Ghost." Most of this had been common from Azusa Street onward. But the movement soon featured more radical tendencies, such as the appearance of demons floating in the air over the congregation, which could be cast out only after being "rebuked in the name of Jesus."[33]

In time, some enthusiasts began to give each other biblical names such as Paul, Timothy, Rebecca, Isaac, and Mary. Prophecies also began to include "divine revelations" as to who should marry and to whom. Finally, a prophecy stated that the United States was shortly to be destroyed and that the only place of safety in the world would be China. Accordingly, a party set out from Virginia for China by way of California. Although most of the churches in the area supported what now came to be known as "the China Movement," others did not. In May of 1916, Taylor was called to Virginia in his capacity of general superintendent to deal with what critics felt were "excesses" and "fanaticism." After a careful investigation, Taylor, with a reluctant and heavy heart, dismissed sixteen preachers from the church in May of 1916, including Superintendent Reeves.

With this action, the movement soon died out and most of the ministers, including Reeves, returned to the church. Although Taylor had dealt firmly with the situation, it was reported that he faced the predicament with such a gentle spirit, at times weeping, that in a short time most of the preachers saw the error of their ways. In later years, Taylor admitted that his action in expelling the ministers "without an investigation" was "my mistake." With this experience behind him, Taylor was more than happy to retire from the general superintendency the next year.[34]

The Pentecostal Holiness Advocate

The general conference of 1917, which convened in Abbeville, South Carolina, elected J. H. King to succeed Taylor and then voted to begin an official church paper to be known as the *Pentecostal Holiness Advocate*. In searching the church for a capable man for this important task, the leaders settled on George Floyd Taylor as the one man best qualified to launch this new undertaking. Taylor had already gained a wide reputation as a writer and publisher and it was natural that he should be the choice.

In the first edition of the *Advocate*, Taylor wrote of his calling to the writing ministry: "For years I have felt a call in this direction. Never was anyone called to the ministry, either in the home land or the foreign, more definitely than I have been called to write. So far back as my memory serves me, I was conscious of my call to the ministry, and parallel with this call was a conviction that I must write, so much so that I am unable to separate the two."[35]

After a few weeks in the work, Taylor stated his editorial policies in regard to the *Advocate*. "I am delighted with my editorial duties. In this capacity I am doing my very best to treat all alike. I am trying to make the paper a blessing to the whole church. I am so much encouraged by the good letters that reach me, telling how the paper is appreciated. I want to keep it full of good things. Of course, I shall be obliged to let some contributions find their way to the waste basket."[36] These "waste basket" contributions seemed to be a constant source of irritation to a perfectionist like Taylor. Periodically he complained about the low quality of some of the material he received. On one occasion he erupted. On July 23, 1923, a three-page editorial appeared that was simply entitled "poetry." Taylor explained himself in the following words: "The Advocate is supposed to confine itself to the religious and ecclesiastical, but from time to time certain subjects so present themselves to the editor that he can hardly resist the temptation to explore other fields of thought. At the present time he feels constrained to write on poets and poetry . . . from time to time we receive what is supposed to be poems for publication in the Advocate . . . some have contained some thought and showed little talent. I have been ashamed to publish them, but I have feared to reject them." Then followed a horrible example from an anonymous donor who sent in a "pome." After this, he delivered a college-type lecture on poetry, dealing with such points as verse, stanza, meter, and explaining the intricacies of monometer, trimeter, pentameter, hexameter, trochee, dactyl, anapest, and all the rest.

Through all his years as editor of the *Advocate*, Taylor served his church well. His editorial work can only be described as brilliant and courageous. He never sidestepped any issue, regardless of how controversial it might be. In fact, the only schism in the history of the church came as a result of a controversy that arose over articles in the *Advocate* while Taylor served as editor. Although Taylor denounced the use of doctors and drugs, he nevertheless published articles by two Georgia preachers, Hugh Bowling and Watson Sorrow, which approved the use of medicines and other "remedies" in addition to prayer. The resulting controversy prompted a schism in the Georgia Conference and the formation of the new Congregational Holiness Church in 1921.[37]

During these turbulent years, Taylor also was given the additional responsibility of organizing and raising support for the world missions program of the church. Elected to serve as the treasurer for the Missionary Society in 1913, he tirelessly appealed for funds in the *Advocate* to support the missionaries of the church. Indeed, the church paper became the leading source of information about the church's missionaries and their needs on the field.

His constant appeals for money kept the missions program alive through many seasons of dire need. A typical appeal was printed in 1917: "we are now standing in great need of funds to carry forward the mission work of the church as it needs to be done. We ask all preachers, workers, and churches to do all they possibly can to help us during this month. Read our call to help on another page of this issue." In another appeal, he said, "We want money for foreign lands, but above all we want souls for those lands for Jesus."[38]

During his tenure with the Missionary Society, Taylor raised money to purchase the first church property in Hong Kong, and helped expand the mission efforts in China, India, and South Africa. Records show that, from 1913 to 1925, Taylor raised $104,401.62 for the missions program of the church, a significant total for that time. In later years, church leaders recognized their debt to Taylor for his years of leadership in the missionary enterprise of the denomination. In a 1935 tribute, R. H. Lee evaluated his influence by saying, "one of the greatest burdens of the church which he labored on so faithfully was that of the cause of foreign missions. The credit for the present organization [of] our church might be rightfully given to him as one who presented and labored for the Missionary Society."[39]

Emmanuel College

In 1918 the church came into the possession of a century-old health resort in Franklin Springs, Georgia. The two hotels and the large skating rink on the property made an ideal situation for a school. Again, the church turned to Taylor to lay the groundwork on a new and difficult endeavor. After accepting the offer of founding the school, Taylor moved everything he had to Franklin Springs in December of 1918 and threw his characteristic energy into the work. He did not leave his home state of North Carolina, however, without a great deal of sadness. Of this experience he wrote, "the thought of my being no more from North Carolina almost made me cry. When I began to see that I must change states, the patriotic fires began to blaze high in my soul. Today I love the Old North State as never before."[40]

The school opened on January 1, 1919, as an academy of eleven grades known as the Franklin Springs Institute. Room and board was $12.50 a month and tuition started at $1.25 a month. There were only three teachers for the entire eleven grades. In the first year a total of fifty-four students enrolled. For four years the school experienced great struggles to survive and largely failed to live up to the visions of its founder. Therefore, in 1922 Taylor decided to open the school on the faith plan and to admit any student regardless of his ability to pay. There would be no charges. The cost of the school would be paid for by contributions from the church, parents of students, and the school farm, which the students would run. Soon the school was overrun with students and many had to be turned away. For four straight years the student body numbered around two hundred boys and girls.

To take care of this great number of students, a new building was begun in 1924 that was to be the first step in organizing a junior college. This building was finished just in time for the general conference in 1925, and, for its time, was a great accomplishment as well as a great financial burden for the church.

The free tuition period represented a great financial sacrifice for G. F. Taylor. According to his own figures, he paid out of his own pocket more to operate the school in those years than the entire church put together. He estimated that he paid out about 70 percent of his annual income to see that the school stayed open.[41]

Taylor was a practical man in the running of the school. A few quotations from his pen might well illustrate his philosophy of Christian education: "We do not have a reformatory department, and do not care to add one . . . please do not think that we are here to manufacture Christians. The fact that he or she is wild and unruly is no reason he or she should come here. We do not need that class. It is the good boys and girls we are after. We are interested in teaching students rather than branches of learning."

Evidently things were much the same then as they are now in regard to romance. Taylor probably excluded all adolescents when he made the following statement: "We do not want boys and girls who desire to spark. We have no objections to young people being together at proper times, but the school room is not the place for these things."[42] Above all, however, Taylor was an idealist. His entire life was spent in the quest of a vision that he had for Pentecostal education. In 1920 he shared it with the readers of the *Advocate*. "When I was a young man I had a vision. It stood before me for months and even for years. I saw a holiness school. I had never heard of such a thing then, and did not know that there was such a thing. I saw about five hundred students in attendance, and everything running like clockwork. Everything was perfectly obedient, all students were well behaved, and it had the approval of everybody." This vision later was altered to be more realistic and practical. Years later, a wiser Taylor wrote: "I found to my sorrow that my vision was nothing but an air castle. When I took charge of my first holiness school, October 12, 1903, visions of sugar plums danced in my head. I was disappointed, not discouraged . . . then my vision of such a school became more practical . . . I used to enjoy the visions very well, but I believe the practical is better."[43]

To Taylor, education was a way of opening the way for the Gospel. In one editorial he defined education thus: "Education is one's ability to think for himself. True education most assuredly does open the way for the gospel, while improper education may close the doors against the gospel. True education brings God into everything, it sees God in everything, and enables one to decide for himself alone whether it is his choice to serve the God of science, the God of wisdom, the God of law and order, the God of the universe."[44]

It was commonly said that Taylor did the work of three men. During these years at Franklin Springs, he carried on several jobs at once. In one issue of the *Advocate* he was unable to write his regular editorial because of fatigue and offered the following reasons: "The things that demand my attention just now are many in number. The editorial work, the business of the printing office, the work in foreign lands, a vast correspondence, the work on the school building, the running of the dormitory, the adjustment of differences, the providing for near one hundred in the home, pastoring the church, praying for the sick; these are a few of the things that demand my attention daily." At another place he described his daily schedule at the school: "At 7:20 A.M. each day I begin my work in the school room. I teach until 1:00 o'clock P.M., assign boys work, get to my office at 2:00 P.M. I often find 15 or 20 letters that need to be answered at once—my Sunday school literature to write, and dozens of things to do with other positions that I hold. Supper at 6:00 P.M. then study hall where I labor with the students for about three hours." Bishop T. A. Melton, a close friend, wrote that he went "in a trot from morning till night." Of course, all this strain was an added burden in that he was physically handicapped and every activity took great physical effort.[45]

Further Education

In February 1926 Taylor resigned his position as head of the Franklin Springs Institute in order to further his education, which had been interrupted twenty-five years earlier. His plan was to earn a college degree so that he could convert the Franklin Springs Institute into a junior college. Accordingly, he moved to Chapel Hill and finished his work for the B.A. degree in history in only two years' time. After graduating from the University of North Carolina in 1928, he took a long-planned trip to Palestine from January to March 1929. As a result of this trip, he published a book entitled *A Tour of Bible Lands*. Later in that year he began work on his master's degree in history at North Carolina. An unusual feature of his college work was that he had to take his classroom notes on a typewriter because of his inability to write with a pen. His thesis was entitled, "Calvinism of the Sixteenth Century Compared with Lutheranism and Zwinglianism." He was awarded the M.A. degree in May 1930. He desired to earn a Ph.D. degree in history, but his major professor discouraged him, since "his books and periodicals had already earned him a Ph.D."[46]

His Final Years

In 1931 the Franklin Springs Institute was forced to close because of the Great Depression. During the time that the school was closed, Taylor made several desperate efforts to reopen a school for the Pentecostal Holiness Church. He first attempted to lease the Franklin Springs campus so that he could reopen the school on his own. He later tried to begin a college in Milford, Texas. He was going to name it Emmanuel College and finance it by selling soap. The soap brand name, Triangle Soap Company, was chosen with the subname BAC (build a college). He abandoned this project, however, when the general conference of 1933 voted to reopen the school at Franklin Springs under new leadership and rename it Emmanuel College. Thomas L. Aaron, the new president of the revived school, appointed Taylor as a member of the faculty, and he served in this capacity until his death on November 16, 1934.

In addition to all his other work, Taylor is said to have read the Bible through exactly one hundred times before he died. The books that he wrote—*The Devil, The Spirit and the Bride, The Second Coming of Jesus, The Sabbath, Daniel's Seventy Weeks,* and *The Rainbow*—established him as one of the seminal theologians and thinkers of the infant Pentecostal movement. He also served the Pentecostal Holiness Church in the various capacities of pastor, conference superintendent, general treasurer, and the highest office of all, general superintendent.

Taylor's ministry and career did not fit the usual stereotypes of the ignorant, poverty-stricken, southern Holy Roller that is so prevalent in popular culture. In the end, Taylor retained much of his Methodist roots. In time, he, along with King and others, created a "micro-Methodist" denomination in the Holiness tradition with the addition of tongues and other Spirit gifts. He insisted on bringing order out of the chaos of the radical Holiness tradition that had formed his Christian experience. When Pentecostalism and tongues appeared, he joined the new movement partly because he saw a biblical order that replaced much that was superficial and ephemeral in traditional Wesleyanism.

Taylor was in one person articulate, intellectual, literate, and persuasive. He did not fit the popular image of the ignorant, disinherited, and deprived Pentecostal. For most of his life he enjoyed the perquisites of middle-class life. His income, lifestyle, and fine home in Franklin Springs spoke of a comfortable life exceeding most southerners of his day. This status owed partly to his restless and enterprising spirit.

Taylor combined two contradictory inclinations—that of revolutionary innovator with that of conservative institutionalizer. As a young revolutionary, he joined and became a leader in the most dynamic religious movement of the century. He explained this when he said of himself, "I believe in progressive theology, in aggressive effort, in conflict, and in crowns."[47]

Yet, after winning the Pentecostal revolution, he settled down to become a churchman who led the church, founded the church literature enterprise, founded the church periodical the *Advocate,* and founded the church's major educational institution, Emmanuel College.

After a 1908 visit to the Falcon Camp Meeting, Frank Bartleman wrote an unforgettable and poignant description of Taylor. "Dear Brother Floyd Taylor reminded me of the little brown bird to whom God has given no fine plumage, but has recompensed with a most beautiful song. Doubtless

God keeps some samples of affliction for His glory. Mephibosheth was also 'lame in both his feet' but he 'ate at the king's table,' and 'dwelt in Jerusalem.' (Brother Taylor was a cripple.) God bless these humble southern brethren. They have been an example to me."[48]

Albert E. Robinson, an early colleague who knew many of the leading early American Pentecostal leaders, commented after Taylor's passing: "George Floyd Taylor was the outstanding character among us in so many respects that it is unlikely that we will see his equal."[49]

Seated with Bible, A. J. Tomlinson, circa 1900; *seated in buggy,* Miles Dickson Kilpatrick, known as "Uncle Dick"; *standing on right,* J. B. Mitchell; *standing in front of Kilpatrick,* Iowa Aletha Anderson; *seated in front of Anderson,* Ella Withrow Hyatt; *seated between Hyatt and A. J. Tomlinson,* Mary Jane Tomlinson; *children, from left to right,* Luther Bryant, Homer Tomlinson, Dolly Anderson, Halcy Tomlinson, Iris Tomlinson, and Julius Bryant. Courtesy of the Hal Bernard Dixon Jr. Pentecostal Research Center, Cleveland, Tennessee.

A. J. Tomlinson: Plainfolk Modernist

Roger Robins

During the course of his seventy-eight years, Ambrose Jessup Tomlinson towered over the third-largest family in American Pentecostalism, the Churches of God, as its beloved patriarch, chief villain, or fallen founder, depending upon where in that then contentious family one happened to stand. Since his death, fate and historiography have subjected his memory to a range of equally conflicted readings. Hagiographers have honored *A. J. Tomlinson: God's Anointed—Prophet of Wisdom*, while others have decried him as an autocrat, a good man of God gone bad, or a magnetic personality who led his fledgling church astray.[1] But whether praised or vilified within the tradition, he has shared the fate of most first-generation Pentecostal leaders in the wider academic world: marginalization. Sorely lacking among these lines of interpretation has been a sense of Tomlinson and his compatriots as natural members of the culture of their times.

The most common species of marginalization found in scholarly literature has involved the depiction of this generation as antimodern. Looking back from the far side of the fundamentalist-modernist controversy, early Pentecostalism has seemed to fit within a multifaceted antimodernist impulse in American popular religion, a vain attempt to circle the wagons of old-time religion against Progressive-era modernity. Conversely, scholars of American religion have generally presumed a special correspondence between social modernization and one particular expression of modern values: the Protestant modernism so ably described by William Hutchison.[2] In short, they have accepted the proprietary claims of a cultural elite that certainly embodied the spirit of its times but by no means exhausted it. Having done so, they have faced a conundrum: why have the heirs of Pentecostalism thrived so luxuriantly in the contemporary world, even

347

distinguishing themselves by their marketing savvy and technological sophistication? The conundrum, however, is illusory, a figment of our imagination of that first generation. Early Pentecostalism, like Protestant modernism itself, did indeed possess antimodern elements. But taken as a whole, the Pentecostal movement gave voice to its own vibrant progressive strain. Its leaders perceived themselves to be decidedly modern and adjusted their inherited culture in ways that were closer to, and in sympathy with, the prevailing trends of their day. They framed those adjustments, however, in the idioms of plainfolk culture, not of high culture or the academy. Nevertheless, like the mainstream elites who won the historiographical rights to the modernist name, they incarnated the robust interplay of progressivism and primitivism that, as Paul Carter has shown, defined their age.[3]

The contours of plainfolk progressivism, for first-generation converts, had been outlined by the radical Holiness movement, which had refit traditional revivalism for new demographic realities, new cultural needs, new marketing methods, and new technological possibilities. Holiness did not offer "the old time religion," one elderly saint explained, "for I have had that for forty years." Rather, it offered "the new kind of religion that . . . turns us loose for God."[4] A. J. Tomlinson ranked among the chief purveyors of that liberating new kind of religion, and his life offers a unique window to first-generation culture and experience. Through Tomlinson we can see the composite nature of the Holiness-Pentecostal tradition and the internal dynamic by which Pentecostalism emerged from its radical Holiness matrix. But in the portrait that follows, I will place special emphasis on another aspect of that generation: its plainfolk modernist cast.

Life in the Middle Landscape

Like the great majority of his native-born contemporaries, Ambrose Jessup Tomlinson began life in rural, small-town America. He was born September 22, 1865, on a farmstead just north of Westfield, Indiana, to Milton and Delilah Tomlinson. Milton had moved west with his own parents, Robert and Lydia Tomlinson, in the Quaker Great Migration of the 1830s. That migration supplied the core of Westfield's social establishment and turned the Indiana Yearly Meeting of the Society of Friends into the largest such meeting in the world. Robert and Lydia, along with most of their children, rose to become pillars of local religious life. But

Milton and Delilah—lapsed Quakers who had been disowned for marriage contrary to discipline—held formal religion in slight regard. The boy grew up in the margins between a devout extended family and his religiously alienated parents.

Despite their religious differences, Robert Tomlinson and his son Milton both enjoyed social prominence and relative affluence in Westfield circles. They farmed but were farmers of the nineteenth-century entrepreneurial sort. The elder Tomlinson had supplemented his farm income by trucking boilers to nearby Indianapolis and operating a steam-powered sawmill. Milton kept an equally mixed portfolio. By the 1850s he had emerged as a notable contractor, helping to stretch the roads and railways that tied Westfield to the expanding national market. Far from backwaters, the small and midsize towns of the Ohio Valley pulsed with lively enterprise, and Ambrose Tomlinson grew up within a family that had carved its niche in that vibrant middle landscape of the new economy.

Milton Tomlinson opened the door for his son to the family brand of mixed agriculture, but his son declined to enter. A psychological distance separated the two men, and it came naturally. Milton was forty-five when Ambrose arrived as a frail, last-born only son. The burly Milton, by contrast, had been the firstborn of five sons. Though gifted academically, Ambrose often fell ill. During one debilitating spell his father—either convinced that his son was poorly suited to the heavy labor on which his own prosperity depended or aspiring to a son in the professional class— began to foster Ambrose's literary side. He sent him to writing school and the boy responded, beginning a diary that he would keep for the rest of his life.

At sixteen Ambrose attended a Quaker high school in Westfield locally renowned for its excellence, and after graduation he continued his literary and civic interests through membership in a literary society, where he joined the drama troupe. At twenty-three he married, completing his progression to young manhood. Perhaps to signal his new status or to please his pious bride, Mary Jane Taylor Tomlinson, he promptly joined a church. It was the local meeting of the Society of Friends organized by his grandparents, built on grounds donated by his uncle, and run by an assortment of cousins, uncles, and friends. For A. J. Tomlinson, the door of that modest Quaker meetinghouse would open to the world of radical Holiness.

By the time the young groom joined the Society of Friends in 1889, western Quakerism had been revolutionized by more than two decades of evangelical and Holiness revivalism. Thomas Hamm has called it the *Transformation of American Quakerism.*[5] The Great Migration had landed Ohio Valley Quakers in a spiritual hothouse where blossoming sects tangled promiscuously, and Quaker attempts to seal the perimeter proved futile. Amid that holy effervescence, silent meetings and plain address gave way to boisterous Methodist-style preaching and revivalistic new methods.

Mary Jane Tomlinson's home congregation at Walnut Ridge, Indiana, formed one of the first centers of this new-style Quakerism, having hosted a revival in 1867 that most Holiness Friends cited as the origin of their movement. But by the 1880s Westfield had surfaced as an epicenter of Quaker Holiness surpassing even Walnut Ridge. Within the confines of his monthly meeting Tomlinson encountered an impressive array of Holiness dignitaries, including his boyhood neighbor, Seth Cook Rees, theologian Dougan Clark Jr., and evangelist John Pennington. William F. Manley, who would later win distinction as a Pentecostal leader, headed the local evangelism committee, and Tomlinson rubbed shoulders with the soon-to-be-celebrated Charles Stalker, a younger contemporary who later embarked on a series of world missionary tours.

Among such company Tomlinson at first left a rather undistinguished record. His most notable service involved a term on the home missions committee, dominated by Holiness figures like his evangelist cousin Orlando Tomlinson. Though brief, the experience introduced him to one of the meeting's chief concerns, industrial schools devoted to the spiritual, intellectual, and moral uplift of poor white children in the South. After one year, however, Tomlinson left the committee for another mission: the social-political crusade of the Populist Party.

The Populist Gospel

Politics came naturally to a Tomlinson. A. J.'s grandfather, father, and uncles were active in local politics and often represented the township at district and state conventions. The only surprising aspect of A. J.'s political turn lay in the banner he chose to wave. Like most Quakers, the Tomlinsons had long ago hitched their wagon to the Whig-Republican trajectory. In 1892 A. J. broke ranks, casting his lot with that Democratic stepchild, heir of the Jeffersonian impulse and champion of the downtrodden, the People's Party. When campaign season reached Westfield, A. J. registered as the

Populist candidate for county auditor while his father trekked off to serve as a delegate to the Republican congressional convention.

Perhaps Tomlinson was drawn to the Populist gospel by its political platform or its fusion of agrarian and industrial concerns. More likely, he was drawn by its potent blend of political cause and plainfolk religion. One reporter described the party's 1892 convention as a "religious revival, a crusade, a pentecost of politics in which a tongue of flame set upon every man."[6] According to Populist orator Mary Lease, "the teachings of Christ and the Constitution" formed the twin pillars of Populism, and the party merely wished to enact into law "the truths taught by Jesus."[7] Furthermore, its animus toward the political and religious establishments was pure Holiness. Ignatius Donnelly decried mainstream religion as "Christianity without Christ" and "the painted shell of a religion." Surveying the pulpits of America, he cried out, "Oh . . . for the man of Galilee! . . . armed with a whip of scorpions, to . . . lash his recreant preachers into devotion to the cause of his poor afflicted children."[8] Like Donnelly and Lease, Populists across the nation couched their political aims in the idioms of plainfolk religion.

Populism and radical Holiness sprang from the same soil, appealed to the same social strata, competed for the same constituency, and shared a common ethos. The founder of Free Methodism, B. T. Roberts, had likewise warned of "an aristocracy of wealth more dangerous" than "titled aristocracy."[9] The Indianapolis-based evangelist Thomas Nelson wanted workers "acquainted with the . . . woes . . . of the oppressed masses" who could "drive degenerate priests, polluted politicians, and plutocratic moneychangers from the temples of piety and politics."[10] The Populist *Nonconformist* hailed one of Nelson's prophetic books as a "'Krupp gun' in the reformed ranks," sure to awaken "the outraged laboring classes."[11] Tomlinson's foray into Populism, then, represented more than a break with the political attachments of his father or an attraction to the concerns of working-class Americans. Populism introduced him to an egalitarian society where unpretentious folk from places like Topeka, Kansas, Corsicana, Texas, and Indianapolis, Indiana, quarried stone from the nation's religious bedrock to hurl at its establishment. It invited him into a biracial alliance welded together by popular discontent, a blue-collar progressivism with room on its platforms for women as well as men. It was a far cry from heaven, but it was almost holiness.

Tomlinson's political career would be as short-lived as the suspense over his party's chances in the 1892 election. Like every other Populist candidate in his county, A. J. took a spectacular beating. With only 135 of 6,200 votes, he finished dead last of four candidates. His only solace came with the recognition that every other Populist candidate in the county had fared even worse. The future for A. J. Tomlinson lay in Holiness, not politics.

Quaker Holiness

Tomlinson had worked closely heretofore with Holiness figures in the Society of Friends but had not yet experienced entire sanctification. Throughout election season, however, a wave of Holiness revivals had been sweeping Westfield. The wave crested in a series of gripping meetings conducted by the famous Quaker evangelists Nathan and Esther Frame. According to one reporter, Esther Frame delivered "the greatest holy ghost sermons that the town has known for years."[12] Shortly thereafter, Tomlinson fell into a bitter struggle with his "old man." When a "sensational power" struck him "like a thunderbolt from the skies," he knew that he had been "sanctified wholly."[13] Tomlinson was now a full-fledged Holiness Quaker.

Holiness Friends struck many as an un-Quakerly lot. Though pacifists in doctrine, their manners were anything but pacific. When the Quaker Holiness patriarch, Amos Kenworthy, asked the Lord to "make a chance" for him to speak at a particular meeting, the Lord replied, "Jump for thy chance."[14] Like evangelist Seth Rees, the "Indiana Earthquaker," Holiness Friends shared a passion for success and regarded mediocrity with withering scorn. "My whole being has revolted against defeat," Rees once blurted. "Win or die!" Their preaching, moreover, sparked outbursts of "genuine Methodist shouting."[15] Ambitious, assertive, pugnacious, inventive, these were Quakers on the go.

Quaker traditionalists lamented the "Methodization of American Quakerism," but the reality was more complex.[16] For one thing, influence ran both ways. True, the encounter with Methodism left Quakers in its wake with names like Asbury Fisher and Lorenzo Dow Williams. But Quaker evangelists bore their testimony widely in Methodist circles, and many Methodists (like Nathan and Esther Frame and William F. Manley) abandoned Methodism for the Society of Friends. Moreover, Quakers enjoyed a prestige beyond their numbers in nineteenth-century America, commanding the respect of even their fiercest competitors. They stood in the public mind as the embodiment of unimpeachable integrity and practical holiness and actively participated in creating the phenomenon that was American Holiness. When Holiness evangelists damned "man-made" creeds and empty rituals, rejected hierarchy and ecclesiasticism, sneered at social pretension, or defined the person and work of the Holy Spirit in terms of extemporaneous inspiration—liable to irrupt in male or female, young or old, clergy or laity—they stood in the shadow of a Quaker anti-structuralism that had leavened popular American piety for more than two centuries. More than mere fancy led B. F. Lawrence, the early Pentecostal historian, to honor them as "our true fathers in the faith."[17]

The Quaker contribution to American Holiness, along with that of thousands of Brethren, Mennonites, German Baptists, Disciples, and others starkly illustrates the composite nature of the movement and suggests that the longstanding habit of dividing Holiness into its Wesleyan and Reformed wings obscures its very essence: a dynamic syncretism that produced a whole greater than the sum of its many parts. Holiness Quakers, then, gave as well as they got. Yet, with success so closely tied to new revivalistic methods and new doctrines like entire sanctification, progress did often come at the expense of traditional distinctives. In addition, Quaker Holiness offered a vista of the more liberating confines of independent Holiness, where the Friend might serve unfettered by any constraint but the call of God. Holiness leaning did not guarantee that one would sell one's Quaker birthright, but it did increase the odds.

Parting with Friends

The lure of Christian service and the encumbrances of daily life converged for A. J. Tomlinson after 1893. His aged parents grew more dependent on their only son. In 1895 a third child, Iris, joined siblings Halcy and Homer in a growing household. Tomlinson tried to provide by imitating his father, combining agriculture with capital venture. In league with an old friend from literary-society days he formed a well-drilling business, hoping to supplement his farm income by providing reliable sources of pure water to local farmers. But A. J.'s business, unlike his father's, had to share time with religious endeavors.

Year by year, the siren song of ministry drew Tomlinson further from the mundane world and closer to the heroic life of Christian service. For one thing, his gifts had begun to be recognized among Holiness Quakers. He represented his meeting at a quarterly conference, superintended a local Bible school, and began to deliver his first tentative sermons. But his engagements also opened doors beyond the Society of Friends. Tomlinson made the acquaintance of a Methodist colporteur and Oberlin graduate, J. B. Mitchell, and in the spring of 1894 the two men founded the Book and Tract Company. That partnership marked the beginning of a long ministry and the beginning of the end of Tomlinson's days as a Quaker.

Mitchell led Tomlinson on short-term missionary excursions into Appalachia, where he distributed literature to poor mountain whites and witnessed a degree of material and spiritual want that moved him deeply. But colportage also introduced him to the more radical spheres of independent Holiness. More precisely, it introduced him to the dynamic evangelist and self-ordained prophet Frank Sandford. After rising through the ranks of New England holiness, the Bates College–educated Sandford had left mentors like A. B. Simpson and Timothy Merritt to champion his own militant brand of Holiness primitivism, which featured an authoritarian ecclesiology, a fervent pursuit of signs and wonders, and a commitment to Christian communalism as described in Acts. In late 1897 Tomlinson traveled to Shiloh, Sandford's Holiness commune near Durham, Maine. While there he was baptized in the Androscoggin River.

Tomlinson's encounter with Sandford convinced him that the Society of Friends, which rejected water baptism and sported an unbiblical name, did not possess the signs of a true church. In the spring of 1898 he submitted his resignation to the Westfield monthly meeting. A year later he led his family and a half dozen other Bible missionaries to the rugged mountains of North Carolina. He had been preceded in the southern mission by a generation of Quaker home missionaries and by advance columns of Holiness evangelists at outposts like the school of the prophets at Beniah, Tennessee, affiliated with B. H. Irwin's Fire-Baptized Holiness Association. But Tomlinson had his own ambitions: a Shiloh in Appalachia.

Visions of Eden

Culberson, North Carolina, posed an unlikely prospect for such aspirations. A mountain village at the state's western edge, run by a few small-town merchants and professionals and surrounded by hardscrabble farms, its chief missionary assets were a railroad and access to the yet more remote hamlets of the poor mountain whites Tomlinson had come to civilize and to save. But the new arrivals saw Culberson through eyes of faith.

The group dropped anchor and settled into a life structured by the Hundred Fold Gospel. That term alluded to the heroic Christianity practiced at Shiloh, where Sandford had read the parable of the sower, with its thirty-, sixty-, and hundredfold yields, as a typology of church membership. Hundredfold members would give their all, selling their possessions and holding all things in common like the early Christians at Jerusalem. Furthermore, the Culberson mission would operate entirely on a faith basis. Following the recently deceased architect of life on faith lines, George Mueller, the missionaries believed that God alone should know and supply, their every need. Tomlinson would publish missionary reports in Holiness papers like Nelson's *Pentecostal Herald,* Martin Wells Knapp's *Revivalist,* the Brethren in Christ *Evangelical Visitor,* and his own small paper, *Samson's Foxes,* but he would make no direct appeal for support.

The work at Culberson began modestly, with scattered colportage, evangelism, and a small elementary school. But Tomlinson did not despise the day of small things. He called his concern Mount Zion Mission Home and saw in it the first fruits of a vast industrial school and orphanage complex inculcating "book knowledge . . . industry and christianity" among the poor. His ultimate goal was grander still. Tomlinson envisioned "a garden of Eaden where God can come and talk with us in the cool of the day, and we will not be ashamed."[18] Of course, the Appalachian soil would have to be prepared before he could plant his paradise.

A. J. Tomlinson tilled that soil with a blend of Holiness rigorism and Yankee hygiene. He denounced "tobacco, opium, pork, tea and coffee" and all other habits "injurious to the health." And he declared "clean hearts . . . clean bodies, clean cloths, clean food and clean homes" to be prerequisites of the Spirit-filled life. That message perfectly echoed the doctrine of uplift preached throughout the North, where agencies like the Children's Aid Society of New York considered soap and water to be moral forces equal to preaching in their line of work.[19]

As an industrial school and Garden of Eden, the mission would fall short. But it marvelously achieved another, unstated objective. Missions like Culberson were only partly concerned with the destiny and welfare of their target population. In the spiritual-warrior culture that was radical Holiness, every mission doubled as a crucible of faith, a purifying tryworks whose end was the proof and perfection of the missionary's own soul. The principles of life on faith lines, plus a remote setting, added to the confrontational Holiness style, equaled an intimate acquaintance with the many faces of hardship: just what a Holiness missionary was looking for. Real saints, according to one esteemed teacher, welcomed suffering as "an opportunity of sweeter union with God." It formed the very terrain of sainthood. Tomlinson's diary chronicled a *via dolorosa* of peculiar efficacy, complete with chronic shortages, grinding poverty, and physical persecution. At the darkest hours he quoted 1 Pet. 1:7 ("the trial of our faith is more precious than gold") and exclaimed, "O this wonderful strain in the trial of my faith."[20]

Tomlinson's neighbors found the mission less edifying and viewed it with mounting suspicion. Its support came almost exclusively from the North and West, and the missionaries themselves supplied virtually the entire Yankee population of the township. The enterprise, then, smacked of Yankee cultural imperialism and arrived—like the expanding national economy, multiplying roads and railways, chain stores, and mail-order catalogs—as a harbinger of that complex blending of regional cultures that spelled doom for southern localism.

These simmering tensions erupted into violence when Tomlinson published an ill-advised missionary report in the July 1901 issue of *Samson's Foxes*. Imagining a northern audience, he introduced "the ignorant whites" served by his mission. By the end of the report he had insulted every segment of the local social order. Area farmers fared poorly because "the dogged tenacity of their prejudice" existed "in proportion to their ignorance." Mountain children were filthy, ill bred, and ate with their fingers. Their parents passed "an unvarying round of reduplicated days," largely "stupefied, dulled, weakened, either by whiskey, tobacco, or poor fare, or all combined." Incompetent teachers offered no help to the illiterate. The Bible, to local "plow handle" preachers, was a "sealed book." Finally, Tomlinson explained that, if his school struggled, it was because the poor whites of the vicinity, "utterly devoid of ambition," viewed education with "an apathy only to be explained by their having been for so many generations without its benefits."[21] The report smoldered with the wrath of a scorned educator.

Unhappily, a paper meant for Yankee eyes fell into the neighbors' hands. Their reaction was not genteel. Toughs accosted some of the missionaries.

A vigilante committee called on Tomlinson and left no doubt about his peril. In mid-August, under cover of darkness, Tomlinson slipped out of town. The following night an angry mob, having lost its prey, stoned the compound and sprayed it with gunfire.

Demoralized and on the run, Tomlinson retreated to Shiloh where he arrived just in time for a grandiose mass rebaptism. Sandford had recently discovered new light on church order and now considered every prior baptism, including his own, to be invalid. Therefore, he promptly rebaptized all of Shiloh into "the Church of the Living God, for the Evangelization of the World, Gathering of Israel, New Order of Things at the Close of the Gentile Age."[22]

Fresh off his new baptism Tomlinson set out again for Culberson. He arrived home in mid-November, but instead of renewal the coming months brought hardship, despair, and live ammunition. Missionaries were stoned and beaten, their homes riddled with bullets. Demoralized workers began to defect. Tomlinson toughed it out for the better part of another year, but in the fall of 1902 he also took a leave of absence. Returning to Indiana, he found refuge near his wife's hometown. His utopian experiment at Culberson had failed, but he had learned valuable lessons. From now on, he would leaven his idealism with a dash of practicality.

Movement Entrepreneur

Eight months in Indiana did wonders for Tomlinson's spiritual and pecuniary circumstances. He worked in a local glass factory and saved his money. His father had died in 1899, and now Tomlinson and his siblings had settled the last of the inheritance. He attended religious meetings, including a conference conducted by George Watson that particularly impressed him. Somewhere along the way he shed his affiliation with Sandford. Appalachia, though, never left his mind. Tomlinson plotted his return, determined that the next time things would be different.

During his years at Culberson, Tomlinson had developed close ties to a number of mountain Holiness preachers, chief among them Richard G. Spurling Jr., William F. Bryant, Frank Porter, and M. S. Lemons. Spurling and Bryant were former Primitive Baptists with Landmark leanings; Frank Porter was a Methodist minister; M. S. Lemons, like Porter, had held credentials with B. H. Irwin's Fire-Baptized Holiness Association. During Tomlinson's absence, Spurling, Bryant, and Porter organized a new church:

the Holiness Church at Camp Creek, North Carolina. The small Appalachian body represented a formidable merger of Landmarkism and Methodist Holiness, the two resurgent religious traditions in the New South.

In May 1903 Tomlinson returned to North Carolina. Shortly after arrival he met up with his old friends and interrogated them about their new church. On June 13, 1903, in a single stroke, he was received in membership, ordained, and appointed pastor of the group's mother congregation. "When A. J. Tomlinson went into anything," Bryant later recalled, "he had to be the head."[23] Though not the founder of the Holiness Church at Camp Creek, Tomlinson would soon make it his own.

The new affiliation wrought a dramatic change in Tomlinson, one strikingly manifest in his diary. Formerly an introspective chronicle of life on faith lines, it resurfaced as a terse ledger of the practical deeds of a tireless minister, tabulating the number of sermons preached, miles traveled, churches organized. The mountain missionary had entered a world where statistics mattered, where success was measured by the indices of institutional growth.

Tomlinson redivivus was an organization man. He took all the work the young sect would give him and in the process created a dependency that placed him at the center of its small orbit. The new style and the new vocation seemed to call for new headquarters, and in the fall of 1904 Tomlinson transferred his base of operations from Culberson, North Carolina, to Cleveland, Tennessee, a midsize town with good schools squarely situated on eastern Tennessee's main thoroughfare. It was a tactical decision of great moment. Now a scant twenty miles from Chattanooga and on a line to Knoxville, Tomlinson had exchanged the remote hamlets of Appalachia for the bustling towns and small cities of the middle South.

In Cleveland, Tennessee, Tomlinson blossomed into a movement entrepreneur. A tireless planter of churches, he tended new churches as tirelessly as he planted them. "There is no chance to rest," he quipped.[24] Tomlinson also cultivated leadership, recruiting, apprenticing, and ordaining fellow workers. By 1906, his attention had turned to the systematic organization of his loosely connected sect. He called a general assembly at Cleveland and a tradition was born. For the next decade delegates of the Church of God, as it would soon be called, came annually to Tomlinson's sanctuary at Cleveland, where he promoted, hosted, and moderated its general assembly.

Tomlinson used his position and prestige to guide the sect toward professionalism. He urged other leaders to look as well as act the ministerial part and even bought new clothes for the rumpled Spurling. Church literature grew more polished, the assemblies more structured and efficient. Tomlinson outfitted a modern business office and had a telephone installed. The Church of God, with Tomlinson at the helm, was a rising enterprise.

The full measure of Tomlinson's talent, however, appeared in his ability to combine administrative gifts with charismatic performance. By the time he joined the Church of God he had developed into a powerful speaker whose sermons provoked startling ecstasies. "People fell in the floor and some writhed like serpents," he noted of one meeting. "Some fell in the road, one seemed to be off in a trance for 4 or 5 hours."[25] His true genius, then, inhered in his knack for striking the fortuitous balance between routine and charisma. The crowds flocked to his meetings, where he lifted them to the transforming heights of religious ecstasy. Then, he incorporated them into the disciplined channels of his church, equal parts charismatic performer and movement builder.

At its general assembly in January 1907, the Holiness Church at Camp Creek adopted a new name: the Church of God. An equally momentous change lay in the offing. For months past, reports of the Azusa Street revival in Los Angeles had circulated in the southern Holiness press. In November 1906 an evangelist with the Holiness Church of North Carolina, G. B. Cashwell, had gone to investigate matters for himself. He returned a month later to publicize Holy Ghost baptism with the evidence of speaking in other tongues and to champion the Pentecostal movement. In June 1907, after investigating a Pentecostal meeting at Birmingham, Alabama, Tomlinson and the principal leaders of the Church of God approved the new doctrine, though none of them could claim the experience. It was just in time for the camp meeting season.

The doctrine proved its worth. Tomlinson's summer campaigns outstripped all of his previous revivals, culminating in a riotous tent meeting in Cleveland that July. For a month solid the night air resounded with old-time Holiness shouting interlaced with bursts of glossolalia. Thousands swarmed into Tomlinson's big top, "praying, singing, shouting, reeling like drunken men." All in all, he boasted, the tent fielded "a mass of happy people."[26] Outside the tent, on the other hand, a mass of disgruntled locals chafed at an intolerable disturbance of the peace.

With Pentecostal baptism on everyone's mind and lips, G. B. Cashwell won an invitation to the Church of God's 1908 general assembly. For more than a year Tomlinson had been preaching an experience that he did not have. And, indeed, for a man who had known his share of eye-popping experiential wonders, it must have been hard to imagine one to top them all—but not for long. With Cashwell behind the pulpit, Tomlinson slid to the floor and commenced a Holy Ghost baptism of epic proportions, complete with ecstatic contortions and reports of levitation, soul travel, and spiritual visions. By the time it subsided, he had spoken, by his count, ten different languages. A. J. Tomlinson had made the short but significant leap from Holiness to Pentecostal.

From Holiness to Pentecost

A. J. Tomlinson had joined the first generation, but his conversion, like the others of that generation, raises perplexing questions. How could men and women habituated to stultifying ecstasies and stark supernatural wonders have been persuaded that their former peak experience had been but a penultimate blessing and not the *real* Holy Ghost baptism at all? An outbreak of glossolalia poses no mystery. It had long existed as a latent necessity, built into the very structure of foundational texts like Acts 2 and Mark 16. The surprising fact is that glossolalia should have acquired such a meaning—the necessary evidence of Holy Ghost baptism—and that it should have become the catalyst for an entirely new movement.

The first step toward comprehending this process may come with the simple recognition that first-generationers were Holiness before they were Pentecostal. That is to say, they shared the assumptions and spiritual idioms of the movement at large and functioned within its interpretive matrix. They could be persuaded, and persuasive, because they weighed evidence on a common Holiness scale and bore witness in the same sacralized forms, the graven narratives whose very predictability convinced hearers of the validity of the experiences they described.

The doctrine of progressive revelation, furthermore, opened the saints to new light. Much has been made, and properly so, of the epistemological gap separating Pentecostals from their cultured despisers. But the ideological difference masked a functional similarity. Liberal modernists stressed the mutability of truth, its historically conditioned and contextually relative nature. Plainfolk modernists like Tomlinson considered truth to be absolute and unchanging. At the same time, however, they taught that its apprehension unfolded gradually and relative to one's "dispensation," and no Holiness saint wished to miss "God's *latest things*."²⁷ When it came to practical adaptability, progressive revelation and cultural relativism were not that far apart.

Finally, glossolalia solved a technical difficulty. The subjective nature of Holy Ghost baptism left an uncomfortable ambiguity. As a spiritual landmark built on potentially shifting sand, it could be questioned and even revised. Tomlinson, for instance, claimed to have been sanctified in 1893. Three years later, he received the Holy Ghost, normally a synonym for sanctification within the movement. Perhaps he understood the 1896 experience as a third blessing on the order of B. H. Irwin's baptism of fire. More likely, his encounter with Sandford had convinced him that his former experience had not in fact been the real thing. Later, after his disaffection from Sandford and in light of his Pentecostal experience, Tomlinson reverted to 1893 as the date of his authentic sanctification. Glossolalia, as the incontrovertible certificate of Spirit baptism, would prove less subject to such vagaries.

Once first-generationers had been persuaded—by the appropriate evidence presented in the appropriate forms—that their earlier baptism had been but a penultimate experience, the new perspective fueled a self-fulfilling expectation. Through the complex algorithm of spiritual consciousness, few would be disappointed in their quest for the ultimate.

Without the exclusivist meaning given by Pentecostals to glossolalia, the phenomenon would probably have been absorbed as a welcome addition to the panoply of Holiness signs and wonders. At the least it could have coexisted uneasily within the broader movement as a doctrinal peculiarity, like Irwin's fire baptism. Glossolalia did, of course, alter Holiness worship subtly but significantly and therefore fostered a distinctive worship experience. But alone it could not have demarcated Pentecostalism from its parent culture. Tongues did not make a difference so much as it was made into a difference, when some of those who experienced it transformed it into something more.

Decisive in this process was the character of the difference-makers. Ambitious, entrepreneurial, independent minded, they were temperamentally inclined to see and therefore to advertise their Pentecostal experience not as a powerful manifestation of Holiness, but as the salient feature of a new dispensation: new wine fit for new wineskins. Following the lead of Charles Parham, they constructed a double dividing wall, using hard doctrine to build hard boundaries. First, they distinguished Holy Ghost baptism from sanctification (previously thought to be identical or at least roughly coterminous). Second, they enthroned tongues as the only and necessary evidence of that baptism. In two fell swoops they disqualified all Holy Ghost baptisms but their own and touched off a civil war within the realm of radical Holiness.

That war, in its own right, yielded important cultural spoils, and none proved more valuable than the renovation of stigma. Radical Holiness had always been what some sociologists call collective religion: costly, exclusive, long on sacrifice. Pentecostalism, with its abrasive ecstasies and angular doctrine, sharpened the oppositional posture on which radical Holiness had depended. For Tomlinson and his church, the Pentecostal turn coincided with a new and more virulent round of persecution. And throughout the movement, converts regaled nodding audiences with stories of mistreatment at the hands of sinners and of former Holiness friends alike. Reviled, persecuted, falsely accused for righteousness' sake: theirs was the kingdom of heaven.

Like a Mighty Army

However one might explain the effect, the Pentecostal experience clearly energized those who embraced it. The Church of God had grown rapidly before. Now, it grew by orders of magnitude. Furthermore, in Tomlinson it had a leader who knew how to make the most of opportunity. For one thing, he understood that, if the organization's structure of management did not expand, any new gains would be lost. So he ordained bishops, deacons, and evangelists with alacrity. He also embarked on extended recruitment tours throughout the South and especially in Florida, by 1909 one of the nation's most rapidly growing regions.

But with new promise came new peril, and Tomlinson ran a gauntlet of challenges. Worldly persecutors severely tried the new sect. Within the burgeoning Pentecostal movement, Tomlinson vied with other ambitious figures for influence and control. Finally, he faced opposition within his own church, on the one hand, from routinizing forces that wished to impose more regularity on worship and on women, and, on the other hand, from localists who resisted his efforts to centralize authority within the Church of God.

By 1910 Tomlinson had weathered the fiercest storm on the routinizing front. An upstart minister, John B. Goins, had attempted to constrain tongues speaking and silence women according to Paul's injunctions in 1 Cor. 11–14. But Tomlinson prevailed, and with him the right of women to speak and of all to enjoy the blessings of freewheeling worship. By 1913 he had outflanked the congregationalists as well. On the heels of persistent behind-the-scenes maneuvering, the general assembly created a position tailor-made for Tomlinson. As general overseer in a now clearly episcopal system, he held final authority over all ordinations and pastoral appointments. In 1914 he was elected to that position for life.

Tomlinson had demonstrated the administrative skills needed to expand and consolidate a movement simultaneously and the finesse to achieve his goals without unduly alienating friends or empowering enemies. Furthermore, he had struck a dynamic balance between primitivism and pragmatism, charisma and routine. Rather than regulate worship (the product) within a laissez-faire organization, as Goins had wished, Tomlinson would regulate the organization (the system of delivery) and let the worship flow freely. "God runs His universe in a systematic way," he explained to the 1913 general assembly. Just as "a machine must be perfectly adjusted to thresh out grain," so the Church of God needed to fine-tune its ecclesiastical machinery to achieve apostolic results. And results followed. In 1903 Tomlinson had encountered a backwoods communion of perhaps two dozen members. Fourteen years later it boasted more than ten thousand members in twenty states and the Caribbean.

Ironically, that rapid growth and Tomlinson's equally rapid accumulation of power contained the seeds of his undoing. By 1915 the overseer had reached a Pentecostal version of high-church ecclesiology. Inspired by the ante-Nicene fathers, he accepted the tradition that James, the Lord's brother, had ruled the church after Christ's death as the bishop of bishops, and he saw himself as the latter-day James for God's latter-day church. Tomlinson also endorsed Cyprian's pronouncement that the bishop is in the church, and the church in the bishop. As his authority increased, anxieties sharpened within the denomination's inner circle.

The strain of leadership, moreover, intensified as the church grew.

Between 1917 and 1922 the Church of God doubled again in size, from ten to twenty thousand members. Ever ambitious, Tomlinson expanded church services apace, adding an orphanage and a new auditorium at Cleveland, vastly enlarging the publishing facilities and launching a Bible school and church brokerage. Always fearful of waste and mismanagement, and always certain that no one could do a job quite so well as himself, he tried to administer all facets of the work. His greatest miscalculation came when he persuaded the general assembly to revise its tithing system by channeling all receipts into a central fund, under his control, from which pastoral salaries would be paid. With unsupervised discretion over all finances, enormous demands on his time, heavy debt hanging over his cherished publishing house, and a vague mandate to apply funds as necessary in emergencies, Tomlinson diverted tithes to pay for publishing. The decision came back to haunt him.

Out in the field, of course, ministers noticed the shortfall, and the elders ordered an audit. In an ostensibly unrelated move endorsed by Tomlinson himself, the 1921 general assembly approved a constitution. The constitution promised to secure the church's claim to its property, but it also created a court of justice with the power to impeach. Later that year the elders confronted Tomlinson with the results of their audit. He confessed to the misappropriation of funds and agreed to disclose his actions fully at the next general assembly.

Disclose he did, but not before blasting his elders and denouncing the constitution. To make matters worse, he spun his arbitrary conduct as a heroic effort to save the church from the shame and reproach of bankruptcy and then introduced a proposal to repeal the constitution. The elders countered with a measure reducing the general overseer's power and transferring his administrative duties to various committees. When the two proposals went before the general assembly, the elders won. By the 1920s the ideal of benevolent autocracy—the swashbuckling captain of industry—had lost much of its luster, and perhaps the new prestige attached to committees and their association with reform, regularity, and expertise worked in the elders' favor. But whatever the explanation, Tomlinson's solitary reign was over.

The end of the 1922 general assembly signaled the beginning of an acrimonious schism. The elders impeached Tomlinson, and Tomlinson excommunicated the elders. The exact size of each faction is impossible to determine, but Tomlinson had clearly lost the lion's share of his denomination. For years the two sides fought over divided congregations and dismayed members. For decades they litigated the right to use the Church of God name, until the elders' party agreed to become the Church of God (Cleveland, Tennessee), while Tomlinson's faction settled on the Church of God of Prophecy.

A New Birth of Freedom

When the patriarch reorganized his loyalists, perhaps six thousand in number, he instituted an authoritarian episcopacy that rendered his power unassailable and set about recouping his losses. The genial autocrat traveled, evangelized, and organized assiduously, wooing the undecided and motivating the faithful. His circumstances had been reduced but his authority was now unencumbered.

Among other things, the new liberty allowed Tomlinson to indulge his taste for theater and spectacle. Together with his son Homer, who divided time between the Church of God and an advertising career in New York City, he orchestrated flamboyant parades to inaugurate each general assembly. The All Nations Parade in 1937 stretched for three miles and drew thirty floats, 123 ribbon-bedecked cars, and three brass bands. The assemblies themselves matched the parades for pomp and circumstance. Congregations and departments delivered "short, snappy" presentations, always full of "pep." The Church of God stood on display and Tomlinson wanted the world to see a "lively, industrious and energetic set of people."[28]

Tomlinson implemented fascinating theological innovations as well, none more so than his speckled-bird doctrine. Reading Jer. 12:9 ("Mine heritage is unto me as a speckled bird"), Tomlinson saw a type of the church. But what might it mean for the church to be speckled? The true church, he divined, would unite all races, "the whites, the colored, the browns . . . the yellow" under "one rule, one faith . . . all one."[29] The Church of God promptly adopted a folksong made famous by Roy Acuff, "The Great Speckled Bird," as its anthem. People of color had been woven into the ecclesiology of the Church of God, and Tomlinson avidly recruited minorities to prove that the "middle wall of partition" had indeed fallen. The results were mixed, but he made an honest effort and always drew attention to minorities at general assemblies. When the church's most prominent African American, Stanley Ferguson, died, flags were lowered to half-mast and the church observed three days of mourning.

Another mark of Tomlinson's liberation appeared in his growing predilection for sacred symbols. In 1933, after commissioning a church flag, he initiated a flags-on-graves ceremony to commemorate departed saints. By 1940 he had begun the rich sacralization of time and space that some have called his mountain theology. Impressed by the prophetic symmetries knit into the tapestry of his life, he returned to Burger Mountain near Camp Creek, North Carolina, to mark the place where in 1903 God had opened his eyes to the true church. A portentous fact had recently dawned on him. In the same epochal year that God had revealed His church, reforming in a humble cabin at the western extreme of North Carolina, the Wright Brothers, at the far eastern extreme, had embarked on their legendary flight. And the same chapter of Isaiah had prophesied both: "Arise, shine; for thy light is come" (Isa. 60:1); "Who are these that fly as a cloud?" (Isa. 60:8). The two events, Tomlinson now perceived, framed the meaning of the end times just as Camp Creek and Kitty Hawk framed the state of North Carolina.

That first marker on Burger Mountain soon blossomed into Fields of the Wood, a pastoral shrine/sacred theme park memorializing those prophetic events. In 1941 Tomlinson conducted the inaugural ceremony, delivering his sermon while church-leased airplanes droned overhead, dropping gospel tracts in fulfillment of Deut. 32:2 ("May my teaching drop as the rain"). Both the airplane and the Church of God, Tomlinson told the gathered saints and reporters, were last-days products. "Trace the airplane," he cryptically averred, "and you trace the final last days Church."[30] A committee was commissioned to mark historic sites related to the rise of the church both in America and in Bible lands.[31] The Church of God would have a myth of origins, complete with an ecclesiastical calendar and the ritual commemoration of sacred time and space.

Tomlinson's mountain theology reflected a triumphalism won through forty years of organizational and personal success, and old age found him more intoxicated than ever with the privilege of the present and the promise of the future. "I do not understand why people want to go back to the early Church," he puzzled. "Those were great days, but look what we are and what is just ahead."[32] If his eyes searched the horizon, however, his daily habits increasingly led him to Fields of the Wood. His strolls there, someone noted, gave him "the happiest moments of his life in his later years."[33] Small wonder. There he served as the curator of his own memory and enjoyed at leisure a shrine to his own legacy.

By then, however, Tomlinson's health had been poor for several years. A stroke in 1937 had left him enfeebled, and, on September 16, 1943, upon returning from his office near midnight after a typically long workday, he collapsed again. Scarcely able to communicate, he lingered for another two weeks. Finally, on October 2, 1943, Ambrose Jessup Tomlinson passed away. His life had spanned the interim between our nation's two greatest wars. Born in the age of the warhorse, he had died at the brink of the atomic age. His legacy includes, in addition to Fields of the Wood, the Church of God (Cleveland, Tennessee); the Church of God of Prophecy; the Church of God (Zion Hill); the Church of God (Scottsville, Kentucky); the Church of God (Original); and the Church of God (Jerusalem Acres). Together they lay claim to one million members in North America, and six million worldwide.

Conclusion

A. J. Tomlinson and his fellow first-generationers would impress any close observer with their restlessness, their insatiable drive and energy. Like the prophet Jeremiah, they had a burning fire shut up in their bones. They had this in common with a great many late Victorians: there seems to have been a surplus of the type in that striving generation. Pentecostals, however, distinguished themselves in their field of endeavor, expending their activism on spiritual reform and the cultural production of religious meaning. They partook in what was perceived to be a spontaneous revival that eluded human instrumentality and control. In fact, that revival was orchestrated by a score of vibrant networks, which were in turn directed by savvy movement builders, men and women who would within a half century transform American Pentecostalism into a religious third force.

A composite profile of that generation would also demonstrate that the weakness for pageantry, self-promotion, and pop culture so characteristic of the movement today does not derive from a recent declension. Contemporary Pentecostalism did not succumb to the seductions of a media- and entertainment-driven culture. Seduction it may have been, but it formed an essential part of the original Pentecostal formula. Likewise, the routinizing impulse visible in today's sprawling Pentecostal empires does not reflect a recent accommodation to worldly bureaucratic means.[34] A passionate desire for the orderly, systematic, and efficient distribution of charisma characterized many among that first generation.

A. J. Tomlinson embodied these several traits. He was the quintessential entrepreneur, stubbornly nonconformist and disinclined to endeavors not of his own choosing. In his mid-thirties he set out to launch an enterprise in Culberson, North Carolina. He took risks and suffered the consequences. But failure did not deter him, and eventually his drive, nerve, and talent paid off in an organization that he did not launch but did commandeer. There, too, he would suffer his share of losses, but the same arrogance, the same sense of destiny and entitlement that undermined him also in the end redeemed him. He died the chief executive officer of a thriving concern, all the more remarkable for the delicate and specialized nature of its product. His was a manufactory of mental worlds, producing and distributing a flourishing line of sacred canopies. He had given it an ancient name: The Church of God, "fair as the moon, clear as the sun, and terrible as an army with banners." But, like the other institutional edifices of Pentecostalism, daily compounding their thousands, its architect was a plainfolk modernist.[35]

Afterword

David Edwin Harrell Jr.

The significance of a historical narrative depends to some degree on the present and the future—on outcomes. Fifty years ago, the life stories told here would have been considered eccentric and ephemeral, hardly worth the attention of serious historians. Even twenty-five years ago, at the very time that the Pentecostal/charismatic movement was exploding in the United States and around the world, few academics were aware of the power of the movement, much less of its roots.

Today, we know better. In the twentieth century Pentecostals reshaped the religious demography of the world. It is difficult to judge accurately their numbers at the present time, but the spread of the movement is probably the most important Protestant story of the twentieth century. Religious demographer David Barrett has judged that worldwide in 2000 around 63 million people were members of 740 Pentecostal denominations; another 295 million were affiliated with "independent neocharismatic denominations and networks"; and an estimated 175 million more were members of "non-Pentecostal mainline denominations with large organized internal charismatic movements."* The yearning for a supernatural outpouring of the Holy Spirit that stirred American religion at the end of the nineteenth century moved the world by the end of the twentieth century.

The men and women discussed in this book were pioneers who crafted twentieth-century Pentecostalism's message, its institutions, and its modus operandi. The editors have gathered this collection into broad groupings, addressing three themes that consumed the movement's first generation. First, these essays throw light on the emergence of a coherent Pentecostal

---

*David Barrett, "The Worldwide Holy Spirit Renewal," in *The Century of the Holy Spirit,* ed. Vinson Synan (Nashville: Thomas Nelson Publishers, 2001), 381–82.

message through the probing of radical Holiness leaders before and after 1900. Second, these biographies illustrate the extraordinary social and theological creativity of a movement that embraced the supernatural power of the Holy Sprit to raise up a new generation of prophets and prophetesses. In a movement where the only heresy was to "quench the Spirit," free spirits explored the boundaries of social and theological convention. Finally, this book introduces a group of organizers and church builders who tried to bring intellectual and institutional order to the freewheeling movement.

To be sure, we have seen idiosyncrasy and fanaticism in the preceding pages. The Holy Spirit led some down roads that few would follow. Still, even those on the margins of early Pentecostalism held a fascination for the millions around the world who embraced the guidance of the Holy Spirit. In a world where all things are possible, every prophet's message was deemed worthy of some honor. Others discussed in this book sought to bring order to a theologically open movement that was driven by private inspiration. Some of these first-generation leaders were gifted and subtle thinkers who constructed doctrinal systems that may deservedly be called popular theology. While none of the men and women in this collection was formally educated, they struggled with theology just as surely as did their contemporary, Reinhold Niebuhr. Out of the maze of new insights and truths they received through their openness to the leading of the Holy Spirit, they constructed a complex but increasingly unified Pentecostal theology.

Often the origins of successful popular religious movements are shrouded in obscurity by the time the movement gains notoriety. Fortunately, the rise of Pentecostalism in the twentieth century has been so precipitous that its founders and early leaders are no more than two generations removed from the present. A new group of scholars has appeared in recent years, arising largely from within the ranks of Pentecostalism, intent on rescuing these early leaders from obscurity. The stories told here are of irresistible interest to the millions around the world who have embraced Pentecostalism. For scholars, they do much to illumine the origins of the century's most vital religious movement.

This book brims with intriguing tales of bold and adventuresome religious pioneers launching out into new and uncharted waters. They proved willing to experiment with the mores of society and with the conventionalities of religious thought in creative and experimental ways. Sneered at by

DAVID EDWIN HARRELL JR.

their more sophisticated contemporaries, labeled Holy Rollers by the popular press and mainstream religious leaders, they sensed that God was doing a mighty work through them. Whatever the source, they were certainly right about the outcome.

NOTES

Introduction
James R. Goff Jr. and Grant Wacker

1. Peter W. Williams, *Popular Religion in America* (Englewood Cliffs, N.J.: Prentice-Hall, 1980), 144. In this editors' introduction we have drawn ideas and passages from James R. Goff Jr., *Fields White unto Harvest: Charles F. Parham and the Missionary Origins of Pentecostalism* (Fayetteville: University of Arkansas Press, 1988), introduction; Grant Wacker, "Searching for Eden with a Satellite Dish: Primitivism, Pragmatism, and the Pentecostal Character," in *The Primitive Church in the Modern World,* ed. Richard T. Hughes (Urbana: University of Illinois Press, 1995), 139–66; and Grant Wacker, *Heaven Below: Early Pentecostals and American Culture* (Cambridge, Mass.: Harvard University Press, copyright 2001), introduction and chap. 9, reprinted with permission of the publisher.

2. Wacker, *Heaven Below,* "Appendix: U.S. Pentecostal Statistics"; David B. Barratt and Todd M. Johnson, "Annual Statistical Table on Global Mission: 2000," *International Bulletin of Missionary Research* 23 (January 2000): 25.

3. *Christian Century,* January 18, 1978, 35; Vinson Synan, "Pentecostalism: William Seymour," *Christian History* 65 (winter 2000): 17.

4. Reuben A. Torrey, *What the Bible Teaches* (New York: Fleming Revell, 1898), 272.

5. For the blending of purity and power themes at the grassroots, see, for example, the *Constitution and By-Laws and Minutes of the First Session of the North Carolina Holiness Convention* (Goldsboro, N.C.: Nash Brothers, 1899), 1.

6. Wacker, *Heaven Below,* chap. 12.

7. See Wacker, *Heaven Below,* 275 n. 21, for an analysis of early Pentecostal growth statistics.

8. Gastón Espinosa, "Borderland Religion: Los Angeles and the Origins of the Latino Pentecostal Movement in the U.S., Mexico, and Puerto Rico, 1900–1945" (Ph.D. diss., University of California at Santa Barbara, 1999), 95–96 and chap. 3.

9. Henry P. Van Dusen, "Force's Lessons for Others," *Life,* June 9, 1958, and Everett Wilson, "World Pentecostalism: Its Emergence and Dynamics," paper presented to the American Society of Church History annual meeting, Washington, D.C., January 1999.

10. *Sacred meteor* is borrowed from Russell P. Spittler, who uses the term in a somewhat different context in "Scripture and the Theological Enterprise," in *The Use of the Bible in Theology: Evangelical Options,* ed. Robert K. Johnston (Atlanta: John Knox Press, 1985), 63. For bibliography on Parham, Seymour, and McPherson, see Augustus Cerillo Jr. and Grant Wacker, "Bibliography and Historiography of Pentecostalism in the United States," in *New International Dictionary of the Pentecostal and Charismatic Movements* (Grand Rapids, Mich.: Zondervan, 2002), by title. For documentation of the interpretation offered in this paragraph, see Goff, *Fields White unto Harvest,* and Wacker, *Heaven Below,* throughout.

11. *Apostolic Faith* (Los Angeles), October 1906, 4. The writer was arguing for the revival's directly supernatural origin—effectively the same as ahistoricity.

12. M. L. Ryan, in *Chinese Recorder,* May 1915, 323.

13. *Faithful Standard,* October 1922, 16.

14. W. J. S. [William J. Seymour], in *Apostolic Faith,* June–September 1907, 3.

15. *Minutes of the General Council of the Assemblies of God . . . 1914,* introduction, 2.

16. Elizabeth V. Baker and Coworkers, *Chronicles of a Faith Life* (1915–16; reprint, New York: Garland Publishing, 1985), 134. Baker was referring to the 1904–5 Wales revival, but clearly the comment applied more broadly.

17. *Pentecost,* November 1908, 3.

18. *Latter Rain Evangel,* October 1908, 1.

John Alexander Dowie: Harbinger of Pentecostal Power
Grant Wacker, Chris R. Armstrong, and Jay S. F. Blossom

This article is partly based on Grant Wacker, "Communitarian Theocracy in the Twentieth Century: John Alexander Dowie and the Christian Catholic Apostolic Church in Zion City, Illinois," seminar paper, Harvard Divinity School, 1972, and "Marching to Zion: Religion in a Modern Utopian Community," *Church History* 54 (December 1985): 496–511. Section heads come from "Marching to Zion," Robert Lowry's 1867 adaptation of the Isaac Watts hymn "Come, Ye that Love the Lord."

1. Ernest Sutherland Bates, *Dictionary of American Biography* 5 (1930): 413–14; Philip L. Cook, *Zion City, Illinois: Twentieth-Century Utopia* (Syracuse, N.Y.: Syracuse University Press, 1996), 6; John Julius Halsey, "The Genesis of the Modern Prophet," *American Journal of Sociology* 9 (November 1903): 311; Rolvix Harlan, *John Alexander Dowie and the Christian Catholic Apostolic Church in Zion* (Evansville, Wis.: R. M. Antes, 1906), 29.

2. Gordon Lindsay, *The Life of John Alexander Dowie, Whose Trials—Tragedies—and Triumphs Are the Most Fascinating Object Lesson of Christian History* (Dallas: Voice of Healing Publishing, 1951), 25.

3. Ibid., 45.

4. Cook, *Zion City,* 9–10; Lindsay, *Life,* 76–79.

5. Lindsay, *Life,* 86.

6. Ibid., 90.

7. Halsey, "Genesis," 314.

8. Lindsay, *Life,* 106, 121.

9. Halsey, "Genesis," 316–17.

10. See for example *Chicago Dispatch,* December 13, 1895, in Lindsay, *Life,* 108.

11. Luther P. Gerlach and Virginia H. Hine, *People, Power, Change: Movements of Social Transformation* (Indianapolis: Bobbs-Merrill, 1970), 173, 180.

12. Halsey, "Genesis," 314–15; "The Dowie Movement in Chicago," *Outlook* 68 (June 22, 1901): 429.

13. Lindsay, *Life,* 152.

14. Cook, *Zion City,* 21–22; Lindsay, *Life,* 162; John Swain, "John Alexander Dowie: The Prophet and His Profits: A Study, at First Hand, of 'A Modern Elijah,'" *Century*

Illustrated Magazine 64 (October 1902): 939; John Alexander Dowie, *Coming City* 1 (November 28, 1900): 140.

15. Zion Historical Society, "Dowie's Dream," *What's in Zion,* ser. 3 (1970): 12; Halsey, "Genesis," 322; *Leaves of Healing* 17 (September 30, 1905): 189.

16. Zion Historical Society, "Dowie's Dream," 19.

17. *Zion Banner* 1 (July 10, 1901): 136; *Leaves of Healing* 8 (April 6, 1901): 750.

18. Lindsay, *Life,* 155; Halsey, "Genesis," 327.

19. Lindsay, *Life,* 234–35. Note the addition of "Apostolic" in the church's title.

20. *Zion Banner* 1 (July 24, 1901): 161–68.

21. *Zion Banner* 1 (June 12, 1901): 65; *Leaves of Healing* 9 (July 6, 1901): 332, 334.

22. *Leaves of Healing* 9 (June 29, 1901): 303; 8 (April 6, 1901): 765.

23. Cook, *Zion City,* 198, 204, 214; Lindsay, *Life,* 230–47; Harlan, *Dowie,* 19–20; Arthur W. Newcomb, *Dowie: Anointed of the Lord* (New York: Century, 1930), 350, 395.

24. *Zion Banner* 1 (July 3, 1901): 114.

25. Lindsay, *Life,* 91.

26. Swain, "Prophet," 943; Harlan, *Dowie,* 71, 78–79.

27. Virtually any issue of *Leaves of Healing* or *Zion Banner.*

28. *Leaves of Healing* 17 (July 1, 1905): 362.

29. Ibid., 361; 17 (April 22, 1905): 8; Harlan, *Dowie,* 17; *Leaves of Healing* 9 (June 29, 1901): 229, 300–303.

30. *Leaves of Healing* 17 (April 22, 1905): 7.

31. Arthur Newcomb, general manager of Zion Printing and Publishing House, some-time ghostwriter for Dowie editorials, and eventual bitter critic, writing in *Coming City* 1 (January 9, 1901): 178.

32. *Zion Banner* 1 (July 17, 1901): 148.

33. *Coming City* 1 (November 28, 1900): 134.

34. Harlan, *Dowie,* 2.

35. Swain, "Prophet," 944.

36. *Zion Banner* 1 (June 12, 1901): 75.

37. *Leaves of Healing* 17 (June 3, 1905): 247.

38. Harlan, *Dowie,* 80.

39. For example, *Leaves of Healing* 17 (June 3, 1905): 238.

40. Harlan, *Dowie,* 140.

41. Gerlach and Hine, *People,* 161.

42. *Leaves of Healing* 17 (April 29, 1905): 43.

43. Wacker, *Heaven Below.*

44. "Sun Interviews New Evangelist," *Waukegan (Ill.) Daily Sun,* September 29, 1906, 1.

45. "Horrors: Dowie Wore Evening Dress," *Waukegan (Ill.) Daily Sun,* October 18, 1906, 3; "Gift of the Tongue: What Means It?" *Waukegan (Ill.) Daily Sun,* October 19, 1906, 7.

46. *Waukegan (Ill.) Daily Sun,* October 22, 1906, 5; November 5, 1906, 7; December 18, 1906, 3.

47. Paul G. Chappell, "The Divine Healing Movement in America" (Ph.D. diss., Drew University, 1983), 350–51.

48. Edith L. Blumhofer, *"Pentecost in My Soul": Explorations in the Meaning of Pentecostal Experience in the Early Assemblies of God* (Springfield, Mo.: Gospel Publishing House, 1989), 171–74.

49. Ibid., 191–208.

50. Chappell, "Divine Healing Movement," 352–56; Blumhofer, *"Pentecost in My Soul,"* 41–46; Edith L. Blumhofer, "The Christian Catholic Apostolic Church and the Apostolic Faith: A Study in the 1906 Pentecostal Revival," *Charismatic Experiences in History,* ed. Cecil M. Robeck Jr. (Peabody, Mass.: Hendrickson, 1985), 139. Gordon P. Gardiner tells the stories of all the former Dowieites mentioned here, plus many others, in his *Out of Zion into All the World* (Shippensburg, Pa.: Companion Press, 1990).

51. John Alexander Dowie's periodicals—*Leaves of Healing, The Coming City,* and *The Zion Banner*—are the best primary sources for his life and work. Many newspapers and magazines published articles on Dowie during his heyday, including *Munsey's Magazine* (September 1902), *Literary Digest* (March 21, 1903; October 24, 1903; October 31, 1903; December 12, 1903), and *The Outlook* (June 22, 1901; October 24, 1903; October 31, 1903; April 14, 1906). *Dowie: Anointed of the Lord* (New York: Century, 1930) is a thinly veiled historical novel written by one of the prophet's top lieutenants, Arthur W. Newcomb. The first full-length academic study of Dowie was Harlan's *Dowie,* while the most recent is the late Philip L. Cook's *Zion City,* which includes an extensive bibliography. Dowie's place in the larger communitarian and faith-healing traditions are assessed in Wacker, "Marching to Zion," and in Jonathan R. Baer, "Redeemed Bodies: The Functions of Healing in Incipient Pentecostalism," *Church History: Studies in Christianity and Culture* 70 (December 2001): 735–71.

E. L. Harvey: The Price of Discipleship
William Kostlevy

1. Jack London, "Holy Jumpers Conduct Their Service," *Boston American,* December 19, 1903.

2. As Holiness and Pentecostal groups have sought acceptance in the wider culture, the crucial roles played by such communities as Zion, Shiloh, Zarephath, and the MCA have disappeared from collective memory. On the Assemblies of God leaders with ties to Zion, see Edith Blumhofer, *The Assemblies of God: A Chapter in American Pentecostalism, Volume 1 to 1941* (Springfield, Mo.: Gospel Publishing House, 1989), 113–16. Also see Robert S. Fogarty, *All Things New: American Communes and Utopian Societies, 1860–1914* (Chicago: University of Chicago Press, 1990).

3. Marian Madison, "Career of a Methodist," *Burning Bush,* June 13, 1950; Mrs. E. L. Harvey, "A Page of My Experience: A Personal Testimony," *Burning Bush,* June 24, 1909; and Mariam Madison, "A Page from the Annuals of Faith," *Burning Bush,* January 2, 1941.

4. Mrs. Edwin L. Harvey, "Our Work from Its Beginning," *Burning Bush,* June 3, 1920.

5. Bernard Farson, "Autobiographical Letters," Metropolitan Church Association Collection, B. L. Fisher Library, Asbury Theological Seminary, Wilmore, Ky.

6. On Farson's role in Chicago Methodism, see "Chicago and Vicinity," *Northwest Christian Advocate,* August 11, 1897.

7. Central to the Holiness movement was Methodism's historic belief that, following

conversion, all Christians needed a second religious experience of purification and empowerment, commonly called "Christian perfection" or "entire sanctification." Among helpful works on the Holiness movement are Charles E. Jones, *Perfectionist Persuasion: The Holiness Movement and American Methodism* (Metuchen, N.J.: Scarecrow Press, 1974), and Melvin Easterday Dieter, *The Holiness Revival of the Nineteenth Century,* rev. ed. (Lanham, Md.: Scarecrow Press, 1996).

8. Although history has been cruel by remembering him primarily as the forebear of a family of prominent actors, Carradine [1848–1931] was one of the most popular and controversial Methodist leaders of the late nineteenth century. Born in Mississippi, he was licensed to the ministry of the Methodist Episcopal Church, South, in 1874 and assigned to an isolated rural circuit. In spite of humble beginnings, Carradine rose to prominence, establishing a reputation as a powerful preacher and social reformer. His attacks upon the highly profitable Louisiana lottery led to the lottery's demise and earned him a national reputation. By 1890 he had become pastor of a large congregation in St. Louis, where he angered wealthy parishioners and denominational leaders with his attacks on the dress, lifestyles, and social activities of upper-class urban Methodists. In 1893, to the relief of the Methodist hierarchy, Carradine entered a full-time evangelistic ministry. See Beverly Carradine, *Graphic Scenes* (Cincinnati: God's Revivalist, 1911), and Martin Wells Knapp, *Pentecostal Preachers* (Salem, Ohio: Convention Bookstore, n.d.), 10–14.

9. On Harvey's struggle to experience entire sanctification, see Farson, "Autobiographical Letters."

10. Edwin L. Harvey, *Sermons on Bible Characters* (Waukesha, Wis.: Metropolitan Church Association, 1909), 186. See also Harvey's description of his experience in "God Answering By Fire, or the Great Chicago Revival."

11. London, "Holy Jumpers Conduct Their Service." The most spirited defenses of demonstrations were by Henry L. Harvey and F. Louis Mitchel. See especially Henry L. Harvey, "A Reasonable Faith," *Burning Bush,* November 16, 1916, 2. On the interracial character of jumping, see the MCA's systematic defense of its worship. G. W. Henry, *History of the Jumpers, or Shouting Genuine and Spurious: A History of the Outward Demonstrations of the Spirit* (Waukesha, Wis.: Metropolitan Church Association, 1909).

12. The point that muckraking journalism had its roots in nineteenth-century evangelicalism is made in Richard Hofstadter, *The Age of Reform: From Bryan to F.D.R.* (New York: Alfred A. Knopf, 1955), 186–214. On the religious roots of the muckrakers and other Progressive Era reformers and on the muckrakers' tendency to see exposé as an end in itself, see Robert M. Crunden, *Ministers of Reform: The Progressives' Achievement in American Civilization* (Urbana: University of Illinois Press, 1984), 165. The very term *muckraker,* from Bunyan's *Pilgrim's Progress,* reflects the moralistic and evangelical world of the muckrakers and their readers. The quotation is from "Is Exposing Sin Wrong?" *Burning Bush,* December 22, 1904, 7.

13. *Burning Bush,* December 4, 1902, 2.

14. See "Who Are the Real Come-Outers," *Burning Bush,* October 30, 1902, 1, and "The Church Situation," *Burning Bush,* January 29, 1903, 1, 4.

15. On Holiness evangelists as cultural figures, see Bud Robinson, *Pitchers of Cream* (Louisville: Pentecostal Publishing Co., 1906).

16. On the use of cartoons, see "The Thirtieth Anniversary of the Birth of the *Burning Bush* and Its Mission through the Years," *Burning Bush,* May 26, 1932, 8–9. The discussion

of the source of the cartoons is from E. L. Harvey, "Herod and Pilate Unity," *Burning Bush,* September 8, 1904, 7.

17. On the Buffalo Rock camp meeting, see W. E. Shepard, "Bloomfield, Iowa," *Nazarene Messenger,* September 25, 1902, 7.

18. The first mention that the Bible school was operating on "apostolic lines" is in the *Burning Bush,* June 23, 1904, issue. Other important early articles in the *Bush* are Mrs. E. L. Harvey, "Faith Line," July 28, 1904, 3; E. L. Harvey, "Real Crucifixion," October 6, 1904, 5; "Bring in the Tithes," October 6, 1906, 9.

19. Membership statistics are in Department of Commerce and Labor, Bureau of the Census, *Religious Census: 1906,* pt. 2 (Washington, D.C.: GPO, 1910), 281–82. On the overcrowded conditions, see F. M. Messenger, "Waukesha," *Burning Bush,* November 16, 1905, 7.

20. On Messenger's experience as a mill superintendent, see "F. M. Messenger," *Burning Bush,* June 6, 1903, 4, and F. M. Messenger, *Catacombs of Worldly Success, or History of Coarsellor Dell* (Waukesha, Wis.: Metropolitan Church Association, 1910), 34, 78–89. Correspondence concerning Messenger's discharge by the Grosvenor-Dale Company is published in F. M. Messenger, "Sowing to the Flesh," *Burning Bush,* December 15, 1904, 11.

21. On the Messenger family's decision to give up their personal property, see Mrs. F. M. Messenger, "Since Giving Up All for Jesus," *Burning Bush,* September 7, 1905, 5.

22. The announcement of the move to Waukesha is in "Our New Location," *Burning Bush,* September 7, 1905, 10. Also see "Is the Band Coming?" *Waukesha Freeman,* December 21, 1905, 1.

23. The resort is described in a four-page pamphlet, Marian L. Madison, "The Fountain Spring House," 1961.

24. Madison, "Fountain Spring House."

25. On the success of A. G. and Lillian Garr, see "Los Angeles Again: Another Nazarene Converted," *Burning Bush,* December 15, 1905, 6.

26. In my research on A. G. and Lillian Garr, I was greatly aided by their son, A. G. Garr Jr. Also on Garr, see William A. Ward, *The Trailblazer: The History of Dr. A. G. Garr and Garr Tabernacle* (Charlotte: by the author, n.d.). Concerning the origins of Pentecostalism, see Robert Mapes Anderson, *Vision of the Disinherited: The Making of American Pentecostalism* (New York: Oxford University Press, 1979), 66–68. Vinson Synan, *The Holiness-Pentecostal Tradition: Charismatic Movement in the Twentieth Century* (Grand Rapids, Mich.: William B. Eerdmans, 1997), and D. William Faupel, *The Everlasting Gospel: The Significance of Eschatology in the Development of Pentecostal Thought* (Sheffield, England: Sheffield Academic Press, 1996).

27. Although it did not seem to deter them, the Garrs' failure to speak in native languages seems to have destroyed any chance they might have had to win Burning Bush missionaries to their cause. On the India perspective, I am especially indebted to Alice Whipple. Also, F. M. Messenger, "Garr in India," *Burning Bush,* July 18, 1907, 6.

28. "The Third Blessing," 4. On the slow start to the Azusa Street revival, see Anderson, *Vision of the Disinherited,* 66–68. On Seymour's preoccupation with the divorce and remarriage issues, see W. J. Seymour, "The Marriage Tie," *Apostolic Faith,* September 1907, 3. On the teachings of the Apostolic Faith Church, Portland, Oregon, see *A Historical*

Account of the Apostolic Faith: A Trinitarian-Fundamentalist Evangelistic Organization (Portland, Ore.: Apostolic Faith Church, 1965), 48–50.

29. On Parham, see James R. Goff Jr., *Fields White unto Harvest: Charles F. Parham and the Missionary Origins of Pentecostalism* (Fayetteville: University of Arkansas Press, 1988). The MCA's first extended attack on Pentecostalism is in the *Burning Bush,* January 24, 1907, 4–8.

30. F. M. Messenger, "Counterfeit Gift of Tongues," *Burning Bush,* September 19, 1907, 5–7. In the years that followed, the MCA lost few people to Pentecostalism.

31. E. L. Harvey, "Save Your Life: Lose Your Life," *Burning Bush,* August 17, 1911, 2–3, and E. L. Harvey, "The Price of Discipleship," *Burning Bush,* December 15, 1910, 2–3. The final quotation is from "Our Front Page," *Burning Bush,* May 3, 1906, 4.

32. E. L. Harvey, "Real Crucifixion," *Burning Bush,* October 6, 1904, 5; "The Property Question," *Burning Bush,* December 15, 1904, 6–7. Lehman first used Luke 14:33 as a defense of the MCA in "The Tithing System," *Burning Bush,* April 13, 1905. It was more fully developed in Lehman, "The Property Question," 6–7, and, in the same issue, see "Wesley on Riches," 5–6.

33. See especially the sermon on 2 Cor. 8:9 in E. L. Harvey, "His Poverty Is Our Riches," *Burning Bush,* July 8, 1909, 2–3. Charles T. Hollingsworth, "Giving All," *Burning Bush,* December 9, 1909, 9.

34. A list of the Scripture texts the MCA used to defend its position is in Charles T. Hollingsworth, "Forsaking All—A Bible Doctrine," *Burning Bush,* January 29, 1920, 9, 15. On what constitutes a rich person, see E. L. Harvey, "The Price of Discipleship," *Burning Bush,* January 15, 1910, 2–3. The first quotation is from "Rich People," *Burning Bush,* August 21, 1919, 4–5.

35. Edwin L. Harvey's sentiments were expressed in "Deeper Truths for Christians," *Message of Victory,* January–March 1980, 1. The memories of Messenger and the African American at the funeral were recounted by Kenneth Kendall, interview by author, tape recording, Milwaukee, Wis., August 1991, B. L. Fisher Library, Asbury Theological Seminary, Wilmore, Ky. The announcement of Harvey's death appears in "Rev. Edwin L. Harvey, Deceased," *Burning Bush,* February 4, 1926, 4.

36. Frank S. Mead, *Handbook of Denominations in the United States,* 2d ed. (New York: Abingdon Press, 1961), 105.

37. The only detailed scholarly discussion of the MCA is in William Kostlevy, "Nor Silver, Nor Gold: The Burning Bush Movement and the Communitarian Holiness Vision" (Ph.D. diss., University of Notre Dame, 1996). Primary sources collected for this dissertation are located in the Metropolitan Church Association Collection at Asbury Theological Seminary. Holiness periodicals, such as the *Nazarene Messenger,* the *Pentecostal Herald,* the *Christian Witness,* and especially *God's Revivalist,* provide the best access to the emergence of the MCA. Also important are the books by E. L. Harvey's principal theological mentors, Seth C. Rees, especially *The Ideal Pentecostal Church* (1899), and Martin Wells Knapp, especially *Lightning Bolts from Pentecostal Skies* (1898). A general introduction to the theology of the MCA is found in W. E. Shepard, *Bible Lessons* (1905). The single most important source for Harvey's thought is the MCA's periodical, the *Burning Bush.* See also a collection of Harvey's sermons, *Sermons on Bible Characters* (1909).

Charles Price Jones: Image of Holiness
Dale T. Irvin

The author wishes to thank Bishop Victor P. Smith of the National Publication Board of the Church of Christ (Holiness) U.S.A. and Dr. David D. Daniels of McCormick Theological Seminary for their assistance in researching this article.

1. "Jesus Only," *His Fullness Songs* (Jackson, Miss.: National Publishing Board of the Church of Christ [Holiness] U.S.A.), 1.

2. From stanzas 2 and 3 of "Jesus Only."

3. The following paragraphs draw upon information found in "Autobiographical Sketch of Charles Price Jones, Founder of the Church of Christ (Holiness), U.S.A.," in *History of Church of Christ (Holiness) U.S.A., 1895–1965*, ed. Otho B. Cobbins, (New York: Vantage Press, 1966) 21–33; J. H. Green, introduction to *An Appeal to the Sons of Africa: A Number of Poems, Readings, Orations and Lectures, Designed Especially to Inspire Youth of African Blood with Sentiments of Hope and True Nobility as well as to Entertain and Instruct All Classes of Readers and Lovers of Redeemed Humanity*, by Charles Price Jones (n.p.: Truth Publishing, 1902), vii–xvi, and idem, *Characters I Have Met* (1927; reprint, Los Angeles: National Publishing Board of the Church of Christ [Holiness], 1996), 2–12.

4. Green, introduction to *An Appeal to the Sons of Africa*, xi.

5. Ibid.

6. See Jones, "Autobiographical Sketch," 25.

7. See *Truth* 8, no. 6 (August 13, 1903): 1, and Jones's notes on his hymns in Cobbins, *History of Church of Christ*, 401–12.

8. Jones, "Autobiographical Sketch," 25–26.

9. On the wider history of the struggle among black Baptists concerning denominational identity, see James Melvin Washington, *Frustrated Fellowship: The Black Baptist Quest for Social Power* (Macon, Ga.: Mercer University Press, 1986).

10. David Douglas Daniels, "The Cultural Renewal of Slave Religion: Charles Price Jones and the Emergence of the Holiness Movement in Mississippi" (Ph.D. diss., Union Theological Seminary, New York, 1992).

11. Jones, *Characters I Have Met*, 30–31; Daniels, "The Cultural Renewal of Slave Religion"; and Jones, "Autobiographical Sketch," 28–29.

12. Cobbins, *History of Church of Christ*, 39.

13. Charles Price Jones, *The Gift of the Holy Ghost in the Book of Acts* (Los Angeles: National Publishing Board of the Church of Christ [Holiness], 1996), 40.

14. Jones, "Autobiographical Sketch," 416.

15. Cobbins, *History of Church of Christ*, 418.

16. Ibid., 426.

17. Mary Esther Mason, comp., *The History and Life Work of Elder C. H. Mason and His Co-Laborers* (n.p., [1931?]), 12–13.

18. Jones, *Characters I Have Met*, 38–39. Regarding Mason's testimony, see *Apostolic Faith* 1, no. 6 (February–March 1907): 7.

19. Jones, *Characters I Have Met*, 39.

20. Jones, *The Gift of the Holy Ghost*, 42.

21. Jones, *Characters I Have Met*, 42 (boldface original).

22. In a letter to the Azusa St. body dated November 28, 1907, and published in

Apostolic Faith 1, no. 12 (January 1908): 4, Mason wrote: "The fight has been great. I was put out, because I believed that God did baptize me with the Holy Ghost among you all."

23. Jones, *Characters I Have Met*, 38–39.

24. Ibid., 41.

25. Ibid., 39–40.

26. Jones, *The Gift of the Holy Ghost*, 42.

27. Douglas J. Nelson, "For Such a Time as This: The Story of Bishop William J. Seymour and the Azusa Street Revival: A Search for Pentecostal/Charismatic Roots" (Ph.D. diss., University of Birmingham, 1981).

28. C. W. Shumway, "A Study of 'The Gift of Tongues'" (A.B. thesis, University of Southern California, 1914), 173.

29. Carhee is listed in Cobbins, *History of Church of Christ*, 58–59, as an evangelist from Louisiana who first met Jones in Jackson, Mississippi, in 1906 and joined the Church of Christ in 1907, being ordained finally in 1910. Nelson does not say how Carhee knew of Seymour's visit to Jackson in 1905.

30. See Dale T. Irvin, "'Drawing All Together in One Bond of Love': The Ecumenical Vision of William J. Seymour and Azusa St.," *Journal of Pentecostal Studies* 6, no. 1 (spring 1995), for a fuller examination of Seymour's teachings. Jones held a moderate millennial view that accepted that the end was near, as seen in "The President's Message," *Proceedings of the Fortieth Annual Session of the Church of Christ (Holiness) U.S.A.* (Chicago: National Publishing Board, 1936), 35–37.

31. *Truth* 9 no. 25 (December 29, 1904): 7.

32. Seymour's own views on the Second Coming and the rapture (or removal) of the saints can be found in a signed article, "Behold the Bridegroom Cometh," *Apostolic Faith* (Los Angeles) 1, no. 5 (January 1907): 2.

33. Personal communication with Cecil M. Robeck.

34. The 1896 booklet, *The Work of the Holy Spirit in the Churches*, was issued under the Truth Publishing imprint and sold at the Baptist Association meeting held that year at Mt. Helms.

35. See C. L. Fisher, "The General Agent, or the Topmost Need in Mission," in *Up the Ladder in Foreign Missions*, ed. L. G. Gordon (Nashville: National Baptist Publishing Board, 1901; reprint, New York: Arno Press, 1980), 189–99.

36. Jones, *The Gift of the Holy Ghost*, 6.

37. Ibid., 18.

38. In his review of other Holiness movements, written around 1910, Jones said of the Christian Alliance: "We are more on their order than any other, except that we were forced by misunderstandings into a separate organization" (Jones, *Gift of the Holy Ghost*, 40).

39. *Truth* 8, no. 11 (September 17, 1903): 1 (emphasis original).

40. *Truth* 9, no. 25 (December 29, 1904): 2.

41. Cobbins, *History of Church of Christ*, 30.

42. *Truth* 8, no. 11 (September 17, 1903): 2.

43. Jones, *The Gift of the Holy Ghost*, 42.

44. Jones, *Characters I Have Met*, 38–39.

45. Ibid., 20.

46. Quinton H. Dixie of Indiana University noted in correspondence with me that Joanna P. Moore was a lay missionary whose work was primarily with family ministry and

education in the South. Thus, Jones's position on women in ministry did not necessarily entail any contradiction.

47. Jones, *Characters I Have Met, 7*.

48. Ibid.

49. Jones, *An Appeal,* preface.

50. Ibid., 5.

51. Ibid., 17.

52. Ibid., 13–14.

53. Ibid., 67 (emphasis original).

54. Ibid., 16.

55. *Truth* 9, no. 9 (September 8, 1904): 6.

56. Jones, *An Appeal,* 101–5.

57. John T. Benson Jr., *A History 1898–1915 of the Pentecostal Mission, Inc.* (Nashville, Tenn.: Trevecca Press, 1977), 47.

58. The writings of C. P. Jones remain difficult to locate, though he authored a sizable body of work. Many of his hymns can be found in *His Fullness Songs.* The best primary source of historical information regarding Jones and the church is Cobbins, *History of Church of Christ.* Several archives across the country hold copies of Charles Price Jones's *An Appeal to the Sons of Africa.* For many years Jones published a paper entitled *Truth* that carried articles by him on biblical and theological topics, as well as information on the churches involved in the convocation and on Holiness efforts elsewhere across the country. Most remaining copies of this paper are now held in personal collections. I have been unable to locate existing copies of two books that Jones published, *The Work of the Holy Spirit in the Churches* and *Progressive Sanctification.* Among the secondary sources, the best is David Douglas Daniels's "The Cultural Renewal of Slave Religion."

Frank Sandford: Tongues of Fire in Shiloh, Maine
Shirley and Rudy Nelson

1. Frank S. Murray, *The Sublimity of Faith: The Life and Work of Frank W. Sandford* (Amherst, N.H.: Kingdom Press, 1981), 96.

2. The account of Parham's first encounter with Sandford's movement is a synthesis of details recorded in Murray, *The Sublimity of Faith,* 231–32, and James R. Goff Jr., *Fields White unto Harvest: Charles F. Parham and the Missionary Origins of Pentecostalism* (Fayetteville: University of Arkansas Press, 1988), 56–61.

3. D. William Faupel, in *The Everlasting Gospel: The Significance of Eschatology in the Development of Pentecostal Thought* (Sheffield, UK: Sheffield Academic Press, 1996), says that "Sandford's major contribution to Pentecostalism came through his impact on the theology and practice of Charles Fox Parham" (158). Edith L. Blumhofer's *The Assemblies of God: A Chapter in the Story of American Pentecostalism,* vol. 1, *To 1941* (Springfield, Mo.: Gospel Publishing House, 1989), 76–81, discusses several of Sandford's influences on Parham. Blumhofer also mentions another strand of the Sandford influence on Pentecostalism; in 1901 he baptized A. J. Tomlinson, who went on to become the leader of the Church of God, Cleveland, Tennessee (79).

4. Vinson Synan, *The Holiness-Pentecostal Tradition: Charismatic Movements in the Twentieth Century,* 2d ed. (Grand Rapids, Mich.: William B. Eerdmans, 1997), 90.

5. *Lewiston (Maine) Evening Journal,* January 6, 1900.

6. Murray, *The Sublimity of Faith,* 927.

7. Grant Wacker, "Are the Golden Oldies Still Worth Playing?: Reflections on History Writing among Early Pentecostals," *Pneuma: The Journal of the Society for Pentecostal Studies* 8 (fall 1986): 90.

8. Hannah Whitall Smith, *The Christian's Secret of a Happy Life* (1870; reprint, Old Tappan, N.J.: Fleming H. Revell, 1966).

9. *The Everlasting Gospel* (Shiloh publication), June 1–30, 1901, 177.

10. Murray, *The Sublimity of Faith,* 58–61.

11. Ibid., 62.

12. Shirley Nelson, *Fair, Clear, and Terrible: The Story of Shiloh, Maine* (Albany, N.Y.: British American Publishing, 1989), 49.

13. Ibid., 66.

14. Murray, *The Sublimity of Faith,* 120–24; Nelson, *Fair, Clear, and Terrible,* 66–67.

15. Glassey is discussed in Goff, *Fields White unto Harvest,* 73.

16. Day is discussed in William C. Hiss, "Shiloh: Frank W. Sandford and the Kingdom, 1893–1948" (Ph.D. diss., Tufts University, 1978), 127–28.

17. Nelson, *Fair, Clear, and Terrible,* 78–80.

18. Hiss, "Shiloh," 214.

19. Murray, *The Sublimity of Faith,* 219–20; Hiss, "Shiloh," 229–30; Nelson, *Fair, Clear, and Terrible,* 125–27, 138–39.

20. Nelson, *Fair, Clear, and Terrible,* 146.

21. Murray, *The Sublimity of Faith,* 333–34; Hiss, "Shiloh," 353–60; Nelson, *Fair, Clear, and Terrible,* 227–42.

22. Blumhofer, *The Assemblies of God,* 18.

23. Hiss discusses Totten at some length, "Shiloh," 166–71.

24. Murray, *The Sublimity of Faith,* 290–95; Hiss, "Shiloh," 291–96; Nelson, *Fair, Clear, and Terrible,* 163–66.

25. Murray, *The Sublimity of Faith,* 312–15; Hiss, "Shiloh," 316–22; Nelson, *Fair, Clear, and Terrible,* 177–80.

26. Murray, *The Sublimity of Faith,* 341; Hiss, "Shiloh," 363–64; Nelson, *Fair, Clear, and Terrible,* 248–49.

27. Nelson, *Fair, Clear, and Terrible,* 299.

28. Murray, *The Sublimity of Faith,* 472–510; Hiss, "Shiloh," 463–78; Nelson, *Fair, Clear, and Terrible,* 312–48.

29. Robert Mapes Anderson, *The Vision of the Disinherited* (New York: Oxford University Press, 1979).

30. Harvey Cox, *Fire from Heaven* (Reading, Mass.: Addison-Wesley Publishing Co., 1995), 30.

31. Dennis A. Smith, "Coming of Age: A Reflection on Pentecostals, Politics and Popular Religion in Guatemala," *Pneuma: The Journal of the Society for Pentecostal Studies* 13 (fall 1991): 131.

32. Cox, *Fire from Heaven,* 315.

33. *The Voice of Faith,* October 22, 1996, 3.

34. Ibid., May 26, 1998, 1. We are indebted to Floyd Hastings of Saco, Maine, for providing copies of recent Kingdom publications.

35. There are three essential secondary sources on Frank Sandford and Shiloh. For the insider's perspective, one should turn to *The Sublimity of Faith: The Life and Work of Frank W. Sandford* by Frank S. Murray, a loyal follower and eventually one of the group's leaders. Although it has a wealth of detail and provides an essential timeline, its portrayal of the movement's history is unambiguously favorable, and its treatment of Sandford is perhaps best classed as a hagiography. William C. Hiss's Ph.D. diss., "Shiloh: Frank W. Sandford and the Kingdom, 1893–1948," is a well-researched history that gives a balanced but essentially sympathetic interpretation. Building on both Murray and Hiss, but adding sources from her family and friends, especially her parents, who grew up at Shiloh at the turn of the century, Shirley Nelson's *Fair, Clear, and Terrible: The Story of Shiloh, Maine* provides the additional perspective of insiders who later became defectors. Like Hiss, Nelson seeks to give a balanced interpretation of Sandford and the movement's controversial history but draws on additional sources that were either unavailable to Hiss or that he chose not to use. Recently two men with strong family connections to Shiloh, Reginald Parker and Richard Sweet, created a Web site (www.fwselijah.com) with a vast array of documentary materials. A perusal of these materials supports the editors' claim that their purpose is "to present the past as objectively as possible" so that people can draw their own conclusions.

Alma White: The Politics of Dissent
Susie C. Stanley

The author wishes to thank John Stanley and David Weaver-Zercher for their helpful comments on drafts of this chapter.

1. *Daily Mail* (London), October 10, 1928, in *Alma White's Evangelism: Press Reports*, 2 vols., ed. C. [Clara] R. Paige and C. [Clifford] K. Ingler (Zarephath, N.J.: Pillar of Fire, 1939–40), 2:104.

2. *Daily Express* (London), October 10, 1928, in Paige and Ingler, *Alma White's Evangelism*, 2:103; and *Daily Mail* (London), October 10, 1928, in Paige and Ingler, *Alma White's Evangelism*, 2:106.

3. Charles E. Jones, *A Guide to the Study of the Pentecostal Movement*, 2 vols., ATLA Bibliography Series, no. 6 (Metuchen, N.J.: Scarecrow Press, 1983), 1:628; and Vinson Synan, *The Holiness-Pentecostal Movement in the United States* (Grand Rapids, Mich.: William B. Eerdmans, 1971), 199.

4. Alma White, *Demons and Tongues* (Bound Brook, N.J.: Pentecostal Union, 1910; reprint, Zarephath, N.J.: Pillar of Fire, 1936), 20; see also 11.

5. See Mel Dieter, "The Wesleyan/Holiness and Pentecostal Movements: Commonalities, Confrontation, and Dialogue," *Pneuma: The Journal of the Society for Pentecostal Studies* 12, no. 1 (spring 1990): 4–13; and Donald W. Dayton, *Theological Roots of Pentecostalism* (Grand Rapids, Mich.: Francis Asbury Press of Zondervan Publishing House, 1987).

6. Dieter, "Wesleyan/Holiness," 13; see also 5.

7. Alma White, *The Story of My Life and the Pillar of Fire*, 5 vols. (Zarephath, N.J.: Pillar of Fire, 1935–43), 2:237; see also 3:236 and Catherine Booth, *Female Ministry: Woman's Right to Preach the Gospel* (1859; reprint, New York: Salvation Army Supplies Printing and Publishing Department, 1975), 7, 10, 16.

8. Phoebe Palmer, *Promise of the Father; or, A Neglected Specialty of the Last Days*

(Boston: Henry V. Degen, 1859; reprint, Salem, Ohio: Schmul Publishers, n.d.), 245.

9. Alma White, *Gospel Truth* (Zarephath, N.J.: Pillar of Fire, 1945), 12.

10. Evan Jerry Lawrence, "Alma White College: A History of Its Relationship to the Development of the Pillar of Fire" (Ph.D. diss., Columbia University, 1966), 26.

11. *Burning Bush,* March 12, 1903, 4.

12. White maintained contact with Godbey after her conversion. Godbey had accepted her invitation to hold a revival in Colorado early in her preaching career. Pillar of Fire published his booklet *Tongue Movement, Satanic* in 1918.

13. Lee Casey, *Rocky Mountain News (Denver),* June 28, 1946, 14.

14. White, *Story,* 2:73–74.

15. *Sun (Attleboro, Mass.),* December 24, 1902; and *Gazette (Colorado Springs),* March 11, 1903, reprinted in *Burning Bush,* March 26, 1903, 2.

16. White, *Demons,* 67–68.

17. Alma White, *What I Saw in a Tongues' Meeting* (Denver: n.p., n.d.), n.p.

18. White, *What I Saw.* Other quotations in this paragraph are from this source.

19. White, *Story,* 1:427.

20. Ibid., 3:146.

21. Ibid., 3:148.

22. Ibid., 3:146.

23. Alma White, *My Heart and My Husband* (Zarephath, N.J.: Pillar of Fire, 1923), 65. This is a collection of four-line stanzas narrating the story of Alma's marital separation.

24. White, *Heart,* 64.

25. Ibid., 69–70.

26. "Bishop Says Her Heart Is Broken," *The World,* 1922 (an incompletely dated, unattributed newspaper clipping in the author's possession).

27. H. D. Ingersoll to Kent White, n.d.

28. White, *Heart,* 77.

29. Kent White, *Victory through Prevailing Prayer* (Bound Brook, N.J.: n.p., n.d.), 9.

30. White, *Story,* 4:55.

31. White, *Heart,* 81 (letter dated June 14, 1915).

32. Ibid., 89.

33. White, *Story,* 5:18.

34. Ibid., 5:24.

35. Alma White, *Modern Miracles and Answers of Prayer* (Zarephath, N.J.: Pillar of Fire, 1939), 231.

36. White, *Story,* 5:82.

37. Kent White to Charles Bridwell, June 24, 1918.

38. Kent White to Arthur White, July 4, 1938.

39. *Rocky Mountain News (Denver),* August 2, 1940, 13.

40. Kent White, "Diary," photocopy, July 8 and 9, 1940.

41. Interview with Arlene White Lawrence, Alma White's granddaughter, on August 2, 1986, in Zarephath, New Jersey. See also Rev. J. Dean Cole, quoted in Harmon Kallman, *(Denver) Post,* August 20, 1955, 5.

42. White, *Demons,* 26.

43. Ibid., 117, 87, 43.

44. Ibid., 66, 10, 43, 38.

45. Ibid., 25–26.

46. Ibid., 10. In her autobiography she attributed the origin of Pentecostalism to Mormons and Spiritualists (White, *Story,* 3:21).

47. White, *Demons,* 52.

48. Ibid., 56, 72, 87.

49. Ibid., 60.

50. Ibid., 83.

51. Ibid., 73.

52. Ibid., 13.

53. Ibid., 24, 93.

54. Ibid., 76.

55. For one example, see *(Denver) Post,* January 8, 1904, 6.

56. White, *Story,* 2:310.

57. *(New York) Herald Tribune,* August 23, 1937, in Paige and Ingler, *Alma White's Evangelism,* 2:193.

58. White, *Story,* 3:145.

59. Paige and Ingler, *Alma White's Evangelism,* 2:193.

60. White, *Story,* 4:267.

61. White, *Demons,* 26.

62. Grant Wacker, "Travail of a Broken Family: Evangelical Responses to Pentecostalism in America, 1906–1916," *Journal of Ecclesiastical History* 47, no. 3 (July 1996): 524.

63. Most of the information on Alma White and the Pillar of Fire Church comes from her writings, particularly her five-volume autobiography, *The Story of My Life and the Pillar of Fire.* Kent White's perspective is limited to several unpublished letters and diary entries. Like most autobiographers, Alma White sought to place her positions in a positive light. White's *Demons and Tongues* is the most frequently quoted source for her anti-Pentecostalism. *Feminist Pillar of Fire: The Life of Alma White* (Cleveland, Ohio: Pilgrim Press, 1993) by Susie Cunningham Stanley remains the only book-length analysis of Alma White and her church. For this chapter, I quoted original sources rather than referencing my biography.

Minnie F. Abrams: Another Context, Another Founder
Gary B. McGee

1. *Indian Witness,* April 26, 1906, 261; cf. P. Ramabai, *Mukti Prayer-Bell,* October 1905, 6–7.

2. Excerpts of this chapter have been reprinted with permission from the following: G. B. McGee, "'Latter Rain Falling in the East': Early-Twentieth-Century Pentecostalism in India and the Debate over Speaking in Tongues," *Church History* 68 (September 1999): 648–65.

3. *Minnesota Census, 1870,* 633.

4. Undated obituary news clipping (ca. 1913) from an unidentified Minnesota newspaper located at Memorial Library, Mankato State University, Mankato, Minnesota.

5. D. Berger, *History of the Church of the United Brethren in Christ* (Dayton, Ohio: United Brethren Publishing House, 1897), 604.

6. "Roll Call" information form for the Woman's Foreign Missionary Society of the Methodist Episcopal Church, dated August 7, 1906; located in the Minnie F. Abrams file (#1465–4–2:06) at the General Commission on Archives and History of the United Methodist Church at Drew University, Madison, N.J.

7. *Latter Rain Evangel,* May 1911, 11.

8. *Missionary Review of the World,* December 1888, 942.

9. I. Horton, *High Adventure* (New York: Methodist Book Concern, 1928), 123.

10. *Missionary Review of the World,* December 1888, 942.

11. D. L. Robert, *American Women in Mission* (Macon, Ga.: Mercer University Press, 1996), 245.

12. *Latter Rain Evangel,* March 1910, 13.

13. "Roll Call"; cf. M. F. Abrams, *Latter Rain Evangel,* July 1909, 7.

14. W. C. Barclay, *History of Methodist Missions* (New York: Board of Missions, 1957), 3:599.

15. Robert, *American,* 245.

16. *Latter Rain Evangel,* August 1910, 8.

17. Ibid., 9.

18. Barclay, *History,* 602–4.

19. E. G. Lindsay, *Missionaries of the Minneapolis Branch* (n.p., 1904), 22.

20. *Latter Rain Evangel,* November 1908, 10. For a somewhat different and more detailed account of the circumstances that led her to the Mukti Mission, see Helen S. Dyer, *Pandita Ramabai: Her Vision, Her Mission and Triumph of Faith* (London: Pickering & Inglis, n.d.), 60–61.

21. "Roll Call." Abrams said her departure from the WFMS "wasn't a tearing away; it was God who took me out and convinced everybody that He was taking me out." *Latter Rain Evangel,* July 1909, 7–8.

22. *Latter Rain Evangel,* March 1910, 14.

23. "Mukti Mission," *World Atlas of Christian Missions,* ed. J. S. Dennis et al. (New York: Student Volunteer Movement, 1911), 68.

24. *Bombay Guardian,* June 30, 1906, 10.

25. W. McDonald and J. E. Searles, *Life of Rev. John S. Inskip* (Boston: McDonald & Gill, 1885), 329.

26. H. P. Beach, *Geography and Atlas of Protestant Missions* (New York: Student Volunteer Movement, 1906), 2:19.

27. S. M. Adhav, ed., *Pandita Ramabai* (Madras: Christian Literature Society, 1979), 216.

28. *Bombay Guardian,* June 30, 1906, 9–10.

29. Cited in "And Fire," *Indian Witness,* December 6, 1906, 772.

30. M. F. Abrams, *Baptism of the Holy Ghost and Fire,* rev. ed. (Kedgaon: Mukti Mission Press, 1906), 84.

31. V. Synan, *Old-Time Power* (Franklin Springs, Ga.: Advocate Press, 1973), 82–83.

32. Abrams, *Baptism,* 26–28, 45–46, 66–67, 84.

33. *Bombay Guardian,* June 23, 1906, 8–9.

34. *Mission World,* May 1, 1906, 20–21.

35. *Mukti Prayer-Bell,* September 1907, 18.

36. *Christian Patriot,* April 22, 1905, 3; reprinted from *Congregationalist and Christian World,* March 4, 1905, 285.

37. *Indian Witness,* December 21, 1905, 804.

38. *Christian Patriot,* October 1905, 6; cf. idem, *Indian Witness,* March 28, 1907, 202–3.

39. G. B. McGee, "Shortcut to Language Preparation: Radical Evangelicals, Missions, and the Gift of Tongues," *International Bulletin of Missionary Research* 25 (July 2001): 118–23.

40. Cited in H. S. Dyer, comp., *Revival in India* (New York: Gospel Publishing House, 1907), 90.

41. L. B. Butcher, "Manmad," *Prayer Circular,* November 1906, 4.

42. D. Gee, *Pentecostal Movement,* rev. ed. (London: Elim Publishing Co., 1949), 28; Abrams, *Baptism,* 69.

43. *Fifty-fifth Annual Report of the Zenana Bible and Medical Mission,* 1906, 22.

44. *India Alliance,* September 1906, 30.

45. *Apostolic Faith* (Los Angeles), November 1906, 1.

46. Ibid., April 1907, 1.

47. *Pentecostal Power* (Calcutta), March 1907, 4.

48. *Indian Witness,* December 13, 1906, 786.

49. M. W. Moorhead, *Apostolic Faith,* September 1907, 4.

50. *Faith Work in India,* July 10, 1907, 4.

51. Ibid., 3.

52. Abrams, *Baptism,* 70.

53. *Mukti Prayer-Bell,* September 1907, 5.

54. Abrams, *Baptism,* 67.

55. *Confidence,* September 15, 1908, 14.

56. *Latter Rain Evangel,* October 1908, 18.

57. Ibid., May 1911, 10.

58. *Pentecostal Evangel,* April 17, 1920, 9.

59. *Pentecostal Power* (Calcutta), March 1907, 3.

60. *Cloud of Witnesses to Pentecost in India,* August 1909, 6.

61. *Latter Rain Evangel,* July 1909, 11.

62. Ibid., July 1909, 6–13; Minnie Abrams, "Brief History of the Latter Rain Revival of 1910," *Word and Work,* May 1910, 138–41.

63. *Cloud of Witnesses,* November 1908, 21–22; for Garr's account, see B. F. Lawrence, *Apostolic Faith Restored* (St. Louis: Gospel Publishing House, 1916), 96–105.

64. See J. Creech, "Visions of Glory: The Place of the Azusa Street Revival in Pentecostal History," *Church History* 65 (September 1996): 405–24.

65. *Latter Rain Evangel,* August 1910, 11.

66. Ibid., 10.

67. *Trust,* October 1910, 15. Whether she intended the agency to be exclusively for women remains unknown. Nevertheless, it was directed and staffed entirely by women. Curiously, Abrams and other independent Pentecostal missionaries were listed under the

category of "Open Brethren" in J. P. Jones, ed., *Year Book of Missions in India, Burma and Ceylon* (n.p.: Christian Literature Society for India, 1912), 596.

68. Undated obituary news clipping (ca. 1913); *Pentecostal Evangel,* October 21, 1916, 13. I am indebted to the research of Mikeuel E. Peterson for locating the latter reference containing information on the friendship of Abrams and Luce.

69. Robert, *American,* 254.

70. Ibid., 244.

71. A. B. Simpson, *Word and Work,* May 1910, 157.

72. *Trust,* October 1910, 16; Robert, *American,* 247.

73. *Bombay Guardian,* December 7, 1912, 3–4; also, *Missionary Review of the World,* February 1913, 156.

74. Resources for the study of Minnie F. Abrams come largely from periodical literature: articles, news notes, and obituaries. The most helpful include the *Latter Rain Evangel, Mukti Prayer-Bell, Confidence, Word and Work, Trust, Missionary Review of the World,* and *Apostolic Faith* (Los Angeles). No less valuable, the *Bombay Guardian, Indian Witness,* and *Christian Patriot* (all available at Yale University libraries, New Haven, Connecticut), serialized the first edition of her *Baptism of the Holy Ghost and Fire* (ca. May 1906). (I have not yet found the first edition in booklet form.) Copies of the second edition (December 1906) and the abridged memorial edition, printed by the Christian Workers Union of Framingham, Massachusetts, are kept at the Flower Pentecostal Heritage Center in Springfield, Missouri. Effie G. Lindsay's *Missionaries of the Minneapolis Branch of the Woman's Foreign Missionary Society of the Methodist Episcopal Church* (1904) contains an informative biographical sketch.

Frank Bartleman: Pentecostal "Lone Ranger" and Social Critic
Augustus Cerillo Jr.

1. Vinson Synan, "Introduction: Frank Bartleman and Azusa Street," in Frank Bartleman, *Azusa Street,* ed. Vinson Synan (Plainfield, N.J.: Logos International, 1980), xii. Cecil M. Robeck, "Introduction: The Writings and Thought of Frank Bartleman," in *Witness to Pentecost: The Life of Frank Bartleman,* ed. Donald Dayton (New York: Garland Publishing, 1985), vii–xxiii.

2. Frank Bartleman, *From Plow to Pulpit, From Maine to California* (Los Angeles: privately published), reprinted in *Witness to Pentecost,* 5–7 (the quotation is on 6); also see Frank Bartleman, *My Story: "The Latter Rain"* (Columbia, S.C.: John M. Pike, 1909), 9.

3. Bartleman, *Story,* 8; idem, *Plow,* 10.

4. Bartleman, *Plow,* 6–12 (quotations in order are on 6, 9, 12).

5. Bartleman, *Story,* 10; also see idem, *Plow,* 12–21.

6. Bartleman, *Plow,* 21–63 (quotations on 22 and 58).

7. Ibid., 64–114 (quotation on 76).

8. Ibid., 113–32 (quotation on 131). In *Plow,* Bartleman indicated the family reached Los Angeles at 10:30 P.M. the night of the twentieth, but in *How Pentecost Came to Azusa Street,* he wrote that the family arrived in Los Angeles on December 22, 1904.

9. Bartleman, *Story,* 19–24 (quotations in order on 20, 21, 22); Bartleman, *Azusa Street,* 2–5.

10. Bartleman, *Azusa Street,* 5; idem, *Confidence* 4 (April 1916): 63.

11. Bartleman, *Story,* 24–30 (quotations on 25, 26); idem, *Azusa Street,* 5–42; idem, *Confidence,* 63–65. John Bartleman was born at 1:45 P.M. on Sunday, March 4, 1906.

12. Bartleman, *Azusa Street,* 37–42 (quotations from the *Way of Faith* and *Christian Harvester* are cited on 37–38); Frank Bartleman, *The Last Call* (Los Angeles: privately published tract, March 1906).

13. Bartleman, *Story,* 30–33 (quotation on 33, italics mine); idem, *Azusa Street,* 43–47; idem, *Confidence,* 65–66.

14. Bartleman, *Azusa Street,* 89–92 (quotation from *Way of Faith* cited on 91).

15. Ibid., 67–78 (quotations in order on 72, 74, 73). On the growth of Pentecostal missions in Los Angeles, see Cecil M. Robeck Jr., *Assemblies of God Heritage* 3 (fall 1983): 3–4, 12.

16. Bartleman, *Azusa Street,* 99–137; idem, *Bridegroom's Messenger,* July 15, 1908, 2; idem, *Way of Faith,* July 23, 1908, 2–3; idem, *Bridegroom's Messenger,* February 15, 1909, 4.

17. Bartleman, *Azusa Street,* 138–46; idem, *The Latter Rain Evangel,* July 1910, 7; idem, *Around the World by Faith, with Six Weeks in the Holy Land,* reprinted in *Witness to Pentecost,* 6.

18. Bartleman, *Azusa Street,* 146–49; idem, *World;* idem, *Two Years Mission Work in Europe: Just before the World War, 1912–1914,* reprinted in *Witness to Pentecost.*

19. Bartleman, *Mission,* 56–60; idem, *Word and Work,* February 15, 1915, 55; May 19, 1917, 245–46; September 15, 1917, 510–11; E. N. Bell, *Christian Evangel,* August 24, 1918, 4. Bartleman's writings from the 1920s and 1930s include *Flapper Evangelism: Fashion's Fools* (tract, circa 1920); *Pentecost or No Pentecost* (tract, 1928); *Waters to Swim in* (tract, circa 1928–29); *A Voice in the Wilderness* (tract, circa 1920s); *A Treasure Chest, Nuggets of Gold* (pamphlet, 1927); *Distilled Dew, 500 Modern Proverbs* (pamphlet, 1934); and essays in *Maran-atha* 6 (November–December 1929): 10–12; 6 (March–April 1930): 8–11; 6 (May–June 1930): 8–11; 9 (June 1934): 6–8; and in *Word and Work,* August 1935, 5, 11. State of California, Department of Public Health, Vital Statistics, *Standard Certificate of Death* (Frank Bartleman), August 23, 1936.

20. Frank Bartleman, *Call;* idem, *Bridegroom's Messenger,* February 1, 1908; idem, *The Latter Rain Evangel,* July 1910 (quotation on 5).

21. Bartleman, *Azusa Street,* 53–60 (quotations in order on 54, 57, 59, 58).

22. The quotations are from Bartleman, *The Los Angeles Work* (Los Angeles: privately printed, circa fall–winter 1906–7); idem, *The Pentecost* (Los Angeles: privately printed, circa fall–winter 1906–7); idem, *The Fullness* (Los Angeles: privately printed, circa fall–winter 1906–7).

23. Bartleman, *Azusa Street,* 85–87, 133 (quotation on 86); *Word and Work,* February 1908, 40–41.

24. Bartleman, *Fragments of Flame,* no. 7 (August 1910); italics mine.

25. Bartleman, *Triumphs of Faith,* December 1906, 247–52; idem, *The Fullness.*

26. Bartleman, *Way of Faith,* 23 (July 1908): 2–3.

27. Bartleman, *Latter Rain Evangel,* July 1910, 2, 6.

28. Robeck, "Introduction," xi.

29. Bartleman, *Bridegroom's Messenger,* February 1, 1916, 4, from which the quotation is taken; idem, *War and the Christian* (tract, circa 1922); and idem, *Christian Citizenship* (tract, circa 1922).

30. Bartleman, *Word and Work,* August 12, 1916, 296–97; idem, *Maran-atha* 6 (March–April 1930): 8–11; and 6 (May–June 1930): 8–11.

31. Bartleman, *Plow,* 40–49; idem, *Weekly Evangel,* August 1915, 1–2. The remark on Native Americans is on page 2.

32. The quotation is from Bartleman, *Bridegroom's Messenger,* March 1, 1916, 4. Other pertinent essays by Bartleman include *War and the Christian* (tract, circa 1922); "Not of this World," *Word and Work* (circa 1917), 296–97; "Christian Preparedness," *Word and Work* (circa 1916), 114–15; *Christian Citizenship* (tract, circa 1922); "The Situation in Europe," *Bridegroom's Messenger* March 1, 1915, 1.

33. Bartleman, *Mission,* 37–55; idem, *Bridegroom's Messenger,* February 1, 1915, 2; idem, *Weekly Evangel,* June 5, 1915, 3; July 10, 1915, 3; idem, *Bridegroom's Messenger,* May 1, 1915, 4; June 1, 1915, 3; July 1, 1915, 3; and January 1, 1916, 4. In addition, see the essays by Bartleman cited in notes 30–31.

34. Quotations are from Bartleman, *Bridegroom's Messenger,* January 1, 1916, 4. Bartleman, *Weekly Evangel,* June 5, 1915, 3; August 7, 1915, 1–2; idem, *Word and Work,* November 1915, 300–301; and September 23, 1916, 393–94.

35. Quotations in order are from Bartleman, *Word and Work,* May 27, 1916, and *Bridegroom's Messenger,* February 1, 1916, 4.

36. Quotations are from *Bridegroom's Messenger,* March 1, 1916, 4. In *Word and Work,* May 27, 1916, 4, Bartleman, after commenting on how the German government contributed to the welfare of its citizens and negatively comparing that nation to the United States, wrote: "Government regulation and development of resources is required to build a nation." That is as close to his supporting government-sponsored reforms as I could find in his writings.

37. Bartleman, *Plow,* 66–69.

38. The major primary sources used in this biographical essay are Bartleman's own published writings. He self-published six books, more than one hundred tracts, and two longer pamphlets, and he published approximately 550 essays in numerous Holiness and Pentecostal magazines. Other than Bartleman's books, probably fewer than one hundred of his articles and tracts are extant. This essay is also informed by the growing historical literature on American Pentecostalism, much of which is described in Augustus Cerillo Jr. and Grant Wacker, "Bibliography and Historiography of Pentecostalism in the United States," in *New International Dictionary of the Pentecostal and Charismatic Movements,* ed. Stanley M. Burgess (Grand Rapids, Mich.: Zondervan, 2002), by title.

William H. Durham: Years of Creativity, Years of Dissent
Edith L. Blumhofer

1. Ethel Goss, *Winds of God* (New York: Comet Press Books, 1958), 124.

2. Durham left only one narrative focused on his Pentecostal experience and published it in his magazine, *Pentecostal Testimony (PT).* Biographical details are culled from census data; military records; social security applications; cemetery, school, and church records and other local history sources; and Rockcastle County, Kentucky, newspapers from the period of Durham's boyhood.

3. "Beloved Windom Pastor Called to Eternal Home," *Cottonwood County Citizen (CCC),* November 8, 1944, 10.

4. Clara Lum, "The Living Gospel, Or a Missionary Family," *Firebrand,* June 1901, 1.

5. *Firebrand,* December 1898, 3.

6. *Firebrand,* April 1900, 3.

7. *The Missionary World (MW),* September 1907, 4.

8. "It Is Finished," *Firebrand,* January 1901, 2.

9. "The World's Faith Missionary Association," *Firebrand,* August 1898, 3.

10. "The Tenth Annual Convention of the Children of God at Windom, Minnesota," *MW,* February 1907, 8.

11. "Currie," *Tracy Trumpet,* October 20, 1893, 8; *Minnesota Signal,* September 23, 1898, 1.

12. *Firebrand,* August 1902, 4.

13. "Arco Items," *Tyler Journal,* January 16, 1903, 5; *Murray County Herald,* June 17 and 24, 1904, 5; *Slayton Gazette and Murray County Pioneer,* June 16, 1904.

14. *MW,* July 1904, 3.

15. Ibid., 5.

16. Ibid., March 1903, 5.

17. This mission may have become the North Avenue Mission. Chicago city directories verify Iverson's home in the area through 1905. See also "Editorial notes," *Bethel Trumpet* 2, no. 2 (March 1901): 12. Certainly Durham first found a welcome as an experienced visiting evangelist in an established mission associated with Scandinavians on North Avenue in Humboldt Park.

18. See, for example, "Camp Meeting," *MW,* July 1904, 2.

19. *MW,* August 1904.

20. "The 7th Annual Convention," *CCC,* December 31, 1904.

21. *Republican Trumpet (RT),* June 16, 1905, 5; *MW,* July 1905, 2.

22. *RT,* January 17, 1902, 7; *TR,* December 24, 1897, 5.

23. *TR,* March 4, 1898, 1; February 10, 1899, 5; October 13, 1899, 5; October 7, 1898, 5.

24. *MW,* September 1905, 3.

25. *MW,* January 1906, 2.

26. Loveless to the Hanleys, *MW,* September 1906, 5.

27. *MW,* April 1906, 8.

28. "Church Notes," *CCC,* January 5, 1907, 5.

29. "Traveling for God," *MW,* April 1906, 8.

30. "Good News from Danville, VA," *Apostolic Faith (AF)* 1, no. 1 (September 1906), 4.

31. "Notes," *MW,* September 1904, 5; *Firebrand,* September 1900, 1; *MW,* September 1902, 3; "Another Missionary, Once at the Training Home," *MW,* December 1906, 1.

32. *MW,* June 1906, 5.

33. *MW,* September 1906, 5.

34. "Field Notes," *MW,* August 1906, 5.

35. *CCC,* December 29, 1906, 5.

36. Frederick G. Henke, "The Gift of Tongues and Related Phenomena in the Present Day," *American Journal of Theology* 13 (1909): 200.

37. *Pentecostal Testimony (PT)* (winter 1909): 5.

38. *CCC,* December 29, 1906, 5.

39. *MW,* May 1907, 8.

40. "A Chicago Evangelist's Pentecost," *AF* 1, n. 6 (February–March 1907): 4.

41. *MW,* May 1907, 8.

42. "Mission in Chicago," *Household of God* 3, no. 11 (November 1907): 10–11.

43. *RT,* April 26, 1907, 5.

44. For example, Thomas Ball Barratt, "En Praedikants Beksendelse," *Folke-Vennen (FV),* December 13, 1906, 1; Hans Lehne, "De nye Foreteelser i Kristiania," *FV,* January 24, 1907, 1; "Pastor Barratts Moder i Kristiania," *FV,* February 14, 1907, 4; Berntsen letter, *FV,* April 24, 1907, 5. *FV* carried translations of articles from *The Upper Room,* a lead article on Pentecostalism by A. S. Worrell, the testimony of George Studd, and remarks by Durham on the dangers of organization. "Tanker om Kirkeorganisation," February 17, 1910, 3.

45. Frederick Link to Robert Cunningham, March 9, 1951, in Link's ministerial file, A/G Archives.

46. Durham, "A Glimpse of a Gracious Work of God in Chicago," *Word and Work* 32, no. 5 (May 1910): 155.

47. The North Avenue Mission helped send Gunnar Wingren and Daniel Berg to Brazil.

48. Cook County Record Book, 1907, 608, 29. Copies in possession of the author.

49. Durham, "Glimpse," 156.

50. "Interpretation of Tongues," *BM* 2, no. 23 (October 1, 1908): 1; ""Budskaber fra Himlen," *FV,* July 1, 1909, 1.

51. Clara Lum, "A Year at Shenandoah," *Firebrand,* August 1898, 3.

52. "Miss Clara Lum Writes Wonders," *MW,* August 1906, 2; "Manifestations Continue; Many Different Experiences," *MW,* November 1906, 8; "Pentecostal Wonders," *MW,* September 1906, 4; *MW,* January 1908, 4.

53. *MW,* September 1904, 5.

54. "Another Missionary, Once at the Training Home," *MW,* December 1906, 1.

55. *MW,* April 1909, 5.

56. A. S. Worrell, "Tongues," *MW,* September 1907, 4; "Dodsfald," *FV,* August 20, 1808, 4.

57. "A Candid Letter," *MW,* April 1908, 4.

58. G. L. Morgan, "What Shall We Do?" *MW,* November 1907, 8; "Letter from Bro. G. L. Morgan," *MW,* September 1907, 8.

59. "Letter from Mrs. E. C. Ladd," *MW,* July 1907, 5; "Religious Leader Here," *Martin County Sentinel,* June 21, 1907, 1.

60. "Other Camp Meetings," *New Acts* 3, no. 4 (August 1907): 1; "Denver Stirred," *Apostolic Light,* August 28, 1907.

61. Durham, "Bible Schools and Training Homes," *Articles Written by Wm. H. Durham Taken from PT* (Pamphlet), AG Archives, Springfield, Mo., 37.

62. Durham, "Glimpse," 155.

63. Ibid.; "A Remarkable Letter," *PT* 1, no. 8 (n.d.): 9–10.

64. *Pentecost,* October 15, 1909, 4.

65. Durham, "Glimpse," 10.

66. Aimee Semple Mcpherson, *This Is That* (Los Angeles: Echo Park Evangelistic Assoc., 1923), 58–61.

67. "Great War," *Upper Room* 1, no. 10 (May 1910): 2; "God Appointed Convention," *Promise,* March 1910, 1–2.

68. "Messages Spoken in New Tongues Interpreted," *BM,* April 15, 1908, 2.

69. Durham, "Our Book and Other Personal Matters," *PT* 1, no. 8 (n.d.): 16.

70. *BM,* August 15, 1909, 2.

71. Ibid.

72. "Londoners Claim the 'Gift of Tongues' (Led by Chicago Missionary)," *Evening Free Press (EFP)* (London, Ontario), February 1, 1910, 1, 8; "32 People Now Claim to Have 'Gift of Tongues' at Pentecost Meeting," *EFP,* February 2, 1910, 1.

73. Zelma Argue, *Contending for the Faith,* 20–23; Durham, "The Winnipeg Convention," *PT* 2, no. 1 (January 1912): 11–12.

74. "Our Canadian Tour," *PT* 1, no. 5 (July 1910): 6.

75. *MW,* June 1904, 6.

76. Durham, "The Great Crisis," *Word and Work* 32, no. 3 (March 1910): 80; *AF* (Ft. Worth) 7, no. 2 (May 1911).

77. "Triumph for Truth," *Reality,* April 1912, 128.

78. Durham, "Sanctification," *PT* 1, no. 8 (1911): 2.

79. Parham, *AF,* Supplement, July 1912; Bartleman, *How Pentecost Came,* 145ff.; Durham, "The Great Battle of 1911, *PT* 2, no. 1 (1912): 6; Durham, "Concerning Self-Defense, Misrepresentations, Etc.," *PT* 2, no. 2 (spring 1912?): 12.

80. Durham, "Battle of 1911," 6.

81. "False Doctrines," *PT* 2, no. 2 (n.d.): 6–7.

82. Durham, "The Great Crisis," *PT* 2, no. 2 (n.d.): 4–6.

83. Durham, "The Great Crisis," 6.

84. Goss, *Winds of God,* 126.

85. "The Lord's Convention," *Midnight Cry* 1, no. 1 (March–April 1911): 8.

86. *AF* (Ft. Worth) 7, no. 2 (May 1911); Harry Van Loon, "Bro. Durham Fallen Asleep," *Word and Work,* August 20, 1912, 3.

87. Durham, "Warning," *PT* 1, no. 8, 14; "Free Love," *AF* (Baxter Springs, Kans.), December 1912, 4–5.

88. "Mass Pentecostal Convention," *PT* 2, no. 2 (spring 1911): 16

89. "The Los Angeles Convention, A Time of Blessing, Power and Results," *PT* 2, no. 1 (n.d.): 12.

90. Durham, "Chicago Revival," *PT* 2, no. 2 (n.d.): 13.

91. Durham, "Revival," *PT* (July 1912): 14.

92. This chapter relies heavily on public records, county histories, and early Pentecostal and other evangelical periodicals. Published and unpublished writings on Durham focus on the content of his doctrine of sanctification rather than on his life.

Thomas Hampton Gourley: Defining the Boundaries
James R. Goff Jr.

This chapter is a revision of an article originally published as "The Limits of Acculturation:

Thomas Hampton Gourley and American Pentecostalism," *Pneuma: The Journal of the Society for Pentecostal Studies* 18 (fall 1996): 171–84.

1. See James R. Goff Jr., "Brother Westbrook Shouted, 'Glory,' and Mother Spoke in Tongues," *Christianity Today* 31 (October 16, 1987): 18–19.

2. Information on Gourley's childhood is sketchy, though his father's affiliation with the Methodist Church (presumably the Methodist Episcopal Church) is confirmed by family records that include a newspaper obituary and by Gourley's own recollections. See *Midnight Cry* 1 (March–April 1908): 4. The *Midnight Cry* hereafter cited as *MC*.

3. Thomas Hampton Gourley Family Collection, Flower Pentecostal Heritage Center, Springfield, Mo.

4. Telephone interview with Ted Gourley, Healdsburg, Calif., January 16, 1996, and "Biographical Sketch" in the Gourley Collection. Also *MC* 1 (May 1908): 1.

5. Effie Gourley's obituary reported that, by her death at age twenty-seven, she had suffered from "an illness that has been growing upon her for the last sixteen years or more." *Lawrence (Kansas) World*, July 13, 1899, 4.

6. Ibid., September 28, 1897, 3.

7. Ibid., July 29, 1897, 6.

8. *Topeka Daily Capital*, September 28, 1897, 1. See also *Kansas City Daily Journal*, September 28, 1897, 1, and *Lawrence (Kansas) World*, September 28, 1897, 3.

9. Compare *Lawrence (Kansas) World*, September 30, 1897, 7; October 7, 1897, 2; and October 14, 1897, 2, with *Kansas University Weekly*, October 2, 1897, 2, 4, and *Kansas City Journal*, October 8, 1897, editorial page.

10. *Lawrence (Kansas) World*, July 13, 1899, 4. Compare *Lawrence (Kansas) Weekly Journal*, July 15, 1899, 6, which attributes Mrs. Gourley's death to an operation, presumably to fight her longstanding bout with poor health.

11. Family records are very sketchy at this point, though the marriage and births are confirmed by documentary evidence in the Gourley Collection.

12. *Seattle Daily Times*, December 2, 1906, 17. Also *Seattle Post-Intelligencer*, December 2, 1906, 11.

13. *Apostolic Faith* (Topeka) 1 (May 17, 1899): 8.

14. *Apostolic Faith* (Topeka) 1 (May 3, 1899): 5. Cf. also p. 8, where the same (or perhaps a similar) account is told without naming the young lady.

15. Family records place the marriage in Topeka on January 17, 1901, in Topeka, just eleven days after local reporters broke the story of the revival. Gourley Collection. On the Topeka revival, see James R. Goff Jr., *Fields White unto Harvest: Charles F. Parham and the Missionary Origins of Pentecostalism* (Fayetteville: University of Arkansas Press, 1988), 62–86.

16. *Seattle Daily Times*, December 12, 1906, 5. Compare also *Seattle Post-Intelligencer*, August 30, 1907, 3, and September 3, 1907, 4.

17. Little is known about Junk other than the articles he contributed to the Azusa Street newspaper. Compare *Apostolic Faith* (Los Angeles) 1 (December 1906): 3, and 1 (January 1907): 1. Earlier references to Junk tie him to a "band of seven" that left Azusa in the fall of 1906 to go north and work in Oakland, Salem, and Seattle. See *Apostolic Faith* (Los Angeles) 1 (November 1906): 1; 1 (November 1906): 4.

18. *MC* 1 (November 1907): 2; 1 (December 1907): 2–3.

19. *MC* 1 (December 1907): 4.

20. *MC* 1 (November 1907): 1.

21. *MC* 1 (January–February 1908): 3.

22. Ibid.

23. On Irwin and the prevalence of the doctrine among Parham's early followers in Kansas and Missouri, see Goff, *Fields White unto Harvest*, 54–57, and Vinson Synan, *The Holiness-Pentecostal Tradition: Charismatic Movements in the Twentieth Century* (Grand Rapids, Mich.: William B. Eerdmans, 1997), 51–60.

24. *MC* 1 (January–February 1908): 1.

25. *MC* 1 (May 1908): 4. The previous issue had also referred to the three men, though in a more neutral light. Compare *MC* 1 (March–April 1908): 4.

26. Compare *MC* 1 (May 1908): 1–2, and 1 (November 1907): 2, noting the addresses for the paper and Gourley's school. No specific explanation was given for the change in address. The November 1907 issue (p. 2) also separated the first two editions of the paper from those that appeared subsequently: "Back numbers of *The Midnight Cry* (except Numbers 1 & 2) can always be had by addressing this office."

27. *MC* 1 (May 1908): 2. While it is possible that the move was coincidental, it is unlikely that a harmonious move would have occurred without recognizing the change openly. See also Frank Bartleman, *Azusa Street: The Roots of Modern-Day Pentecost*, ed. Vinson Synan (Plainfield, N.J.: Logos, 1980), 118. It is unclear whether Bartleman visited the mission on Seventh Avenue or on Olive Street.

28. Exceptions were the announcements of William Piper's "Latter Rain Convention" and of Gourley's own "Pentecostal Camp Meeting" to be held alongside Seattle's World's Fair. See *MC* 1 (August 1908): 2, and 1 (September 1908): 2. Gourley's camp meeting plans were also announced in the Midwest by J. R. Flower. See *Pentecost* (July 1909): 12.

29. On Parham's struggle with the issue of organization, see Goff, *Fields White unto Harvest*, 140–46.

30. *MC* 1 (August 1908): 3. The title "Projector of the Apostolic Faith" is one that Parham consistently used during this period. See Goff, *Fields White unto Harvest*, 106–35.

31. *Seattle Post-Intelligencer*, March 17, 1911, sec. 2, 1. Ballard Beach remained a popular site for Pentecostal revivalists. See *Word and Work* (Framingham, Mass.) 26 (September 1914): 281.

32. *Seattle Post-Intelligencer*, March 17, 1911, sec. 2, 1; *Seattle Star*, March 16, 1911, 8; and *Seattle Daily Times*, March 16, 1911, 8.

33. *MC* 1 (January–February 1908): 1, 4, and supplement. A smaller rendition of the supplement sketch had already appeared in the previous issue, *MC* 1 (December 1907): 1.

34. *MC* 1 (March–April 1908): 1, and 1 (September 1908): 3.

35. The reference is to the case of Leslie Crim, whose death in 1911 left an undetermined value in stock to the colony. The subsequent court case found in favor of Crim's relatives. For a description of life on the island, see Charles P. LeWarne, "'And Be Ye Separate': The Lopez Island Colony of Thomas Gourley," in *Pacific Northwest Themes: Historical Essays in Honor of Keith A. Murray*, ed. James W. Scott (Bellingham, Wash.: Center for Pacific Northwest Studies, 1978), 86–91. Also *Seattle Times*, December 4, 1955, 11.

36. *MC* (Port Stanley, Wash.), Lesson No. 15, 2. These later editions of the newspaper are easily distinguished from the earlier run; they were printed on smaller size paper and were not dated. Each issue included a single, sometimes continuing, article by Gourley.

37. *MC* (Port Stanley, Wash.), Lesson No. 13, 3.

38. For Parham's views on World War I, see Goff, *Fields White unto Harvest*, 156–57.

39. *American Reveille* (Bellingham, Wash.), January 10, 1919, 4. Though news reports referred to the Espionage Act, passed June 15, 1917, Gourley was actually tried according to revisions added in the Sedition Act of May 16, 1918.

40. *American Reveille* (Bellingham, Wash.), January 11, 1919, 6; January 12, 1919, 2; and LeWarne, "'And Be Ye Separate,'" 91–92. The colony, still with at least a hundred members at the time of the trial, continued briefly after Gourley's departure but was abandoned sometime in 1922.

41. For an early explanation of the doctrine by Gourley, see *MC* (Seattle) 1 (September 1908): 3.

42. *St. Louis Post-Dispatch*, March 2, 1923, 3. An earlier *Dispatch* article confirmed that Gourley and his entire family (he and Mary ultimately had five sons) now resided in St. Louis. See *St. Louis Post-Dispatch*, February 27, 1923, 20. Gourley supporters maintained that the evangelist claimed he would not die from sickness, thus leaving him vulnerable only to accidents.

43. Gourley's remarkable health was a legend even among the settlers at Lopez Island. When the Spanish flu afflicted the colony in 1918, only Gourley and one other man were unaffected. Transcript of interview with Peter Hampton Gourley, Thomas Gourley's son, by Irma Margaret Gourley, 1984, Gourley Collection. The testimony is confirmed by J. R. Moseley, *Manifest Victory: A Quest and a Testimony*, rev. ed. (New York: Harper and Brothers, 1947), 115–16.

44. This is the clear implication of Moseley, who visited Moise's home immediately after Gourley's death. Moseley, *Manifest*, 118–19. On Moise and her acceptance of this doctrine, see Wayne Warner, "Mother Mary Moise of St. Louis," *Assemblies of God Heritage* 6 (spring 1986): 6–7, 13–14.

45. *Macon Daily Telegraph*, April 17, 1923, 4. On Moseley's Pentecostal experience, see J. Rufus Moseley, *Perfect Everything*, rev. ed. (St. Paul: Macalester Park Publishing Co., 1952), 141–43. According to news accounts, Gourley, Moseley, and Henry H. Buhl of Irvington, Illinois, were headed north to collaborate on a publication and a series of tracts based on their religious views. See *Macon Daily Telegraph*, February 27, 1923, 1, and *Atlanta Constitution*, February 27, 1923, 6.

46. Moseley, *Manifest*, 118–19. According to this account, Gourley was in charge of the ministry at the Moise home at 2829 Washington Avenue in St. Louis. After the wreck, Moise attempted to replace Gourley with Moseley but Moseley refused, citing a specific warning from the Holy Spirit not to take such a position. The Macon theologian then informed Moise that the Spirit had told him that Gourley was to have no successor and that "we are all to be taught of the Lord and led by His Spirit" (119). For news coverage of the wreck, see *Macon Daily Telegraph*, February 27, 1923, 1, and *Atlanta Constitution*, February 27, 1923, 1, 6. The reference to John the Baptist also made the St. Louis papers. *St. Louis Post-Dispatch*, March 2, 1923, 3. The article further suggests that Gourley created a brief division between Moise and Ben Pemberton, another minister at the mission.

47. The connection with similar doctrine among Word of Faith followers in the 1980s and 1990s is intriguing, though there is no apparent direct link with Gourley. See James R. Goff Jr., "The Faith That Claims," *Christianity Today* 34 (February 19, 1990): 18–21.

48. The best source on Gourley's thought remains the scattered issues of the *Midnight Cry*, a number of which are held in the archives of the Assemblies of God in Springfield, Missouri. Secondary sources on Gourley are few. The pioneering description of life on Lopez

came in Charles P. LeWarne's "'And Be Ye Separate.'" See also James R. Goff Jr., "Thomas Hampton Gourley (1862–1923): American Pentecostal Pioneer," in *The New International Dictionary of Pentecostal and Charismatic Movements*, ed. Stanley M. Burgess (Grand Rapids, Mich.: Zondervan, 2002).

Alice E. Luce: A Visionary Victorian
Everett A. Wilson and Ruth Marshall Wilson

1. Gladys Fillmore, as told to Ruth Marshall Wilson. RMW's unpublished notes on Alice Luce are found in the Assemblies of God Archives, Springfield, Mo.

2. *Proceedings* of the Church Missionary Society (hereafter *Proceedings*), 1898, 202, 203.

3. Ibid., 1903, 241.

4. Ibid., 1905, 195.

5. Ibid., 1906, 164, 165.

6. Alice E. Luce, *The Messenger and His Message: A Handbook for Young Workers on the Preparation of Gospel Addresses*, rev. ed. (Springfield, Mo.: Gospel Publishing House, 1930), 65.

7. Gary B. McGee, "Pentecostal Phenomena and Revivals in India: Implications for Indigenous Church Leadership," *International Bulletin of Missionary Research* (July 1996): 112–17.

8. Alice Luce, *The Little Flock in the Last Days* (Springfield, Mo.: Gospel Publishing House, 1927), 94, 95.

9. Gary McGee to Everett Wilson, April 18, 1998 (in Assemblies of God Archives). See also Stanley H. Frodsham, *With Signs Following* (Springfield, Mo.: Gospel Publishing House, 1941), 109, and William T. Ellis, "Christians in India Are Given Gifts of Tongues," in B. F. Lawrence, "The Works of God," *Weekly Evangel* 9 (June 24, 1916): 4–6.

10. Luce, *The Little Flock*, 195, 196.

11. Ibid., 203–5.

12. Gladys L. Fillmore, who knew Luce in California, refers to her recurrent malaria. RMW, unpublished notes.

13. Alice Luce, "Paul's Missionary Methods," *Pentecostal Evangel*, January 8, 1921, 6. The correct title is Roland Allen, *Missionary Methods: Saint Paul's or Ours?* (1912).

14. Ibid.

15. Ibid.

16. RMW, unpublished notes.

17. *Pentecostal Evangel*, October 13, 1917.

18. *Pentecostal Evangel*, March 3, 1917.

19. Frodsham, *With Signs Following*, 202–4.

20. *Pentecostal Evangel*, July 17, 1917.

21. *Pentecostal Evangel*, November 17, 1917.

22. Ibid.

23. *Weekly Evangel*, April 20, 1918.

24. Additional information on the relationship of Luce with Francisco Olazábal is found in Victor De León, *The Silent Pentecostals* (n.p.: privately published, 1979), 22. Also

see Jennifer Stock, "George S. Montgomery: Businessman for the Gospel," *Assemblies of God Heritage* (summer 1989): 12–14, 20, and Miguel Guillén, *La Historia del Concilio Latino Americano de Iglesias Cristianas* (Brownsville, Tex.: Latin American Council of Christian Churches, 1982), 104, 105.

25. *Weekly Evangel*, April 20, 1918.

26. *Pentecostal Evangel*, June 15, 1918.

27. Clifton L. Holland, *The Religious Dimension in Hispanic Los Angeles: A Protestant Case Study* (South Pasadena, Calif.: William Carey Library, 1974), 356.

28. Luce, *The Messenger and His Message*, introduction.

29. *Pentecostal Evangel*, December 14, 1918.

30. Ibid., January 24, 1920.

31. Ibid., May 24, 1921.

32. See Gastón Espinosa, "El Azteca: Francisco Olazábal and Latino Pentecostal Charisma, Power, and Faith Healing in the Borderlands, "*Journal of the American Academy of Religion* 67, no. 3 (September 1999): 597–616.

33. Nellie Bazán, *Enviados de Dios* (Springfield, Mo.: Gospel Publishing House, 1987), 42.

34. Luce, *The Little Flock*, 35; *Pentecostal Evangel*, December 9, 1922.

35. See the memoirs of Ralph D. Williams in *Hands That Dug the Well*, ed. Lois Williams (n.p.: privately published, 1998). The work begun by Ralph Williams in Central America followed the "indigenous model" he learned from Alice Luce. That national church is analyzed in Melvin Hodges, *The Indigenous Church* (Springfield, Mo.: Gospel Publishing House, 1953).

36. *Pentecostal Evangel*, April 21, 1923.

37. Ibid., February 9, 1924.

38. Alice Luce, "Pentecost on the Mexican Border," *Pentecostal Evangel*, November 11, 1939.

39. "Portions for Whom Nothing Is Prepared," *Pentecostal Evangel*, December 9, 1922; "The Strangers within Our Gates," *Pentecostal Evangel*, August 13, 1927; and "Pentecost on the Mexican Border," *Pentecostal Evangel*, November 11, 1939.

40. Alice Luce, "Latin American Bible Institute of California," *Pentecostal Evangel*, June 6, 1942.

41. "Lighthouse That Once Led Souls to the Rock of Ages Now Is Gone," *(Torrence, Calif.) Daily Breeze*, February 6, 1997. Also, RMW, unpublished notes, and RMW, *Declare His Glory*, a commemorative volume published by the Southern California District of the Assemblies of God, 1994, 58.

42. Luce, *The Little Flock*, 164, 165.

43. Alice Luce, *Pictures of Pentecost in the Old Testament*, 2d ser. (Springfield, Mo.: Gospel Publishing House, 1930).

44. *Pentecostal Evangel*, July 8, 1947.

45. RMW, unpublished notes.

46. Ibid.

47. De León, *Silent Pentecostals*, 22.

48. RMW, unpublished notes.

49. Estéban Camarillo to E. Wilson, April, 14, 2000.

50. De León, *Silent Pentecostals*, 22. Estéban Camarillo, who was associated with Alice Luce at LABI in the 1950s, characterized her as a "sweet person who was devoted to training Mexican leaders." Camarillo to E. Wilson, April, 14, 2000.

51. De León, *Silent Pentecostals*, 22. Other assessments of Alice Luce and her work include Gary McGee's entry in the *Dictionary of Pentecostal and Charismatic Movements*, ed. Stanley Burgess and Gary McGee (Grand Rapids, Mich.: Zondervan, 1988), and McGee, "Pioneers of Pentecost: Alice E. Luce and Henry C. Ball," *Assemblies of God Heritage* 2 (1985): 5–6, 12–15. Luce's own writings for the most part are available in the Flower Pentecostal Heritage Center, Springfiled, Mo., and at the Latin American Bible Institute, La Puente, California. Because her writings are so diffuse, it is possible that not all of them can be found. The unpublished notes of Ruth Marshall Wilson, found in the Flower Center, heavily inform this chapter.

Francisco Olazábal: Charisma, Power, and Faith Healing in the Borderlands
Gastón Espinosa

The author wishes to thank Glenn Gohr and Juan Hernandez for their assistance in securing sources and Catherine Albanese, Mario T. García, Sarah Cline, Colin Calloway, John Watanabe, Robert Gundry, and Rick Pointer for their critical feedback on early drafts of this chapter, which is the basis for a critical biography to be published by Oxford University Press.

1. Barry A. Kosmin and Seymour P. Lachman,. *One Nation under God: Religion in Contemporary American Society* (New York: Harmony Books, 1993), 137–42.

2. Andrew Greeley, "Defection among Hispanics," *America*, July 30, 1988.

3. Max Weber argues that the charismatic prophet is someone who possesses "extraordinary powers" that are either a natural endowment or artificially produced. This charismatic power often manifests itself through a prophetic voice that develops in opposition to the priestly religion out of which it arises. Charismatic leaders do not receive their power and mission from the established religion but rather seize it. The prophet's authority is based on personal, direct revelation from God, not service to an already established tradition. Peter Berger argues that rather than interpreting the prophet as an outsider to society, it may be best to interpret the prophet as an insider who attempts to reform or transform the tradition from within but is gradually driven to the social periphery. The key to the charismatic prophet's success is the allegiance of his followers, who enable him to exercise charisma. Ironically, this noninstitutional charisma is bureaucratically institutionalized after the founder's death in accordance with the emerging body of tradition. This transition from charismatic prophet to routinization often creates an unstable period that can end in fragmentation. For further discussion, see Max Weber, *The Sociology of Religion* (New York: n.p., 1922), and Michael J. McClymond, "Prophet or Loss? Reassesssing Max Weber's Theory of Religious Leadership," paper presented at the American Academy of Religion, San Francisco, Calif., November 1997.

4. Gastón Espinosa, "Borderland Religion: Los Angeles and the Origins of the Latino Pentecostal Movement in the U.S., Mexico, and Puerto Rico, 1900–1945" (Ph.D. diss. University of California, Santa Barbara, 1999).

5. For evidence and a discussion of Mexican popular Catholicism and folk healing, see Ari Kiev, *Curanderismo: Mexican American Folk Psychiatry* (New York: Free Press, 1968); William and Claudia Madsen, *A Guide to Mexican Witchcraft* (Mexico, D.F.: Minutiea Mexicana, 1972), and June Macklin, "*Curanderismo* and *Espiritismo:* Complementary Approaches to Traditional Health Services," in *The Chicano Experience,* ed. Stanley A. West and June Macklin (Boulder, Colo.: Westview Press, 1979), 207–26.

6. Juárez Cano," El Rev. Francisco Olazábal: Datos Biograficos" *El Mesanjero Cristiano* (June 1938): 6–8, 12–13; Roberto Domínguez, *Pioneros De Pentecostés: Noreamerica y Las Antillas,* vol. 1, 3d ed. (Barcelona: Editorial Clie, 1990), 41–42; Luís Villaronga, "¿Quién es Olazábal?" *El Mundo* (1934): 31; Luís Villaronga, "Datos para la Biografía del Rvdo F. Olazábal," *El Mensajero Cristiano* (October 1938): 5–6; Frank Olazábal Jr., Latino Pentecostal Oral History Project (LPOHP), telephone interview, May 1998, Hanover, N.H. LPOHP housed at Hispanic Churches in American Public Life Program, University of California, Santa Barbara.

7. Cano, "El Rev. Francisco Olazábal," 6–8, 12–13; Domínguez, *Pioneros De Pentecostés,* 41–42; Luís Villaronga, "¿Quién es Olazábal?" 31; Luís Villaronga, "Datos para la Biografía del Rvdo F. Olazábal," 5–6.

8. Homer A. Tomlinson, *Miracles of Healing in the Ministry of Rev. Francisco Olazábal* (New York: Homer Tomlinson, 1939), 6; Domínguez, *Pioneros De Pentecostés,* 32–35.

9. Domínguez, *Pioneros De Pentecostés,* 36.

10. Methodist Episcopal Church, Official Minutes of the Sixty-fourth Session of the California Conference of the Methodist Episcopal Church, Santa Cruz, Calif., 1916, 26, 34; Methodist Episcopal Church, Official Minutes of the Sixty-fifth Session of the California Conference of the Methodist Episcopal Church, Santa Cruz, Calif., 1917, 185.

11. Tomlinson, *Miracles of Healing,* 6–7; Domínguez, *Pioneros De Pentecostés,* 32, 35; Francisco Olazábal, "A Mexican Witness," *Pentecostal Evangel,* October 16, 1920.

12. Tomlinson, *Miracles of Healing,* 6–7; Domínguez, *Pioneros De Pentecostés,* 32, 35.

13. H. C. Ball, "A Report of the Spanish Pentecostal Convention," *Christian Evangel,* December 28, 1918, 7; Francisco Olazábal, "God Is Blessing on the Mexican Border," *Weekly Evangel,* October 1, 1921, 10; Victor De León, *The Silent Pentecostals* (Taylors, S.C.: Faith Printing Co., 1979), 28–29.

14. J. W. Welch to H. C. Ball, November 11, 1924; H. C. Ball to J. R. Flower, December 8, 1924; Francisco Olazábal, "The Mexican Work at El Paso," *Pentecostal Evangel,* September 30, 1922, 13; Francisco Olazábal Jr., Latino Pentecostal Oral History Project; Miguel Guillén, *La Historia Del Concilio Latino Americano De Iglesias Cristianas* (Brownsville, Tex.: Latin American Council of Christian Churches, 1991), 83; Latin American Council of Christian Churches, *Seminario Del CLADIC 25 Año Aniversario* (Brownsville, Tex.: Latin American Council of Christian Churches, 1979), 7.

15. H. C. Ball to Pastor J. R. Kline, February 7, 1933, 1–2; Tomlinson, *Miracles of Healing,* 7; De León, *Silent Pentecostals,* 99.

16. Guillén, *La Historia,* 93–114.

17. Tomlinson, *Miracles of Healing,* 7–8.

18. "La Hermana McPherson en la Carpa de Watts y el Hno. Francisco Olazábal en 'Angelus Temple' de Los Angeles," *El Mensajero Cristiano* (October 1927): 6–8; J.T.A., "Un Servicio Evangelio Para Los Mexicanos," *El Mensajero Cristiano* (November 1927): 7–8.

19. "La Hermana McPherson en la Carpa de Watts y el Hno. Francisco Olazábal en 'Angelus Temple' de Los Angeles," 6–8; Francisco Olazábal Jr., *Revive Us Again!* (Los Angeles: Christian Academic Foundation, 1987), 81; idem, LPOHP.

20. "La Hermana McPherson en la Carpa de Watts y el Hno. Francisco Olazábal en 'Angelus Temple' de Los Angeles," 6–8; Olazábal, LPOHP.

21. "Primera Sesion De La Iglesia Interdenominacional de Chicago," *El Mensajero Cristiano* (September 1929): 8–9; "Iglesia De Chicago, IL.," and "Testimonios de Sanidad Divina," *El Mensajero Cristiano* (September 1930): 12–16; Tomlinson, *Miracles of Healing,* 11.

22. "Cuatro Meses con el Rev. Francisco Olazábal en la Ciudad de Nueva York," *El Mensajero Cristiano* (January 1932): 11–12. Circular flyer, in possession of the author.

23. Ibid.

24. Tomlinson, *Miracles of Healing,* 1–2.

25. Ibid., 1.

26. Gastón Espinosa, "'Your Daughters Shall Prophesy': A History of Women in Ministry in the Latino Pentecostal Movement in the United States," in *Women and Twentieth Century Protestantism,* ed. Virginia Brereton and Margaret Bendroth (Champaign: University of Illinois Press, forthcoming).

27. "Cuatro Meses con el Rev. Francisco Olazábal en la Ciudad de Nueva York," 11–12.

28. Homer A. Tomlinson, "Letter to the Pentecostal Evangel," October 13, 1931.

29. Robert A. Brown to H. C. Ball, October 13, 1931; H. C. Ball to J. R. Evans, October 14, 1931; J. R. Flower to H. C. Ball, October 21, 1931; H. C. Ball to J. R. Evans, October 27, 1931; J. R. Kline to J. R. Evans, February 4, 1933; J. R. Flower to J. R. Kline, February 7, 1933. Copies of letters in possession of the author.

30. Olazábal, LPOHP.

31. Domínguez, *Pioneros De Pentecostés,* 18.

32. Luís Villaronga, "El Evangelista Olazábal en Rio Piedras," *El Mundo* (San Juan, Puerto Rico), May 5, 1934; Guillén, *La Historia,* 122–31; Spencer Duryee, "The Great Aztec," *Christian Herald* (August 1936): 6.

33. Ernest Gordon, "Revival among Spanish-Speaking," *Sunday School Times,* August 24, 1935, 550–51; Spencer Duryee, "The Great Aztec," 5–7; Luís Villaronga, "El Evangelista Olazábal en Rio Piedras"; Tomlinson, *Miracles of Healing,* 12, 17, 24.

34. Tomlinson, *Miracles of Healing,* 16–17; Domínguez, *Pioneros De Pentecostés,* 18.

35. Tomlinson, *Miracles of Healing,* 17; Domínguez, *Pioneros De Pentecostés,* 44.

36. Tomlinson, *Miracles of Healing,* 18–19; Domínguez, *Pioneros De Pentecostés,* 45–46; "La Campaña Olazábal en Puerto Rico," *El Mensajero Cristiano* (April 1936): 3.

37. Tomlinson, *Miracles of Healing,* 18–19.

38. "Campaña Olazábal de El Paso, Texas," *El Mensajero Cristiano* (July 1936): 6, 15; Carlos Sepúlveda, "La Campaña Olazábal en el Paso, Texas," *El Mensajero Cristiano* (August 1936): 6–7; Carlos Sepúlveda, "Glorioso Servicio De Despedida," *El Mensajero Cristiano* (August 1936); Tomlinson, *Miracles of Healing,* 19–20.

39. "Campaña Olazábal de El Paso, Texas," 6, 15; Sepúlveda, "La Campaña Olazábal en el Paso, Texas," 6–7; Sepúlveda, "Glorioso Servicio De Despedida"; Tomlinson, *Miracles of Healing,* 19–20; Father Lourdes F. Costa to Francisco Olazábal, June 9, 1936; Father

Lourdes F. Costa to Francisco Olazábal, June 11, 1936; Rev. Francisco Olazábal to Father Lourdes F. Costa, July 13, 1936.

40. "Campaña Olazábal de El Paso, Texas," 6, 15; Sepúlveda, "La Campaña Olazábal en el Paso, Texas," 6–7; Sepúlveda, "Glorioso Servicio De Despedida"; Tomlinson, *Miracles of Healing*, 19–20; Olazábal, *Revive Us Again!;* Domínguez, *Pioneros De Pentecostés*, 280–81.

41. Francisco Olazábal Jr., an eyewitness to the event, stated that his father was surprised by Homer Tomlinson's insistence that he swear allegiance to the Church of God at the convention. Olazábal had no intention of doing this prior to his arrival in Cleveland, Tennessee. He later told his son that he had reluctantly agreed to the act. Olazábal, LPOHP; Travis Hedrick, "Hundreds Seek Faith Healing," *Chattanooga Times*, September 12, 1936, 1, 7; Tomlinson, *Miracles of Healing*, 16. The Tomlinson Church of God had split from the Church of God (Cleveland, Tennessee) in 1923. In 1952 the main body of the former named itself the Church of God of Prophecy.

42. Hedrick, "Hundreds Seek Faith Healing," 1.

43. "Hundreds Pray All Night at Unique Healing Service," *Cleveland Daily Banner,* September 12, 1925.

44. Tomlinson, *Miracles of Healing*, 20.

45. Homer Tomlinson, "Big Parade of 2,000 Lead Down Fifth Avenue New York City," *White Wing Messenger,* November 7, 1936, 1, 4.

46. "Rev. F. Olazábal, Evangelist Here," *New York Times,* June 12, 1937.

47. "A Mighty Man of God Has Fallen in the Midst of His Labors," *White Wing Messenger,* July 3, 1937, 4.

48. A. D. Evans, "Brother Olazábal Killed in Auto Accident," *White Wing Messenger,* June 19, 1937, 1; "A Mighty Man of God Has Fallen in the Midst of His Labors," 1, 4; Tomlinson, *Miracles of Healing*, 23–25; Domínguez, *Pioneros De Pentecostés*, 50–56.

49. Guillén, *La Historia,* 187–300.

50. "Overseer of Latin-American Churches," *White Wing Messenger,* August 28, 1937, 1; Tomlinson, *Miracles of Healing*, 26–27; "Miguel Guillén Leaves New York for Another Visit to the Churches," *White Wing Messenger,* April 23, 1938, 1.

51. The fourteen denominations Olazábal directly or indirectly contributed to include the Hispanic United Methodist Church; the Hispanic Districts of the Assemblies of God; the Latin American Council of Christian Churches; the Hispanic International Foursquare Gospel; the Hispanic Church of God of Prophecy; the Defenders of the Faith; the Missionary Church of Christ; the Church of Christ of the Antilles; the Assembly of Christian Churches; the Damascus Christian Church; the Concilio Cristiano Hispano Pentecostés (former Olazábal Council of Christian Churches); Evangelical Assemblies, Inc.; the Pentecostal Council of Christian Churches; and the Pentecostal Assembly of Jesus Christ. There are also many other smaller Latino Pentecostal denominations that trace their roots back to Francisco Olazábal.

52. Villaronga, "¿Quién es Olazábal?" 31; Duryee, "The Great Aztec," 5–8; Cano, "El Rev. Francisco Olazábal," 6–8, 12–13; Domínguez, *Pioneros De Pentecostés,* 41–42.

53. The Chicano movement (1965–75) was a political-social movement that fought for civil rights against the social and racial indignities many Mexican Americans faced in the United States. Rudy L. Busto, "Like a Mighty Rushing Wind: The Religious Impulse in the Life and Writings of Reies López Tijerina" (Ph.D. diss., University of California,

Berkeley, 1989); Carlos Muñoz Jr., *Youth, Identity, and Power: The Chicano Movement* (New York: Verso Books, 1992).

Maria B. Woodworth-Etter: Prophet of Equality
Wayne E. Warner

1. Clarence Macartney, "Shall We Ordain Women as Ministers and Elders?" *Presbyterian* (November 7, 1929): 7. Quoted in Margaret L. Bendroth, "Fundamentalism and Femininity: The Reorientation of Women's Role in the 1920s," *Evangelical Studies Bulletin* (March 1988): 2.

2. E. N. Bell, editorial, *Christian Evangel* (February 13, 1915): 2

3. Woodworth, *Marvels and Miracles* (Indianapolis: author, 1921), 12, 13. Maria B. Underwood (1844–1924) married Philo H. Woodworth in 1863. She divorced him in 1891, charging him with adultery. He died in 1892. After she married Samuel Etter in 1902, she was known as Maria B. Woodworth-Etter, or Sister Etter. For simplicity, I have used Etter throughout.

4. "Says She Is Insane," *St. Louis Post-Dispatch,* August 31, 1890.

5. Woodworth, *Marvels and Miracles,* 11.

6. "Camp Meeting," *Time,* August 19, 1935, 34, 35.

7. Aimee Semple McPherson, *The Story of My Life* (Waco, Tex.: Word Books, 1973), 74, 75.

8. Kathryn Kuhlman, *A Glimpse into Glory* (Plainfield, N.J.: Logos International, 1979), 32.

9. Wayne Warner, *Kathryn Kuhlman: The Woman Behind the Miracles* (Ann Arbor, Mich.: Servant Publications, 1993), 110.

10. Woodworth, *Life, Work and Experience of Maria Beulah Woodworth* (St. Louis, 1894), 38.

11. Woodworth, *Life, Work and Experience,* 51. This is only a sample of the powerful results Etter experienced even before she began praying for the sick and seekers began going into trances.

12. *Kokomo (Ind.) Dispatch,* May 28, 1885. The *Dispatch* and the rival *Gazette Tribune* took sides on Etter's trances, healings, and other practices.

13. *Kokomo (Ind.) Dispatch,* May 28, 1885.

14. "Camp Meeting in Indiana," *Church Advocate* (June 9, 1886).

15. *Cincinnati Enquirer,* February 17, 1885.

16. After the Dallas meeting in 1912, Etter could not keep up with the demands on her ministry. The next year she was the featured speaker at the World-Wide Camp Meeting in Los Angeles. And she preached and prayed for the sick at key Pentecostal centers across the country.

17. Woodworth, *Life, Work and Experiences,* 41, 42.

18. Woodworth, *Life, Work and Experiences,* 342, 343. Police arrived within a few days and established order. Etter reported that many of the hoodlums were converted and united with a church she established in St. Louis.

19. "Quackery and Emotional Religion," *St. Louis Republic,* September 3, 1890.

20. Oral history interview with David Lee Floyd, conducted by Wayne Warner in 1981, Flower Pentecostal Heritage Center.

21. Robert Craig, "The San Francisco Etter Meetings," *Weekly Evangel*, December 16, 1916, 15.

22. Everett A. Wilson, "Robert J. Craig's Glad Tidings and the Realization of a Vision for 100,000 Souls," *Assemblies of God Heritage* (summer 1988): 10.

23. Goss, *The Winds of God*, 159.

24. Quoted in Wayne Warner, *The Woman Evangelist: The Life and Times of Charismatic Evangelist Maria B. Woodworth-Etter* (Metuchen, N.J.: Scarecrow Press, 1986), 190.

25. Four of the best-known women preachers in the twentieth century, in addition to Etter, experienced divorces. They were Florence Crawford, Kathryn Kuhlman, Aimee Semple McPherson, and Uldine Utley.

26. Woodworth, *Life, Work and Experiences*, 446.

27. McPherson, *This Is That*, 149, 150. The 1918 influenza epidemic had closed public meeting places prior to McPherson's arrival in Indianapolis.

28. Woodworth-Etter, *Signs and Wonders* (Indianapolis, 1916); reprinted as *A Diary of Signs and Wonders* (Tulsa: Harrison House, 1980), 211.

29. Ibid.

30. Ibid., 215. Concerning her credentials, C. H Forney, in *The History of the Churches of God in the United States of North America* (Findley, Ohio: Churches of God Publishing House, 1914), 440, wrote that Etter was granted a license to preach and was appointed "Eldership Evangelist" at that 1884 meeting, credentials that were withdrawn in 1904.

31. Carrie Judd Montgomery edited a Christian periodical, *Triumphs of Faith*, from 1881 until her death in 1946. A faith home could be described as a Christian communal home, or a bed and breakfast for Christian travelers. Here temporary and permanent residents would conduct Bible studies and prayer meetings. Children growing up in a faith home never knew who would show up for breakfast—perhaps an old friend or a total stranger.

32. An Etter descendant told me during the 1980s that, as a result of discovering and reading Etter's life story, she sold her business and entered the ministry.

33. Woodworth, *Life, Work and Experiences*, 208.

34. Ibid., 304–5.

35. Ibid., 305.

36. Ibid., 306. Etter mentions meeting a "Sister Foot, a colored evangelist," who participated in the Louisville meetings. "She was highly esteemed by the people of the East. She had labored with the white people. For years I had desired to meet her . . . She is a firebrand for God." This is possibly Julia Foote, a Methodist evangelist.

37. It is unknown what happened to the African American mission. In her updated *Signs and Wonders* (1916), Etter deleted the line "We organized a colored mission."

38. *Oakland Tribune*, December 9, 1889.

39. Reprinted in Woodworth-Etter, *Signs and Wonders*, 253. Haywood (1880–1931) was a leader in the Pentecostal Assemblies of the World and was an Indianapolis pastor.

40. Woodworth-Etter, *Signs and Wonders*, 359–60; *Atlanta Journal*, April 13, 1914.

41. Woodworth, *Marvels and Miracles*, 408–9.

42. Woodworth, *Life, Work and Experiences*, 346.

43. "Neglect Not the Gift That Is in Thee," a sermon Etter preached at Chicago's Stone Church, July 17, 1913, and published in *Latter Rain Evangel* (August 1913).

44. Considerable material in this chapter came from my research in writing *The Woman Evangelist, The Life and Times of Charismatic Evangelist Maria B. Woodworth-Etter,* included in the Studies in Evangelicalism series. Other valuable sources include C. H. Forney, *The History of the Churches of God in the United States of North America;* Ethel Goss, *The Winds of God;* Roberts Liardon, comp., *Maria B. Woodworth-Etter: The Complete Collection of Her Life Teaching* (Tulsa: Albury Press, 2000); Aimee Semple McPherson, *This Is That;* and Wayne Warner, *Kathryn Kuhlman: The Woman Behind the Miracle.* Etter's books published before 1902 are under the name of Mrs. M. B. Woodworth or Maria Beulah Woodworth; books published after 1902 (following her marriage to Samuel Etter) show the author's name as Mrs. M. B. Woodworth-Etter. Several of her journal-type books were updated periodically and given new titles. Etter self-published her books.

Florence Crawford: Apostolic Faith Pioneer
Cecil M. Robeck Jr.

1. F. L. Crawford, "*Teaching* [on Sanctification]: John 17:1–23, I Corinthians 13:1–6" (December 28, 1921), 3. Crawford's unpublished sermons are in the Archives of the Apostolic Faith Mission in Portland, Oregon.

2. "Last Honor Paid Faith's Founder," *Oregonian,* June 25, 1936, sec. 1, 9.

3. But see "The Same Old Way," *Apostolic Faith* (Los Angeles) 1 (September 1906): 3.

4. "Pioneer of 1849 Is Dead at Age of 79," *Portland Telegram,* November 28, 1921, 9; "One of First White Children of This Section Succumbs," *Oregon Sunday Journal,* June 5, 1927, sec. 1, 7; "Emigrant Wagon That Crossed Plains in 1850 Prized Possession of Oregon Man," *Oregonian,* September 8, 1929, sec. 1, 14.

5. *A Historical Account of the Apostolic Faith: A Trinitarian-Fundamental Evangelistic Organization: Its Origin, Functions, Doctrinal Heritage, and Departmental Activities of Evangelism* (Portland, Ore.: Apostolic Faith Publishing House, 1965), 54.

6. F. L. Crawford, "Sermon: Acts 1:1–8," (July 10, 1924), 2.

7. Cf. F. L. Crawford, "Sermon: Hebrews 1:1–4, 6, 8–9" (January 10, 1924), 5.

8. *A Historical Account,* 54.

9. Ibid., 55.

10. *The Light of Life Brought Triumph: A Brief Sketch of the Life and Labors of Florence L. [Mother] Crawford, 1872–1936* (Portland, Ore.: Apostolic Faith Publishing House, 1936, 1955), 5.

11. F. L. Crawford, "Sermon: Malachi 5:1–2, *et al.*" (September 17, 1922), 5; "Sermon: Joel 2:21–23, *et al.*" (March 16, 1930), 5.

12. "Highland Park Happenings," *Highland Park Herald,* August 11, 1906, 5.

13. *The Light of Life Brought Triumph,* 5.

14. F. L. Crawford, "Sermon: Acts 3:1–10, 4:9–12" (August 13, 1922), 5.

15. *Saved to Serve: A Sketch of the Life and Theology of Raymond Robert Crawford* (Portland, Ore.: Apostolic Faith Publishing House, 1967), 21.

16. F. L. Crawford, "Sermon: Acts 17:15–21, 23–30, Matthew 11:2–6" (October 1, 1922), 4.

17. Crawford, *A Historical Account of the Apostolic Faith,* 55–56.

18. *Saved to Serve,* 21.

19. Crawford, "Sermon: Acts 1:1–8," 1; "Building on the foundation 'Which Is Jesus Christ'" (July 2, 1919), 2; and *The Light of Life Brought Triumph,* 6.

20. *Saved to Serve,* 21.

21. Los Angeles City Directory, 1899, 36, and 1903, 40.

22. "W.C.T.U. Delegates Are Here," *Los Angeles Express,* October 24, 1905, sec. 1, 13.

23. "Untitled Note," *Highland Park Herald,* April 7, 1906, 5.

24. F. L. Crawford, "Sermon: Acts 17:15–21, 23–30, Matthew 11:2–6" (October 1, 1922), 4.

25. F. L. Crawford, "What It Means to Be the Bride of Christ: II Peter 1:1, II Corinthians 11:2, Matthew 22:1" (August 4, 1919), 8.

26. F. L. Crawford, "Sermon: Joel 2:22–26" (March 5, 1922), 1; idem, "Teaching on the Baptism of the Holy Ghost" (July 21, 1925), 6.

27. F. L. Crawford, "Sermon: Hebrews 6:1, *et al.*" (September 30, 1934), 1; idem, "Teaching on the Baptism of the Holy Ghost," 6.

28. "Last Honor Paid Faith's Founder," *Oregonian,* June 25, 1936, sec. 1, 9.

29. Crawford, "Teaching: The Baptism of the Holy Ghost (Cont.)" (July 21, 1933), 8.

30. F. L. Crawford, "Sermon: Malachi 3:1" (December 31, 1916), 2.

31. "Rev. Joseph Smale Holds Revival," *LA Express,* June 17, 1905, sec. 2, 7.

32. Frank Bartleman, "The Pentecostal or 'Latter Rain' Outpouring in Los Angeles," in Bernard F. Lawrence, *The Apostolic Faith Restored* (St. Louis: Gospel Publishing House, 1916), 71.

33. "New Church Is Organized," *LA Express,* September 25, 1905, 7; "Curb Preacher Scores Theater," *LA Express,* May 1, 1906, 7.

34. F. L. Crawford, "Sermon: Acts 1:1–8, Isaiah 35:2–6, Joel 2:25, 23, 24, 27–29" (December 14, 1930), 3.

35. Crawford, "Building on the Foundation 'Which Is Jesus Christ,'" 2. Cf. idem, "Teaching on the Baptism of the Holy Ghost," 3.

36. Cf. Crawford, "Teaching: The Baptism of the Holy Ghost (Cont.)," 9.

37. Crawford, "Sermon: Malachi 3:1," 6. The dates vary. Cf. Crawford, "Teaching: Baptism of the Holy Ghost," 6, which notes "just three days after that He baptized me with the Holy Ghost and fire."

38. *The Light of Life Brought Triumph,* 14–16.

39. Crawford, "Teaching: The Baptism of the Holy Ghost" (August 2, 1929), 9.

40. Nils Bloch-Hoell, *The Pentecostal Movement: Its Origin, Development and Distinctive Character* (New York: Humanities Press, 1964), 48.

41. "Highland Park Happenings," *Highland Park Herald,* August 4, 1906, 5.

42. "Fire Falling at Oakland," *Apostolic Faith* (Los Angeles) 1 (September 1906): 4, and "Spreading the Full Gospel," *Apostolic Faith* (Los Angeles) 1 (November 1906): 1. Cf. "Missionaries to Jerusalem," *Apostolic Faith* (Los Angeles) 1 (September 1906): 4.

43. "Fire Falling at Oakland"; untitled item, *Apostolic Faith* (Los Angeles) 1 (October 1906): 1; "A Portuguese Minister Receives His Pentecost," *Apostolic Faith* (Los Angeles) 1 (October 1906): 1.

44. "Local Holy Rollers to Invade Oregon," *LA Express,* October 5, 1906, 2; "Slow to Arrive," *(Salem) Daily Oregon Statesman,* October 10, 1906, 2.

45. Clara E. Lum, "Wonderful News from Los Angeles," *Apostolic Light* (November 1906): 4.

46. "Ask Police Aid," *Daily Oregon Statesman*, November 15, 1906, 3.

47. "Under Wings of Police," *(Salem) Daily Capital Journal*, November 14, 1906.

48. "'New Tongues,'" *Daily Oregon Statesman*, November 20, 1906, 6.

49. "Anonymous Visitor, The Other Side," *Daily Oregon Statesman*, November 20, 1906, 6.

50. "Sister Crawford Departs," *Daily Capital Journal*, December 29, 1906, 5.

51. "Specimen," *Topeka Daily Capitol*, January 6, 1901, 6; cf. two untitled items *Apostolic Faith* (Los Angeles) 1 (September 1906): 1; "Baba Bharati Says Not a Language," *Los Angeles Daily Times*, September 19, 1906, 1.

52. "Pile of Queer Lore Gets Fat," *(Portland, Ore.) Evening Telegram*, December 22, 1906, 4; "Claims Gift of Tongues," *(Dallas) Polk County Observer*, December 28, 1906, 1; Florence Crawford, untitled item, *Apostolic Faith* (Los Angeles) 1 (January 1907): 4; B. H. Irwin, "My Pentecostal Baptism—A Christmas Gift," *Triumphs of Faith* 27 (May 1907): 114–17; F. L. Crawford, "Portland Is Stirred," *Apostolic Faith* (Los Angeles) 1 (January 1907): 1.

53. "Azusa to Portland: A Moment in History Revisited," *Higher Way: The Magazine for Spiritual Growth* 89 (November–December 1996): 6.

54. "Padded-Cell Religion in Two Forms Is Rampant in Portland," *(Portland, Ore.) Evening Telegram*, December 31, 1906, 1.

55. "Frazer after Holy Howlers," *(Portland, Ore.) Evening Telegram*, January 1, 1907, 1.

56. Crawford, "Portland Is Stirred," 1, describes the meeting of December 30.

57. "Fanatics Must Go into Court," *(Portland, Ore.) Evening Telegram*, January 2, 1907, 7.

58. "Judge Frazer Issues Ukase," *(Portland, Ore.) Evening Telegram*, January 3, 1907, 8.

59. "'Bride of the Lord' Now Has a Severe Cold," *(Portland, Ore.) Evening Telegram*, January 4, 1907, 12.

60. Crawford, "Portland Is Stirred," 1.

61. "Azusa to Portland: A Moment in History Revisited," *Higher Way* 89 (November–December 1996): 7.

62. F. L. Crawford, "Soldiers Receive Pentecost," *Apostolic Faith* (Los Angeles) 1 (April 1907): 4.

63. F. L. Crawford, "Pentecost in the North," *Apostolic Faith* (Los Angeles) 1 (February–March 1907): 5.

64. "Pentecost in San Jose and Portland," *Apostolic Faith* (Los Angeles) 1 (May 1907): 4.

65. "Broken Arm Unattended," *Los Angeles Herald*, July 14, 1907, 1; "Doctor Sets Child's Arm," *Los Angeles Herald*, July 15, 1907, 2.

66. "Trotter Released from Union Rescue Mission," *Los Angeles Herald*, July 24, 1907, 6; "To Continue Rescue Work," *Daily Times*, July 25, 1907, sec. 2, 3; untitled item, *Apostolic Light* (Spokane, Wash.) 183 (August 28, 1907): 3.

67. "Call Melville Trotter to Rescue Mission," *Los Angeles Herald* (August 14, 1907): 3.

68. Gal. 6:17; cf. untitled item, *Apostolic Faith* (Los Angeles) 1 (September 1907): 1.

69. "Pastor's Funeral Set for Saturday," *Oregon Daily Journal,* November 11, 1935, 13.

70. "Winnipeg, Can.," *Apostolic Faith* (Los Angeles) 1 (January 1908): 1.

71. Loyce C. Carver, "History and Beginnings of Our Church: Roots from Azusa," typescript, 8, archives of the Apostolic Faith Mission, Portland, Ore.

72. F. L. Crawford, "A Cheering Testimony," *Apostolic Faith* (Los Angeles) 1 (October–January 1908): 4; "Portland Oregon," *Apostolic Faith* (Los Angeles) 1 (January 1908): 1.

73. Carver, "History and Beginnings," 8–9.

74. The Biola University Library and Archive holds the papers of Lyman Stewart. On Stewart and *The Fundamentals,* see George M. Marsden, *Understanding Fundamentalism and Evangelicalism* (Grand Rapids, Mich.: William B. Eerdmans, 1991), 41.

75. "Women with Men Embrace," *LA Daily Times,* September 3, 1906, 11; "Wife Prefers Holy Rollers to Husband," *LA Express,* September 7, 1906, 4; "Says Wife Went with Jumpers," *Los Angeles Record,* September 7, 1906, 1; "Found with Holy Rollers," *(Los Angeles) Herald* (September 8, 1906): 3.

76. "Bible Teaching on Marriage and Divorce," *Apostolic Faith* (Los Angeles), 1 (January 1907): 3.

77. G. W. Shumway, "A Study of 'The Gift of Tongues'" (A.B. thesis, University of Southern California, 1914), 179–80. For additional details, from different perspectives, see C. M. Robeck Jr., "Seymour, William Joseph," in *New International Dictionary of Pentecostal and Charismatic Movements,* ed. Stanley M. Burgess (Grand Rapids, Mich.: Zondervan Publishing Co., 2002), 1056, and Edith Blumhofer and Grant Wacker, "Who Edited the Azusa Mission's *Apostolic Faith?*" *Assemblies of God Heritage* 21 (summer 2001): 15–21.

78. *Saved to Serve,* 25, 28.

79. Owen "Irish" Lee was a colorful figure from Azusa Street who became a successful evangelist; Ned Caswell, Sunday No. 1 (diary), September 27, 1908, David du Plessis Archive, Fuller Theological Seminary, Pasadena, Calif.

80. Caswell, Sunday No. 1, October 4, 1908.

81. Ibid.

82. Ibid.

83. Ibid.

84. Ibid.

85. Will C. Trotter to Mr. Lyman Stewart, January 4, 1909; Will C. Trotter to Mr. Lyman Stewart, April 19, 1909, and April 20, 1909. Trotter even named one son Lyman Stewart Trotter.

86. Will C. Trotter to Mr. Lyman Stewart, May 13, 1909.

87. Will C. Trotter to Mr. Lyman Stewart, July 22, 1909; October 22, 1909; and March 3, 1911.

88. Will C. Trotter to Mr. Lyman Stewart, December 24, 1909.

89. Ned Caswell, Sunday No. 1.

90. Ibid.

91. Crawford, "Teaching: Baptism of the Holy Ghost," 6.

92. Will C. Trotter to Lyman Stewart, April 29, 1913.

93. H. A. Ironside, *Apostolic Faith Missions and the So-Called Second Pentecost* (New York: Loizeaux Brothers, Bible Truth Depot, n.d.), 15, 14, 10.

94. Cf. J. C. Vanzandt, *Speaking in Tongues.* (1911; reprint, Portland, Ore.: J. C. Vanzandt, 1926), 38.

95. Cf. Robert Bryant Mitchell, *Heritage and Horizons: The History of Open Bible Standard Churches* (Des Moines: Open Bible Publishers, 1982).

96. To date, the only substantive biographical data on Florence Louise Crawford may be found in *A Historical Account of The Apostolic Faith*, especially 53–72. A smaller, useful treatment is *The Light of Life Brought Triumph.*

G. T. Haywood: Religion for Urban Realities
David Bundy

1. *Apostolic Faith* (Los Angeles) 2 (May 1908): 1.
2. Ibid., 1 (September 1906): 1.
3. Ibid., 1 (January 1907): 1.
4. Alice Reynolds Flowers, *Grace for Grace: Some Highlights of God's Grace in the Daily Life of the Flower Family* (Springfield: n.p., 1961), 18–24.
5. *Indianapolis Star,* February 1, 1907, 6.
6. Glen Cook, "Pentecostal Power in Indianapolis," *Apostolic Faith* (Los Angeles) 1 (February–March 1907): 3.
7. "'Gliggy Bluks' Meet," *Star,* April 17, 1907, 1. "Bluk" (overheard glossolalia?) was used by the newspaper to designate Pentecostals.
8. David Bundy, "Bishop William Taylor and Methodist Mission: A Study in Nineteenth Century Social History," *Methodist History* 27 (1989): 197–210; *Methodist History* 28 (1989): 3–21.
9. "Negro Bluk Beats Demon from Girl," *Star,* May 5, 1907, 1.
10. "Bluk's Patron Saint," *Star,* May 9, 1907, 9.
11. "Negro Bluk Coming," *Star,* May 9, 1907, 3.
12. "Negro Bluk Kissed," *Star,* June 8, 1907, 3.
13. "Bluks Divide Home," *Star,* June 4, 1907, 1.
14. "Negro Bluk Blows. Why? Husband May Know," *Star,* June 5, 1907, 20.
15. "Oddy Asks Divorce Because of Bluks," *Star,* June 6, 1907, 3.
16. "Bluk Crowd Runs Over," *Star,* June 10, 1907, 12.
17. "The Gliggy Bluk Language," *Star,* June 15, 1907, 10.
18. "Bluk Feet Big and Little Washed," *Star,* June 16, 1907, 10.
19. "Police after Bluks," *Star,* June 11, 1907, 15.
20. G. T. Haywood, "Autobiographical Text," cited by Morris E. Golder, *The Life and Works of Bishop Garfield Thomas Haywood (1880–1931)* (n.p.: n.p., 1977), 32.
21. Ibid.
22. *Voice in the Wilderness* 2 (July 1910): 2.
23. G. T. Haywood, "The Marriage and Divorce," *Voice in the Wilderness* 2 (July 1910): 3.
24. C. K., "An Open Letter," *Voice in the Wilderness* 2 (July 1910): 3.
25. G. T. Haywood, "Autobiographical Text," 32.
26. Oral history interview with Rachel Johnson, October 7, 1988.
27. "A Closer and Deeper Fellowship," *Christian Evangel* 1 (July 19, 1913): 1–2.
28. "A Closer and Deeper Fellowship," 1.

29. Golder, *Life and Works,* 36, citing Haywood writing in *Voice in the Wilderness* (1921).

30. James L. Tyson, *The Early Pentecostal Revival* (Hazelwood, Mo.: Word Aflame Press, 1992), 293–300. Cf. Golder, *History,* 50–60.

31. Prints (which do not do justice to the original) of the photograph appear in Morris E. Golder, *History of the Pentecostal Assemblies of the World* (Indianapolis: n.p., 1973), 55, and Tyson, *Early Pentecostal Revival,* 205.

32. Hilda Reeder, *A Brief History of the Foreign Missionary Department of the Pentecostal Assemblies of the World* (Indianapolis: Foreign Missionary Dept, n.d.).

33. Oral history interview, Raymond Moore, July 7, 1991.

34. G. T. Haywood, *The Marriage and Divorce Question in the Church* (Indianapolis: Christ Temple, n.d.). See his "The Marriage and Divorce," *Voice in the Wilderness* 2 (July 1910): 3.

35. Golder, *History,* 93–95.

36. The essential sources on Haywood are the books by Morris E. Golder (*The Life and Works of Bishop Garfield Thomas Haywood (1880–1931)* and *History of the Pentecostal Assemblies of the World*) and periodicals, especially *Voice in the Wilderness.* The best archives are those of the United Pentecostal Church (Hazelwood, Missouri) and the Assemblies of God (Springfield, Missouri).

Charles Harrison Mason: The Interracial Impulse of Early Pentecostalism
David D. Daniels

1. William B. Holt, comp., *A Brief Historical and Doctrinal Statement and Rules for Government of the Church of God in Christ* (n.p., circa 1917), 9.

2. Ibid., 9.

3. C. Eric Lincoln and Lawrence H. Mamiya, *The Black Church in the African American Experience* (Durham, N.C.: Duke University Press, 1990), 1, 76–91.

4. In an interview of Bishop Mason by Lucille J. Cornelius, Mason gave 1862 as his birth year. See Lucille J. Cornelius, comp., *The Church of God in Christ* (n.p., 1975), 16; Mason's birth date is also listed as 1866.

5. Cornelius, *History,* 16; James Courts, ed., *The History and Life Work of Elder C. H. Mason, Chief Apostle and His Co-Laborers* (n.p., circa 1920), 14–17; Courts identified 1880 as the year of Mason's conversion.

6. Paul Harvey, *Redeeming the South: Religious Cultures and Racial Identities among Southern Baptists, 1865–1925* (Chapel Hill: University of North Carolina Press, 1997), 62–74.

7. Courts, *History and Life Work,* 22.

8. Lowell Barks Sr. et al., *Glorious Heritage: The Gold Book, Documentary—Historical, Church of the Living God, Motto: (CWF) 1899–1964* (n.p., 1967), 22–23, 9–11; William Christian, *Poor Pilgrim's Work* (Texarkana, Ark.: n.p., 1896), 14.

9. Barks, *Glorious Heritage,* 17. There is no record of Mason's view on the polygenesis theory.

10. Courts, *History and Life Work,* 18.

11. Ibid., 26.

12. David Daniels, "Pentecostalism," in *Encyclopedia of African American Religions*, ed. Larry Murphy, J. Gordon Melton, and Gary Ward (New York: Garland Reference Library of Social Science, 1993), 585–90.

13. Otho B. Cobbins, ed., *History of Church of Christ (Holiness) USA, 1895–1965* (New York: Vantage Press, 1966), 28; David Douglas Daniels, "The Cultural Renewal of Slave Religion: Charles Price Jones and the Emergence of the Holiness Movement in Mississippi" (Ph.D. diss., Union Theological Seminary, New York, 1992), 153–55; *Truth* (Jackson, Miss.), March 15, 1906, 10; Jones began publishing *Truth* in 1896.

14. Daniels, "Cultural Renewal," 585–89; John T. Benson Jr., *Holiness Organized or Unorganized: History 1895–1915 of the Pentecostal Mission, Inc. Nashville, Tennessee* (Nashville: Trevecca Press, 1977), 47.

15. Susie Cunningham Stanley, *Feminist Pillar of Fire: The Life of Alma White* (Cleveland: Pilgrim Press, 1993), 70; Timothy Smith, *Called unto Holiness: The Story of the Nazarenes, The Formative Years* (Kansas City, Mo.: Nazarene Publishing House, 1962), 180–204.

16. Douglas J. Nelson, "For Such a Time as This: The Story of Bishop William J. Seymour and the Azusa Street Revival" (Ph.D. diss., University of Birmingham, United Kingdom, 1981); Cecil M. Robeck, "Azusa Street Revival," in *Dictionary of Pentecostal and Charismatic Movements*, ed. Stanley M. Burgess et al. (Grand Rapids, Mich.: Zondervan, 1988), 33.

17. Earlie Simmons Truitt, "Elder William T. Simmons," *The St. Paul Church of God in Christ* (Lexington, Miss.), 1987 Homecoming Celebration Souvenir Book (n.p., n.d.).

18. Frank Bartleman, *Azusa Street* (Plainfield, N.J.: Logos Books International, 1980), 54. The Boddy quotation is cited in Lawrence Neale Jones, "The Black Pentecostals," in *The Charismatic Movement*, ed. Michael P. Hamilton (Grand Rapids, Mich.: William B. Eerdmans, 1975), 147.

19. Robert Mapes Anderson, *Vision of the Disinherited: The Making of American Pentecostalism* (Oxford: Oxford University Press, 1979), 122–24.

20. Charles Price Jones, *Characters I Have Met* (Jackson, Miss.: National Publishing Board Church of Christ [Holiness] USA, 1927), 41–42.

21. The minutes of the second annual session of the Pentecostal Alliance convention are cited in Benson, *Holiness Organized*, 93. For L. P. Adams, see Minutes of Second Annual Session of the Pentecostal Alliance Convention, November 15–20, 1900; for H. G. Rodgers, see *Zion's Outlook* 11 (November 17, 1901): 9; for M. M. Pinson as early as 1902, see Benson, *Holiness Organized*, 231.

22. Wayne Warner, "Church of God in Christ (White)," and "Pinson, Mack M.," in Burgess et al., *Dictionary*, 203, 715–16; Ithiel Clemmons, *Bishop C. H. Mason and the Roots of the Church of God in Christ* (Bakersfield, Calif.: Pneuma Life Publishing, 1996), 54.

23. Paul S. Carter, *Heritage of Holiness: An Eyewitness History, First Assembly of God, Memphis, Tennessee* (Memphis: Paul's Press [self-published], 1991), 18–21, 29, 33, 69–70; Adams's congregation included a Latino family (two daughters of a Mexican–white American couple, Emmanuel and Lucy Trevino). For the earlier use of the name Church of God in Christ that counters Carter's claim, see *Truth* (Jackson, Miss.) 10 (March 15, 1906): 10. Carter contended that Adams first used the name Church of God in Christ; however, there were published accounts of the name within Jones and Mason's fellowship as early as 1906.

24. Clemmons, *Bishop C. H. Mason,* 70–71; Harold Vinson Synan, *The Holiness-Pentecostal Movement in the United States* (Grand Rapids, Mich.: William B. Eerdmans, 1971), 150.

25. *Truth* (Jackson, Miss.) 10 (March 15, 1906): 10.

26. Bureau of Investigations file, Monroe, Louisiana, April 2, 1918, 6, Special Agent H. D. Gulley to Bureau, case file OG64788, BI, NA.

27. Lillian Coffey, comp., *1926 Yearbook of the Church of God in Christ* (n.p., n.d), 125; Charles H. Pleas, *Fifty Years of Achievement (History) Church of God in Christ* (n.p., circa 1957), 12; Holt, *Brief Historical,* 3, 5.

28. Theodore Kornweibel Jr., "Bishop C. H. Mason and the Church of God in Christ during World War I: The Perils of Conscientious Objection," *Southern Studies: An Interdisciplinary Journal of the South* 26 (winter 1987): 277.

29. Kornweibel, "Bishop C. H. Mason," 271, 265.

30. Holt, *Brief Historical,* 9.

31. Coffey, *1926 Yearbook,* 125; April 6, 1926, letter with February 1924 as incorporation date on the letterhead along with the name "The White Churches of God in Christ," Flower Pentecostal Heritage Center, Springfield, Mo.

32. The minutes omit the particulars of the doctrinal issue; Minutes of the General Assembly, 1928; December 5, 1931 (private collection of Juanita Faulkner, Madison, N.J.).

33. Wayne E. Warner, *The Woman Evangelist: The Life and Times of Charismatic Evangelist Maria B. Woodworth-Etter* (Metuchen, N.J.: Scarecrow Press, 1986), 261. Minutes of the General Assembly, 1933 (private collection of Juanita Faulkner, Madison, N.J.).

34. The first full-length study of Charles Mason is Clemmons's *Bishop C. H. Mason and the Roots of the Church of God in Christ,* which has a good bibliography. The scholarly analysis of Mason's pacifist activity during World War I is Kornweibel's "Bishop C. H. Mason and the Church of God in Christ during World War I." An overview of Mason's life can be found in David C. Tucker's chapter on Mason in his *Black Pastors and Leaders: Memphis, 1819–1972* (Memphis: Memphis State University Press, 1975). The primary text that serves as the basis of the outline of Mason's life is James Courts's *The History and Life Work of Elder C. H. Mason.*

Carrie Judd Montgomery: The Little General
Jeannette Storms

1. Carrie F. Judd is shortened to CFJ and Carrie Judd Montgomery to CJM in the notes. Articles from the *Triumphs of Faith* appear as *T/F* with only the volume number, year, and pages given. CJM, *The Secret of Victory* (Oakland: Triumphs of Faith, 1921), 19–21, 106–9; CFJ, *The Prayer of Faith* (New York: Fleming H. Revell Co., 1880), 9–21; CJM, *Under His Wings* (Oakland: Triumphs of Faith, 1936), 54–56, 69–72, 98–102.

2. CJM, *Under,* 69–73, 79–81; CJM, *T/F* 29 (1909).

3. "Wealthy Warriors: A Rich Salvationist and His Wife," *Buffalo Morning Express,* May 8, 1892, 4; CJM, *Under,* 9–13. I have woven this overview around the word *faith,* which succinctly expresses the major theme of Montgomery's life and teaching.

4. CJM, *Under,* 12–47; CJM, *Secret,* 24.

5. CFJ, *Prayer,* 9–17; CJM, *Under,* 49–59; CJM, *Secret,* 24–26.

6. CJM, *Under,* 59–68; Daniel E. Albrecht, "Carrie Judd Montgomery: Pioneering

Contributor to Three Religious Movements," *Pneuma: The Journal of the Society for Pentecostal Studies* 8 (fall 1986): 112–14.

7. CJM, *Under,* 76–77; Ralph Judd, "Knave," *Oakland Tribune,* July 26, 1964, sec. 5-FL.

8. Robert L. Stanton, "Gospel Parallelisms," *T/F*3 (March 1883): 73–77. *T/F* carried this series from March to December in 1883. Miroslav Volf argues that this emphasis on the materiality of salvation is a unique contribution of Pentecostalism to Protestant theology. Miroslav Volf, "Materiality of Salvation: An Investigation in the Soteriologies of Liberation and Pentecostal Theologies," *Journal of Ecumenical Studies* 26, no. 3 (summer 1989): 457.

9. CFJ, *T/F*2 (December 1882): 187–88.

10. CJM, *Under,* 78–79; CFJ, *T/F* 1 (November 1881): 144.

11. CFJ, *T/F*2 (February 1882): 20; (April 1882): 59–60; (December 1884): 265–69.

12. CJM, *Under,* 98–102. W. E. Boardman, International Conference for Divine Healing and True Holiness, to Carrie Judd, Bethshan, London, archives of the Home of Peace of Oakland in Oakland, California (hereafter cited as S/C, Oakland).

13. CJM, *Under,* 69–72; CFJ, *T/F*9 (May 1889): 117–19.

14. CFJ, *T/F* 7 (September 1887): 203–4; (December 1887): 265–69; 8 (February 1888): 47–49; (November 1888): 241–44; 9 (May 1889): 117–19; (June 1889): 138–40.

15. CFJ, *T/F* 1 (January 1881): 1–4; 4 (February 1884): 25–27. Irving Ford, interview by author, Oakland, Calif., December 17, 1997.

16. CFJ, *Prayer,* 130–31.

17. James E. Webb, "Announcement Summer Convocation Christian Workers, Western Springs, Cook County, Illinois, from June 7th to 16th" (Chicago: Foster Roe & Crone Art, 1889), S/C, Oakland. CJM, *Under,* 127–28.

18. George S. Montgomery, *T/F* 12 (December 1892): 265–67. Reprinted in tract form and translated into Spanish and Portuguese. Jennifer Stock, *Assemblies of God Heritage* (spring 1989): 4–5, 17–18.

19. CJM, *T/F* 22 (March 1902): 50. "Vast Fortune Given Away by Montgomery," *Oakland Tribune,* September 9, 1930.

20. CJM, *Under,* 132–41. Anna W. Prosser, *T/F* 10 (June 1890): 121–24. CJM, *T/F* (July 1890): 165–67; (August 1890): 187–91.

21. CJM, *Under,* 140–45. CJM, *T/F* 10 (October 1890): 232–33; 12 (January 1892): 16–17; 13 (June 1893): 94–95.

22. CJM, *T/F* 12 (October 1892): 257–60; 13 (June 1893): 125–26; 14 (July 1894): 166–67; 20 (August 1900): 190; 21 (June 1901): 143; 34 (June 1914): 140–44.

23. CJM, *T/F* 12 (September 1892): 214–15; (October 1892): 261; 13 (April 1893): 94–95.

24. CJM, *T/F* 12 (May 1892): 118; 13 (December 1893): 198–99; 14 (April 1894): 86–87; 16 (July 1896): 167–68; (August 1896): 187–88; 27 (December 1907): 280.

25. CJM, *T/F* 14 (February 1894): 30–31; 19 (November 1899): 234–35; 22 (April 1902): 80–82; 25 (July 1905): 179; 27 (November 1907): 254–55.

26. S.I.D., "The Home of Peace," *Oakland Enquirer,* October 1895, S/C Oakland.

27. CJM, *T/F* 12 (April 1982): 73–74; 13 (January 1893): 1, 5–9; (March 1893): 54–55.

28. CJM, *The Life of Praise* (Oakland: Triumphs of Faith; reprint, n.d.); CJM, *T/F*

13 (May 1893): 98; 19 (July 1899): 145–47; (March 1899): 49–51; 22 (September 1902): 193–97.

29. Frank Bartleman, "Letter from Los Angeles," *T/F* 26 (December 1906): 247–52. Pandita Ramabai, *T/F* 27 (December 1907): 267. CJM, *Under,* 161–65.

30. CJM, *T/F* 28 (July 1908): 146–48; 29 (July 1909): 145–49. CJM, "Speaking in Tongues" (tract) (Framingham, Mass.: Christian Workers Union, n.d.). Sophie Hansen, "Gift of the Chinese Language" (tract) (Oakland: Triumphs of Faith, n.d.).

31. CJM, *T/F* 28 (October 1908): 229–30. S. R. Break, *T/F* 29 (April 1909): 82–83.

32. "Pentecostal fullness" was her preferred terminology. CJM, *Under,* 165–66.

33. CJM, *T/F* 31 (November 1911): 241–44; (December 1911): 265–67. Reprinted as one tract.

34. CJM, *Under,* 215. *T/F* 32 (October 1912): 216.

35. CJM, *Under,* 163, 171–85. CJM, Personal Journal, 1909, Assemblies of God Archives in Springfield, Missouri (hereafter cited as S/C, Springfield). CJM, *T/F* 28 (November 1908): 258–61; (December 1908): 267–68; *T/F* 29 (July 1909). Future references to CJM use only her last name, with her husband referenced as George Montgomery.

36. CJM, *T/F* 29 (January–August 1909). CJM, Personal Journal, 1909, S/C, Springfield. CJM, *Under,* 187.

37. CJM, *T/F* 30 (June 1910): 121; (July 1910): 145–47; (September 1910): 193–95; (October 1910): 217–20. CJM, *Under,* 186–87, 231.

38. CJM, *Under,* 195–99. CJM, *T/F* 30 (March 1910): 71; (October 1910): 215–16; 34 (February 1914): 47; 33 (January 1933): 24.

39. "Credentials," or "Certificate of Ordination & Unity," Church of God in Christ, January 11, 1914, and "Application for Ordination," November 30, 1917, S/C, Springfield. Beulah Chapel was listed as an Assemblies of God Church in *The Assemblies of God, Northern California-Nevada District Presents Its Chronicle of the Past 50 Years* (San Jose: Assemblies of God, Northern California & Northern Nevada District Council, Inc., 1971), 24. Edith Blumhofer, *The Assemblies of God,* vol. 1 (Springfield: Gospel Publishing House, 1989), 199–202.

40. CJM, Personal Journal, 1900, S/C, Springfield. CJM, *T/F* 33 (December 1913): 269–71; 35 (April 1915): 86; 36 (March 1916): 65–67. Jennifer Stock *Assemblies of God Heritage* (summer 1989): 20.

41. CJM, *T/F* 28 (August 1908): 169–70; 30 (January 1910): 1–3; 30 (February 1910): 25–26; 33 (March 1913): 49–51; 33 (May 1913): 97–99; 33 (June 1913): 121; 33 (December 1913): 265–67; 34 (October 1914): 217–19.

42. CJM, *Under,* 196. CJM, *T/F* 30 (December 1910): 266. CJM, *Secrets,* 19–21, 106–9.

43. CJM, *Under,* 250–56.

44. William DeArtegea, *Quenching the Spirit* (Lake Mary, Fla.: Creation House, 1992), 121.

45. "With Christ," *Pentecostal Evangel,* August 17, 1946, 7. J. Narver Gortner, "Carrie Judd Montgomery—A Tribute," S/C, Springfield. *T/F* 65, no. 9 (August 1946): 105–11.

46. CJM, *Under,* 140. Loren Berry, interview by author, Oakland, Calif., December 17, 1997.

47. Primary sources of autobiographical materials most useful in deciphering

Montgomery's life were the *Triumphs of Faith* (vols. 1–65), with monthly notes of her life, ministry, and travels as well as her autobiography, *Under His Wings*. The primary source that detailed her healing was Carrie F. Judd, *The Prayer of Faith*. Her views on the victorious life were contained in *The Secret of Victory*. Two archival collections containing primary documents were the Assemblies of God Archives in Springfield, Missouri, and the archives of the Home of Peace of Oakland in Oakland, California. Secondary sources and biographical overviews included Albrecht's, "Carrie Judd Montgomery" and J. D. Douglas, ed., *Twentieth Century Dictionary of Christian Biography* (Grand Rapids, Mich.: Baker Book House, 1995), 258. Jennifer Stock's biographical overview of the life of George S. Montgomery added another perspective. It appeared in the 1989 spring and summer issues of *Assemblies of God Heritage*.

Antonio Castañeda Nava: Charisma, Culture, and Caudillismo
Daniel Ramirez

The author wishes to acknowledge the contribution of Bernice Nava Ares, as well as the debt owed to Jose Ortega, Manuel Gaxiola, and Issac Cota, historians of the Apostolic movement, and to the late Maria Mendoza de Ramírez and Mary Lou Carrillo, two of Antonio Nava's many lay contemporaries, without whom the *caudillo* and his collaborators could not have built a movement.

1. I suggest the term *apostolicism* to encompass this cultural and doctrinal tributary of Pentecostalism both for sake of leaner nomenclature and to reflect the more common self-designation (*apostólico* or *apostolic*) by practitioners. Oneness Pentecostals affirm a proto-Hebrew monotheism and a functional, i.e., nonontological, view of the Godhead: God as Father in creative work, as Son in redemptive work, and as Spirit infilling the Church. As primitivists, Oneness Pentecostals also eschew postapostolic conciliar creeds and confessions, e.g., Nicea and Chalcedon, as unacceptable contextual compromises with Graco-Roman philosophy.

2. The Pentecostal movements headed by Lugo and Olazábal also produced considerable indigenous hymnody. See Juan Concepción, ed., *Ecos de vida: Selección especial de himnos y canciones espirituales por compositores hispanos* (Brooklyn: Editorial Ebenezer, n.d.); and Felipe Gutiérrez, ed., *Nuevo himnario de melodías evangélicas selectas* (Brownsville: Latin American Council of Christian Churches, 1944).

3. Lalive d'Epinay, *Haven of the Masses: A Study of the Pentecostal Movement in Chile* (London: Lutterworth P., 1969).

4. Robert Mapes Anderson, *Vision of the Disinherited: The Making of American Pentecostalism* (New York: Oxford University Press, 1979), 113.

5. Harvey Cox, *The Rise of Pentecostal Spirituality and the Reshaping of Religion in the Twenty-first Century* (Reading, Mass.: Addison-Wesley, 1995), xv.

6. Louis Dupré, "Mysticism," in *The Encyclopedia of Religion*, ed. Mircea Eliade (New York: Macmillan, 1987), 246.

7. Arvind Sharma, "Ecstasy," in *The Encyclopedia of Religion*, ed. Mircea Eliade (New York: Macmillan, 1987), 11.

8. Dupré, "Mysticism," 247.

9. Antonio Castañeda Nava, *Autobiografía del Hermano Antonio Castañeda Nava* (Rancho Cucamonga, Calif.: Apostolic Assembly of the Faith in Christ Jesus, 1994), 1.

10. Schleiermacher considered praxis beyond intuited religious feeling an "absor[ption] in[to] an unholy superstition." Friedrich Schleiermacher, *On Religion: Speeches to Its Cultured Despisers,* trans. and ed. Richard Crouter (Cambridge: Cambridge University Press, 1996), 29–30.

11. Nava, *Autobiografía,* 2.

12. Ibid.

13. Max Weber, *From Max Weber: Essays in Sociology,* trans. and ed. H. H. Gerth and C. Wright Mills (New York: Oxford University Press, 1946), 246.

14. For Oneness Pentecostals, soteriology follows theology; hence, they reject a Trinitarian baptismal formula (Matt. 28:19) in favor of water baptism "in the name of Jesus" (Acts 2:38).

15. Alice Luce, "Mexican Work along the Border," *Pentecostal Evangel* (Springfield, Mo.), June 15, 1918. Luce's 1920 application for license renewal with the denomination stressed the orthodoxy of recent converts: "All our converts have been immersed according to Matt. 28:19. The 'new issue' error is the greatest difficulty here. They are trying to steal away our flock all the time." Alice Luce, License Application, 1920, Assemblies of God Archives.

16. "The Missionary Department," *Pentecostal Evangel,* November 1, 1919, 23.

17. "Report of the Pentecostal Mexican Work in Texas, New Mexico, Colorado, Arizona, and Old Mexico," *Pentecostal Evangel,* November 1, 1919, 22.

18. "Supervision by Americans will always be helpful, if not necessary, however." Alice Luce, "Report of Trip through Texas," *Pentecostal Evangel,* November 1, 1919, 11. For an appraisal of the LABI and Luce, see Arlene Sanchez Walsh, "Workers for the Harvest: The Latin American Bible Institutes and the Institutionalization of the Latino Pentecostal Identity," *ACHTUS: Journal of Hispanic/Latino Theology* 8, no. 1 (August 2000): 54–79.

19. H. C. Ball, "A Call for More Laborers for the Mexican Work," *Pentecostal Evangel,* March 24, 1917, 13.

20. For a critical assessment of the "pious paternalism" of Ball and Luce, see Gastón Espinosa, "Borderlands Religion: Los Angeles and the Origins of the Latino Pentecostal Movement in the U.S., Mexico, and Puerto Rico, 1900–1945" (Ph.D. diss., University of California, Santa Barbara, 1999).

21. Antonio Nava interview, July 3, 1984, David du Plessis Archive, Fuller Theological Seminary, Pasadena, Calif.

22. Nava interview, September 13, 1994; Luis Herrera interview, September, 16, 1994, both interviews du Plessis Archive.

23. Garfield T. Haywood, "Baptized into the Body," in *The Bridegroom's Songs,* comp. G. T. Haywood (Indianapolis: by author, republished by Christ Temple Bookstore, n.d. [song composed 1914]), 20; Antonio C. Nava, "El Nombre del Mesias," in *Hymnos de Consolacion* (Los Angeles: Apostolic Assembly of the Faith in Christ Jesus, 1972); English translation of Nava's lyrics by Daniel Ramirez. "El Nombre del Mesías" used by permission, Bernice Ares.

24. Jose Ortega interview, July 10, 1991, du Plessis Archive.

25. For a study of such Gramscian strategies, see Manuel Peña, *The Texas-Mexican Conjunto: History of a Working-Class Music* (Austin: University of Texas Press, 1985).

26. That such Black-Latino contacts and influences were reciprocal is hinted at by the continued interracial fellowship among these two groups through the 1920s and 1930s (e.g.,

Watts, California) and reports of African American enthusiasm for Mexican worship, even in the Jim Crow setting of south Texas: "The brethren worship in a large room in a private house, perhaps some thirty gathering there, and in the back part the colored people gather. These colored people are anxious to hear Pentecost preached in their own language, but a white man could hardly preach to them in this part of the country. Yet, these colored people have learned to sing the Spanish songs with the Mexicans, even though they know very little Spanish. I hope that some colored Pentecostal preacher will go to Edna sometime and hold a meeting among them." H. C. Ball, "The Work Prospers on the Mexican Border," *Pentecostal Evangel,* July 8, 1922, 13.

27. Nava was elected *anciano ejecutivo* in the inaugural 1925 convention (and reaffirmed in that post in the 1927 convention) of the fledgling Iglesia de la Fé Apostólica Pentecostés. Francisco Llorente headed up the movement as *pastor general.*

28. Nava, *Autobiografía,* 13.

29. Jose Ortega interview, July 10, 1991, du Plessis Archive. The break with the PAW may not have been as clean and consensual as official Apostolic Assembly historiography has presented it. As late as 1945, several prominent dissidents (Guadalupe Lara, Ramón González, Sotero Carranza, Bautista Castro, and Heriberto Soto) claimed to operate under the aegis of the PAW as its "Spanish Department," an affiliation they relinquished when their following was received into fellowship that year with the Iglesia Apostólica in Tijuana, Mexico. "Libro de Registro de la Iglesia de Tijuana, B.C., Mexico" (Tijuana, 1945). The continued strength of African American ecclesial influences upon this group during the 1930–45 period is unclear.

30. Manuel J. Gaxiola, "Tiempos de Cambio: Breve Análisis Histórico-Teológico de la Relación entre la Asamblea Apostólica de los Estados Unidos y la Iglesia Apostólica de Mexico" (unpublished paper, Mexico D.F., 1990).

31. Clause 3, "Alianza Internacional Concertada entre los Representantes de la Iglesia Apostólica en Estados Unidos de Norte America y Mexico," *Constitución de la Asamblea Apostólica* (Mexico D.F.: Maclovio Gaxiola, 1945).

32. Antonio C. Nava, ed., *Himnos de Consolación,* 2d ed. (Los Angeles: A. C. Nava, 1932).

33. Maclovio Gaxiola Lopez, ed., *Himnos de Suprema Alabanza a Jesús* (Guamúchil, Sinaloa: Maclovio Gaxiola, 1941).

34. Max Weber, "The Routinizaton of Charisma," in *Max Weber: Sociological Writings,* ed. Wolf Heydebrand (New York: Continuum, 1994), 60:40.

35. Efraín Valverde letter, "A los Pastores y Ministros de la Asamblea Apostólica," September 21, 1969, du Plessis Archive.

36. "Declaración Oficial de los Acontecimientos que Constituyeron el Problema Manifestado en Salinas, California en los Meses de marzo, abril y mayo de 1971," Apostolic Assembly of the Faith in Christ Jesus, August 18, 1971, du Plessis Archive.

37. Arnold Cedillo, e-mail message, March 13, 1999, du Plessis Archive.

38. The chief primary sources on Nava and the Apostolic Assembly consist of two official histories: Ernesto S. Cantú, Jose A. Ortega, et al., eds., *Historia de la Asamblea Apostólica de la Fé en Cristo Jesús* (Mentone, Ca: Sal's Printing Service, 1966), and *Autobiografía del Hermano Antonio Castañeda Nava.* Jose Ortega's memoir, *Mis memorias en la Iglesia y la Asamblea Apostólica de la Fé en Cristo Jesús* (Indio, Calif.: author, 1998), devotes considerable attention to Nava and other pioneer evangelists, especially Felipe Rivas of the Iglesia

Apostólica in Mexico, with whom Ortega served at the helm of the Apostolic Assembly's sister church. In both the *Historia* and his memoir, Ortega, an avid photographer since the early 1920s, offers a rich visual collage of religious and cultural life in the U.S.-Mexico borderlands over the span of eight decades. A recent video documentary project commissioned by the Apostolic Assembly, *Nuestro Canto/Our Song: Apostolic Music and History from 1906 to Today* (Jack Genero, director, 1995), gathered a series of oral history interviews of Nava and other songwriters that await transcription. Bernardo Hernández's published record of the first conclave, *Estatutos acordados en la 1a. convención mexicana de la Iglesia de la Fé Apostólica Pentecostés* (Los Angeles: Bernardo Hernandez, 1926), and Maclovio Gaxiola's edition of the *Constitución de la Asamblea Apostólica*, the joint charter of both the Apostolic Assembly and the Iglesia Apostólica, provide contemporaneous evidence of Nava's prominence. In terms of secondary and critical sources, Manuel J. Gaxiola's published version of his master's thesis in church growth at Fuller Seminary, "La serpiente y la paloma: Análisis del crecimiento de la Iglesia Apostólica de la Fé en Cristo Jesús de Mexico" (South Pasadena: William Carey Library, 1970), appends a valuable summary on Apostolic Assembly history. Finally, my article, "Borderlands Praxis: The Immigrant Experience in Latino Pentecostal Churches," *Journal of the American Academy of Religion* 67, no. 3 (September 1999): 573–96, foregrounds Nava's pivotal role in the articulation of an ethos of borderlands solidarity and in the construction of networks to embody this praxis.

Ida B. Robinson: The Mother as Symbolic Presence
Harold Dean Trulear

The author wishes to acknowledge the ongoing support of Bishop Joseph Bell and the important cooperation of the late Bishops Amy Stevens, Sylvester Webb, and James Brown in the gathering of information for this article. Elder Minerva Bell deserves special mention for her lengthy history of the Mount Sinai Holy Church. Also to be recognized are Drew University, the Association of Theological Schools of the United States and Canada, Eastern Baptist Theological Seminary, and New York Theological Seminary for financial and structural support.

1. Stephen Breck Reid calls this principle the "Unity of Life" in his outstanding volume *Experience and Tradition: A Primer in Black Biblical Hermeneutics* (Nashville: Abingdon, 1991), 25–33.

2. See Cheryl Townsend Gilkes, "The Roles of Church and Community Mothers: Ambivalent American Sexism or Fragmented African Family-hood?" *Journal of Feminist Studies in Religion* 2 (spring 1986): 41–59.

3. C. Eric Lincoln, *The Black Church since Frazier* (New York: Schocken, 1973), 104.

4. Victor Turner, *Dramas, Fields, and Metaphors: Symbolic Action in Human Society* (Ithaca: Cornell University Press, 1974), 96.

5. Of the treatments of the "black religious experience" as a category for organizing and analyzing life, see especially Carl Ellis, *Beyond Liberation: The Gospel in the Black American Experience* (Downers Grove, Ill.: InterVarsity Press, 1983); C. Eric Lincoln and Lawrence Mamiya, *The Black Church and the African American Experience* (Durham: Duke University Press, 1990), especially chap. 1; Peter Paris, *The Social Teaching of the Black Churches* (Philadelphia: Fortress, 1985), 1–81; Talbert Shaw, "Religion and Afro-Americans: A Propaedeutic," *Journal of Religious Thought* 32 (spring–summer 1975): 65–73.

6. *Manual of the Mount Sinai Holy Church of America, Inc.,* 10.

7. Chester W. Gregory, *The History of the United Holy Church of America, Inc., 1886–1986* (Baltimore: Gateway Press, 1986), 77.

8. Minerva Bell interview with Mary Jackson, Mount Sinai archives, n.d. See also *Commemorative Journal of the Mount Sinai Holy Church of America* (1989), 9.

9. Episcopal remarks by Presiding Bishop Amy Stevens at New York–New England District Convocation, Stamford, Conn., August 1991.

10. Bell interview with Jackson.

11. "Minutes of First Holy Convocation," September 1925, quoted in *Commemorative Journal,* 10–11.

12. "Minutes of First Holy Convocation," September 1925.

13. *Manual,* 10.

14. Trulear, "Reshaping."

15. See William Clair Turner's important dissertation, "The United Holy Church of America: A Study in Black Holiness-Pentecostalism" (Ph.D. diss., Duke University, 1984), especially 49–101. See also his "Singing in the Holy Convocation of the United Holy Church of America," *Journal of Black Sacred Music* 2 (fall 1988): 19–22. Also note specifications on sanctification in *Manual,* 29–31.

16. Trulear interview with Bishop Joseph Bell, September 1985.

17. *Manual,* 45.

18. "Report on Foreign Inspired Agitation among American Negroes in Philadelphia Division," Federal Bureau of Investigation File 100-135-37-2, August 9, 1942. Special thanks to Pentecostal bibliographer extraordinaire Dr. Sherry Dupree of Santa Fe Community College (Fla.) for supplying this reference. Subsequent interview by Bishop Joseph Bell with longstanding member Walter Spain in September of 1991 has shed further light on this subject.

19. Lillian Sparks, "Women's Rights," *Latter Day Messenger of the Mount Sinai Holy Church of America* 2 (1934): 3.

20. Trulear interview with Bishop Joseph Bell, August 1991.

21. Noted by Minerva Bell in her address, "Confirming Our Earthly Heritage: Mount Sinai History and Roots," delivered at the Sixtieth Annual Holy Convocation of the Mount Sinai Holy Church of America, September 1984, in Philadelphia. Such sentiments were also echoed by Rev. James Pollard of Ardmore, Pennsylvania, during an October 1991 interview. As a young man, Pollard attended Mount Olive.

22. Wardell Payne, ed., *Dictionary of African American Religious Bodies* (Washington, D.C.: Howard University Press, 1991), 101.

23. Remarks made at celebration of the 100th anniversary of the birth of Bishop Ida B. Robinson by adopted daughter Ida Robinson at New York–New England District Convocation in Stamford, Conn., August 1991.

24. Bell, "Confirming."

25. Trulear interview with Bishop Amy Stevens, September 1985.

26. Trulear interview with Elder Minerva Bell, September 1985.

27. This is not to suggest that women in ministry are universally accepted today; rather it is to say that acceptance was much more difficult in Ida Robinson's time, especially with so few precedents set for women in pastoral ministry.

28. See William Bentley, "Bible Believers in the Black Community," in David Wells and John Woodbridge, *The Evangelicals: What They Believe, Who They Are, Where They Are Changing,* rev. ed. (Grand Rapids, Mich.: Baker Book House, 1977), 133–36.

29. Elder Thelma Richey, "Eve, the Woman," address given at Sixtieth Annual Holy Convocation, September 1984.

30. Trulear interview with Bishop Amy Stevens, September 1985.

31. Recalled and sung as part of the Founder's Day address by Bishop Amy Stevens, September 1985, at Wilmington, Del.

32. See Leonard Lovett's careful rehearsal of this issue in his entry "Black Holiness-Pentecostalism" in *Dictionary of Pentecostal and Charismatic Movements,* ed. Stanley Burgess and Gary McGee (Grand Rapids, Mich.: Zondervan, 1988), especially 82–83.

33. *Manual and Course of Study for the Mount Sinai Holiness School* (n.p., n.d.).

34. Sparks, "Women's Rights," 2.

35. The archives of the Mount Sinai Holy Church of America are located at the Mount Olive Holy Church, Broad and Jefferson Streets, Philadelphia. Arthur Huff Fauset's *Black Gods of the Metropolis: Negro Religious Cults and the Urban North,* published by the University of Pennsylvania in 1944 and 1971, includes a chapter on Ida Robinson's church. This chapter includes extensive transcriptions of interviews with members. No new research appeared on Robinson until my "Reshaping Black Pastoral Theology: The Vision of Bishop Ida B. Robinson," *Journal of Religious Thought* 46 (summer–fall 1989): 17–31. Several of her sermons, with biographical commentary, appear in Bettye Collier-Thomas's *Daughters of Thunder: Black Women Preachers and Their Sermons, 1850–1979* (San Francisco: Jossey Bass, 1998).

George Floyd Taylor: Conflicts and Crowns
Vinson Synan

1. G. F. Taylor, Diary, April 14, 1901, North Carolina State History Archives, Raleigh, N.C.

2. Ibid., August 10, 1908; *Pentecostal Holiness Advocate* (henceforth *PHA*), April 6, 1922, 8.

3. Joseph E. Campbell, *The Pentecostal Holiness Church, 1898–1948* (Franklin Springs, Ga.: Pentecostal Holiness Publishing House, 1948), 479.

4. *PHA,* January 13, 1921.

5. G. F. Taylor, "Fanatical," from "Our Church History," *Pentecostal Holiness Advocate,* January 20, 1921, 9.

6. Taylor, "Our Church History," *Pentecostal Holiness Advocate,* January 27, 1921, 8.

7. Vinson Synan, *The Old Time Power: A Centennial History of the Pentecostal Holiness Church* (Franklin Springs, Ga.: Lifesprings Press, 1998), 68–92.

8. Ibid., 77–82.

9. Jeffrey Trexler, "G. F. Taylor and the Evolution of Southern Pentecostalism," (Ph.D. seminar paper, Duke University, 1988), 7, Regent University Archives, Virginia Beach, Va.

10. H. W. Taylor, *A History of William Taylor and Sarah Jones and Their Descendants* (Raleigh, N.C.: n.p., 1972), 88–91; Trexler, "G. F. Taylor," 8.

11. G. F. Taylor, *Spirit and the Bride* (Philadelphia: Winston Publishing Co., 1908), 39. For a time, Watson preached a third-blessing-type "baptism of fire."

12. Trexler, "G. F. Taylor," 12.
13. *PHA*, April 6, 1922.
14. Ibid.
15. Trexler, "G. F. Taylor," 23.
16. Synan, *Old Time Power*, 96.
17. Ibid., 94–113.
18. *PHA*, March 17, 1921; Trexler, "G. F. Taylor," 14.
19. Taylor, *Spirit and Bride*, 39; Synan, *Old Time Power*, 99.
20. Trexler, "G. F. Taylor," 15.
21. Ibid.
22. Synan, *Old Time Power*, 100.
23. Ibid., 108–9.
24. More on King can be found in his series "History of the Fire-Baptized Holiness Church," which appeared in the *PHA* March–April 1921 in a series of four articles. Also see his autobiographical *Yet Speaketh: The Memoirs of the Late Bishop Joseph H. King* (Franklin Springs, Ga.: Publishing House of the Pentecostal Holiness Church, 1949). Taylor and King played major roles in the merger of the Pentecostal Holiness Church and the Fire-Baptized Holiness Church in 1911.
25. Taylor, *Spirit and the Bride*, 96. Although *The Spirit and the Bride* claimed a publication date of September 1907, it did not appear in print until February of 1908. Taylor was the first Pentecostal to develop fully a "latter rain" theology, which had been hinted at by William J. Seymour. See Seymour's "The Promised Latter Rain Now Being Poured Out on God's Humble People," *Apostolic Faith* 1 (October 1906): 1.
26. This fact was commonly reported to the author by those who knew Taylor well. See Charles Bradshaw, *Profiles of Faith* (Franklin Springs, Ga.: Advocate Press, 1984), 196–200. His daughter Havens once said that she had never heard her father speak in tongues.
27. Synan, *Old Time Power*, 107.
28. See Grant Wacker, "Travail of a Broken Family," in Edith Blumhofer, Russell Spittler, and Grant Wacker, eds., *Pentecostal Currents in American Protestantism* (Chicago: University of Illinois Press, 1999), 28.
29. Synan, *Old Time Power*, 109.
30. Taylor, "Union," *PHA*, May 29, 1930, 1–8; Synan, *Old Time Power*, 121–24.
31. *PHA*, May 11, 1922.
32. Thomas L. Aaron Papers, Emmanuel College, Franklin Springs, Ga.
33. Synan, *Old Time Power*, 134.
34. Ibid., 135; Bradshaw, *Profiles of Faith*, 197. A full treatment of this movement is given by Dan Woods in his "Living in the Presence of God" (Ph.D. diss., University of Mississippi, 1997), 240–80.
35. *PHA*, May 3, 1917, 8.
36. *PHA*, June 21, 1917, 9.
37. Synan, *Old Time Power*, 162, 166–67, 260–61.
38. *PHA*, August 30, 1917, 1; October 30, 1919, 1. For a discussion of Taylor's work as a missiologist, see Stan York, "The Formation of the Pentecostal Holiness Missionary Endeavor" (master's thesis, Duke Divinity School, 1997).
39. *PHA*, January 10, 1934.

40. *PHA,* December 16–19, 1918, 8. According to Stan York, before accepting King's offer, Taylor had made plans to move his family and the *Advocate* to Birmingham, Alabama.

41. Taylor Manuscripts, "School Review," Emmanuel College Archives, Franklin Springs, Ga.

42. *PHA,* July 29, 1920, 9.

43. *PHA,* April 8, 1920, 9.

44. *PHA,* April 11, 1918, 8–9.

45. *PHA,* October 11, 1923, 1; November 23, 1922, 4.

46. Personal interview with Stan York, April 8, 2000.

47. Taylor, *Spirit and the Bride,* 97.

48. Frank Bartleman, *Azusa Street,* ed. Vinson Synan (Plainfield, N.J.: Logos Press, 1974), 122–23.

49. Taylor's diary contains his personal comments from his adolescence until his death in 1934. His *Spirit and the Bride* contains much autobiographical information, as does his twelve-part series "Our Church History" in the *Pentecostal Holiness Advocate,* January 20, 1921–April 14, 1921. Secondary sources include Joseph E. Campbell's *The Pentecostal Holiness Church, 1898–1948;* Vinson Synan's *The Old Time Power* and *Emmanuel College: The First Fifty Years* (Washington, D.C.: North Washington Press, 1968). More recent scholarly studies include Stan York's "The Formation of the Pentecostal Holiness Missionary Endeavor" and Daniel Wood's "The Gift Movement Controversy of 1916," a paper delivered at the Society for Pentecostal Studies, Cleveland, Tenn., 1998.

A. J. Tomlinson: Plainfolk Modernist
Roger Robins

1. Avery D. Evans, ed., *A.J. Tomlinson: God's Anointed—Prophet of Wisdom* (Cleveland, Tenn.: White Wing, 1943); Wade Phillips, "The Corrupted Seed" (master's thesis, Church of God School of Theology, 1990).

2. William R. Hutchison, *The Modernist Impulse in American Protestantism* (Harvard University Press, 1976).

3. Paul Carter, *Spiritual Crisis of the Gilded Age* (De Kalb: Northern Illinois University Press, 1971).

4. Quoted by A. B. Crumpler, *Way of Faith* (January 15, 1896): 1.

5. Thomas Hamm, *Transformation of American Quakerism: Orthodox Friends, 1800–1907* (Bloomington: Indiana University Press, 1988).

6. Quoted in James Davidson et al., *Nation of Nations: A Narrative History of the American Republic,* 2d ed. (New York: McGraw-Hill, 1994), 787.

7. Rhys Williams and Susan Alexander, "Religious Rhetoric in American Populism: Civil Religion as Movement Ideology," *Journal for the Scientific Study of Religion* (March 1994): 8.

8. Ibid.

9. *Free Methodist* (July 30, 1890): 490.

10. *Pentecostal Herald* (Indianapolis), June 1, 1895, 2.

11. Ad for *Midnight Cry,* reprinted in *Pentecostal Herald* (Indianapolis), June 15, 1896, 8.

12. *Republican Ledger,* December 9, 1992, 6.

13. A. J. Tomlinson, *Answering the Call of God* (Cleveland, Tenn.: White Wing, n.d.), 5–7.

14. Lydia Williams-Cammack and Truman Kenworthy, *Life and Works of Amos M. Kenworthy* (Richmond, Ind.: Nicholson Printing, 1918), 231.

15. Paul Rees, *Seth Cook Rees: The Warrior Saint* (Indianapolis: Pilgrim Book Room, 1934), 5.

16. "The Methodization of American Quakerism," *Friends Review* (November 10, 1892).

17. B. F. Lawrence, *The Apostolic Faith Restored* (St. Louis: Gospel Publishing House, 1916), 36.

18. A. J. Tomlinson, diary, vol. 1, April 14, 1901, Manuscripts Division, Library of Congress, Washington, D.C.

19. Richard Bushman and Claudia Bushman, "The Early History of Cleanliness in America," *Journal of American History* (March 1988): 1231.

20. Tomlinson, diary, vol. 1, May 1, 1901.

21. *Samson's Foxes* (July 20, 1901): 4.

22. Tomlinson, diary, vol. 1, October 1, 1901.

23. Transcript of oral interview, n.d., Hal Bernard Dixon Jr. Pentecostal Research Center, Cleveland, Tenn.

24. Tomlinson, diary, vol. 1, August 28, 1906.

25. Ibid., vol. 1, September 5, 1905.

26. Ibid., vol. 2, July 22–26, 1907.

27. Ibid., vol. 1, August 10, 1901; *Everlasting Gospel* (July 1–30, 1901).

28. Lillie Duggar, *A. J. Tomlinson* (Cleveland, Tenn.: White Wing, 1964), 788–93.

29. Duggar, *Tomlinson*, 406, quoting from 1932 general assembly address.

30. Ibid., 666.

31. Ibid., 677–79.

32. Ibid., 389.

33. Ibid., 690–91.

34. On the balance of routine and charisma in the contemporary Assemblies of God, see Margaret Poloma, *The Assemblies of God at the Crossroads: Charisma and Institutional Dilemmas* (Knoxville: University of Tennessee Press, 1989).

35. Valuable treatments of A. J. Tomlinson and the Church of God can be found in Charles W. Conn, *Like a Mighty Army Moves the Church of God, 1886–1955* (Cleveland, Tenn.: Church of God Publishing House, 1955); Mickey Crews, *The Church of God: A Social History* (Knoxville: University of Tennessee Press, 1990); and Roger Robins, "Plainfolk Modernist: The Radical Holiness World of A. J. Tomlinson" (Ph.D. diss., Duke University, 1999). The most important primary source is A. J. Tomlinson's diary in five volumes, Manuscripts Division, Library of Congress, Washington, D.C. The preeminent archival holdings are found at the Hal Bernard Dixon Jr. Pentecostal Research Center, Lee College, and the Archives of the Church of God of Prophecy, both in Cleveland, Tenn.

CONTRIBUTORS

Chris R. Armstrong is a Ph.D. candidate in the Graduate Program in Religion at Duke University, Durham, North Carolina.

Jay S. F. Blossom is a Ph.D. candidate in the Graduate Program in Religion at Duke University, Durham, North Carolina.

Edith L. Blumhofer is professor of history and director of the Institute for the Study of American Evangelicals, Wheaton College, Wheaton, Illinois.

David Bundy is associate provost for Library Services and associate professor of history at Fuller Theological Seminary, Pasadena, California.

Augustus Cerillo Jr. is provost and professor of history at Vanguard University, Costa Mesa, California.

David D. Daniels is associate professor of church history at McCormick Theological Seminary, Chicago.

Gastón Espinosa is assistant professor of religion at Westmont College, Santa Barbara, California.

James R. Goff Jr. is professor of history at Appalachian State University, Boone, North Carolina.

David Edwin Harrell Jr. is Daniel F. Breeden Eminent Scholar in the Humanities and professor of history at Auburn University, Auburn, Alabama.

Dale T. Irvin is professor of world Christianity at New York Theological Seminary, New York.

William Kostlevy is archivist and special collections librarian at Asbury Theological Seminary, Wilmore, Kentucky.

Gary B. McGee is professor of church history and Pentecostal studies at Assemblies of God Theological Seminary, Springfield, Missouri.

Rudy Nelson is emeritus professor of English at State University of New York-Albany.

Shirley Nelson is an independent scholar and writer.

Daniel Ramirez is a Ph.D. candidate in the Graduate Program in

Religion at Duke University, Durham, North Carolina.

Cecil M. Robeck Jr. is professor of church history and ecumenics at Fuller Theological Seminary, Pasadena, California.

Roger Robins is archivist of the David du Plessis Archive, Fuller Theological Seminary, Pasadena, California.

Susie C. Stanley is professor of historical theology at Messiah College, Grantham, Pennsylvania.

Jeannette Storms is professor of practical theology at The King's College and Seminary, Van Nuys, California.

Vinson Synan is dean of the School of Divinity, Regent University, Virginia Beach, Virginia.

Harold Dean Trulear is senior pastor at Mt. Pleasant Baptist Church in Twin Oaks, Pennsylvania, and also serves on the faculty at the Center for Urban Theological Studies, Philadelphia.

Grant Wacker is professor of church history at The Divinity School, Duke University, Durham, North Carolina.

Wayne E. Warner is director of the Flower Pentecostal Heritage Center of the Assemblies of God, Springfield, Missouri.

Everett A. Wilson is president and professor of history at Bethany College, Scotts Valley, California.

Ruth Marshall Wilson is a freelance researcher and writer.

INDEX

divorce, 30, 150, 251, 316
Dowie, John Alexander, 3–19, 21, 63–64, 127, 278
Durham, Bessie Mae Whitmore, 128–32, 135, 140–41, 234
Durham, William H., 44, 115, 123–42. *See also* Stone Church, Chicago

Elijah, persons claiming to be, 8, 63–65, 69
end times, 13, 19, 27, 66, 114, 143, 149, 151, 154–55, 172, 306–7, 366. *See also* latter rain; Second Coming of Christ
ethnic relations. *See* race and ethnic relations
Etter, Maria Woodworth, 174, 199–216, 277

Farson, Marmaduke "Duke" Mendenhall, 22, 26
Fink, George, 129, 131, 133
Fisher, C. L., 38, 46
Flower, J. Roswell, 18–19, 187, 244, 247–48
Foursquare Gospel Church. *See* International Church of the Foursquare Gospel
Franklin Springs Institute, Georgia, 340–43
Frazee, J. J., 249

Garr, A. J. and Lillian, 29–30, 99–101
Glad Tidings Bible Institute, 169–70
glossolalia. *See* tongues
Godbey, William, 75
Gordon, A. J., 10, 41, 56, 271, 330
Goss, Howard, 207–8, 264
Gourley, Thomas Hampton, 143–58
grapholalia, 226, 334
Gray, James M., 181

Hanley, Charles and Minnie, 126, 132–33, 136
Harvey, E. L., 21–35

Harvey, Gertrude Ford, 21–22, 27
Haywood, Garfield T., 212, 237–53, 291, 299–300
healing: and atonement, 275, 281, 286, 330; controversies, 61, 107–8, 228–29; gift, 97–98, 337; ministries, 4–6, 179–80, 188–90, 192–93, 285; specific instances, 4, 11, 60, 146, 182, 184–87, 205, 212–13, 224, 271, 274, 278, 298; theories, 10–11, 38, 182, 276–77, 286–87
Higher Life movement, 54–55, 92–94, 281. *See also* Keswick movement
Holt, William B., 266–69
Hoover, Willis and Mary, 103
hymnody, 299–301, 303

Iglesia de la Fé Apostólica Pentecostés. *See* Apostolic Assembly of the Faith in Christ Jesus
India, revival of 1905–6, 87–88, 93–97, 101
Inskip, John S., 93, 260
International Church of the Foursquare Gospel, 184–85. *See also* McPherson, Aimee Semple
International Divine Healing Association, 4–6

Jackson, Mary, 313, 314, 318–21
Jeter, John A., 39–43, 260, 263
Jones, Charles Price, 37–50, 260–61, 264–66
jumping during worship, 24, 82, 328

Keswick movement, 93, 136, 159, 281. *See also* Higher Life movement
Kuhlman, Kathryn, 202–3, 277

Ladd, Emma C., 131–33
Last Things. *See* end times
Latin American Bible Institute, 171
latter rain, 77–78, 100, 109, 163, 173, 219, 222, 334. *See also* end times; Second Coming of Christ